W9-BRR-895

ATLAS OF THE SUPER-NATURAL

ATLAS OF THE SUPER-NATURAL

Derek and Julia Parker

NEW YORK · LONDON · TORONTO · SYDNEY · TOKYO · SINGAPORE

ATLAS OF THE SUPERNATURAL
Derek and Julia Parker
To David and Pauline with love

PRENTICE HALL PRESS
15 Columbus Circle
New York, NY 10023

Copyright © Mitchell Beazley Publishers 1990
Text Copyright © Derek and Julia Parker 1990

All rights reserved, including the right of reproduction in whole or in part in any form.

PRENTICE HALL PRESS and colophons are registered trademarks of Simon & Schuster, Inc.

Library of Congress Cataloging Card Number: 89-43591

ISBN 0-13-050576-5 (cloth)
0-13-050634-6 (pbk)

Edited and designed by Mitchell Beazley International Limited, 14-15 Manette Street, London W1V 5LB.

Photoset by Bookworm Typesetting, Manchester
Reproduction by Mandarin Offset, Hong Kong
Printed in Spain by Printer Industria Grafica S.A., Barcelona

10 9 8 7 6 5 4 3 2 1

First Prentice Hall Press Edition

Editors	Frank Wallis Frances Gertler
Art Editor	Eljay Crompton
Illustrations	Maggie Kneen
Maps	Swanston Graphics Ltd Sue Sharples Pavel Kostal
Map Research	Sarah Polden
Editorial Assistant	Jaspal Bhangra
Picture Research	Brigitte Arora Ellen Root
Production	Ted Timberlake Sarah Schuman

Although all reasonable care has been taken in the preparation of this book, neither the publishers, nor the authors or editors can accept any liability for any consequences arising from the use thereof or from the information contained herein.

42

CONT

E N T S

Introduction

A man dreams of the death of a friend and wakes to the letter announcing it. A spoon bends into a hoop while being gently stroked with a forefinger. A woman stands terrified as crockery moves unaided through the air or bells ring although no hand has moved them. Another, under hypnosis, describes in detail a life lived in another country, a hundred years ago.

Almost everybody, at one time or another, has had an experience, perhaps less startling than these, that they would describe as "supernatural". That term suggests we know what is "natural".

But do we? Many famous scientists and thinkers have had the unpleasant experience of being dismissed as lunatics because their ideas outraged the conventional view of the "natural". There was a time when it seemed unnatural that anyone should suppose that the earth moved round the sun. There was a time when a man, standing on the cliffs at Poldhu, in Cornwall, could exclaim with contempt that it was as impossible that Marconi should be able to send messages through the air to America as that man should ever stand upon the face of the moon. Yet within a lifetime it seemed perfectly natural to send a telegram by "wireless" to San Francisco; indeed, not too long after that it became possible to send moving pictures through the air (and how many rationalists, in the past, scoffed at the alleged ability of some saints to "see" things happening many miles distant? Unnatural, you see).

The supernatural is not, however, quite the same as the "unnatural". A definition of the supernatural is that it is natural but not yet generally recognized or scientifically understood. Some events which have too often been experienced to be dismissed remain impossible to explain: ghosts, poltergeists, premonitions, fire-walking, metal-bending, finding a lost object by means of a pendulum. . . .

Scientists will describe these experiences as "supernatural" – often pejoratively. What they mean is that they consider them "unnatural", and therefore impossible. If they are relatively open-minded, they may prefer the word "paranormal", used to define phenomena at present inexplicable, but for which a scientific explanation is thought to be possible. There are examples of both in this book.

Many scientists take the view that if a phenomenon cannot be scientifically tested and explained, then it cannot exist. Yet there are many experiences shared by a large number of people for which science has been able so far to find no explanation. A message passed by extra-sensory perception cannot be traced as a telephone wire or a wireless wave can be traced; science cannot show how red-hot stones fail to burn the foot of the fire-walker, or explain how a man can apparently bend a metal spoon simply by stroking it. Most scientists therefore presume that such events are misreported or faked, and it is remarkable how ill-tempered they may become should one try to discuss the matter seriously. The great Dr Johnson was clearly one such: when Boswell talked to him about Bishop Berkeley's theory of the non-existence of matter, and suggested that it couldn't be refuted, Johnson simply gave a large stone a hard kick, and limped away muttering "I refute it thus". Bernard Levin, the English journalist with a passing interest in the subject, has described how an eminent scientist once took him to task for taking such nonsense seriously and then, as the discussion continued, began to turn purple, beads of sweat appearing on his brow!

Occasionally – indeed, in the present century, increasingly often – the supposedly "supernatural" becomes so common that science has in the end to accept it, although no scientific explanation can be produced: this has most recently been true of acupuncture, which until lately was regarded by Western doctors with the same respect as they afford the practices of witch doctors. Some still cling to that view; but most have been forced to concede that the Chinese system unquestionably works, and to cast around – so far, hopelessly – for a "rational" explanation. Most people now concede that dowsers are capable of finding water or minerals beneath the earth's surface; there is a steadily increasing confidence in the existence of extra-sensory perception and even of psychokinesis – and more and more scientific investigations are being mounted to examine them.

The great American psychologist William James had his doubts about working with mediums: but although (as he wrote) "the phenomena are as massive and widespread as is anything in nature, and the study of them as tedious, repellent, and undignified, to reject [psychical research] for its unromantic nature is like rejecting bacteriology because *penicillium glaucum* grows on horse dung and *bacterium termo* lives in putrefaction. Scientific men have long ago ceased to think of the dignity of the materials they work in . . . The first difference between the psychical researcher and the inexpert person is that the former realises the commonness and typicality of the phenomenon here, while the latter, less informed, thinks it so rare as to be unworthy of attention. I wish to go on record for the commonness."

But if it is unreasonable for scientists to dismiss all the material produced by psychic research as rubbish, it would be equally silly to accept that material uncritically. Some of it, perhaps a great deal of it, may well *be* rubbish; it is very difficult indeed to overestimate man's capacity for credulity. The example of the famous picnic at Hanging Rock is an excellent one (see p.194).

One of the problems is that an enormous number of people "know", from their own experience, that supernatural events occur, and regard those scientists whose minds are entirely closed to the mysteries of the paranormal with even more scorn than those mediums or conjurers whose frauds have been properly exposed. They are often impervious to the argument that there are rational explanations for the phenomena they cherish. They cling to their belief in strange powers or apparitions for sentimental reasons, or because they long to believe in life after death, or merely because they do not like to think that everything around them conforms to strict sets of scientific rules.

Both extremes are wrong. The "supernatural" may be "natural" – or rather, may once have been so. We have all had experience of watching animals react to situations or atmospheres of which we are unaware. Humanity may once have shared instincts the vestiges of which we can still see; and there is increasing conviction that in ignoring or ridiculing such powers we are – apart from anything else – denying faculties which could be of great practical value.

We have tried to take a middle line in this book. One of us has, to the best of his belief, never had a psychic experience of any kind; has never had a predictive dream, a precognition which has proved true, never seen an apparition, never seen (except on television) metal-bending. The other has had dreams, and sometimes waking premonitions, which seem to have predicted, with reasonable accuracy, events which have later taken place, but would deny being in any sense "psychic." Yet both have certainly seen events which science cannot explain – for example, fire-walking; and both would claim to have open minds on the subject of the supernatural and/or paranormal.

Although the field is too large to explore completely in a single volume, we have tried to include some "classic" examples of each *gene* – some well-known, some relatively unknown. We have made attempts to check details, and believe that the evidence produced for each reported event is – to put it at the lowest – worth careful consideration. We have given little space to those anecdotes for which, however firmly they are believed by some people, there is no vestige of real support: there are no articles here on the First World War bomber allegedly discovered on the moon, or on the proposition that Elvis Presley is alive and well and running a drug store in Middle America.

One interesting aspect of our research has been the universality of some of the phenomena: poltergeists have made themselves heard in old houses in Dorset, New England, Heidelberg, Rome and Adelaide, and also in native villages in Africa, fragile homes in Japan and Indian tents in Canada. All over the world, it has at one time or another been supposed that some illnesses – and by no means only emotional ones – have been caused by possession: the casting out of spirits is not exclusive to the Christian religion. It has been practised in almost every country in the world.

Forms of witchcraft are found everywhere, as are forms of Psychokinesis (see pp.61-2) and extra-sensory perception (see pp.63-6), ghosts know no boundaries; trance states and hypnosis have always been associated with medicine men, doctors and saints (of several religions). The use of dancing and drumming to induce trance is world-wide; sexual magic has been used by every civilization, although with greater discretion in the Christian world than elsewhere.

One of the interesting puzzles of the history of astrology (not included in this book because the researches of the Gauquelins and others have now shown that its cause and effect can be scientifically evaluated) is how the *glyphs* or symbols for the sun and some other planets appear written or carved in various parts of the world from the very earliest times – and are the same in areas which have never communicated with one another. Something of the same mystery appears in the history of the supernatural and paranormal, suggesting that what is being examined are real forces rather than the speculations of a few superstitious cranks.

There is a great deal of evidence available to those interested in the supernatural and paranormal. It is well to remember Murphy's Law of Research: enough research will tend to confirm your theory. But that law works both ways – it is as difficult to prove that something did not occur as to prove that it did. Seriously disturbed by that proposition, the American Society for the Scientific Investigation of Claims of the Paranormal, for example, has been reduced to commissioning magicians to duplicate the feats of (among others) Uri Geller (see pp.61-2), on the dubious grounds that if a magician can successfully counterfeit the Indian rope trick, make objects appear out of thin air, appear to bend metal, this must prove that those phenomena when produced by psychical researchers cannot be paranormal. Of course it proves nothing of the kind. It simply demonstrates that magicians are good at *legerdemain.*

Again, even if a paranormal event is obviously not – or turns out not to be – supernatural, this does not always make it less interesting. Whether or not the stigmata phenomenon (see pp.151-2) has a psychological cause, it is really rather remarkable that it can be responsible for the production of such extraordinary wounds as those suffered by Padre Pio – total piercing of hands and feet. Science and psychology, pooh-poohing a supernatural explanation, has done nothing to advance any other solution to a well-documented and so far inexplicable occurrence.

In writing this book we take the risk of upsetting both believers and sceptics: the first because we are not credulous enough, the second because we are insufficiently sceptical. On the whole, we prefer to leave the matter with Hamlet: "There are more things in heaven and earth than are dreamed of in your philosophy . . . ."

Derek and Julia Parker.

The Supernatural in History

The earliest history of the supernatural is as unknowable as the earliest history of man; there is no possible way to discover whether every human being once had extra-sensory perception, was able to communicate in that way, could use "natural magic" for curative purposes. The nearest we can get to guessing is to look at the unusual powers which some members of more or less primitive societies still recently commanded, and of which we have reliable records.

By the time such records were being made the development of humanity was well advanced, and there is some merit in the argument that even a small degree of sophistication had already resulted in the desuetude of our supernatural powers. It is a well-supported fact that the presence of one unbeliever in a group attempting to demonstrate extra-sensory perception can inhibit success; and the strange powers observed by early explorers in primitive tribes were at their strongest and most remarkable when every member of the tribe took them for granted. Once "civilization" arrived – and in particular, the missionaries who regarded all "magic" as diabolical, and did their best to abolish it – this soon ceased to be so. It became necessary to search out those young men (and they usually were men) in whom "supernatural" powers seemed strongest, and train them to be able to call on them at will, and focus them most usefully.

Primitive African tribes continued to do this until well into the 20th century. It was fairly easy to recognize someone with the potential to make use of supernatural powers: even a young child might be seen to have premonitions, to "know" things of which he could not rationally have learned. Poltergeist noises may have been heard around or near him; he may have appeared to someone else in a dream; he may have seemed able to read thoughts.

Such a boy would immediately be regarded as a potential witch doctor (to use a useful term), and a process of initiation would begin. This was always arduous and sometimes cruel, but aimed at sharpening the faculties which the tribe believed the subject to possess. He would be turned out into the wild to support himself as best he could. He would often suffer great privations, but these were believed to sensitize and strengthen the spirit by the very process of subjugating the body. Unsurprisingly, he often became deranged, spoke in strange languages, saw visions; all of which were signals of increasing spirituality and a sharpened awareness of his supernatural powers.

Once the ordeals were over, the wise men who emerged from them were highly regarded by their society – and, if they actually commanded even a small proportion of the powers attributed to them, rightly so.

In our own time, tribes entirely unaffected by "civilization" are now extremely rare; and one has only to compare the records of 19th-century explorers and missionaries with those of our own time to conclude that although in some parts of Africa, in particular, the witch doctor or his equivalent is still respected and his powers both feared and enjoyed, the strength of those powers is clearly less than it once was.

The Old Testament

The latest appearance of those powers among relatively civilized people can most readily be found in the Old Testament, which is full of reports of the activities of "prophets" who can perhaps also be described as witch doctors. Moses heard voices, possessed a magic wand which turned into a serpent, produced fire and food from nowhere; Shadrach, Meshach and Abednego performed feats of fire-walking which would have put the Fijians to shame; many prophets had predictive dreams, out-of-body experiences, were dowsers, and used crystals for divination. Modern Christians who denounce "fortune telling" can certainly not do so on the basis of the Old Testament.

But even here there are indications that critics were already accusing practitioners of the paranormal of cheating. The spiritualist writer Mrs St Clair Stobart, arguing in the 1920s

Witchcraft is still practised *in Africa: the Ghanaian priestess from Kumasi* (opposite) *may wear a modern dress, but her face and feet have been daubed with ash from a fire through which she has walked; and the circle has been pierced by a sword.*

Goats play a major role *in many witchcraft ceremonies, either as the embodiment of the Devil or as sacrificial victims. The history of the "scapegoat" in Jewish religious practice – when a goat assumes the burden of human sins and suffers for them – indicates the extent to which the animal has been associated with supernatural practices. The witch doctor* (left) *from the Congo will kill the goat at the peak of the ceremony.*

Evidence that Socrates (right) *had a mystical temperament is plentiful. Plato speaks of his once standing spellbound for 24 hours and also records that from childhood he heard a "voice". According to Plato, the voice foretold good or bad luck, often on trivial occasions. In his play* The Birds, *Aristophanes depicts Socrates presiding over a fraudulent seance.*

for properly controlled experiments, suggested that the first recorded one was mounted by the Hebrew prophet Elijah, who, in competition with the priests of Baal, guaranteed to call down fire from heaven. He went out of his way to demonstrate that what his audience saw was truly magical.

He dug a trench around the altar, and having placed an offering on some wood he instructed his followers to throw no less than 12 jars (about three gallons or 14 litres) of water over it, which ran down and filled the trench. He then summoned fire, which burned the offering and the wood, and evaporated all the water. This was quite impressive enough for his followers to reject the priests of Baal and follow Elijah, who now called down water and ended the drought, and also – presumably while possessed – outran Ahab's chariot in a demonstration of supernatural speed.

His successor Elisha had similar powers, but was perhaps less single-mindedly concerned with the public good, for although he purified undrinkable water and guaranteed that a widow's oil-jar should remain permanently full, he also did conjuring tricks (making an axe-head float) and made use of his supernatural powers in moments of ill-temper (42 boys, having called him "baldy", were cursed and promptly torn to pieces by she-bears).

Although some of the feats of Biblical witch doctors seem now to be slightly risible, records of some of their powers coincide remarkably with those claimed by living men and women. For example, Elisha, apart from his sharp way with juvenile delinquents, was also adept at psychic travel, and while out of the body could transport himself into his enemies' presence and hear their plans. There is a tenuous link between reports of supernatural powers from the earliest recorded text to our own time, and if there is also a history of disbelief, the strength of the current of well-authenticated strange supernatural powers is undeniable.

Egypt and Greece

No-one in ancient Egypt, nor in the contemporary civilizations of Babylonia or Assyria, seems seriously to have questioned the fact that magic was a part of everyday life. In classical Greece, while the supernatural was less superstitiously regarded, it still played a large part in everyday life. It is tempting to look at Homer (*c.*700 BC) and produce passages from the *Iliad* and *Odyssey* as evidence similar to that found in the Old Testament, but they do not contain the same sort of magic. The tricks described in Homer's chronicles are performed by the gods themselves, not (as in the Bible) by men whose powers were given to them by God. And on the whole they are feats which we recognize either as fictional (gods transform themselves into animals or men in order to seduce women) or as miracles of wishful thinking. In fact, they are not magical at all.

However, one strong strain of the paranormal which does run through Greek history, is the alleged ability to foretell the future. This is a tricky area for modern men and women, for it involves a criticism of freewill, a concept to which most of us are temperamentally attached. The Greeks had no such inhibitions, and the ways in which they obtained their visions of the future – although some of them were curious and even comic (for example, visions seen reflected in oil spread on the fingernails of a male virgin) – had something in common with the methods of modern visionaries.

The great oracles of Greece were originally worked by the equivalent of witch doctors, who spoke from self-induced trances, and often in symbols as scrambled and all-embracing as those of Nostradamus, centuries later. Contemporary descriptions of these trance-states bear a strong resemblance to modern cases of "possession".

The great Athenian philosopher Socrates (*c.*470-399 BC) is not usually considered a witch doctor, or even someone with a strong interest in the paranormal; yet the periods of intense philosophical speculation in which he was regularly lost sound remarkably like trances – trances in which, he claimed (according to Plato) that his "demon" spoke to him.

Later Greeks found it difficult to accept the idea of "voices", and like Aristotle (384-322 BC), questioned the idea that man could voluntarily put himself in touch with the supernatural. The Romans, led by Cicero (106-43 BC) in his *De Divinatione*, went further – Cicero was perhaps the first intelligent man to suggest that most of the evidence of supernatural powers was too anecdotal to be conclusive ("who vouches for them?" he asks).

Jesus healed the sick (left) *when pressed to do so – an example of his magical powers that is not unlike those of a witch doctor. But Christ never took money for these cures and always emphasized that such miracles were secondary to his religious message – which distinguishes him absolutely from ordinary magicians.*

Moses set up a copper serpent (opposite, bottom) *at God's command during the Israelites' wanderings in the desert. It had a therapeutic effect on anyone who looked upon it having been bitten by a poisonous snake – an example of magical healing. Later, King Hezekiah of Judah had it destroyed to stop it being worshipped as a false idol by the Jews. Serpents, symbolizing life and death, were commonly worshipped in the region at the time.*

Christianity and Magic

With the spread of Christianity, the situation became very confused indeed. On the one hand, Christians were happy to accept the miracles recorded in the Bible and biographies of the Saints; on the other any ordinary person who appeared to have unusual paranormal powers was highly suspect. The confusion arose even before Christianity – when supernatural events were invariably linked to "gods" or "spirits". It was never considered that the ability to "read the thoughts" of someone else might be a "natural" ability: no – it was "supernatural", and therefore explicable only in religious terms.

There were exceptions to this view; but not many. One focused on Apollonius of Tyana, a contemporary of Jesus, who seems to have been an old-fashioned witch doctor, but with more extraordinary powers. These were described more than a century after his death by Philostratus. Although the phenomena in which he was involved bear some resemblance to those of the New Testament, there is no connection with Christian thought or morality – but with pagan religions of Greece and Egypt and, while it is safest to regard the biography of Apollonius at least as sceptically as that of Jesus, many elements ring true.

Other non-Christian cults have also left evidence of supernatural powers. For example, Theurgy has the delightful fable of *The Golden Ass*, told by Apuleius (born *c.*AD 123). The tale includes an account of a *Discourse on magic* which spoke of a magic mirror, and gave accounts of boys with clairvoyant abilities.

Perhaps the most respectable of all Roman philosophers who possessed supernatural capabilities, was the Greek, Plotinus (*c.*AD 205-70). When a pupil was contemplating suicide, Plotinus, at a distance, became aware of the fact, and appeared just in time to stop him. He claimed that such powers were natural and that he was using the forces inherent in human nature – which included artistic powers. Indeed, what is more magical than the composer's power to move us to tears by a mere pattern of sounds?

The pupil whom Plotinus saved from suicide was Porphyry (*c.*AD 234-305), whose account of the "magic" of his time is enormously valuable. He was particularly interested in the many varied ways in which different "magicians" attempted to achieve their results and, with his friend and pupil Iamblichus, set up several experiments in spiritualism. With practice, they found it relatively easy to contact "spirits". Porphyry's descriptions of seances read remarkably like those of Victorian sessions, with accounts of apparent manifestations, speaking in tongues and "entranced" people being stuck with needles without feeling pain.

Christ cast out devils *from people in His lifetime. Later, He came to be regarded as a defender of Jerusalem* (right)*, the symbol of the Heavenly City on earth, surrounded on all sides by devils led by Satan. Such a transformation of Satan into the leader of diabolical armies, which Christ had only hinted at in the Gospels, was emphasized by the new Church in an attempt to damn all its opponents, be they pagans or unorthodox Christians. If the true Church was like a besieged city, all outside its walls were clearly on the side of the enemy – the Devil.*

Christianity attributed all "supernatural" events to God, His son and His saints. In a sense, all religions have their supernatural aspects – they propose a supernatural force. However, not all of them are so replete with miracles as Christianity. If the Old Testament, on the whole, is preoccupied with what might be called "coarse magic", the New Testament is rather different, for while there are some events which today would probably be denounced as mere conjuring tricks – for example, turning water into wine – these were mostly performed for moral instruction.

All the same, there are strong connections between the supernatural feats performed by Jesus and those of the witch doctors or wise men of primitive tribes. Jesus not only had out-of-body experiences, but he could control them, transporting himself to a mountain-top or the highest point of a temple; he could turn a stone into bread, or feed 5,000 people with a few loaves and fishes. Not only this, but he underwent the same sort of training as the young seers of the tribes – physical self-denial and abasement, hunger and thirst, the rejection of sensual pleasure.

If there can be no really conclusive proof of the divinity of Jesus, it seems unquestionable that such a man existed, and that he had remarkable psychic powers. These were rendered more impressive by his assurance that his followers would outlive the experience of death; and it was perhaps the force of this promise, backed up by his extraordinary displays of supernatural power, that persuaded so many people so soon after his death to regard him as divine.

None of Jesus' followers had quite as extensive psychic powers as he. But many of them could apparently also transfer themselves from one place to the other by psychic means, go into trances, hear voices, produce articles out of thin air, perform remarkable psychic cures. They also confirmed what Jesus had suggested – that as well as a spiritual power of good, there was a darker power of evil. Many of the saints combated evil spirits which strongly resembled those that had plagued more primitive people.

The Birth of the Devil

The concept of Satan was useful to the Church, for if a powerful devil existed, it would be possible to condemn the spiritual statements of anyone with whom the establishment disagreed, on the unprovable basis that they emanated from the power of Evil rather than that of Good. For example, Satan was clearly in charge of the pagan Oracles which were still being consulted during the early years of the Christian era – or at least that was the argument that was used to demolish them.

Not all early Christian fathers were prepared to consider all non-Christian psychic powers as diabolical. For example, St Augustine preserved a balanced view of the subject, accepting that dreams could be useful conveyers of psychic messages, that some people had mind-reading powers or powers of psychic travel which were not necessarily evil. And he made one statement which is intensely sympathetic to modern explorers of the subject: divine portents, he said, were "not contrary to nature, but contrary to *what is known* of nature."

But Augustine was out on a limb even in his own time; and for the next 1,500 years the Church regarded magic as either something divine and therefore good (that magic that the saints could command) or a tool of the Devil and therefore bad (that magic which non-Christians or even ordinary people seemed able to perform). It was an attitude which was to lead inevitably to the torture chambers and stakes of the Inquisition and then later the witch burners.

Many of the acts for which people were condemned – or, very occasionally, canonized – are similar to those which modern psychics claim to perform today – or which primitive people have performed throughout recorded history. The fire-walkers of Fiji are no cleverer than Peter Aldobrandini, who in 1062 underwent an ordeal by fire to prove that he was the rightful Bishop of Florence. Those psychics who claim to be able to "see" events occurring many miles away, are following in the footsteps of Raymond, Lord of Carosse, who in 1385 is purported to have kept his friend the Count de Foix, Governor of Languedoc, informed by psychic means of the progress of the battle of Aljuberota.

Because the Church was careful to record supernatural events – either in order to condemn their perpetrators for witchcraft or to celebrate them as saints – we can follow a psychic trail which is marked by phenomena similar to those recorded in the 19th and 20th centuries, when people became interested in the psychic for its own sake. There are many records of poltergeists, such as the spectacular outbreak that occurred in 858 in a village on the Rhine, or the more restrained example recorded in the 12th century by Giraldus Cambrensis, who went to two Welsh houses in which lumps of dirt were thrown about, and clothes were damaged while locked away in presses. Monasteries were particularly subject to such visitations, and their more saintly members were often tried by being knocked about or showered with human excrement.

Some, at least, of the psychic events recorded must surely actually have occurred. It is more difficult to come to a safe conclusion about the "heavenly voices" heard by some of the saints – notably St Catherine of Siena (1347-80) and St Joan of Arc (1412-31). But at least it seems likely that both were clairvoyant, for there were many occasions on which their voices "told" them things which they could not have known.

There have been a few attempts throughout history to persuade the Church to regard the supernatural as an acceptable aspect of God's creation, and today many churchmen and women are interested in the psychic and pursue it no less clear-mindedly than other investigators. A precursor of these was Cornelius Agrippa (1486-1535), a secretary to the Emperor Maximilian I, who took advantage of the appearance in the West of ancient books of magic, and was deeply read in Hermetic tracts which recorded some of the theories passed down from Babylon and Egypt, via Greece, and in the Cabala, a mystical Jewish approach to God.

Agrippa, in a book published in 1530, attempted to rationalize what was known about the supernatural – or "magic" – by considering the mathematics involved, and then looking at its relationship to religion. He concluded that the material world was balanced by a spiritual world, that everything – animate and inanimate – was shot through with the spirit, and that particularly sensitive men and women were able to capture that spirit and translate it into visual terms – which was how they could, for example, be aware of things happening at a distance.

It was during the same century that one of the most famous, or notorious, of all clairvoyants lived – Michael Nostradamus (1503-66). For some reason best known to himself, Nostradamus' prophesies were made in the form of quatrains so vague and abstruse that it is possible to interpret them to fit almost any situation, although in a few cases they seem to fit events too closely for the comfort of sceptics.

Nostradamus left no account of how he arrived at his predictions; his contemporary John Dee (1527-1608) recorded his attempts at divination in some detail. A trusted friend and agent of Queen Elizabeth I, Dee shared Agrippa's belief that the world was full of spirits, and believed that there were innumerable ways of contacting them – by using a mirror, a pendulum, a crystal, dreams or waking visions. He and a colleague, Edward Kelley (1555-95), conducted a number of experiments, including one in which Kelley, as a medium, answered questions in a code which only Dee could transcribe. Unfortunately, the spirit-messages were no more illuminating than those usually purveyed at modern seances.

Dee believed that some people naturally possessed what he called "super-normal" powers – "not those of a magician, but of a peculiar and scientific quality." The Roman Catholic Church regarded such powers as tantamount to witchcraft, and during Dee's own lifetime burned a Dominican friar, Giordano Bruno (1548-1600), at the stake for arguing that magic was a natural phenomenon which should be at everyone's command. Indeed, it was during the 16th century that the Church most jealously guarded its own rituals, while condemning those who made use of the natural powers they possessed.

Levitation

The idea of levitation may seem slightly comic, especially as there is rarely any good reason for it. But it has been a characteristic of many saints. St Francis of Assisi (*c.*1182-1226), St Dominic (*c.*1170-1221), Catherine of Siena (1347-80), Edmund of Canterbury (*c.*1170-1240), St Teresa of Avila (1515-82) and St Joseph of Copertino (1603-63) all from time to time freed themselves or were freed from the trammels of gravity. St Teresa seems to have found the experience rather embarrassing (she left an account of how it felt). The case of St Joseph is particularly interesting, because his levitation was a source of considerable exasperation to his superiors of the Copertino Franciscan order, who far from regarding it as a miraculous proof of heavenly powers, cordially wished that the young man would stop. On one occasion in full view of a large congregation he soared 40 feet (12m) into the air; on another, his sandals fell off while he was in flight.

He took off despite himself, and at the least provocation. Out walking with a brother, the latter's casual remark about the fine weather sent Joseph soaring up to the branch of a tree, from which he had to be rescued by means of a ladder. Granted an audience by Pope Urban VIII, he was so overcome that he left the floor and had to be ordered down by his Superior – an event to which the Pope was a witness.

Comic though the incidents sound, many of them were witnessed by well-known people with no particular motive for lying about them. No doubt it is possible that all these people were suffering from mass hysteria, but it scarcely seems likely.

Inanimate objects such as holy books *have sometimes been said to levitate. This painting* (above), *from the Prado, in Madrid, shows the orthodox burning books written by Cathars, members of an heretical Christian sect that flourished in Europe in the 12th and 13th centuries and which believed, among other things, that Satan was not a fallen angel of God but an independent deity. But, as the flames consume the works of evil, a book written by Saint Dominic, founder of the Dominicans, flies up and is saved.*

Nostradamus used a magic mirror (left) *when casting the horoscopes of Catherine de Médicis' children. He began as a doctor in 1529 and became well known for his treatment of plague at Aix and Lyon in 1546-7. He started making prophecies in around 1547 and published them in 1555. He was appointed physician-in-ordinary by Charles IX in 1560. In 1781 the Roman Catholic Church placed his prophecies on the Index of Forbidden Works.*

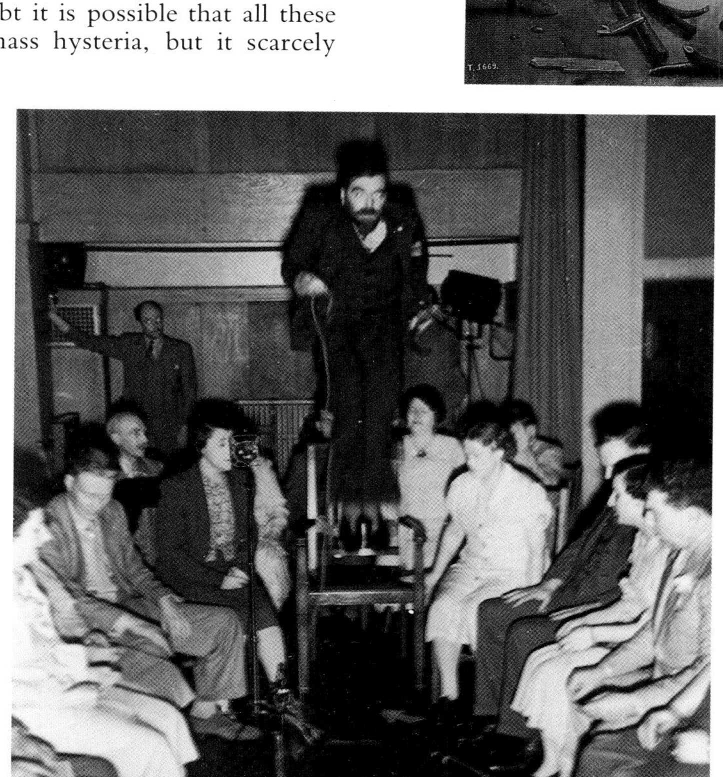

Medium Colin Evans was photographed levitating (right) *in London on November 27, 1937. If the event was faked, he chose a bad moment: most of his audience have their eyes closed, either in meditation or in a trance state.*

St Joseph's powers of flight were merely an embarrassment to the Church. Ordinary people with similar powers were in greater danger, for levitation was allegedly at the command of witches. There are innumerable "confessions" of levitation by unfortunates at witch trials – confessions invariably obtained after torture. Very occasionally, there may have been actual cases, observed by reasonable people – for example, that of Françoise Fointaine of Louviers who, in 1591, rose into the air in front of a magistrate, his clerk, a jailer, and a number of independent witnesses. In England at a time when witch-hunting was not a national sport, there are reports of levitation by members of the nobility – for example, the Countess of Dumfries was given to flying around her garden, and Lord Orrery had a neighbour whose butler rose into the air despite the efforts of two strong men to hold him down.

Sorcery and witchcraft

The simple fact that both good and evil exist necessarily implies that those who possess or acquire supernatural powers will use them differently; and there is plenty of evidence that this happened – not only outside but inside the church. Occult powers used for evil purposes leave a trail more memorable than those used, for example, to heal.

The connection between sorcery and witchcraft and sexual gratification is too strong to be ignored (see pp.32-3). That sexual magic was to be found in many monasteries and nunneries is unsurprising considering the amount of sexual frustration that must have built up in communities of avowed chastity. No doubt many monks and nuns were able successfully to sublimate their sensuality; however, others found it more difficult, and we find many accounts of sexual magic in monastic environments.

Among these is insufflation – the technique of arousing desire in a woman simply by breathing upon her. Women who knelt for long periods before a priest in the close confines of the confessional were particularly susceptible to this, and Augustine, Jerome and Gregory all publicly condemned the

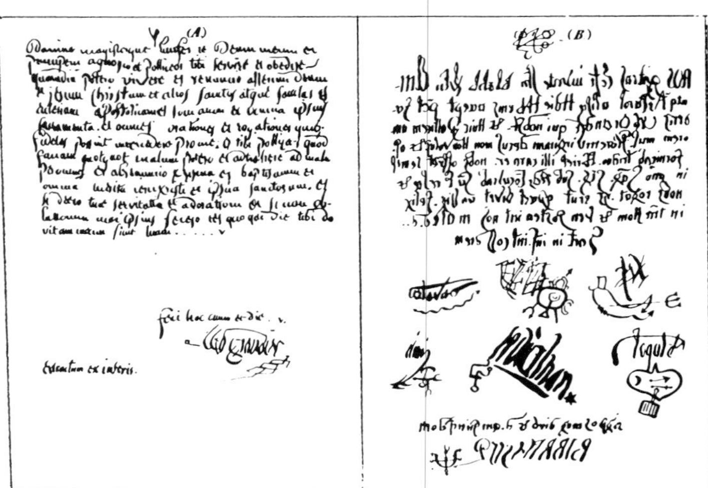
(A)

(B)

***Pacts with the Devil** are a popular theme in literature – that recorded in Goethe's* Faust *is perhaps the best known – but may also have been signed in real life. The document* (left) *is (allegedly) a pact made in Loudun, France, in 1634 between Father Urbain Grandier, a parish priest, and Lucifer, Beelzebub, Satan, Leviathan, Asteroth and Baalberith. In return for his immortal soul, Grandier was granted success with women. Eventually, he was accused of bewitching a convent of nuns. The charge did not lead to a conviction, but he was accused a second time, found guilty, and burned at the stake.*

***Ghostly shapes can appear in photographs**. The Rev K.F. Lord, vicar of Newby church, near Ripon, in North Yorkshire, England, did not notice the hooded form here when he took the photograph in the early 1960s: it showed up only when the film was developed.*

practice as prevalent. Several priests were burned at the stake for it. The best-known instance took place at Loudon in the 17th century, when Urbain Grandier (1590-1634), confessor to the convent there, allegedly turned the nuns into salacious concubines and suffered at the stake for his pleasures (the story is rivetingly told in Aldous Huxley's *The Devils of Loudon*). Joan of Arc's protector, Gilles de Laval, Seigneur de Rais (1404-40), was an alchemist who killed more than 200 children in the practice of black arts.

The mental and physical paraphernalia required by the genuine magician is considerable. The raising of demons or the powers of evil is not a simple technique. Nor is it easy to assess how often it has been successful. There are naturally far fewer witnesses to this kind of activity than to, say, levitation; and those witnesses who have left accounts saw what were, on the whole, often activities as innocent as those already recorded – disembodied voices, hysteria in children, and so on. No doubt such occasions were often excuses for sexual excess – "black magic" has almost always had sexual connotations, including those of the Black Mass, traditionally celebrated on the naked body of a young virgin. But very often, the supernatural events which sorcerers or witches evoked were no more evil than those of "white magic".

Ghosts

Ghosts have been around since man was first conscious of death. Reluctance to believe in extinction naturally led to belief in an afterlife – from which it was but a short step to the belief that the dead sometimes visited the living, to warn or encourage, to help or hinder them. Primitive tribes in particular "used" the dead to help them, evoking them in dreams, trances or by spells. Civilized man continued the belief, although it took various forms.

The Egyptians believed that the soul, or *ka*, remained for some time in the vicinity where its body died; or sometimes, as the *khu*, returned to perform certain tasks. The *ka* had no visible form; the ghost with which we are more familiar has the shape of the dead person, sometimes appearing solid, sometimes transparent.

Not only Greek and Roman literature, but that of civilized Europe up to the Age of Enlightenment, and to a lesser degree since, testifies to a steady belief in this kind of ghost. Apparitions are not, generally speaking, harmful – although frequently frightening. Too many people have had the experience either of seeing a ghost or "being aware of its presence" for us to be able to dismiss the phenomenon – although it is possible, of course, to offer all kinds of rational explanations for it. In some cases – for example, where an apparition has signalled the death of the person it resembles – this is difficult.

Modern ghost-hunting has proved an exacting art, and has not provided conclusive evidence. The best-known modern practitioner, Harry Price (see pp.130-1), failed to do so under test conditions – although once again, the presence of antagonistic or unbelieving observers does seem to inhibit apparitions. Poltergeists seem to have no such inhibitions.

Franz Mesmer's methods *involved a large tub* (right) *to which was fixed pieces of cord (which the patients tied around their limbs) or iron hooks (which they applied to whatever part of the body was proving a problem): "the patients, especially women, have fits, which bring about their recovery". Mesmer also had a hundred "magnetizers" who assisted the action of the cords and hooks by placing their hands on the ailing parts. Mesmer was described as "seeming always to be absorbed in profound reflections."*

Goethe (below) ***had a vision*** *of meeting a friend on the Weimar road at the time the friend was asleep, dreaming he had met Goethe.*

Poltergeists

Poltergeists are heard and not seen. Sometimes they seem to have human voices, speaking or muttering or giggling; more usually they merely throw objects about in displays of psychokinesis that any living practitioner would envy. The Church was less inhibited about paying serious attention to poltergeists, and there are many cases in which investigation took place, under carefully controlled conditions that any modern scientist could respect.

Some became famous. The earliest English example is that of the Phantom Drummer of Tidworth. In 1661, William Drury, a vagrant former soldier, was arrested in Wiltshire and charged with creating a nuisance by continually beating a drum in order to blackmail people into paying him to move on. He was jailed, and the drum was taken home by the magistrate in the case, one John Mompesson. Very curious things then began to happen: objects flew about the house, the Mompesson children were thrown out of bed, a Bible was hidden in the ashes of a grate, voices were heard – and all the time, the drum beat steadily by itself.

These phenomena were carefully recorded by a chaplain to Charles II, the Rev Joseph Glanvil (1636-1680), who was a Fellow of the Royal Society, and a trustworthy witness. Mompesson too was a respectable man, with no possible motive for setting up a hoax. The circumstances remain mysterious.

In 1759 the Cock Lane ghost, which operated near Holborn, in London, became even more notorious. The ghost, which signalled its presence by knocking, was thoroughly tamed, and answered questions with one knock for yes and two for no (it sometimes made a scratching noise when rendered impatient by stupid visitors). This poltergeist was connected with the presence of an adolescent girl, Elizabeth Parsons; so much so that the sceptical Dr Johnson, looking into the case, concluded that "the child has some art of making or counterfeiting particular noises." However, others were careful to watch the child, even to hold her hands and feet while the knocking continued, and were sure that the sounds were supernatural.

The Supernatural Under Attack

The gradual growth of scepticism about the supernatural had one excellent result: people were a great deal more careful about how they recorded apparently magical events when they knew that they would not be too readily accepted. A less welcome result was the growing tendency for people to believe that only events which could be "rationally" explained or accounted for could take place.

The lead in this attempt to rationalize the unexplained was taken, oddly enough, by the Church, at least, the Protestant Church: although founded on events that were entirely supernatural – a man who performed miracles, walked on water, rose from the dead – it now asserted that the supernatural did not exist. Taking the new tendency to an extreme, some people indeed actually questioned the New Testament miracles (although they landed in gaol for blasphemy: some beliefs were not to be doubted). The Catholic Church began to be a great deal more rigorous in its examination of "miracles". But strange happenings continued – literally under the nose of Lambertini (1675-1758), Archbishop of Bologna, a critic who went out of his way to point out that the supernatural frequently, upon examination, turned out to have natural explanations. One Alfonso Liguori, as though to teach the Archbishop a lesson, levitated so determinedly that he collided with the cleric, and almost knocked him out.

Scepticism grew throughout the 18th century, and the Scottish moral philosopher David Hume (1711-76) went so far as to say that even when proof of miraculous events seemed irrefutable, they must still be doubted because ordinary people must be convinced of their "absolute impossibility". It is an attitude shared, quite irrationally, by many modern scientists, whose creed seems to be "I doubt, therefore I am."

Arguments about the supernatural took a new turn in the second half of the century, when Franz Mesmer (1734-1815) sparked a new interest in "mesmerism" (hypnotism), and in the effects of magnetism and electricity on human beings. Mesmer argued that all living things – indeed, the whole known universe – were linked together by a subtle force whose nature was so far not understood. His subjects certainly did remarkable things when in a state of trance – they recognized hidden objects, became impervious to pain, read books without being able to see. It became for a time relatively respectable – particularly in France – to study the effects of "animal magnetism", although many scientists declined to believe that a hypnotic state could be induced. Now, of course, it is a commonplace – and has become associated with other marvels such as regression (see p.60), in which a subject is hypnotized and encouraged to describe events during past incarnations.

In Germany, meanwhile, some of the country's most distinguished philosophers, while not particularly interested in animal magnetism, were coming to the conclusion that human beings had abilities not obvious to the casual observer. Arthur Schopenhauer (1788-1860) believed there was some irrational instinct similar to that possessed by animals, which could connect the minds of human beings; Georg Hegel (1770-1831) agreed, and accepted the idea of clairvoyance. Johann Wolfgang von Goethe (1749-1832), the founder of modern German literature, was convinced by his own experiences – which included meeting his old friend Frederick von Schiller on the road to Weimar, incongruously wearing some of Goethe's clothes. Finding that his companion on the road had not seen Schiller, Goethe checked – and discovered that at precisely the time of the vision, Schiller, soaked in a rainstorm, had dressed himself in Goethe's clothes, sat by the fire, fallen asleep, and dreamed that he had met Goethe on the Weimar road and exchanged with him the very words Goethe himself remembered speaking.

In England, the interest in clairvoyance and animal magnetism remained at the level of music-hall entertainments, scientists being resolutely unwilling even to investigate the clearly useful aspects of hypnotism (dentists in France were now extracting teeth while patients were "entranced"). A few experiments were carried out, often as the result of wagers; and some were spectacularly successful – like one held in Plymouth in 1846 when a youth so thoroughly blindfolded that his eyelids could scarcely be unstuck after the experiment accurately "read" papers and advertisements.

The "mesmerists" seem not to have been especially interested in any other kind of psychic phenomena, nor did they connect their powers with religion, believing they were entirely natural. However, in America there were one or two instances in which, in a trance state, subjects had claimed to see and talk with spirits. In 1844, Lyman B. Larkin, a Massachusetts doctor, mesmerized his housemaid, Mary Jane, in order to cure her of epilepsy; while she was under the influence, he heard rappings, furniture moved about, and a flatiron travelled about the house in a random manner.

More interestingly, a semi-literate leatherworker's son of Poughkeepsie, New York, when mesmerized, dictated lectures on philosophy and science. Andrew Jackson Davis claimed to have spoken with the spirits of Galen and Swedenborg – of whom, waking, he said he had never heard. There seems to have been no way in which he could have "known" anything about the matters he discussed in trance.

***Harry Houdini** mounted a crusade against fake mediums. One of his devices was a fraudproof wooden box* (left)*, shown here with medium Margaret Crandon locked inside.*

***The Fox sisters** (left) became famous for the odd things that happened in their presence: musical instruments began to play, objects began to float, and people felt mysterious, unseen hands brushing their faces. The strictest investigations failed to find any evidence of trickery.*

An interest in what is now known as "spiritualism" began to sweep the United States not long afterwards, partly because of the case of the Fox sisters, of Hydesville, Rochester, New York. In 1848 the children – 15-year-old Margaret and 12-year-old Kate – were the focus of various mysterious noises and rappings, and claimed to be in touch with the spirit of a man who had been murdered in the house, and buried in the cellar.

Whether or not this was true (and no body was ever found in the cellar), it became clear that the sisters attracted psychic phenomena, which followed them about the country and, encouraged by an elder sister who seems to have recognized moneymaking potential when she saw it, they soon began to perform other tricks, but tricks the trickery of which was impossible to establish. The fame of the Fox sisters and the phenomena attending them resulted in an interest in the psychic that within a few years produced a flood of anecdotal evidence, some of which was meticulously investigated.

Soon, very respectable men and women were professing themselves "spiritualists", believing that for the most part the phenomena which so puzzled rationality were connected with the spirits of the dead, for some reason driven to attempt to communicate with the living. Spiritualism in time acquired a capital S, and became a new faith.

It came to England in the middle of the 19th century, at first attracting not only scepticism but ridicule. Then, as groups of people began to experiment with table-turning, a popular proof of the presence of spirits, they found themselves frequently startled by things they did not understand. In small houses throughout the country knockings allegedly announced the presence of spirits; at Osborne House, a table stirred itself under the amazed palms of Queen Victoria and Prince Albert. Electricity, the Queen thought. By 1853, thousands of people were sitting in semi-darkness asking with bated breath whether Anyone was There.

The problem was that while there was undoubtedly some chicanery about, a number of rational people were sufficiently impressed to stir the scientists. The latter spent a great deal of time inventing equipment which would enable tables to move about, apparently without the intervention of any human agency. They did not explain how similar equipment could be manufactured by ordinary people all over the country. The mystery remained.

It might be supposed that the most famous mediums of the time were those who were cleverest at concealing fraud. Certainly, the better-known the medium, the harder the sceptics tried to catch him or her out. The best-known medium of the early years of spiritualism was probably Daniel Dunglas Home, born in Edinburgh, Scotland, in 1833, but brought up in Connecticut. He was 17 when he first began to have psychic experiences. Sceptical observers failed to discover how he could have faked the table-turnings which occurred in his presence. He levitated in the presence of a number of witnesses, and there were various materializations, including dismembered hands which wrote messages.

In 1855 Home journeyed to Britain, and there and

throughout the Continent startled thousands of people with displays of apparently inexplicable psychic powers. Some witnesses admitted that the convictions of many years were upset by his remarkable seances. Others were impressed but declined to admit it: Sir David Brewster (1781-1868), a lifelong sceptic, in public claimed that Home was a fraud, but in a private letter to his daughter admitted that he could not imagine any rational explanation for what he had seen at Home's seances. The list of eminent men and women convinced that Home was the centre of supernatural phenomena is too long to reproduce – and although there were attacks (Robert Browning portrayed Home in a famous poem as "Mr Sludge the Medium"), these were on the whole based on repugnance rather than rational argument.

Unfortunately for those who took spiritualism seriously, a number of people saw great opportunities for defrauding the gullible – especially those who had recently been bereaved and would cling desperately to the idea that their loved ones could communicate with them after death. The detection of some frauds naturally supported those sceptics who found the whole idea of the supernatural too worrying for serious contemplation. In 1876 they were given additional ammunition when two mediums were found guilty of fraud.

However interesting one finds the subject, it is impossible when reading about the spiritualist craze which took over Britain and America during the second half of the 19th century not to have some sympathy with those who regarded the whole thing as bunkum. Even if one discounts the obvious frauds, what went on at spiritualist meetings was in itself comic: disembodied spirits might communicate with the spiritualists – but what they told them was rubbish; furniture might move about – but to what possible purpose? A medium might levitate – but what was the point of that?

Yet however ludicrous the goings-on might appear, among them were some which seemed genuinely inexplicable, and people with open and inquisitive minds could not resist – and felt they should not resist – seriously examining them.

Medium Eusapia Palladino (opposite page, left) *so impressed the eminent Italian professor Cesare Lombroso that he renounced his former sceptical view of spiritualism. Professor Lombroso, best known as a criminologist, had to admit that in Mrs Palladino's presence, pianos played themselves, objects moved and strange imprints appeared in clay; she also levitated. Lombroso, who had always been a severe critic of the supernatural, and who examined Mrs Palladino with three colleagues, told a friend that he was ashamed to have so vehemently opposed the possibility of "so-called spiritist facts"; although he seems to have believed that the force she exerted was the result of a kind of hysterical epilepsy.*

Daniel Dunglas Home (opposite page, right) *was the best known medium of the early years of spiritualism. He claimed he could turn tables, levitate, and materialize disembodied hands, which wrote messages. Some people disbelieved, and even attacked him in print: but thousands of people were convinced.*

Disaster struck Aberfan, *a Welsh village* (left), *on October 21 1965 when an avalanche of coal slid down a mountainside, burying the local school and killing 128 children. The day before, a woman in Plymouth, England, told six witnesses at a spiritualist church, that in a trance she had "seen" an avalanche of coal sliding down a Welsh mountainside towards a terrified child.*

A woman in Sidcup, Kent, had a premonition of a similar disaster a week before the event; another in Aylesbury, Buckinghamshire, dreamed of it two days before the disaster; a child victim of the incident told her mother, the day before the event, "I dreamed I went to school and there was no school there. Something black had come down all over it." All these premonitions were reported to reliable witnesses.

In 1882, a Society for Psychical Research (SPR) was founded in London. It was certainly associated with leading spiritualists but also included a core of firm-minded academics. Its first President was Henry Sidgwick (1838-1900), a leading British academic philosopher and Lecturer in Moral Sciences at Cambridge. The purpose of the Society was (as its literature still announces) "to examine without prejudice or prepossession and in a scientific spirit those faculties of man, real or supposed, which appear to be inexplicable on any generally recognized hypothesis." An American Society was founded not long afterward.

As might have been suspected (and is still, sadly, the case) even those academics who felt sympathetic to the notion of a serious examination of psychic phenomena hesitated to associate themselves with the new Society, and some condemned it out of hand – including Sir William Thomson (1824-1907), a leading scientist who among other things believed flight in a heavier-than-air machine to be impossible, and X-rays a delusion, and who called the whole idea "wretched".

However, the Society prospered, and its membership in the early years included not only some reputable scientists but a number of well-known public figures, including Gladstone (1809-98), Tennyson (1809-92), Ruskin (1819-1900) and the artist G. F. Watts (1817-1904). Its range was considerable – it looked not only at table-turnings and rappings and the various forms of spiritualism, but at "ghosts", hypnotism, thought-transference and physical phenomena.

Although no society was yet in being on the Continent of Europe, serious experiments were taking place there: the most notable perhaps in Italy. Reports were received of a medium, Eusapia Palladino, to whom poltergeists appeared to have attached themselves. Following claims that she was a cheat, in 1908 the Society for Psychical Research, organized a series of seances in Naples which were attended by several SPR members experienced in exposing cheats. Thoroughly sceptical, they were nevertheless unanimous in their conclusion: Eusapia Palladino "was not detected in fraud in any one of the 470 phenomena that took place at 11 seances." During a tour in America in 1909 she was caught cheating and her reputation collapsed. Nevertheless, many people best placed to judge remained convinced of her powers.

The growth of interest in the new science or art of psychology was bound to attach itself to such people as mediums, and to offer explanations of their powers which were within its own domain – although while these theories claimed to discover strange states of mind, they could never offer any rational basis for them.

Enter PSI

Although in the 20th century the British SPR and similar bodies throughout the world have continued to look at what might be called traditional supernatural events – "ghosts", automatic writing, poltergeists and so on – attention has recently been focused on what has become known as PSI, and which is roughly divided into two categories: ESP and PK.

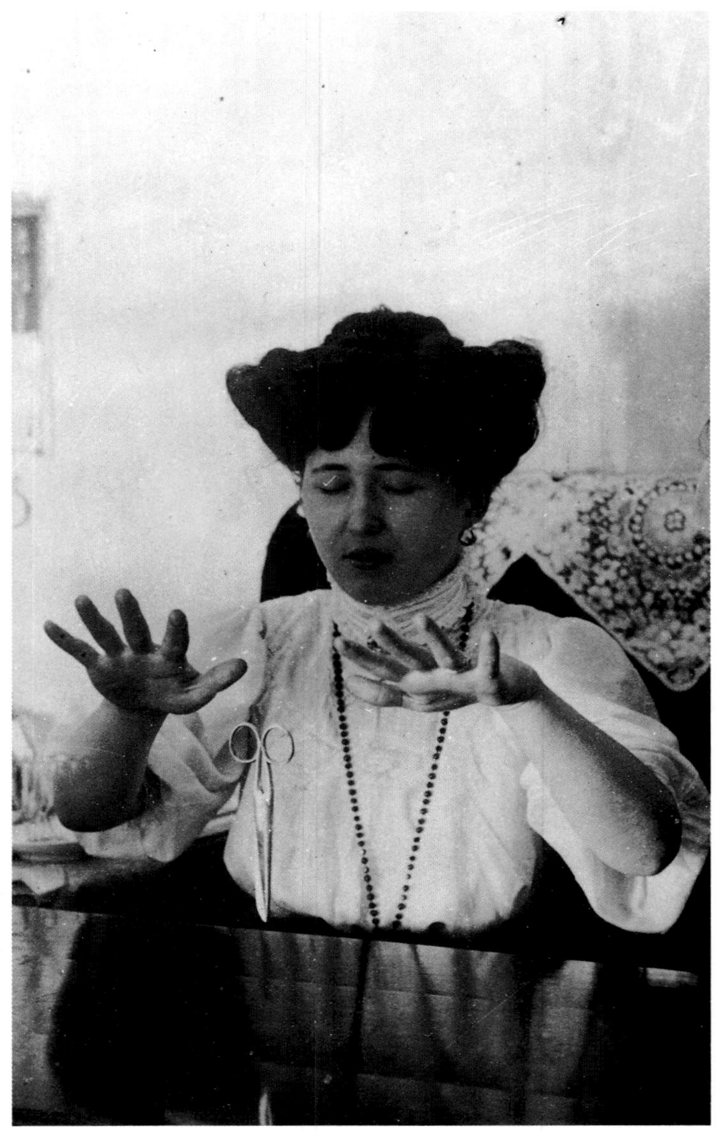

Scissors lift from a table (above), *levitated by Polish medium Stanislawa Tomczyk. Mrs Tomczyk (who was the widow of an Englishman called Fielding) levitated many objects during the early 1900s, but then abandoned spiritualism.*

A video camera *caught lamps swinging* (right) *as a German girl, Anne-Marie, walked down a corridor of a law office in Rosenheim, West Germany. Anne-Marie was the centre of intense poltergeist activity: there were telephone calls at a rate beyond what was technically possible, electrical fuses exploded, and pictures swung on the walls. The phenomena were witnessed by more than 40 people, including scientists.*

ESP, or extra-sensory perception, includes the means by which it is possible for certain people to "receive" in some way knowledge which they could not possibly acquire in any "rational" way. PK, or psychokinesis, is related to table-rapping or object-moving, and deals with an alleged ability to move objects or influence people by a simple act of will not involving any recognizable physical force. There are various sub-categories: ESP includes telepathy, clairvoyance and precognition, while PK includes metal-bending.

There has been no shortage of modern examples of alleged supernatural powers in all these areas, particularly perhaps in precognition. Some of these can be ignored – for example, there have been several instances of people who dreamed of the assassination of President Kennedy. But given that everyone in the world dreams several dreams a night, and given Kennedy's high profile, it would have been amazing if a number of people had not dreamed of his assassination.

But there are instances far more difficult to explain away – for example, that of a woman in Plymouth, England, who on October 20 1965, told six witnesses at a spiritualist church, that in a trance she had "seen" an avalanche of coal sliding down a Welsh mountainside towards a terrified child. On the following morning a coal tip at Aberfan in Wales slid down a mountainside and killed 128 children. Does simple coincidence seem a sufficiently persuasive explanation?

The SPR has innumerable records of apparently well-supported instances of PSI ability. There are also many recorded instances of telepathy or clairvoyance – an apparent link between two people (sometimes lovers or relatives, or at any rate two people with a strong emotional bond).

There are obviously many difficulties in checking anecdotes of PSI ability; we all know people who have stories of precognition or telepathy, and may even have experienced them ourselves. The difficulty is in knowing whether they – or we – have misremembered or embroidered the anecdotes. If we have written them down or told them to witnesses, the evidence is strengthened – there is no apparent reason why witnesses should lie about such matters, especially if they are uninterested in PSI.

So the relatively few people interested in proving that PSI exists have had to attempt to devise foolproof tests. One of the most notable of these was Joseph Banks Rhine (1895-1980), of Duke University, North Carolina, who devised a five-card test (see p.64). Subjects were asked to "guess" which card would turn up next in random experiment. The scientific viability of such a test depends on the well-established laws of chance: if in a run of 25 cards, a score higher than 5 is achieved, this is greater than chance dictates.

One of the more interesting facts to have emerged from this and other tests confirms the assertion that scepticism actually weakens a person's ability to participate in PSI experiments: indeed, there is some reason to suppose that it damages what ESP abilities one may have. Experiments mounted by Dr Gertrude Schmeidler at the City University of New York in 1942 with 1,308 subjects not only showed that those who believed in ESP or at least accepted that it might exist, consistently scored more highly in Rhine's tests than sceptics; more interestingly, the latter's scores were actually *below chance*. Thirty years later a Californian, John Palmer, looked at similar data collected from experiments held as far afield as India, Argentina and Czechoslovakia and found that they confirmed Schmeidler's experiments.

Raymond B. Cattell in America and Professor Hans Eysenck in England have subsequently attempted to discover whether there is any correlation between personal psychology and PSI ability, and seem to have found that extroverts achieve better results in ESP tests than introverts. This claim has been supported by independent experiments mounted in South Africa, Sweden and India. Dr Eysenck has suggested that this has something to do with the fact that there is a lower level of activity in the cortex of the extrovert's brain than in the introvert's. Ramakrishna Rao, an Indian researcher, believes that social attitudes may play their part – the extrovert's more open, relaxed attitude to life may be more receptive to PSI influences than the closed, sometimes tense psychological state of the introvert.

A much clearer relationship seems to exist between PSI ability and gender: more women have ESP experiences than men – or at least, more women report them. This may be because they are less inhibited about admitting them; or there may be a genuine sexual difference (women certainly seem to "receive" telepathic messages more easily than men).

A comparatively recent development in the examination of ESP has been the attempt to examine the different physical or psychological conditions under which it flourishes. Particular attention has been paid to apparent cases of telepathy or precognition in dreams (something reported in literature for at least 4,000 years).

During the 1960s and 70s, Dr Montague Ullman ran a Dream Laboratory at the Maimonides Medical Center in Brooklyn, New York, where, with Dr Stanley Krippner, he attempted to discover (among other things) whether sleeping people could receive, telepathically, messages sent to them by others who were awake. He did this by offering the "senders", at random, pictures on which they concentrated while the "receivers", asleep in another room, were awakened at the end of REM sleep (Rapid Eye Movement Sleep, during which dreams are known to occur) and asked to describe what they had seen. Experiments over a considerable period came up with a success rate of more than 75 percent.

The Maimonides Center then turned its attention to precognitive dreams, with almost equal success, especially with an English psychic, Malcolm Bessent.

One of the Center's researchers, Charles Honorton, came to the conclusion that the PSI sense was one not unlike the other five senses, but much weaker – for it seemed to thrive best under calm, noiseless conditions, or in sleep. He tested this, first by equipping volunteers with blindfolds and earmuffs, then by using sensory-deprivation equipment. This turned out to be too disturbing and frightening to most subjects to be of service; but a relaxed state induced by white noise and low lighting had results considerably above chance in a picture-guessing experiment. This seems to confirm the suspicion that PSI functions best under calm, stressfree conditions – not achievable in the presence of highly antagonistic sceptics, and perhaps explaining the bad results achieved by psychics under test conditions.

A connection has also been made between PSI abilities and meditation. Indian yogis have achieved strange feats which have astonished Western observers (for example, Swami Rama once stopped his heartbeat for so long that one of the doctors observing him had a coronary from anxiety). The highest results in tests have often been achieved not when the subject is in a meditative state, but just afterward.

Modern research into PK has shed very little light on its nature. However, there have been cases which have been so thoroughly examined by serious researchers that their strangeness cannot be doubted. Perhaps the best-known of these centred around a 19-year-old girl, Anne-Marie, who worked in a law office in Rosenheim, West Germany. Post Office engineers having failed to trace mysterious telephone calls, and electrical engineers being unable to discover why electrical fuses regularly exploded, Professor Hans Bender of the University of Freiberg began an investigation.

It was soon discovered that the strange events occurred only when Anne-Marie was in the building, and the physicists' equipment monitored inexplicable electrical surges in her vicinity. When she left the office, the effects ceased. As well as the visiting scientists, more than 40 witnesses confirmed the phenomena.

A somewhat similar case was examined in North California in 1967 by the Psychical Research Foundation there: the psychokinetic effects were connected with a 19-year-old boy, Julio, a shipping clerk in whose presence objects flew from shelves. The investigators were able to record ten occasions on which target objects moved in their presence, and while they were carefully observing the boy. This case, like that of Anne-Marie, proved inexplicable except in terms of PSI.

Less work has been done on PK than on ESP; perhaps because it is less interesting to the layman – or was until, in 1973, Uri Geller (b.1946), a one-time amateur conjurer, stunned Britain by his dramatic feats of metal-bending on television. His appearances sparked off such controversy that it is almost impossible to discuss him rationally; quieter investigation of PK went on elsewhere (see pp.61-2).

Meanwhile, there is a slowly growing consensus, articulated first by the American parapsychologist Rex Stanford, that we *all* possess PSI. Stanford asserts that even those who resolutely refuse to believe in the paranormal unconsciously use PSI every day – and that this explains the strange coincidences which often occur in our lives. He suggests that we also use those powers in ways which we do not suspect.

Some odd but interesting experiments have been devised to attempt to confirm this supposition. In one case, James Carpenter, of Duke University divided a number of subjects into two groups – one of relatively high-anxiety personalities, the other with low-anxiety. He asked them to guess the ESP cards placed in a number of sealed envelopes: but they did not know that in half of the envelopes Carpenter had also placed pornographic pictures. The result quite clearly showed that the high-anxiety group scored better when the envelopes held only the cards; the low-anxiety, more relaxed people scored more highly when the pornographic pictures were included. Why had there been a noticeable reaction to an element about which none of the subjects could possibly have known, if not by some unconscious use of PSI?

It is clear that if we accept this theory it explains many apparent "magical" elements of life. For example, for centuries it has been generally accepted that there is a form of sexual magic which can be used by one person to attract another: some men seem able to attract a woman simply by concentrating upon his desire for her. Is PSI at work?

Science and the Supernatural

In an interesting book written with his colleague Carl Sargent (*Explaining the Unexplained,* 1982) Dr Eysenck claimed that "a clear majority of scientists believe that ESP is either an established fact or a likely possibility, and that parapsychology is a bona fide scientific enterprise." But, he points out, parapsychology remains relatively disreputable.

One reason for this is that the history of the supernatural is full of unverifiable tall stories; another is that in comparatively recent times a number of frauds have been unmasked; yet another that those most interested in the paranormal have tended to be "outsiders", as antagonistic to science as scientists have been antagonistic to them.

But perhaps the major obstacle has been the relentlessly closed minds of those scientists who unhesitatingly assert that they are now aware of all the laws of physics, and that anything which appears to contradict them cannot possibly exist. This attitude is, of course, anti-scientific. The necessity of accepting the unbelievable is as strong now as it has ever been, if we are to make progress. Of course it is true that some "evidence" for PSI or other areas of supernature has been shown to be doubtful (frequently by other parascientists!); but any honest man must assert that the positive evidence now far outweighs the negative.

Powers and Phenomena

Witchcraft

Witchcraft, sorcery and simple spell-casting are as ancient as humankind: there is some evidence from cave markings that palaeolithic man indulged in it. It is also universal: African tribesmen chanted much the same invocations as the witches in Shakespeare's *Macbeth*.

We may not fully realize the extent to which ancient magical ideas have coloured our culture. Many of the customs of Western people who may not be in the least interested in magic derive from ancient beliefs. They also survive in children's rhymes. The mother who croons "Sing a song of sixpence" to her child has no idea that she is recalling the legend of the Celtic spirits of the Underworld to whom Rhiannon sent 24 blackbirds to announce the death of Man. Many of us, when children, were told how to cure warts – perhaps by rubbing them with a piece of meat and then burying it: as the meat rotted, the warts would disappear. These are small examples of ritual folklore, or domestic magic. Real witchcraft, seen as far more attractive or repulsive, is something different.

Witchcraft and sorcery traditionally differ from other forms of spell-casting in that they involve always doing evil to others by supernatural means. And witches are distinguished from sorcerers in that witches are deemed essentially evil while sorcerers merely perform the occasional evil act.

Although in all societies there was a relationship between witchcraft and evil, personified by witches, witches were by no means always outcasts; most people used the more innocent charms they taught.

In medieval Europe almost every village had its healer or wizard, much as every African tribe until recently had its witch doctor. These village magicians were often more or less innocent healers, who simply knew, for example, a lot about the healing properties of plants.

Covens, local groups of witches, met at their secret places – and many churches were built near groves which custom had made magical – for their *Sabbath* or *Sabbat* (the name probably derives from the Hebrew word for the seventh day) at least once a week. Two more important ceremonies – April 30, the eve of May Day or Walpurgis Night, and October 31, All Hallows Eve or Hallowe'en – may have been linked to older, pagan festivals. The so-called grand Sabbats were supposed to take place on the four pagan seasonal festivals – winter or Candlemas (February 2), spring (June 23), summer or Lammas Day (August 1), and autumn (December 21).

The agenda for a Sabbat began with homage to the Devil and the initiation of new witches. A banquet and dancing followed. The ceremony concluded with a good deal of sex. The Devil would attend important Sabbats in person – the person of a man who had probably inherited the right to play the part, and who wore the mask of a diabolical face on his backside, beneath an animal's tail; this would be kissed by everyone present before some of the women took part in ritual copulation with him. For the purpose he was equipped with an artificial horn phallus.

Sexual magic (see pp.32-3) has always played a major part

These modern witches (above), *photographed dancing around a bonfire near Lough Leane, County Kerry, Eire, in 1981, have fulfilled age-old criteria: they are naked, the time is midnight, and sticks are placed in the ground to form a pentagram. These witches' purpose was to invoke a water monster, and to build power for magical purposes.*

Pan plays his pipe *on the left of this painting* (right) *by Sidney Lang, 1898, while on the right two satyrs dance with their nymphs. Elementary spirits of the forests and mountains, satyrs were half-human, half-goat. They spent their time sleeping, playing pipes, or cavorting with nymphs (for they were lewd and lascivious by nature). They were originally associated with the god Dionysus.*

in witchcraft ritual. The Christian church's preoccupation with the sinfulness of sex may have encouraged witches to indulge in "the sins of the flesh" – demons often appeared even to upright citizens as *succubi*, irresistibly beautiful seductive women, or as *incubi*, comely young men. Nuns suffered particularly from assaults by incubi; when the Inquisition was at its height, intercourse with an incubus was an act expected of a witch, and women were tortured until they confessed to it. Ritualistic invocations of the life force were frequently accompanied by behaviour that in other public contexts would be considered wildly improper – the anal kiss, perhaps, or the feigned rape.

The magical force released by these goings-on were sometimes used (allegedly) for good; sometimes for evil. The latter was generally believed to be the case in the 16th century, although it was commonly suggested that it was a massive, planned operation by many covens of English witches which raised the storm that led to the defeat of the Spanish Armada – perhaps the Establishment was not above using magic when there was advantage in it.

There is little doubt that there was a lot of witchcraft about in 16th and 17th century Europe; although the witch trials that soaked so many places in blood often fixed on innocent old women whose "guilt" consisted merely of a smattering of knowledge of herbalism, or some minor physical defects such as a mole or a wart in the wrong place. One of the most infamous trials took place in 1692 in the New England village of Salem. A group of eight girls began behaving in a bizarre fashion: they eventually claimed that spells had been cast on them and named three villagers as witches. Panic and terror spread until 200 people had been charged with witchcraft and imprisoned. A special court was set up to try them and only after 34 had been hanged did Salem come to its senses. A revulsion against witch-hunting led in 1736 to legislation that made it an offence to accuse someone of witchcraft.

Witchcraft displays universal characteristics. Those Scottish witches who insisted that they flew to Elfland with the Queen of the Fairies were no more and no less mad than the American Indians who said that they visited the Land of the Dead, to see their relatives in their new homes; or the children of Java who flew through the air on the backs of animal spirits. Flying, incidentally, was a witch's usual mode of transport – on broomsticks, in Europe; in saucer-shaped baskets in Central Africa; on the backs of animal familiars in Africa. Witches loved to be contrary – indeed, black magic was "the left-hand path", and witches presented themselves all over the world as mirror-images of normality: the Logo and Keliko witches of the Congo went about upside down, and those of the Kaguru people of Tanganyika walked about on their hands. In our own time, the initiation of newcomers to the witches' covens of the Ozark Hills in America ended with the recitation of the Lord's Prayer – backwards.

Witchcraft became extremely unrespectable during the 18th and 19th centuries: apart from public feeling, there was also the spectre of the bonfire. Yet witches survived – in England, in the remote New Forest and the Welsh marches; in France in the Vosges and in Brittany; in Germany in the Brocken and the Black Forest. In Italy small groups of naked villagers would meet to pray to Tana, the moon-goddess whom the Romans called Diana.

As with other occult phenomena, interest in witchcraft has greatly increased during the present century; there are probably more people around now who would call themselves witches than there have been for centuries. Some of them are clearly extraordinarily unpleasant individuals: there have been desecrations of churchyards, the digging up of bodies, the decapitation of animals, and so on.

In England one man was particularly responsible for a renewed interest in witchcraft during and after the Second World War. Gerald Gardner (1884–1964) seems to have formed his first coven during the war for the admirable purpose of focusing the powers of good to help the Allies to win. He did this by encouraging the members of his coven to perform nude dancing rituals, with a certain amount of harmless bondage and mild flagellation. He also revived the legendary Great Rite, during which the High Priest (himself) and High Priestess (elected for the occasion) copulated in full view of the coven.

It is difficult not to conclude that his preoccupation with witchcraft was to some extent centred on sexuality; and that may be true of some contemporary covens, whose activities are led by the High Priest, often bearing a ceremonial phallus, and High Priestess, accompanied by a Witch Queen or Magus. The ceremony begins with the fivefold kiss – High Priest and Priestess kissing each other's feet, knees, genitals, breasts and lips – after which new members are initiated with the help of various rites. The proceedings usually end with the Priest and Priestess copulating either symbolically or actually.

Although the part played by sexuality in witchcraft rites is often denied by modern witches, it certainly still plays its part – as does nudity (in a charming phrase, a naked person is described as "sky-clad"). A clothed witch has always been considered less powerful than a naked one: even removing the shoes increases one's magical muscle.

According to modern witches, any orgies that take place are about as exciting as a church social – wine is drunk and buns marked with crosses (symbolizing a disc marked into seasonal quadrants) are eaten, and there is general gossip and agreeable conversation.

The connection between modern witchcraft and magic seems somewhat tenuous. The activities of 20th-century covens may or may not harness ancient powers; but the members do not seem to do a great deal with them, although some covens have been looking at ancient magical arts and attempting to test them – and at new theories, such as the possible relationship between ley-lines (see pp.42-3) and the ancient, positive powers of the earth. Ancient rituals, magic circles and symbols, traditional prayers (many of them from Leland's *Arcadia*, a well-known authority much consulted by Gardner) continue to be used by modern witches, whose activities are at worst harmless and at best positive.

Satanism

There is one obvious exception to the relative innocence of most witchcraft rituals, and that is Satanism or Devil-worship, of which vestiges still exist in Europe and America (in North America, experiments appear to have been provoked by some of the recent movies based on the powers of the Devil).

The name Satan is derived from the Hebrew word for "adversary"; it is in the Biblical Book of Job that Satan first appears as a malignant force; in the Book of Enoch, which influenced early Christians, "satans" appeared as angels of punishment; gradually the Satan became a false accuser, a slanderer, and was identified with the Devil, whom Jesus saw as the protagonist of worldliness, luxury and pride. Later, the Christian church, with its intense mistrust of sensuality, identified him also with sexual desire.

Devil-worshippers do not, of course, see him as evil, but as the enemy of Christianity, and therefore good (for the Christian god is seen by them as wicked). Traditionally, Satanists have loved sensual pleasure, violence and cruelty, and their worship has therefore involved acts which most people would regard as repellent, if not "evil" – including human sacrifice and bizarre sexual acts.

The central ceremony of the Roman Catholic church being

Cecil Williamson (above), *a well known witch from Castletown in the Isle of Man, passes a "poppet" image through flames in order to defeat a curse laid on him in a letter written by a woman. Williamson directed the "Witches Kitchen" in Castletown.*

The goat (right) *has a long relationship with mystical religion. It was venerated in ancient Egypt as a symbol of fecundity and may have been the idol Baphomet, worshipped by the medieval Knights Templar. It was turned by Judeo-Christianity into the devil, and thereafter was worshipped at witches' sabbats.*

The pentagram (left) *is a potent religious and magical symbol. However, in this collection of black-magic accoutrements, it is inverted, the central arm pointing downwards instead of upwards. The devilish goat is placed in the centre.*

the Mass, diabolists have concentrated on parodying it, not only to insult those whose beliefs they despised, but to give the participators mystical strength.

Black Masses have been held for at least 1,700 years (St Irenaeus reported one in the 2nd century AD). The *grimoires* (see p.144) are full of allusions to them, and instructions for holding them. Classically, this involves the killing of a black cock at sunrise, the drying and powdering of its eyes, heart and tongue, and the writing of magic characters with one of its feathers, using consecrated wine as ink. In the ensuing ceremony the "host", represented by a turnip, was abased rather than elevated, water or urine took the place of wine, and there were cries of "Beelzebub!" The robes of the priest were embroidered with naked women, pigs or goats.

Sexual excess is almost always involved in Black Masses. Madeleine Bavent, a nun of Louviers in Normandy, left in her autobiography vivid accounts of black masses in which she participated in the early 17th century, after she had been seduced by a priest. The trouble started with the convent's eccentric chaplain, Fr Pierre David, who insisted that God should be worshipped naked, in the manner of Adam. This led to certain familiarities between himself and the nuns; after his death Fr Mathurin Picard was appointed chaplain, and the Black Masses began, during which there were regular ceremonial rapes on the altar, nuns wore grotesque animal costumes, roasted human flesh was eaten, and the nuns enjoyed coitus with Fr Picard and with Fr David's ghost.

Similar accounts can be found all over Europe, although it is difficult not to believe that some at least are fictional, for Satanism has often been an ingredient of pornography. Indeed, accounts of Black Masses in the 19th century became so scatological that we must suspect this – though there is little doubt that Satanism continued to be practised. In 1889 a reporter of *Le Matin* described a ceremony he attended with 50 worshippers, during which mass was said on the naked body of a woman strapped to an altar, while black hosts were consecrated and eaten before the enjoyment of an orgy.

More modern accounts also exist. William Seabrook reports in his *Witchcraft* (1940) attending Black Masses in London, Paris, Lyons and New York where the ancient tradition was observed of a male or female prostitute acting as acolyte, and the naked body of a virgin used as altar. Julio Caro Baroja attended a ceremony in the Basque country in 1942 at which a cat was boiled alive, and the soup drunk by six naked men and women who chanted obscene prayers between mouthfuls.

Rumours of Black Masses have surfaced during the past 30 years, perhaps particularly in Italy and England: in Sussex and Bedfordshire the altars of churches have been reconsecrated after obscene rites had been observed.

Whether Satanism can actually release occult powers remains to be seen. Many people strongly believe that it can. Certainly it is believed by some of the participants, though many others must surely take part – as some, no doubt, participate in white witchcraft – because of the sexual element in the ceremonies.

Laurie Cabot (above) *is a self-confessed Salem witch today. She runs a black magic boutique called Crow Haven Corner.*

Charles Manson (right) *used sexual magic to enhance his control over the "family" – the commune of disciples he set up in the Los Angeles Hills, where bizarre rites of initiation bound them in absolute obedience to all his orders – including murder.*

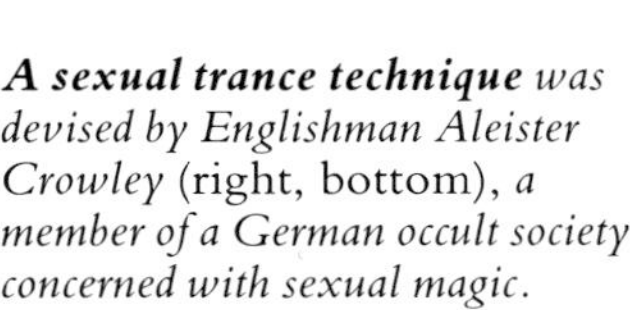

A sexual trance technique *was devised by Englishman Aleister Crowley* (right, bottom), *a member of a German occult society concerned with sexual magic.*

Sexual Magic

The energy and engrossing power of sex being what it is, it is not surprising that it has had throughout history a powerful magical connotation.

The magical element of human love is commonly experienced in the pull that is felt – not only sexually, but spiritually – between one person and another, often at first meeting, and sometimes even before that. It has resulted in innumerable happy lifetime partnerships. On the other hand, the erotic element in such an attraction has often proved destructive, and sometimes all-consuming. The greatest seducers have recognized that the total concentration of desire, strongly focused, is an almost irresistible aphrodisiac – Don Juan's secret weapon.

But it is the similarity between a person in the grip of powerful sexual passion and someone allegedly "possessed" by a demon, which is most marked. We speak of a lover "possessing" his mistress – the urge seems to be to be not so much the taking or giving of pleasure, as the desire to be one with the loved one. And of course the actions and sounds associated with lovemaking are very common in states of demonic possession.

The religious ceremonies of many civilizations have had strong sexual elements, from the days of Aphrodite onward – even Christianity, which for so long regarded human sexuality as bestial, spoke of Christ as the Bridegroom and the human soul (even the masculine soul) as His bride. *The Song of Solomon*, that most erotic poem so surprising a part of the Bible, was made acceptable to Christians by claiming it was a paeon of Christ's love for his Church, and the very marriage ceremony speaks of the groom "adoring" the bride with his body, just as the worshipper must "adore" God.

It is not surprising, then, that sexual excitement has been a part of many occult ceremonies – even in Christianity, although this was heavily disguised in medieval monasteries and nunneries, and John Wesley was being naive when he innocently referred to his meetings as "love feasts". Some early American evangelist meetings were less innocent, the faithful achieving physical orgasm during their celebratory praises. Several religious sects have used *carezza* – prolonged sexual intercourse without reaching orgasm – in order to attain a state of ecstasy in which – or after which – spiritual delight is said to reach unparalleled heights.

In the West, sexuality has only been fully acknowledged by Christianity in the context of marriage. Outside marriage it has been (and sometimes still is) associated with evil, even with witchcraft. The *Malleus Maleficarum* or *Hammer of Witches*, printed in 1486, in which Jacob Sprenger and Heinrich Kramer set out the rules for discovering and questioning a witch, goes out of its way to emphasize the ways in which witches copulated with incubi.

This was believed quite literally (in 1485 in one German city alone, 41 witches were burned for publicly affirming – no doubt after dreadful torture – that they had copulated with devils). Great attention was paid to illicit dealings in semen: "A succubus devil draws the semen from a wicked man; and if he is that man's own particular devil, and does not wish to make himself an incubus to a witch, he passes that semen on to the devil deputed to a woman or witch; and this last, under some constellation that favours his purpose that the man or woman so born should be strong in the practice of witchcraft, becomes the incubus to the witch."

Puritans emphasized that the pleasures of sex were particularly likely to lead to the downfall of young virgins, male or female, supporting their homilies with cautionary tales:

"A certain young girl, a devout virgin, was solicited one Feast Day by an old woman to go with her upstairs to a room where there were some very beautiful young men. And when she consented, and as they were going upstairs with the old woman leading the way, she warned the girl not to make the sign of the Cross. And although she agreed to this, yet she secretly crossed herself. Consequently it happened that . . . the virgin saw no one, because the devils who were there were unable to show themselves in assumed bodies to that virgin."

Sprenger and Kramer emphasized that one of the devil's regular occupations was making love to witches: "The witches themselves have often been seen lying on their backs in the fields or the woods, naked up to the very navel; it has been apparent from the disposition of those limbs and members which pertain to the venereal act and orgasm, as also from the agitation of their legs and thighs, that, invisibly to the bystanders, they have been copulating with incubus evils."

The best known modern western practitioner of quasi-tantric diabolic sexual religion was the Englishman Aleister Crowley, who in London at the beginning of the 20th century was a member of the Golden Dawn Society; between 1902 and 1906 he travelled in the Orient and began to experiment with drugs. In Germany, with the Ordo Templi Orientis, an occult society concerned with sexual magic, he began those practises which were to preoccupy him for the rest of his life. In 1911 he devised his own sexual trance technique, which he later described:

"The candidate is made ready for the ordeal by general athletic training and by fasting. On the appointed day he is waited on by one or more experienced attendants whose duty it is to exhaust him sexually by every known means. The candidate will sink into a sleep of utter exhaustion, but he must be again sexually stimulated and then again allowed to fall asleep. This alternation is to continue indefinitely until the candidate is set free by perfect exhaustion of the body . . . and communes with the most Highest and the Most Holy Lord God of its Being, Maker of Heaven and Earth."

In the course of the activities which followed, potions containing blood and semen were prepared and consumed, allegedly allowing total communication with spirits, giving the ability to foretell the future or to utter efficient curses.

Crowley died a confirmed heroin addict in 1947. There are strong parallels between his obscene delusions and those of a number of criminals whose cases have shocked Western society since then: most notably, perhaps, Charles Manson. The use of heightened sexuality to induce trance-states and alleged possession persists but it has obvious dangers.

Explicit temple carvings *at Khajuraho in India* (right) *show how closely sexual and religious ecstasy can be identified. The Tantric cults of India, among the oldest of all that country's cults, had ceremonies involving not only sexuality but terror, sadism and masochism, often stimulated by drugs (hashish in particular); one Hindu scholar has described them as "the most revolting and horrible that human depravity could think of." In order to store up sexual energy, all amorous activity was forbidden for some days before a ceremony, when the participants, further stimulated by drugs, participated in ritualistic intercourse while chanting special mantras. It was believed that the energy released enabled the worshippers to be united with demons (good and bad) and gods. Temple prostitutes were often available to help arouse male worshippers to the necessary pitch of excitement.*

HEALING

The late 1980s saw an enormous growth of interest in the alleged healing power of crystals. As a by-product, they also began to be used as a predictive device (although there is little evidence of an ancient tradition of that use, except in the form of the crystal ball, which acted as a focus for instinctive seers).

There seems to be no general agreement about the relative healing powers of various crystals: some healers seem to attribute certain powers to certain stones solely because of their colour, others allot powers to them by using the Hindu *chakras*, the seven energy centres of the body. Yet again, some simply "feel" that a crystal has a particular influence.

Crystal healers also argue about the precise way in which the crystals should be used: some suggest that they should be placed in a specific pattern on the patient's body; others that the relevant stone should be placed on the relevant *chakra*. Yet others place crystals around the body, but not touching it.

Perhaps the most respected healer to use crystals is the Englishman Harry Oldfield, who works with the electromagnetic field of the body, which can often indicate at an early stage the onset of disease (see his book, *The Dark Side of the Brain*). Because crystals also possess electromagnetic forces (he claims), they can be used on the same basis as homeopathic medicine, "treating like with like." He uses Kirlian photography (see pp.161-2) to match human auras with the discernible aura of crystals.

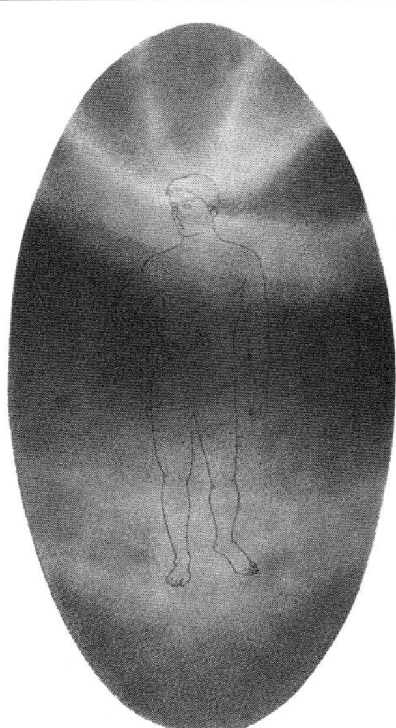

Quartz crystals *(silicon dioxide),* (above) *are the most important healing crystals. They are also a main source of piezoelectricity – when compressed (for example, struck with a hammer) they (and other crystals) give off a tiny electrical charge; a lithium battery connected to a crystal will emit electrical energy at a constant rate (this can be used to drive a watch). Healers claim that this electrical energy – usually provoked, it is claimed, not by a battery but by the power of the healer's mind – has curative properties.*

The aura*, or "astral body" of the average human is an envelope of coloured light* (left)*, egg-shaped and slightly broader at the head than at the feet.*

THE AURA

Most mediums claim to be able to see the "aura", or cloud of visible energy, in the form of bands of coloured light, which is supposed to surround us all.

Although the idea had been current for many years – indeed, centuries, for the saints shown in the earliest religious paintings are often surrounded by a golden light which very much resembles our idea of an aura – it was a doctor working at St Thomas' Hospital in London who gave it a certain respectability, claiming in *The Human Atmosphere*, a book published in 1911, that by looking through coloured glass, he could see an aura of light surrounding the bodies of patients, and that the shape and colour of this aura changed with the

These crystals (left) *are used by Zulu witch doctors for divination and sometimes to cast spells. This link with the murky, even "black" magic associated with witch doctors, may surprise many who now use crystals. To such people of the New Age, crystals seem "pure" and white in their magic but, like most aspects of the supernatural, they can be used for evil purposes as well as for good.*

EXPERIMENTING WITH CRYSTALS

There are various ways to experiment with crystals. They may simply be worn: use as jewelry the crystal which allegedly has the effect you desire – or simply the one you like most (it is alleged that a crystal will "choose" its owner). According to some healers, merely holding your favourite crystal and willing it to be a channel for your desires may help you attain them.

Crystals can be steeped in pure (preferably distilled) water for 10 minutes, and the water drunk: peridot treats indigestion; rose quartz, migraine; agate gives energy; sodalite cures hangovers. Some healers suggest that the water containing the crystals be stood in the morning sun for three hours, and the resulting potion used sparingly (a few drops placed in water, or directly under the tongue).

It should be said that as far as we can discover no scientific work has been done on the powers of crystals; it is at least possible that they work most efficaciously simply by being a channel for the subconscious, conveying the will to be healed from mind to body.

health of the patient. According to some people, the colours represent specific qualities – for example, purple is supposed to have healing or therapeutic powers.

It has been suggested that he – and those others who claim to be able to see the aura – may have had extraordinary eyesight which enabled them to see the electromagnetic waves which can now be photographed by the thermographic technique, and are used to detect tumours, cancer and arthritis, which show up as "hot areas" in thermographic photographs. But there are differences between the electromagnetic waves as photographed, and the aura as described by mediums.

Descriptions of the aura have been remarkably consistent over centuries: it has a bright inner layer and a hazier outer layer, and occasionally a much brighter ray leaps out, sometimes several feet, before vanishing again. A Cambridge biologist, Oscar Bagnall, has recently discovered that the aura can be distorted by a magnet, although other forces (for example, currents of air) have no effect on it.

It is difficult, now, to deny the presence of an aura (see also the work of the Kirlians in Russia, pp.161-2); and it can at least be surmised that it is the visible evidence of a force of whose power and constituents we are at present ignorant. It is possible that the aura is more closely connected with the mind than with the body; and if that is indeed the case, may be related to PSI and PK.

Laying on of Hands

The use of crystals is just one aspect of healing – the curing of illnesses by the laying on of hands, is more traditional. The history of the subject is long, complex and controversial. The Bible, of course, quotes many instances, and so do other historical sources.

For centuries, the talent was exclusively claimed by the Church, and much associated with the casting out of devils. In the 18th century, Friedrich Anton Mesmer (see p.12) claimed that the human mind could cure most ills through the medium of induced trance: and indeed his chief successes were in the kinds of condition – convulsions and paralysis, hysteria and so on – whose roots may well have lain in the mind.

He did not claim to cure by invoking religion; but nor did he cure by traditional medical treatment. Something stranger and more interesting was clearly afoot. And it was happening not only in Europe, but in the New World – for in New England, Phineas Pankhurst Quimby was, by the middle of the 19th century, treating an enormous number of sick men and women simply – he claimed – by telling them the truth about their illnesses.

The French Zouave Jacob (near right), *originally a trombonist in a military band, discovered a talent for healing and in the middle of the 19th century became famous for his many successes: indeed, he was discharged from the army when the great crowds of people coming to the barracks to ask him to heal them became a serious inconvenience. Jacob refused all payment for his healing, and always said that he had no idea where his power came from, or what it consisted of; however, he believed firmly that it was not supernatural – although sometimes he achieved a cure simply by looking at the patients, or merely by instructing them to "be well."*

The Archbishop of Lusaka, *Emmanuel Milingo* (right, top), *is a notable faith healer who lost his archdiocese when the Vatican, disturbed by his view that most illness was caused by evil spirits, and his use of exorcism, summoned him to Rome, made him undergo medical and psychiatric examinations, and then permitted him to exercise his powers only in one church in Rome.* ***Milingo's ceremonies*** (right, bottom) *usually last five hours and end with his touching the temples and scalps of the ill.*

"I tell the patient his troubles, and what he thinks is his disease, and my explanation is the cure. If I succeed in correcting his errors I change the fluids in the system and establish the patient in health. The truth is the cure . . . Disease is false reasoning; false reasoning is sickness and death."

If this statement has a familiar ring it is because it also lies at the heart of the teaching of a much better-known healer, Mary A. Morse Baker Glover Patterson Eddy, the founder of the Christian Science movement. Mrs Eddy, a lifelong invalid, was cured by Quimby – and to his enormous irritation (for he was an agnostic) insisted that the cure was founded on "the truth of Christ."

In 1875 she published her *Science and Health*, a book which insists that pain and illness are "all in the mind":

"You say a boil is painful – but this is impossible, for matter without mind is not painful. The boil simply manifests a belief in pain, and this belief is called a boil."

Mrs Eddy wore spectacles and false teeth, and used drugs (the malicious animal magnetism of her enemies forced these upon her, she explained); but she claimed that faith cures could be effected by strict adherence to her discipline. Sometimes, no doubt, they were; Christian Science is said at present to have a total of three million followers in 50 different countries, but in its services there is no great emphasis on healing.

There are roughly speaking three types of modern healers: those who work within the Christian church (and are sometimes actually ministers), those who are members of spiritualist churches specializing in healing, and individual healers, adherents of no special church or creed, often uncertain where their power lies.

Christian healers have no monopoly of success in this field: similarly good results have been obtained by Islamic and Jewish healers, and by agnostics. Origen, the great 3rd-century Christian thinker, pointed out that the power to cure people by unconventional means was "within the reach of godless as well as honest folk. The power of curing diseases is no evidence of anything specially divine."

Nor does healing seem, on the face of it, to be supernatural, and it is interesting that the great surge of belief in healing by unconventional means – either by the laying on of a healer's hands, by the simple assurance that one is cured, or by what seems a kind of self-hypnosis – has coincided with professional medical interest in the degree to which most illnesses are psychogenic.

***A Kenyan schoolgirl**, Margaret Wangari* (right)*, became the country's most popular faith healer after she had attended a Christian camp in the Great Rift Valley. Her home village is called Banana Hill: she has become known as "the Bernadette of Banana Hill".*

***Native faith healing** practised by Nguema Antoine, in northern Gabon, is divided into the rite of the chicken and the rite of water. The child* (opposite) *was discovered to have had a spell put on him through a gift of food from his uncle. His uncle, having admitted his wrong-doing, was sent into the bush to find the plants that caused the child's anaemic state. Then the chicken was placed on the child's head. It is supposed to stay there until all aspects of the case have been aired in public, and the child has also confessed anything relevant. Then, with all revealed, the chicken will leave him and the faith healer can proceed to the rite of water by means of which the child is blessed. Antoine has been practising for almost 40 years.*

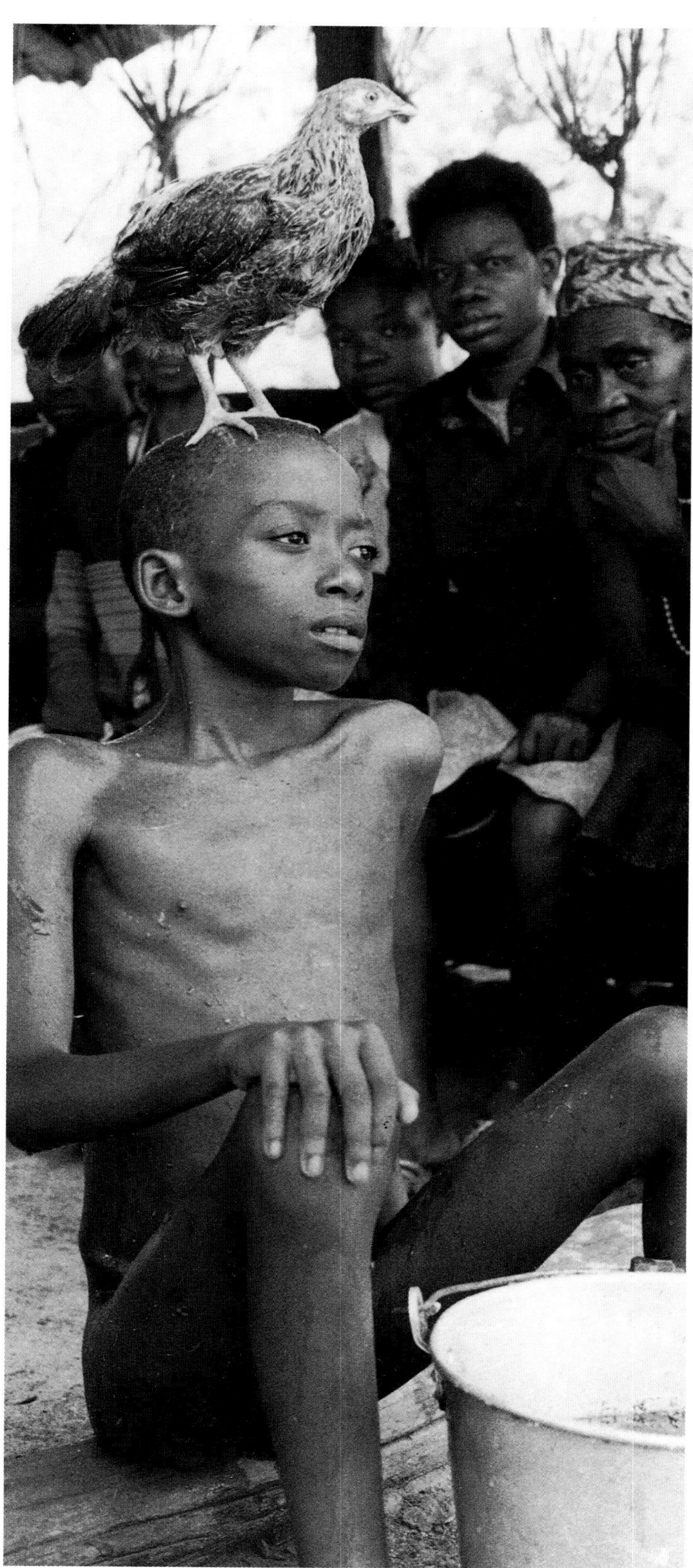

It may be that the best healers succeed in tapping that mental power which is now recognized as important by conventional medicine: a patient who can in one way or another be assured, or assure himself, that he will recover, very often *will* recover – or at least will often win a remission, even from a fatal illness. The difficulty is that the cure is too often temporary: the healers may relieve the symptoms, but they do not succeed, in general, in removing their origin.

Emile Coué, a self-taught 19th century French apothecary whose work was virtually unknown in his own time but who is now highly regarded, believed that auto-suggestion was valuable in curing patients: he was really an early proponent of "positive thinking", and claimed to have taught hundreds of patients to cure themselves.

A major difficulty in looking at unconventional medicine is that the progress of illness is still often mysterious, and real evidence hard to come by. Louis Rose, who in 1968 published a sympathetic but critical examination of faith healing in the modern world, found that despite the vast number of successes claimed by healers, he could not collect sufficient evidence of conclusive cures. "After well over 15 years of work, I have still to find one 'miracle cure'," he wrote. He goes on to quote the British Medical Association committee which advised a church commission on faith healing:

"We can find no evidence that there is any type of illness cured by 'spiritual healing' alone which could not have been cured by medical treatment . . . We find that, while patients suffering from psychogenic disorders may be 'cured' by various methods of spiritual healing, just as they are by methods of suggestion and other forms of psychological treatment employed by doctors [there is] no evidence that organic diseases are cured solely by such means. The evidence suggests that many such cases claimed to be cured are likely to be either instances of wrong diagnosis, wrong prognosis, remission or spontaneous cure."

Nevertheless, Mr Rose found what is generally true – that exceptional cases of apparently successful faith-healing do take place, sometimes at a distance; and it cannot be doubted that some faith healers are of enormous help to sufferers, even if this is often temporary.

In Europe and North America many healers work within the framework of spiritualist churches. In 1939, the British Home Office recognized spiritualism as a religion, and granted it the right to appoint ministers. Since then, it has resolved itself into two factions – the Greater World Christian Spiritualists, which recognizes Christ as its leader, and the Spiritualist National Union. There are few rules of conduct other than the Seven Principles, which range from the Brotherhood of Man and Personal Responsibility to the notion that External Progresss is Open to Every Human Soul.

Healers use various methods, some partly physical, some wholly spiritual. Many members of the churches are not healers, although everyone is encouraged to participate in the experience by, at the very least, becoming a channel through which spirit guides can communicate healing powers. Others simply seek messages from the Other Side.

Charms and amulets *are used by faith healers in north Togo, in Africa* (right) *to cure madness, or folly, thought to be caused by the evil eye or a bad spell. The faith healers, or witch doctors, employ techniques passed down through the generations. As well as charms, other traditional methods of curing insanity or apparent insanity in the region include bathing the patient with hot water infused with plants and herbs; releasing the malignant spirit by making small incisions with razor blades; and persuading the patient to inhale the vapours of a preparation of plants and roots placed on incandescent ash.*

Dowsing and the Pendulum

Dowsing – the finding of water (in particular) by the use of wooden or metal rods – is now so widespread that it cannot be regarded as supernatural, although it is certainly paranormal in the sense that the talent cannot be explained by science. Some scientists, unable to explain the phenomenon, even contrive against all the evidence to believe that it does not exist.

But dowsing has been going on for millennia: cave-paintings show dowsers working in prehistoric times, and the Egyptians and ancient Chinese civilizations also used this system to find water.

Traditionally a forked stick – of hazel, willow or peach – is used. Held out before the dowser as he or she walks across the countryside, it reacts to the presence of whatever is being sought (see p.40) – not only water, but minerals, oil, or a number of other things. Metal rods can also be used.

It was in France that serious research into dowsing began, in the early 20th century. The Vicomte Henri de France founded dowsing societies in France and in England. After the Second World War the Russians took a serious interest, and much research on the subject has been done in the USSR.

Teacher Lee Kachdorian (below), *teaches dowsing to children at a special school in Vermont. She says that learning to dowse is like tuning a radio; you must keep trying until a signal comes through loud and clear.*

Dowsing can be fine-tuned for *particular purposes. "Grattan's sandwich"* (left, top), *is sensitive enough to remain unaffected by the nearby surface waters of the Schwarm river as he dowses for water along its banks.*

Dowsing for oil *is another practical variation, as Clayton McDowell* (left, bottom), *demonstrates with his rod, which dips where there is oil underground. Dowsers can also trace the course of electrical cables beneath the ground or within walls.*

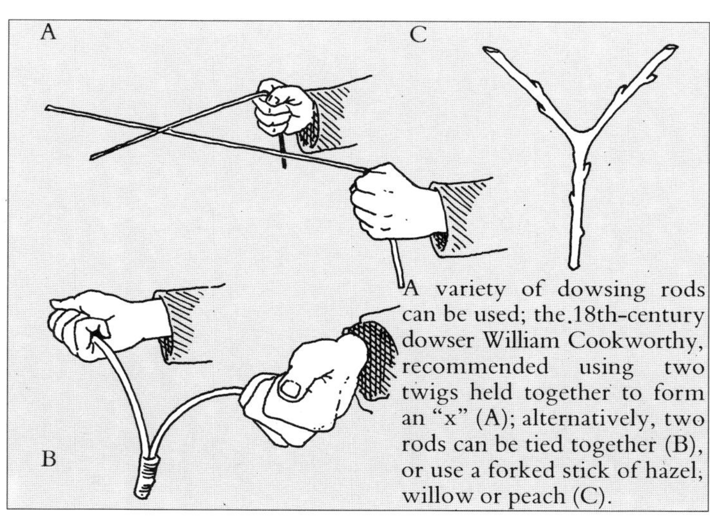

A variety of dowsing rods can be used; the 18th-century dowser William Cookworthy, recommended using two twigs held together to form an "x" (A); alternatively, two rods can be tied together (B), or use a forked stick of hazel, willow or peach (C).

Whether the dowser is using metal rods, willow, hazel or peach wood, walking sticks, whalebone, or even plastic, to find water or minerals, these materials cannot work unaided: there must be a human medium. Dowsers seem to have a special relationship to the earth's magnetic field – and this is to some extent measurable. While dowsing, their blood pressure and pulse rate increase. More women are successful as dowsers than men – but it has been claimed that animals (for example, antelope and wild pig) can find hidden water by using their tusks as divining equipment. At least one dowser – a twelve-year-old South African boy – successfully found water; he "saw" it "shimmering like green moonlight" through the earth.

Among other things, it has been shown that dowsers are particularly sensitive to the earth's magnetic field, and are capable of detecting an artificial field only one two-hundredth the strength of the earth's field. There are other, stranger, manifestations of dowsing talent: in Japan, the pendulum (in this case merely a bead on a piece of silk thread) is used to sex day-old chicks: the factories claim a 99 percent success rate using this method.

Many modern dowsers earn their living by advising oil-companies – or farmers – where to drill wells; the Canadian Ministry of Agriculture employs a permanent dowser, and dowsers have been used to locate buried explosive mines or mortar shells. The Czechoslovakian Army has a permanent corps of dowsers.

This kind of dowsing may be a matter of the physical effect of radiation on the dowser. But there is another, far more curious, means of dowsing, which does not apply only to water or oil – and does not depend on the dowser's personal presence. If this indeed works, it is impossible to offer any scientific explanation for its success.

It consists of the dowser using a pendulum and a map: searching for whatever is lost, he or she simply holds the pendulum over the map, and it begins to swing when above the spot where the object is to be found. This is very strange indeed, and would be unbelievable were it not that, using this method, dowsers have from time to time scored remarkable successes. In the hands of the most talented dowsers the results have generally been better than is statistically consistent with chance.

Andrew Archer, a dowser who works in the East Anglian area of England, claims that everyone has the power to dowse – to find water, at least, and possibly other buried material by means of a wand made of metal or wood.

The main thing to do, he claims, is to relax – and to believe that you can command the technique. Even a metal coat-hanger, the wires unwound and held out before you in the form of a V with the two separated ends pointing away from

Hamish Miller (left) *checks the alignments of standing stones at Merry Maiden's Circle near Land's End, Cornwall with his dowsing rod. The alignment of megalithic circles is thought by some people to be influenced by underground waters.*

The German army (opposite page) *used water diviners in the First World War to search for water on the Eastern Front, despite some officers' scepticism.*

you, should react to an underground stream as you pace a piece of ground, walking steadily and concentrating on what you hope to find.

"You will feel not so much a tug as a steady pull towards the ground," he says. "With some people, who are naturally good dowsers, this pull can be so strong that the rods are almost dragged from your hands. Many people are extremely startled the first time they experience this!"

More complex techniques are partly a matter of practice: although simple concentration on the material you are seeking – oil or metal or water – should be enough to allow you to differentiate between them. The ability to estimate the depth at which it is buried, the direction of a stream, or the quantities involved, comes only with repetition.

One of the most remarkable dowsers of recent years was Tom Lethbridge, sometime Keeper of Anglo-Saxon Antiquities at the Cambridge University Museum of Archaeology and Ethnology.

Lethbridge became interested in dowsing in the late 1950s, and discovered that by varying the length of thread by which a pendulum was suspended he could "tune" it to find various materials – 22 inches (56cm) for silver and lead, for example, 30½ inches (77.5cm) for copper. He believed that the power of dowsing was allied to lines of force or ley-lines (see pp.42-3), which encircled the earth.

Following up his interest, he performed many extraordinary experiments – concluding among other things that a pendulum can react to emotion, such as anger, and to physical states, including cold, sleep and death. The lines of force in the earth thus seem to interact with the human mind and body. Lethbridge expanded his theories in many books, including *Ghost and Divining Rod* (London, 1963) and *The Power of the Pendulum* (London, 1976).

WORKING WITH A PENDULUM

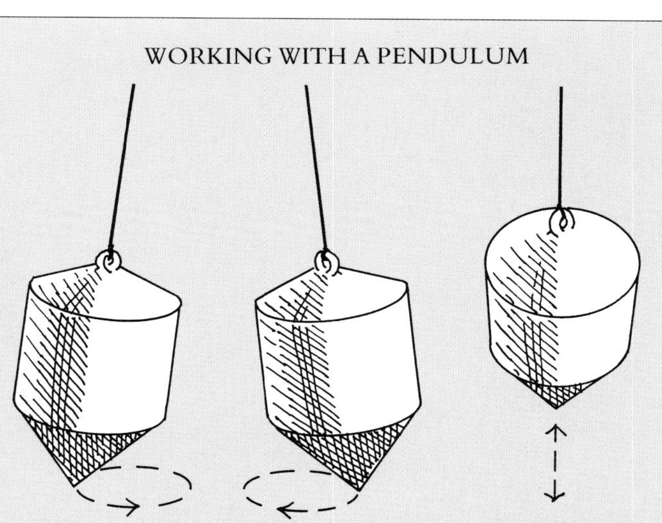

It is easy to test whether a pendulum will work for you. You can use almost anything – a button on the end of a piece of cotton will do, or wooden and other pendulums can be bought from occult stores. The thread should be between three and four inches (7.5-10cm) long. Hold the pendulum about an inch above your left hand. You will find that after a short time, it will begin to describe a small circle. If you now transfer the pendulum to your other hand, so that it hangs over your right hand, you will probably find that the circle it describes moves in the opposite direction (usually clockwise over the right hand, anti-clockwise over the left).

Now go on to a simple experiment – place a coin under a pile of books – the pendulum should begin to move almost immediately it finds itself over the metal. From this, you can move on to more complex experiments.

Ley-Lines

GLASTONBURY LEY

N
St Nicholas', Brockley
Holy Trinity, Burrington
Gorsey Bigbury
Westbury Beacon Camp
Yarley crossroads
Glastonbury Tor
St Leonard's, Butleigh

The imposing Glastonbury Tor, or hill, presides over the area of Glastonbury, one of the sites on the ley that passes through Avon. The end of the ley is Butleigh, which is near the centre of the so-called Glastonbury zodiac, a 10-mile (16 km) area marked by natural features said to represent animal and human forms.

OLD SARUM LEY

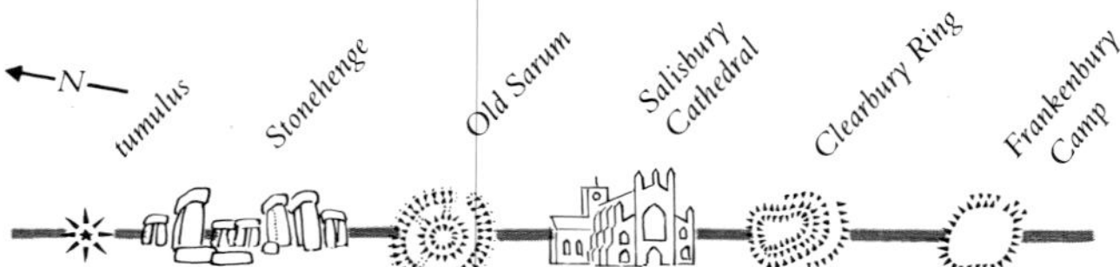

This 18½-mile (29.5 km) ley runs in Hampshire, through Stonehenge (see pp.124-5) and Salisbury Cathedral, dedicated to the Blessed Virgin Mary. The area has been the focus of inexplicable natural phenomena: dense clouds of flying ants have swarmed round the Cathedral spire, and mysterious white birds allegedly appear whenever a bishop of Salisbury is about to die.

SPEYER CATHEDRAL LEY

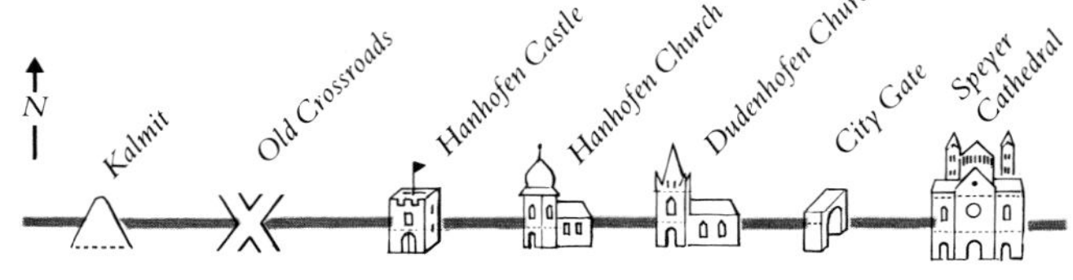

Speyer's Romanesque cathedral, dating back to the 11th century, is the largest in Europe and is built on a site regarded as sacred for some 2000 years. It is aligned with the Kalmit mountain, the highest in the region.

There has been much speculation among psychics and dowsers as to the use of ley-lines – the lines of energy that allegedly run through the earth – and whether any force they may convey can be usefully harnessed (see pp. 40-1).

Some believe that ley-lines were only instinctively understood by prehistoric man, who constructed the primitive stones and emphasised the sites which mark them. Others suggest that they are part of the structure of the earth, according to universal rules allied to the balance of the known universe. Another theory is that they were magicked into being by the scientists of Atlantis.

It may be possible to validate or measure the force of ley-lines – for example, through deviation in the behaviour of radio waves. If so, in the distant future we may understand more about these forces. Until then, we can only conjecture.

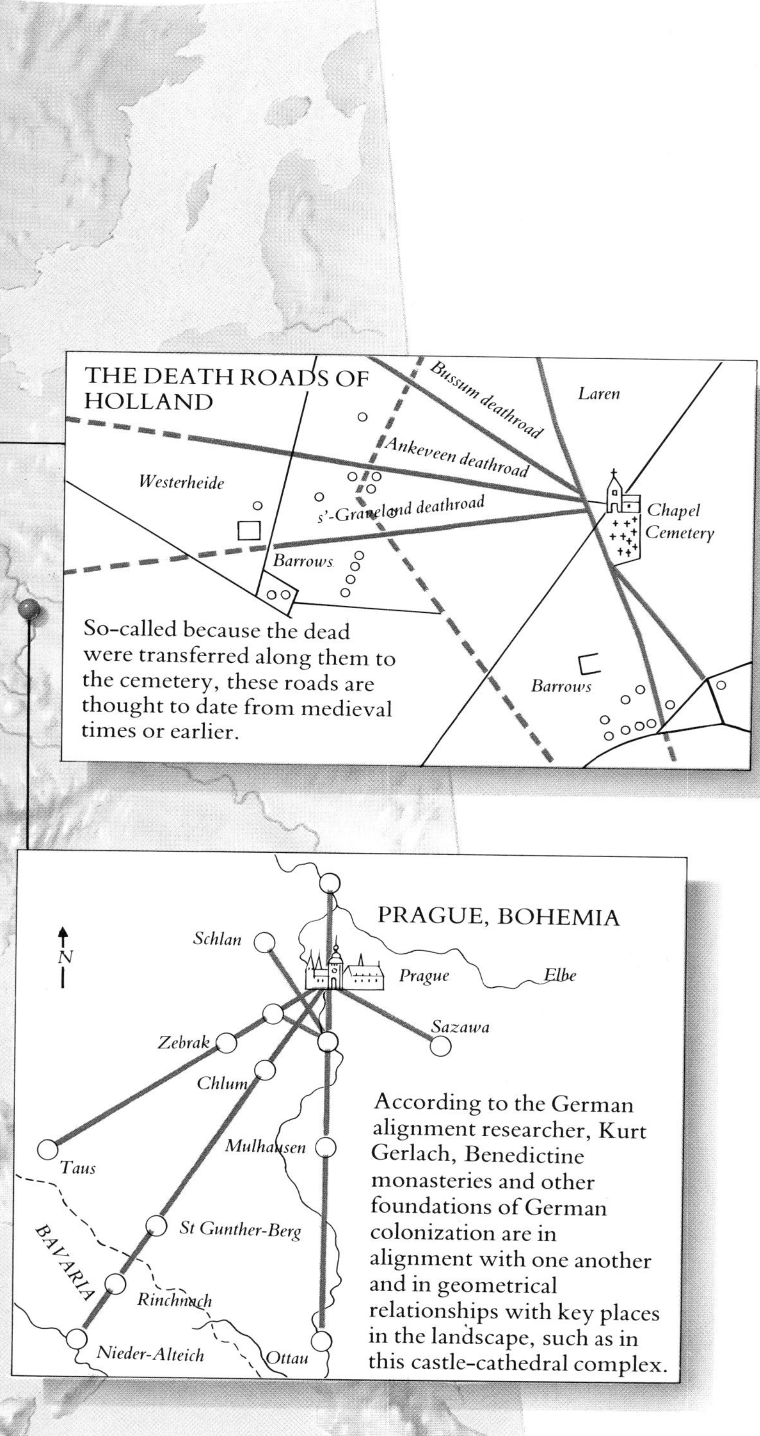

So-called because the dead were transferred along them to the cemetery, these roads are thought to date from medieval times or earlier.

According to the German alignment researcher, Kurt Gerlach, Benedictine monasteries and other foundations of German colonization are in alignment with one another and in geometrical relationships with key places in the landscape, such as in this castle-cathedral complex.

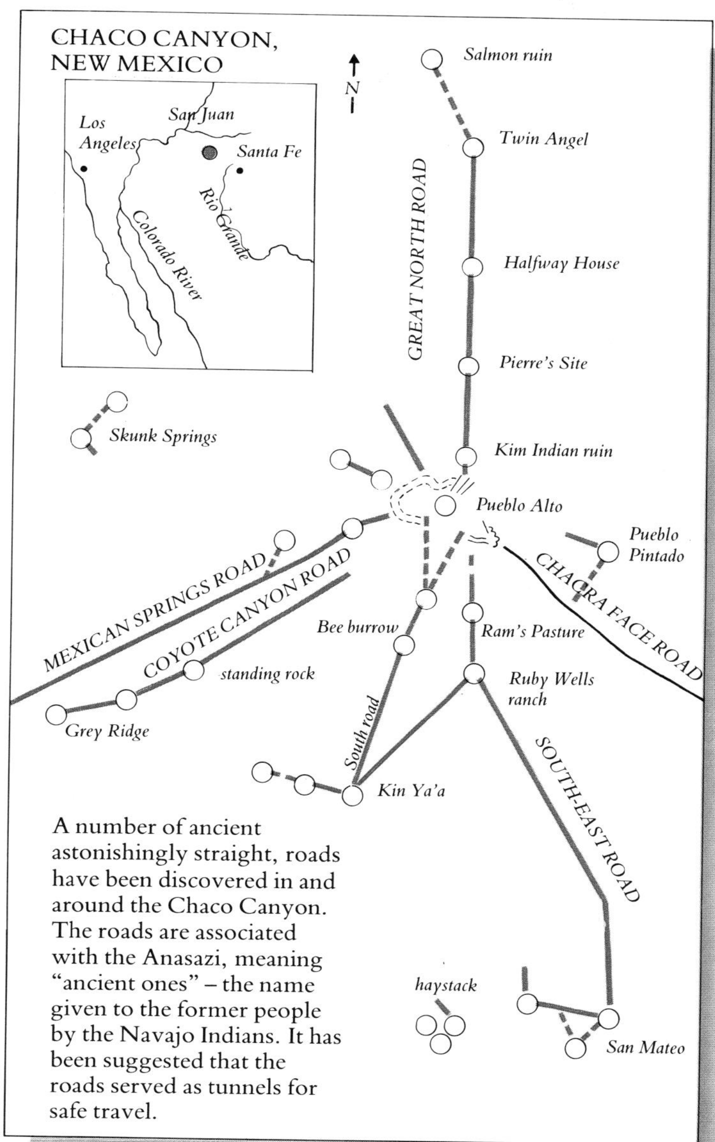

A number of ancient astonishingly straight, roads have been discovered in and around the Chaco Canyon. The roads are associated with the Anasazi, meaning "ancient ones" – the name given to the former people by the Navajo Indians. It has been suggested that the roads served as tunnels for safe travel.

Ghosts and Hauntings

Mention "the supernatural" to most people and they immediately think of ghosts. A ghost is popularly considered an apparition, generally of a dead person but sometimes of an animal. Such an apparition may come to warn the living of impending trouble or (if the deceased died vowing revenge) to haunt them. Ghosts usually seem to be tied to the places in which their beings lived and suffered – it is rare for there to be no apparent connection between a place and an attendant apparition – and to be universally unhappy. Indeed, so rare is contentment in the world of apparitions that to speak of a happy ghost seems a contradiction in terms.

Ghosts have been recorded from the earliest times: Greek and Roman literature, in particular, are full of them, and innumerable instances of their appearance have been recorded up to the present day. Neither religion nor rationalism has managed to damage the general assumption that some places can be haunted, either by particular ghosts or simply by an atmosphere which somehow places them apart from other, happier places.

There are many different kinds of ghosts and few rules that can be applied to their appearances. Beyond an occasional lowering of the temperature, they do not seem to affect the environment much – for example, lights do not brighten or dim – and they can be seen in bright sunlight or in dark shadow. Very occasionally, the figures seem to have some inner illumination.

The ghost is seen obliquely – for example, out of the corner of the eye; indeed, some people claim that one can never look *directly* at a ghost. Nevertheless, there are many records of conversations purported to have been held with apparitions. Sometimes, more than one person has seen the same ghost; occasionally observers claim to have actually touched ghosts, or have made physical contact with a human being who, it has later been proved, could not actually have been there.

Many ghosts have the reputation of appearing again and again in the same environment – for example, houses in which their living counterparts have died. In such cases they usually seem to haunt one room, typically the one in which they were murdered; but sometimes they will move from room to room.

We usually speak of "seeing" a ghost, yet there have been reliable reports of people merely sensing a presence in the room with them, and of having been able to describe it without actually observing it. Perhaps the best-known example is of a woman who awoke one night in a room at the Château de Prangins, near Nyon in Switzerland, and was convinced that a man was sitting writing at a desk in the room, dressed in a long, flowered dressing-gown. She described him vividly to her husband; but when she was persuaded to look directly at the desk, could see no-one there. Next morning she was told she had described the figure of Voltaire, who often used the room during his lifetime and was regularly seen there.

Some people, of course, go out of their way to seek out ghosts. However, to most people they appear unannounced and unexpected, often "out of thin air." They simply look up and there is the apparition standing before them. Most ghosts seem to disappear right under the eye of the beholder, sometimes gradually fading away, sometimes simply vanishing if the observer makes a sudden movement, switches on a light, tries to touch the ghost or speak to it. It is a cliché that ghosts have the ability to walk through walls or closed doors, but there are many reports of those who seem to have done so.

***This ghostly figure of a woman**, draped in a veil, descending the main staircase in Raynham Hall, in Norfolk, north-east England, was taken in 1936 by Indre Shira. Ghost-hunter Robert Thurston Hopkins, a professional photographer, said: "It may well be the most genuine ghost photograph we possess." The Hall is the seat of Marquess Townshend, whose wife commissioned Shira to photograph it. He and his assistant were setting up their equipment when the figure appeared. Experts who examined the plate agreed that it had not been faked. The apparition, which had been seen before, is known as the Brown Lady of Raynham Hall. According to one legend, she foretells a death in the family.*

***A Scotland Yard detective** took this photograph of a ghostly – and apparently headless – dog* (below, top) *in Bucks., England, in about 1916. The detective, Arthur Springer, was a retired criminal investigation department inspector, well trained in the art of observation – but he did not see the dog when he took the photograph.*

***A hundred years after she died,** on June 27 1967, this University of Missouri student* (below, bottom) *appeared to members of the University's Society for Research into Rapport and Telekinesis (SORRAT). The society made contact with "Myra", as she became known, by using a "rap" code.*

The transparent ghost is another cliché; but most ghosts appear solid enough to cast shadows, although very occasionally transparent apparitions are reported to have been seen, or ghosts have gradually seemed to become transparent as they disappear. The idea of the headless ghost is not well supported, although sometimes only a head, or a pair of hands, has been seen, apparently suspended in mid-air. Among the strangest of ghosts is the *doppelganger*, or ghost of oneself, whose appearance is thought always to precede death.

It is a mistake to suppose that all ghosts are of people. There is a well-known case of a ghostly bus which was said to run on a London route. The ghost of a bombed house has been seen, standing on the site it once occupied. Ghostly clothing, letters, money, even machinery has appeared. Ghostly animals have sometimes been seen – or heard, without any human apparitions. Interestingly, ghost cats seem almost always to appear alone, while ghost dogs more usually appear in ghostly human company (a reflection of living canine and feline characteristics, perhaps).

In the search for rational explanations, it is fair to concentrate on the physical state, as well as the state of mind, of the person concerned. Ghosts seen from bed, during the night, or just upon awakening – and a good many of these have been recorded – must be suspected of being part of a dream. Those encountered in broad daylight are another matter. Some have appeared to people under much the same conditions as poltergeists – that is, when the observers have clearly been awake and unaffected by exhaustion or mental instability.

The fact that most people merely *see* ghosts (one researcher records that of the people who see ghosts, 84 percent *only* see them, while 37 percent hear them and 15 percent touch them) must suggest at least the possibility of hallucination. A relatively few people also have other senses affected: a few record that they feel a drop of temperature in the presence of a ghost, and even fewer suggest that ghosts are accompanied by a curious smell.

It is extremely difficult to produce any generally acceptable proof of the appearance of a ghost. Even if two or three people see the same apparition, there is the possibility of group illusion; while the very circumstances under which apparitions usually appear preclude careful scientific observation – ghosts are notorious for their failure to appear under test conditions (no good reason for claiming they do not exist, but a hindrance to proving that they do). The most famous ghost-hunter, the Englishman Harry Price (1881-1948), had no real success at proving the existence of ghosts, but he witnessed, and recorded many strange experiences, especially at Borley Rectory (see p.131).

Occasionally people have claimed that ghosts have told them things that they could not know, have uttered warnings or provided information about the future. Very few of these are any more reliable, as proof, than simple anecdotes. The case for ghosts, although sometimes extremely interesting, must be regarded as unproven.

THE MYSTERY OF POLTERGEISTS

***Simon and Béatrice Sithebe**, of Durban, in South Africa, have suffered poltergeist attacks since July 1987. During a photo session, a kettle flew across their living room* (above) *– but that was only one recorded instance of innumerable disturbances. The Sithebes have been bombarded with stones and potatoes, fires have been started, and Mrs Sithebe was hit with a Bible whenever the couple began to pray. Some of the items hurled at them, or broken are shown on the right. Journalist Richard Compton, of the local Daily News, verified the phenomena; an apostolic minister, the Rev John Hadabe, came to exorcise the demon but collapsed as soon as the ceremony began, declaring he was incompetent in the face of a superior diabolic power. Until a more powerful exorcist is found, the Sithebes and their three children seem condemned to live under siege.*

A poltergeist is generally described as some unknown force that makes inexplicable noises or invisibly moves objects or throws them about. It is a reasonable definition, and can be applied to a very long list of strange incidents.

The activities of poltergeists have been recorded for as long as man has been startled by the supernatural, and not only stretch back in time, but also extend throughout the world (one of the earliest cases of which we have reports was recorded in China in AD 900).

Poltergeist activity – whether it consists merely of rapping noises and the throwing about of small objects, or rather more seriously turns to lighting fires or making physical attacks – tends to be centred on one person, usually known as the "agent". There are innumerable cases of "simple" poltergeists at work: noises clearly heard when no-one seems in a position to make them, furniture seen to rise from the floor and move, small objects observed to float.

Happily, there are relatively few accounts of serious attacks on people – although these are not unknown. One of the most unpleasant is a series of assaults made on the Blessed Christina of Stommeln in the 13th century, into whose flesh nails were thrust, she was bitten, her clothes were cut to pieces and her room was smothered in excrement. Although there were many witnesses, and their accounts are persuasive, the passage of 700 years makes her case seem remote. Nearer our own time, there are the well-documented cases, set out overleaf, of a Romanian peasant girl, Eleanore Zugun, and of the events at Mulhouse (see p.49).

If poltergeist activity is not faked by human agencies, whence does it arise? Of course it has been associated with the dead, and with spirits, whether angelic or demonic; there have been many cases in which it has been regarded as part and parcel of a "haunting", sometimes associated with spectral appearances. There was a famous case, recorded in Brighton in the 1880s, when a house in Prestonville Road (in which a woman was said to have hanged herself) was "haunted" by the spectre of "a little woman" with a white face, who peered around doors at visitors, sometimes sobbing and moaning. She apparently did a thorough job of haunting, for researchers who visited the house not only heard knockings, but footsteps, paper being screwed up, bells ringing, doors opening and shutting and a piano and musical-box being played; they also saw things being thrown around, and furniture being moved.

This all sounds like a comic-book account of a classic haunted house. However, various witnesses gave extremely convincing and rather frightening accounts of the time they spent there, and the documents on the case (in the files of the London Society for Psychical Research, which published them in 1889) are remarkably – even chillingly – persuasive.

There have, of course, been cases in which fraud has been detected, and some phenomena have been found to have been caused – sometimes cleverly – by human agency. However, there are many others where no fraud has been proved; and some in which extremely careful observation by independent witnesses under test conditions has failed to explain some remarkable occurrences for example, see the Indridason case, p.138).

It is certainly true that in almost every case someone *could* have caused *some* of the phenomena seen or heard. However, it is unlikely that they could all have been caused by a single human agency; and even less likely that they are the result of collusion. Occasionally, conjurers or professional magicians have succeeded in counterfeiting or reproducing "effects" similar to those in classic poltergeist cases, and it is fair to point out that not only deception but self-deception may have occurred. Strange voices and other noises, even the opening and closing of doors and similar phenomena, are often the result of natural phenomena technicolored by remarkable imagination.

However, when it comes to the matter of objects apparently rising into the air – either large and heavy objects, moving with slow deliberation, or lighter objects sometimes violently thrown – a rational explanation becomes much more difficult: and it must be said that there are far too many cases in which this kind of thing has been recorded by reliable witnesses, for it to be possible to dismiss them all (for example, see the Sauchie case, p.133).

Assuming that some at least of these phenomena are genuine, how do they happen? There have been various attempts to suggest how the "agent" may "cause" the noises

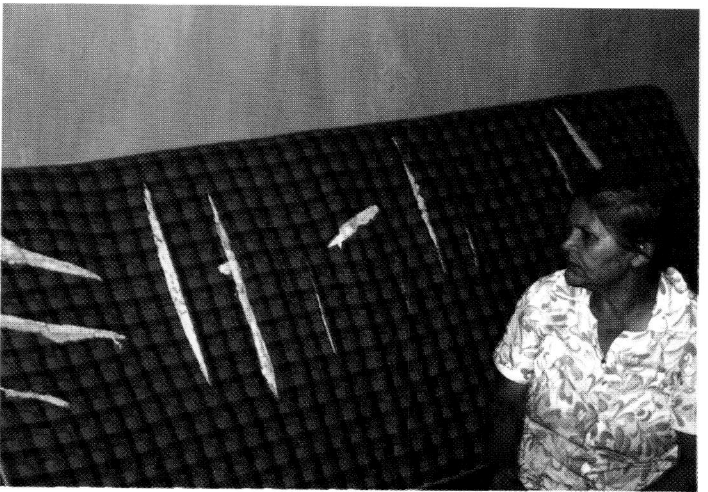

***Poltergeists** do not confine their attacks to humans. While someone was sitting on it, the settee* (above) *was slashed, allegedly by a Brazilian poltergeist using an unseen instrument; also in Brazil, the parrot* (left), *had its wing scorched by a mysterious force.*

Elenore Zugun (left, *with Countess Wassilko-Serecki), endured vicious poltergeist attacks from the age of 12. She claimed to have been bitten, pricked with invisible needles, slapped, pushed to the ground and had her hair pulled. She was rescued from a mental asylum* (below) *by Countess Wassilko-Serecki, who was interested in the paranormal. The Countess took her to Vienna where, in 1926, when Elenore was 13, the British psychical researcher Harry Price witnessed some of the activity and brought both her and the Countess to London. He photographed the teeth marks and contusions that appeared on her flesh; samples of the spittle that frequently appeared on her were analysed and found to be neither a secretion of her skin nor her own saliva. Fraud was never proved: the attacks ceased soon after Elenore reached puberty.*

or movements – for the most part, unconsciously. None of these have been very successful or persuasive. As early as the mid-18th century there were suggestions that poltergeist activity might be connected with terrestrial forces such as a build-up of underground water or mild earthquake shocks which might have the necessary effect. However, attempts made by the contemporary researcher A. D. Cornell to reproduce poltergeist effects by physically "shaking" a house (by mechanical means) entirely failed to produce anything like the desired effect.

We are left with two alternatives: the phenomena are somehow either caused by the "agents" themselves or by some other inexplicable force.

Perhaps the most persuasive aspect of the argument that poltergeist phenomena are the result of tension within the "agent" is simply the meaninglessness of those phenomena: they seem more often than not simply to be displays of incoherent irritation or anger. More light-hearted manifestations – the playing of musical instruments, or hiding of clothes or other objects – are less easily explained.

There are relatively few examples of poltergeist activity which can be more or less firmly linked to the dead. Occasionally young children who seem to have been "agents" have referred (for example) to dead grandparents, while the objects moved have had the same association. But such clear-cut cases are rare. There is a general supposition that poltergeist activity is most frequently centred on the presence of adolescent boys or (particularly) girls, and that there is perhaps a connection with sexual frustration. In fact, recent research suggests that the sex of the "agent" is immaterial; his

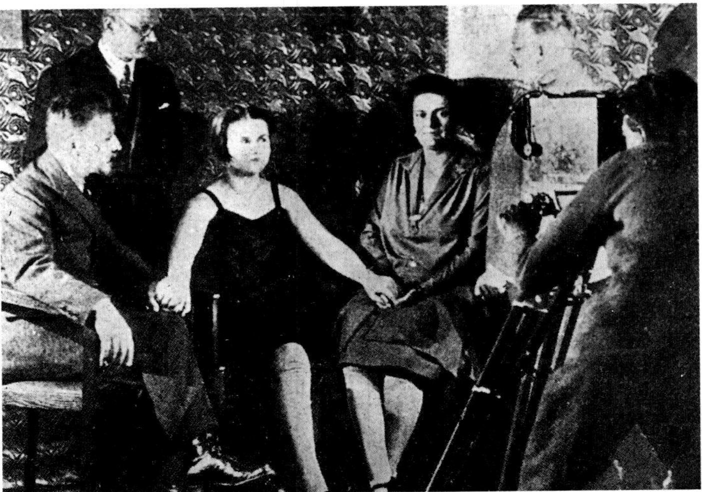

or her average age is about 20 – although a lot of "agents" are indeed pubescent children (a number of whom, curiously enough, are adopted).

The most common link between "agents" is depression and neurosis of some kind, and the people concerned seem above all to be seeking attention. This of course suggests an excellent reason why they should fake poltergeist activity, but even the most suspicious investigators have in many cases failed to discover any evidence of this. In such cases we must either conclude that respectable witnesses have been deluded, or are lying, or accept that we are in the presence of the truly supernatural.

The Mulhouse Case

The Mulhouse case is one of the most inexplicable poltergeist phenomena of recent times. It first came to scientific attention in November 1980, when a Dr Fleur, a physicist, called Professor Hans Bender at the Freiburg Institute for Border Areas of Psychology and Mental Hygiene, in West Germany, to ask for help. Dr Fleur had recently become involved in the experiences of a young couple, Thierry and Carla, who lived in Mulhouse, in eastern France. For three years they had been under attack by a poltergeist: Dr Fleur, in an attempt to monitor temperature fluctuations in their home which sometimes produced 27°C (80°F) when the heating was off, had installed a temperature recorder. The printout he got (far right) was technically impossible.

Professor Bender and other investigators from the Institute decided to interview Thierry and Carla and to examine the notes Thierry had kept since 1978. Both Thierry and Carla were under great stress and concerned for the mental health of their four-year-old son, Jean. Carla had an unusual history: she had begun to sleepwalk at the age of three and at five could detect pregnancy, even in its earliest stages. On one occasion she and some friends had been locked in an empty house – even though there was no lock on the door – and had had to be released by a passer-by (who had no difficulty opening the door). She had also had premonitions, and seemed to be the person on whom the poltergeist activity centred. This activity ranged from tables being moved, rugs levitating, and doors being locked, to personal attacks: she was punched, pinched, scratched, cut and felt cold hands trying to strangle her.

The investigators established through glass-rolling, a variation on the ouija board, that the poltergeist was called Henri and decided to hypnotize Carla, with Henri's consent. The hypnotist said he had received a message about a bed; and when the bed was moved two designs found under it were similar to those found on Carla's thigh five days earlier.

Two weeks later the investigators tried again, this time with a radar-controlled camera. The camera was designed to film, for 10 seconds, any movement of objects put on a table in a locked room. During the experiment the camera was triggered, but ran for three minutes until Thierry switched it off, from outside the room. The film, when developed, showed no movement. In the weeks that followed, Carla's son Jean began to talk in his sleep, claimed he heard music that others could not hear, and spoke of visitors who came to his bedside at night.

In desperation, Thierry and Carla decided to seek help from an exorcist. But the day before he was due to come, Carla cancelled the appointment. She and Thierry had decided to leave Mulhouse and move to Antilles. An alarming increase in paranormal activity had produced this decision. Carla began to see a dark figure in the apartment; Thierry found he could not open the cellar door without digging out the ground beneath it; and, on April 17 1981 Carla went into a spontaneous trance. Thierry kept a camera loaded in case he wanted to record something – he seized it to photograph Carla, but knew at once that it had no film in it, even though he had sealed it. When he broke the seal he found the film was gone. In its place was a piece of paper with the same designs as those found under the bed.

The final act came at the airport, when Carla found all her identity papers missing from her handbag. She was allowed on the aircraft. A few weeks later she wrote from Gaudaloupe to say she had found her papers – under the mattress of the bed in her new apartment.

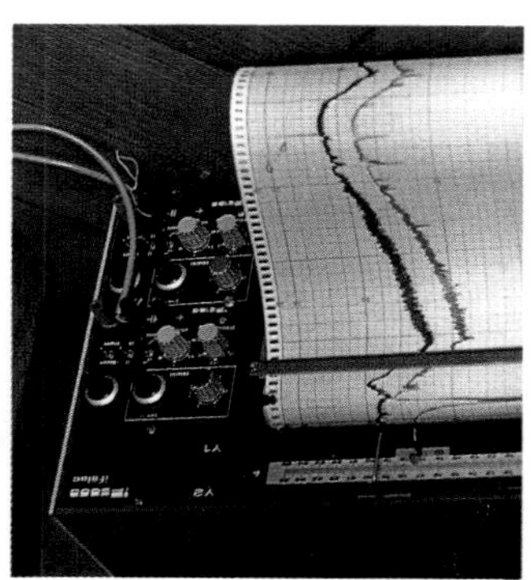

Poltergeist activity *plagued the lives of Thierry and Carla, living in Mulhouse, France, during the late 70s and early 80s.* ***The chart of temperatures*** (above) *in Thierry and Carla's apartment showed not only unexplained fluctuations in temperature, but also broken and horizontal lines that were technically impossible.* ***Books on shelves*** (left top) *in Thierry and Carla's apartment were constantly turned round by unseen forces. Thierry's sealed camera had lost its film, which was replaced by a* ***piece of paper*** (far left) *bearing the same designs found under the bed and on Carla.* ***Poltergeist graffiti*** *found on the floor* (near left) *repeated patterns found earlier on Carla's thigh.*

Channels and Mediums

During the past decade or so, there has been an increased interest – especially on the West Coast of America – in what is known as channelling.

The term is rather difficult to define, as different people seem to mean different things by it. But in general, a channel is someone who is able to transmit information and advice to individuals in this world from spirit guides in some other world. In most senses, a channel is simply what was formerly known as a medium.

Channelling can concern one person, or more than one. That is, someone can learn to relax sufficiently to allow information to come through to him or her from "the other side", which is then used in order that he or she can solve problems, know themselves better, or simply lead more fulfilling lives. On the other hand, the channel can simply be a medium through which a message is to be passed to someone else – sometimes a client, for many mediums now earn considerable sums by receiving messages for those who are not able to hear for themselves. However, it is claimed that anyone can learn to be a channel.

It goes without saying that this is an area very susceptible to fraud, for it is particularly difficult to apply a test of any kind to someone who says he or she is a channel. Zoe Hagen, the author of a book on the subject (*Channelling*, New York, 1989) says that the person in search of a good channel should "look for one who has experienced much personal growth . . . who has cleared many of his/her own emotional blocks, who has his/her feet firmly planted on the ground while still being in contact with the higher energies." This is perhaps more easily said than done, but in the final analysis everyone must be his or her own judge, for it is results that count; the bottom line is whether one receives enough help to justify whatever expense is incurred.

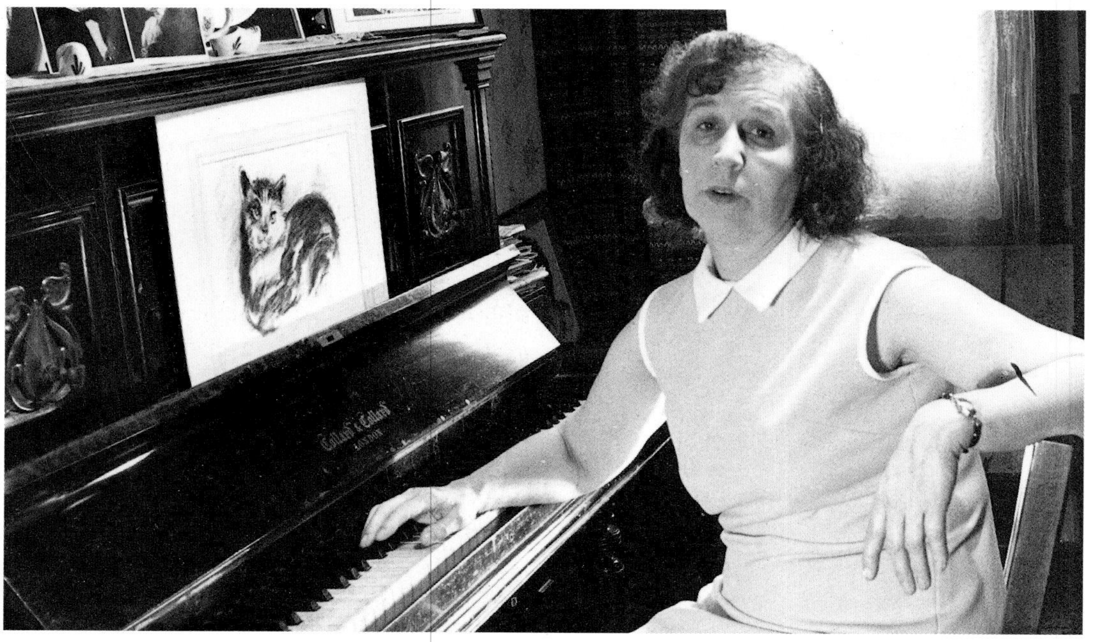

***Great composers** such as Beethoven and Bach seem to have chosen Mrs Rosemary Brown, a London housewife* (left)*, as the channel through which to publish compositions written from beyond the grave. Mrs Brown claims to have been first visited by Franz Liszt when she was seven years old, and says she has since become the amanuensis of Chopin, Beethoven, Bach, Brahms, Schumann, Debussy, Grieg, Berlioz, Rachmaninov, Monteverdi and others. She purports to have written down music at their dictation, and has performed it in public, as well as recording it on disc – although her musical training was very sketchy, and her piano technique is barely good enough to cope with the pieces she has transcribed. Experts say that more than pastiche is involved.*

Asked to explain just what goes on when they are in contact with "the other side" (the term is an old-fashioned one, but still rather apt), channels find it difficult to explain. Many claim to be in touch with their own personal spirit guide. A surprising number of these – and not only in America – are AmerIndians ("Silver Birch" was one of the most famous; it – despite keen questioning, its sex was never revealed – was the eloquent teacher of the Hannen Swaffer circle in London). A Washington housewife, J. Z. Knight, channels the advice of Ramtha, a 35,000 year-old warrior from Atlantis whose message was presented in 1987 to more than 500 people at a session in Sydney, Australia. Jane and Robert Roberts are in contact with Seth, whose antecedents are unknown, but who is perhaps Egyptian (another popular identity for spirit guides) and have written a book (*Seth Speaks*). It is fair to say that people in general probably hear what they want to hear from their spirit guides, or from their spiritual selves, or from whatever source they contact when – often in trance – they become a channel. Sometimes the voices are alleged to aid them when they are giving a Tarot reading, or using psychometry; they may speak in tongues, or dictate by automatic writing; they may recall the previous lives led by themselves or their clients; at other times they enable otherwise inartistic people to draw and paint, or to write or compose.

While many people are utterly convinced that they are guided by spirits, or by a supernatural power, some channels admit (or claim) that channelling has nothing to do with the supernatural: in going into meditation, a self-induced trance, or some other mystical state, what the genuine channel is doing is putting him- or herself in touch with the collective unconscious, and drawing on the pool of wisdom to which everyone in the last resort has access.

The traditional seance (above) *often took place around a table in a private home. The participants touched hands to establish an unbroken circle through which psychic power could flow – an act that also prevented anyone surreptitiously knocking on the table or making it move. The medium – the central figure in this photograph, taken in Berlin between the wars – went into a trance in order to make contact with "the other side". Modern channels, especially in the United States, often operate in larger, more relaxed and more informal groups.*

Psychic sketching *was a technique employed by Frank Leah, a British medium* (right), *who attracted much attention in the 1940s. He is seen here in 1947 completing an oil painting of a Mr Sutton, who had died two years previously in Brazil. During an initial telephone conversation between Leah and Mr Sutton's widow, Leah told her he had the impression of two men standing by him, and accurately described her late husband and her father. Mrs Sutton then joined Leah at his studio, where he produced a pencil sketch of her husband in the last months of his illness. When they were compared by Mrs Sutton (on the right), the sketch and the photograph appeared remarkably similar, the proportions of the features in each being exactly the same.*

***When in a trance**, a Brazilian psychologist, Luis Antonio Gasparetto* (left), *is able to paint like Rembrandt, Picasso and Modigliani using only his bare fingers. He calls himself a "psycho-pictographer" and says he does it by communicating with the spirits of dead Masters. He was born into a family interested in spiritualism. At the age of 13 Gasparetto was sent to a special school and there perfected his mastery of inner trance. He works very fast: a "Rembrandt" takes three minutes and 46 seconds, a "Picasso" two minutes and 27 seconds, and a "Modigliani" 50 seconds. So far, Gasparetto has produced some 9,000 works, most of which have been sold for charity or hang in Brazil's mediumenical museum.*

***New novels by dead authors** are the speciality of Stella Horrocks* (below left), *a retired teacher who lives in Bradford, England. Once in a trance she writes at lightning speed, turning out works she says have been communicated to her by such literary giants as Jane Austen, Virginia Woolf and Winston Churchill. Each author has different handwriting.*

It is, of course, impossible to prove anything either way. There is certainly considerable anecdotal evidence of channels or mediums speaking of personal matters of which it seems unlikely they could have previous knowledge, describing dead relatives or friends of others, or past events in the lives of their clients.

Unfortunately, these anecdotes are often related by the channels themselves. For example, Coral Page, the British medium, has written of being inhabited by the spirit of a girl who had committed suicide, when she heard herself saying "I have a young lady here who died of something which made her feel very giddy; I feel as if I can't breathe – everything is floating away." She drew a portrait of a girl, who was later recognized by a woman in the audience as a daughter of hers who had committed suicide by breathing in carbon monoxide.

So, again, everyone must judge for themselves, for to the best of the authors' knowledge there has not yet been a successful controlled experiment which has shown that channels have any extraordinary pass to an occult world. (although such an experiment would be very difficult to mount). At all events, lack of proof has not prevented channelling from becoming one of the most popular of all occult experiences.

Immortality

Most religions offer the hope of some kind of personal or general immortality; but, apart from reports of alleged miracles, they have produced no evidence to support this conviction. However, from time to time people have claimed to have experienced a condition very different to life as we know it, and have taken this to be a glimpse of a life to come.

Near-death Experiences

Near-death experiences have something in common with out-of-body experiences. Both concern the separation of the "spirit" or "soul" from the often suffering body, and most have a profound effect on their subjects. A classic example is that of a private soldier in America, George Ritchie, who in December 1943 was suffering from influenza when a sudden deterioration in his condition resulted in his apparent death. A doctor was called, and the death certificate signed. Nine minutes later, an orderly noticed faint signs of life, and an injection of adrenalin into the heart resulted in his recovery.

Ritchie clearly recalled finding himself separated from his body, travelling through the air to a large town, then returning to the hospital, examining a number of bodies, recognizing his own ring on the finger of one of them, and after a religious vision, rejoining his body. He later became a psychiatrist, and wrote a book – *Return from Tomorrow* – about the experience.

Many similar experiences have been recorded, as have many "visions" seen by people at the point of death. Man's deep longing for immortality might, of course, be expected to surface during serious or terminal illness, and logically would express itself in such visions. More interesting is the fact that those who have come very close to death have tended to record much the same experience. In two books published in the 1970s, *Life After Life* and *Reflections on Life After Life*, the American philosopher Raymond Moody identified the similarities in a great number of such anecdotes.

Most common was the experience of being detached from the physical body, and travelling down a long tunnel, often to the accompaniment of a rather unpleasant noise – a ringing or a buzzing – although sometimes to the sound of triumphant music. In an atmosphere of intense joy and peace, figures of dead friends or relatives would appear, apparently expressing welcome; and they would be accompanied or followed by a supernatural figure, "a creature of light" whose purpose is apparently to help the newly-dead to place his or her past life in a general context: subjects often said that the whole of their life passed vividly before them.

Just after this, some barrier, either physical or spiritual, appeared, and the choice had to be made: to pass finally into the land of the dead, or to return to life. Naturally, in the cases recorded, the latter decision was made. Despite the consciousness that the state of death is a blessed and happy one, the subject returns to life, aware that no effort can convey the true nature of the experience to the living.

These common elements are subject to certain personal views of life and death: for example, the mystic figure is

Paradise (above, top), *as envisaged by the 15th century Netherlandish painter Hieronymus Bosch, shows a remarkable correlation with the visions described by those who have undergone a near-death experience. Welcoming friends, supernatural beings and a long tunnel figure widely in accounts by those who have elected to return to the world of the living.*

Many age-old cultures include belief in an afterlife. *Bobby Holcomb's painting* Ancestral Spirits (above, bottom) *shows a Polynesian view of spirits, still tied to their dead bodies, rising toward heaven.*

usually identified by Christians as Christ, by Buddhists as Buddha, by Jews as an angel. The landscape in which the figure is set differs according to the subject's ideas of beauty, as does the atmosphere: some people have found it extremely unpleasant, usually those who have contemplated suicide, or were depressives.

Incidentally, artists throughout the ages have recorded scenes very like those above: Hieronymus Bosch's *Paradiso* in the Gallery of the Accademia in Venice shows spirits travelling down a dark tunnel leading towards the light, while there have been many landscapes of the heavenly gardens.

Proof of a human spirit *was claimed by Hyppolite Baraduc, a noted French psychical researcher, who took these photographs of his wife in October 1907 a quarter of an hour after her death* (left), *and* (below) *an hour after death. Baraduc identified the three luminous globes with his wife's soul: they first appeared when his wife sighed three times as she died, and then combined into one. Baraduc had photographed his son's death six months earlier and had obtained an image of a similar misty, formless mass.*

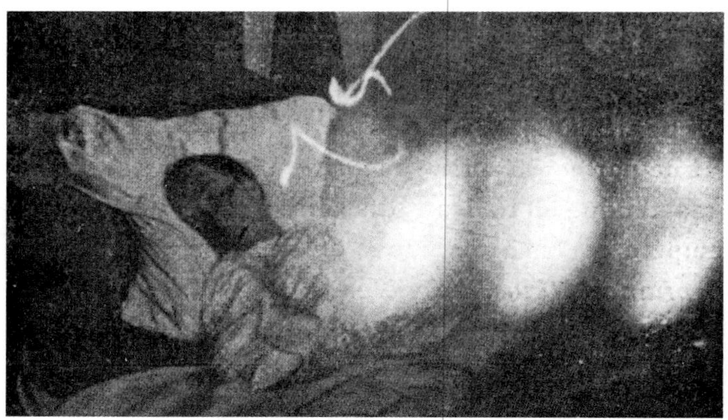

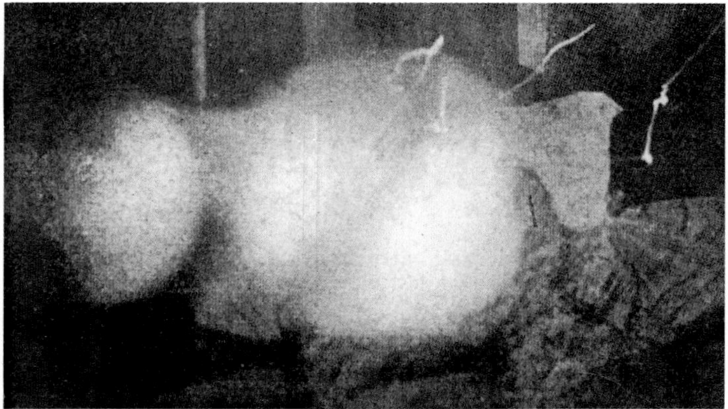

Those who have had near-death experiences are extremely difficult to persuade that they are anything other than true religious visions. It is also the case that people working over lengthy periods in hospices, or under circumstances where they are in close proximity to death, are frequently convinced that the dying undergo deep spiritual experiences.

It has also been suggested that chemical changes in an injured or dying brain may be responsible. For example, a depleted supply of oxygen to the brain might induce hallucinations – and the idea of travelling down a dark tunnel is common to those under severe psychological stress. Medically administered drugs might also have an effect.

Many alleged near-death experiences have also taken place when people have been in extreme danger. Soldiers have described the phenomenon, but so have people lying dangerously ill. Near-death experiences have an extraordinary similarity, whether they are described in ancient literature (there is an example in Plato's *The Republic*; the Tibetan *Book of the Dead* vividly elaborates the theory), or more recently.

Sometimes people who have apparently "died" on the operating table have been able, on recovery, to describe accurately the conversation of doctors, and even events occurring in the operating-theatre and in rooms nearby.

It has been suggested, notably by Kenneth Ring, an American psychologist (head of the International Association for Near Death Studies at the University of Connecticut), that something very like a near-death experience can be undergone while under hypnosis, during intense personal crisis, or in a state of religious ecstasy, and he speculates that it may be connected with some means of raising the level of one's experience of living.

Out-of-body experiences

One of the most common of all psychic experiences is the separation of body and spirit – out-of-body experiences (OBE's). Very recently, the actress Shirley MacLaine gave the topic a new lease of life by describing the journeys her own spirit has taken when apparently separated from her body.

But human beings seem always to have taken these journeys: they are described in the literature of ancient Egypt and Greece, and there are many examples in the Bible – for example, the Old Testament prophet Elisha is said to have sent his spirit into the tent of a Syrian king, thus discovering and frustrating his plan to attack the Israelites.

With the advent of spiritualism in the mid-19th century, people began to record out-of-body experiences in detail: in *Phantasms of the Living*, published in 1886, two members of the Society for Psychical Research recorded more than 700 of them, although the authors (Edmund Gurney and Frederic Myers) noted that most of these were occasions when people had received very strong impressions of the presence of other people, rather than cases in which individuals claimed that their own spirits had left their bodies.

It is not surprising that a few individuals have attempted to cultivate a technique – rather in the way in which some people cultivate lucid dreams – by which they could leave their bodies and slip the bonds of everyday existence. Two of them have left voluminous reports of their experiences.

The Italian front *in the First World War produced a near-death and out-of-body experience for the novelist Ernest Hemingway. While serving with the American Red Cross at Fossalta di Piave* (left) *in 1918 he was almost killed by a mortar shell. He believed that he felt his spirit leaving his body and described the experience in* A Farewell to Arms:

"I tried to breathe but my breath would not come. I felt myself rush bodily out of myself and out and out and out and all the time bodily in the wind. I went out swiftly, all of myself, and I knew I was dead and that it had all been a mistake to think you just died. Then I floated, and instead of going on I felt myself slide back. I breathed and I was back."

Hugh G. Calloway, who used the pseudonym Oliver Fox, became interested in the psychic when he was an adolescent and both his parents died. He became adept at lucid dreaming – that is, commanding his dreams to bring him certain experiences: usually of travel. Eventually, he became so adept at this that he could rise out of his sleeping body and hover hundreds of feet above the ground, could pass through walls or closed doors. He also claimed to have travelled in time and space to unidentifiable cities and even into outer space.

Calloway published his experiences in 1938 in a book entitled *Astral Projection*. A younger man, the American Sylvan Joseph Muldoon, had by then stolen his thunder in a rather similar book, *The Projection of the Astral Body*, which had come out in 1929. In this, he recalled as a child of 12 finding himself one night rising some feet above the bed on which he saw his body still lying; his astral and real bodies were connected by a kind of umbilical cord. He wandered about in the spirit for some time, before being painfully reunited with his earthly body.

Among many similar excursions Muldoon claimed to take during his life the most spectacular was probably that in which he travelled many miles to an unknown room in which a girl sat, sewing. Some time later he coincidentally met and recognized the girl, and was able to describe the room to her in great detail.

The activities described by Calloway and Muldoon (who were later collaborators) are uncheckable: the reader either accepts or rejects them, according to temperament.

A 19th dynasty Egyptian papyrus (above) *depicts the soul, or ka, re-uniting with the body. The Egyptians believed that the soul, which left the body at death, could also do so during life, chiefly when the body was asleep. This belief was widespread: most early cultures have a word for the spiritual or astral body. In Norwegian it was* vardger, *in German* doppelgänger, *in Scottish* taslach *and in Old English* fetch. *The Christian Church strongly supported the theory, Catholic literature records examples of saints who contrived to be in two places at once.*

What attempts have been made at a scientific examination of the phenomenon of OBEs?

In 1961, Robert Crookall and Celia Green were involved in the foundation of an Institute of Psychophysical Research at Oxford. Crookall has subsequently published, in a number of books, an analysis of many descriptions of out-of-body experiences, and recorded several factors which seem common to them all – for example, the fact that they seem to begin at the hands and feet, and that they are often accompanied by clicking noises.

But the most interesting research so far has probably been that undertaken by Dr Charles T. Tart at the University of Virginia School of Medicine. It involved Robert Monroe, an American advertising executive whose first out-of-body experience occurred in 1958, and who became so involved in the subject that in 1982 he was invited to read three papers to the American Psychiatric Association.

Under close scrutiny, Monroe was invited to project himself from one room into another and to read a five-figure number on a high shelf (which would ordinarily be out of sight to anyone standing on the floor). He failed to do so; but reported that while "out of the body" he had seen the woman who had been monitoring his heartbeat and brain-waves talking to a man in the corridor. The technician later admitted that at the time she had been in the corridor with her husband.

Tart regarded the experiment as inconclusive. However, later, an unidentified woman subject succeeded in "reading" a five-figure number while "out of the body"; monitoring equipment recorded that at the time she showed no signs of being in deep sleep, or of dreaming.

Other experiments have sometimes succeeded, but more often failed – there seems to be some evidence that the atmosphere in which such tests take place is as inimical to this kind of psychic experience as in other circumstances.

Beyond the Body

Out-of-body experiences are by no means as uncommon as might be thought. In 1953, J. H. M. Whiteman published a report summarizing more than 500 cases of "detachment from the physical body" reported to a parapsychological congress at Utrecht; most of them had been as thoroughly checked as is possible in such cases. In 1960 the Society for Psychical Research published in its Proceedings more than 300 incidents of out-of-body experiences – and these were selected from more than 1,500 collected by Sir George Joy and Celia Green.

Occasionally, people apparently remaining in their bodies saw themselves elsewhere: Frederica Hauffe, of Prevorst, was being attended by a doctor when she saw herself sitting on a chair near her bed. Another woman, Violet Tweedale, woke in her sunny bedroom and saw her spirit hurrying back toward the bed to rejoin her body.

It is possible, of course, that some such occurrences may be dreams: the poet Shelley (1792-1822) was lying in bed one night reading, when a muffled and hooded man appeared and beckoned Shelley to follow him. Outside the room, he revealed his face – which was Shelley's own. The poet's screams woke the household. It seems most likely that he had fallen asleep over his book. However, the same could not be said of the writer Guy de Maupassant (1852-93) who, returning home from walks, would find himself sitting in his armchair.

More recently, there have been cases in which people have apparently been able to project themselves beyond their bodies so successfully as to have been recognized by other people. For example, during the Second World War a French lieutenant in charge of Italian prisoners-of-war at Guelma in Algeria was returning to his quarters one night when he met the medical officer of the camp.

"What are you doing outside the wire?' he asked. The medical officer, a Captain Lefebure, replied "It's not me – it's my double." Back in the camp, the lieutenant found Lefebure asleep in his bunk. Awakened, he admitted that he had been trained by an orientalist to be able to leave his body while asleep, and that he had decided to startle his colleague. The camp was well guarded, and no-one had seen him leave.

Others have used similar powers in conscious display: while on a train travelling to Los Angeles for a spiritualist conference in 1922, Mrs Mary C. Wlasek successfully manifested herself at seances there. A Danish engineer, Olle Jonsson, has been spectacularly successful in performing similar feats.

A sensible attitude was taken by Lord Byron. In 1811, when King George III was seriously ill, several witnesses saw Byron signing the visitors' book at the palace, while he was in fact in Patras, in Greece. When this was reported to him, the poet remarked: "I hope my double behaves like a gentleman."

AN EXPERIMENT IN OBE

Robert Monroe believes that anyone can enjoy astral travel – the projection of the "soul" from the body – and indeed it has been suggested that up to 20 percent of the population can expect to have an out-of-body experience at some time during their life.

He recommends the subject should lie down comfortably, without constricting clothing, in a warm, dark room, and with the head toward the north. He or she should relax, breathe rhythmically with the mouth slightly open, and focus on a single image until they feel themselves almost over-taken by sleep.

In his experience, an OBE is heralded by vibrations; these are introduced by focusing the mind on a point about 12 inches (30.5cm) above the forehead, then "pushing" it upward until it is about six feet (1.8m) away and imagining a line there parallel to the body. Imagine that line vibrating, and thus introduce the vibrations into your mind and thence into the whole body. The presence of the vibrations is immediately obvious, when the technique is achieved; and at that point it is enough to imagine oneself floating free of the body, in order actually to do so.

In order to return to normality, when you are ready you simply will the two entities – the floating body and the "home" body – to rejoin and become one.

REINCARNATION

The doctrine of reincarnation – that the human soul or the spirit of an animal or plant can, after death, enter another human or animal body – is an extremely ancient one, and can be found in the teachings of Egyptian religion, Greek philosophy, Buddhism, Hinduism, Jainism, Taoism, theosophy, and the philosophies of Plato and Pythagoras.

Belief in reincarnation depends, of course, on belief in the soul. If we accept that man has a soul, merely housed in a physical body, it is not unreasonable to propose that it may survive death. But if it does survive death – is, in fact, immortal – may it not also have existed before birth? If time is infinite, it is surely surprising that a soul should have been created at a particular moment in it. Is it not more sensible to assume that immortality stretches both ways?

Although we associate reincarnation chiefly with non-Christian religions, the idea is not entirely foreign to Christianity. The Jews believed in the periodic return of their great prophets – Moses was a reincarnation of Abel, and the Messiah was to be the reincarnation of Adam (the Samaritans believed that Adam was reincarnated as Seth, then as Noah, Abraham and Moses). Several early Christian scholars were intrigued by reincarnation.

Nor is the idea confined to the West. Many African tribes accept it: when a child is born to the Yoruba tribe, the first thing the elders do is look for signs that will tell them which ancestral spirit has returned wrapped in the infant's body. Several Australian aboriginal tribes (among them, the Warramunga, the Urabunna and the Tasmains) accept that the souls of men and women can exist in growing plants, as well as animals. The Okinawans (among most Oceanic people) believe that human souls can exist only in human bodies: when the body dies, the soul remains in the family home for 49 days, then enters *Gusho*, the afterlife, whence within seven generations it must return to earth, inhabiting the body of someone who will be very similar to its previous host. The AmerIndians share a belief in reincarnation in various forms – the Maryland Indians held that white men were an ancient generation of Indians who had come to life again, and set out to seize their ancestral lands.

In Europe, a general belief in reincarnation was common in historic times, when the Finns and Lapps, the Danes and Norse, the early Saxons and Celts, Prussians and Teutonics held it. Modern Western man remains, on the whole, unattached to the theory – although it strongly appeals to some. While he stopped short of actually affirming a belief in reincarnation, C. G. Jung (1875-1961), the great psychiatrist and psychologist, wrote in his memoirs, *Memories, Dreams, Reflections*:

"My life as I lived it had often seemed to me like a story that has no beginning and no end. I had the feeling that I was an historical fragment, an excerpt for which the preceding and succeeding text was missing . . . I could well imagine that I might have lived in former centuries and there encountered questions I was not yet able to answer; that I had to be born again because I had not fulfilled the task that was given me."

Jung's theory of the collective unconscious – a shared pool of memories inherited from ancestors, which he believed coexists with individual unconscious recollections – is clearly related to the theory of reincarnation; although some scientists deny that – for example, musical knowledge or a craft or

A belief in reincarnation *sometimes produces practical results: Umberto di Grazia* (near left)*, who lives in Rome, believes he used to live in Etruscan times: he dreams about them and from those dreams, and inexplicable "memories", gathers information that enables him to find hitherto unknown Etruscan sites. He is seen here by an early Estrucan grave he found.*

Steps lead up (far left) *from an early Etruscan tomb found by di Grazia in 1987.*

a language can be transmitted from father or mother to children, they are able to accept the fact that a person may have shadowy "memories" of strange cities they have never seen, perhaps in some way passed on through the genes from remoter ancestors. The idea is only different from that of reincarnation in that such "memories" are passed on by the genes rather than by the spirit: and so we return to a dependence on belief in such a spirit – in the "soul", whatever that is.

Mohandas K. Ghandi (1869-1948), the Indian social philosopher, once wrote to a disciple:

"It is nature's kindness that we do not remember past births. Where is the good of knowing in detail the numberless births we have gone through? Life would be a burden if we carried such a tremendous load of memories. A wise man deliberately forgets many things, even as a lawyer forgets the cases and their details as soon as they are disposed of. Yes, 'death is but a sleep and a forgetting'."

Regression

Almost everyone has had the experience of suddenly thinking – "I have said that before", or "I have done this before." Sometimes the fact is, of course, that one *has* done so – and has forgotten the circumstances. But in many cases there seems to be no explanation for the experience – and occasionally, people have remembered, and described in great detail, places, people and events of which they could have had no knowledge.

This often happens under hypnosis – and for some time hypnotists have been "regressing" subjects: placing them under hypnosis and inviting them to remember their past lives. These sessions have often been tape-recorded and sometimes filmed, and many seem genuinely remarkable.

In 1952, an American hypnotist, Morey Bernstein, worked with a 29-year-old Wisconsin woman, Virginia Tighe, regressing her until she was one year old, and then inviting her to remember previous lives.

She began talking in an Irish accent, announcing herself as four-year-old Bridey Murphy, of Cork. During six tape-recorded sessions, she recalled her life in Ireland – where she had been born in 1798 – with details of her relatives and friends – until her death in 1864 as the result of breaking her hip in a fall. The case was discussed at great length, and of course attempts were made to discredit Mrs Tighe – the charge being made that her knowledge of 19th century Ireland had probably been gathered from the recollections of an Irish aunt (although the aunt had been born in Chicago, and apparently knew little about Ireland).

There is absolutely no reason to suppose that either Mrs Tighe or Mr Bernstein were engaging in any fraud: although some of her "memories" might certainly have been obtained from general reading or conversation, the amount of detail was such that it is very difficult to dismiss the whole, long, detailed account as imaginary.

Graham Huxtable, a swimming instructor, was regressed by the founder of the British Reincarnation Institute, Arnold Bloxham, in 1975, and under hypnosis began recalling life on a 32-gun frigate in Nelson's navy. His recollections were by no means vague, and included references to specialized naval terms of the period, to the rigging and organization of the ship, and on one occasion, an account of a battle, recorded and transcribed:

"Wait for the order, wait for it! Swing those matches. Aye, siree! Stand clear from behind! Now, you fool! Now, up, fool, now! – now! [Screams in exultation as the shot is fired]. Well done, lads! run 'em up! run 'em up! get 'em up! get 'em up the front! [Shrieks] Pull that man out! Pull 'im out! Send him in the cockpit . . . The shot in . . . ramrods! Swab it, swab it, you fool, swab it first! The shot in, shot in! Come in, number four, you should be up by now! . . . Aye, aye, sir. Ready! And again, lads! You had him then! Hurry, men! By God, you bastard! Got him that aim! That's the way to lay a gun. By Christ, they've got old Pearce, they've got Pearce! [Sudden terrible screaming] My bloody leg! [Screaming and moaning uncontrollably] My leg, my leg!"

Mr Huxtable denied any knowledge of 19th century life at sea; and while it might be suggested (and has been) that very few people can have escaped seeing films about the period, the detail given in his accounts is very considerable.

Colour Sergeant Reuben Stafford, of the 47th Lancashire Regiment of Foot, served at the Battle of Alma in the Crimean War and then, having left the army, became a waterman on London's River Thames. He drowned at Milwall Dock in 1879 and was buried at Plaistow, in Essex. Under hypnosis, Ray Bryant, a journalist from Reading, near London seems to become Colour Sergeant Stafford.

To test the authenticity of Bryant's "memory", he was taken to the headquarters of what used to be the 47th regiment, hypnotized, and then questioned by the regimental archivist, who had access to letters written home from the

HOW IT WORKS

Regression is a technique practised by only a few hypnotists: it is advisable to check that they have been properly trained before you commit yourself to an experiment.

The hypnotist will put you at your ease, and will first encourage you to relax completely. Once you are relaxed, that state of relaxation will be made deeper and deeper. Eventually, you will enter a stage where, as in depth analysis, you will be encouraged to remember in detail events and emotions experienced at a very early age in your present life, but which, in a thoroughly wakeful condition, you may not be able or ready to recall. The hypnotist will then ask you to "go back" to a time before you were born as your present self; and you may well recall, even in some detail, two, three, or even more previous lives.

Some people remain conscious throughout the session of what they are saying. Occasionally subjects will "wake" with no recollection of what they have said. In most cases subjects find that during the few days following the experience they are able to embellish the images they "saw".

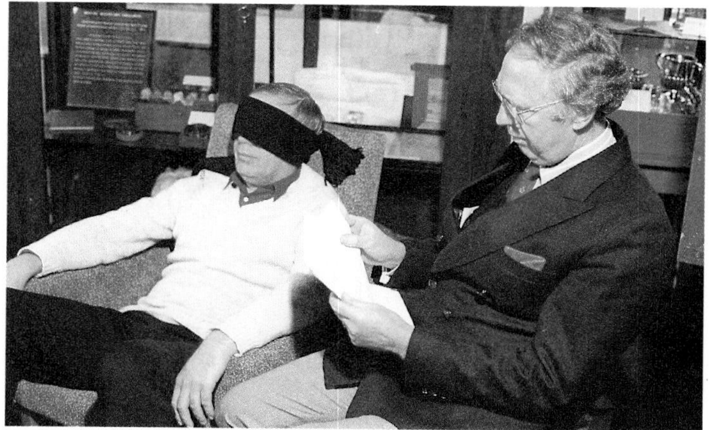

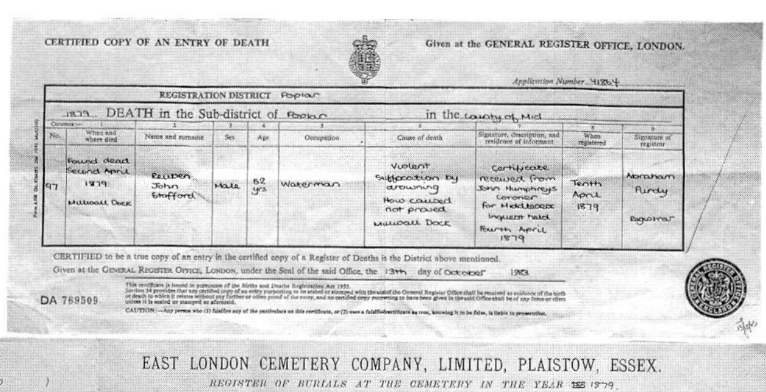

CERTIFIED COPY OF AN ENTRY OF DEATH

Given at the GENERAL REGISTER OFFICE, LONDON.

Application Number 41364

REGISTRATION DISTRICT Poplar

1879 DEATH in the Sub-district of Poplar in the County of Mid

No.	When and where died	Name and surname	Sex	Age	Occupation	Cause of death	Signature, description, and residence of informant	When registered	Signature of registrar
97	Found dead Second April 1879 Millwall Dock	Reuben John Stafford	Male	52 yrs	Waterman	Violent suffocation by drowning How caused not proved Millwall Dock	Certificate received from John Humphreys Coroner for Middlesex Inquest held Fourth April 1879	Tenth April 1879	Abraham Purdy Registrar

CERTIFIED to be a true copy of an entry in the certified copy of a Register of Deaths in the District above mentioned.

Given at the General Register Office, London, under the Seal of the said Office, the 13th day of October 1983

DA 769509

CAUTION:—Any person who (1) falsifies any of the particulars on this certificate, or (2) uses a falsified certificate as true, knowing it to be false, is liable to prosecution.

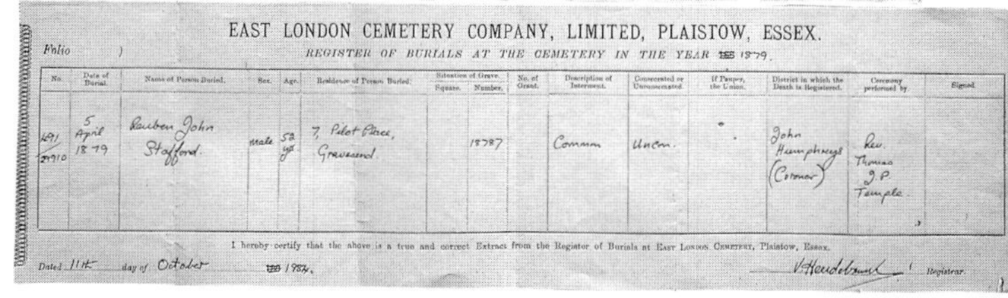

EAST LONDON CEMETERY COMPANY, LIMITED, PLAISTOW, ESSEX.

Folio)

REGISTER OF BURIALS AT THE CEMETERY IN THE YEAR 1879.

No.	Date of Burial.	Name of Person Buried.	Sex.	Age.	Residence of Person Buried.	Situation of Grave. Square.	Number.	No. of Grant.	Description of Interment.	Consecrated or Unconsecrated.	If Pauper, the Union.	District in which the Death is Registered.	Ceremony performed by	Signed
691 / 27910	5 April 1879	Reuben John Stafford	male	52 yrs	7, Pilot Place, Gravesend		18787		Common	Uncon.		John Humphreys (Coroner)	Rev. Thomas J.P. Temple	

I hereby certify that the above is a true and correct Extract from the Register of Burials at East London Cemetery, Plaistow, Essex.

Dated 11th day of October 1984. Registrar.

With Crimean War trophies *behind him, hypnotist Joe Keeton* (above, left) *regresses Ray Bryant. Bryant becomes Rueben Stafford, whose* ***death and burial certificates*** *are shown* (above right) *and recalls experiences at the* ***Battle of Alma*** *on September 20, 1854* (left).

Crimea but never published. Bryant's – or Stafford's – recollection of detail was astonishing. He recalled crossing the River Alma under heavy fire from Russian guns. When asked what the river was like, he said "Cold, and slippery with mud; so slippery you couldn't get a grip, 'ardly." This was almost word for word what was in the letters held by the regiment. He remembered that the regiment captured some Russian side drums – "brassy, with animal 'eads on 'em, like they 'ave in churches." The drums, brass and decorated with eagles' heads, are among the regimental trophies. Yet he could not correctly name the commander nor the type of rifle issued to the troops: the Hammond he named was not even tested for another 10 years.

Leonard Wilder, a London hypnotist who has been interested in regression for more than 30 years, (see right), has experienced cases in which there was some degree of verification of events "remembered" from past lives; but it is always extremely difficult to do, and is very rare. From the subject's point of view there is usually a degree of conviction.

"I had a young woman who had a feeling that she had been someone of importance in the medical world, and I hypnotized her, and she had been a drunk living in the East End of London in the latter part of the 19th century – the lowest of the low – and I have never seen her since; she was disgusted with the whole thing; but *she* had done it, not I."

To an extent, these regressions resemble dreams: they present images which are not consciously summoned by the subject, but clearly come from his or her subconscious mind. Could they be recollections from a past life?

The main question is the degree of cryptomnesia which may be involved: that is, to what extent subjects may under hypnosis be recalling memories or events or experiences – including perhaps books and films – which they have in ordinary wakeful life completely forgotten, and which are presented as "new". Many psychiatrists would claim this as an explanation of the whole phenomenon of "regression"; and in Julia's experience (see right), which was a very brief, grossly telescoped one, the images could certainly be explained in that way – although why, for example, she should have fixed instantly and unhesitatingly on the year 1727 would require considerable explanation.

In July 1989 Julia Parker was hypnotized by Leonard Wilder. (above). *Having taken her first into light, then deeper hypnosis, he invited her to recall her life at 20, then at 15, then five, then two. Then he asked her to:*

"go back in time a long, long time, to a time before you were born as your present self . . . to a time before you were born as Julia – when you were someone else living on this earth; and as you go back in time a memory, a scene, an emotion, an event will come to you. Start talking about the first thing that comes into your mind . . ." Julia almost immediately responded: ". . . it's a wood . . . it's a big tree-trunk. It seems quite dark. It's late afternoon. Annie, I'm Annie. I'm wearing something green. I'm 37 . . . I'm in the Black Forest. I live a mile away; a lonely house. [I have] two boys . . . Husband is away. It's 1727, [the boys' names are] Heinrich and Peter." At this stage Julia became slightly distressed. "It's the wood . . . it's the tree. I'm frightened of it . . . it's just standing. It's big, it's beautiful, but it frightens me. I want to like it . . ."

Wilder then suggested that Annie was 25. She "recalled" living by a river, and being married to a man called George. They had no children. She spent her time digging, growing potatoes. "I sell them to people . . . [I charge] two pfennig."

The session was relatively short, lasting only about an hour. It was clear that Julia said nothing which need have related to a previous life. It is perhaps significant that she had very recently begun to teach herself German. Julia noted that she did not "return" to any of those periods of history in which she has been particularly interested. Her feelings about regression – that it need not indicate a previous life – have not changed, but she finds it interesting that images and symbols from her unconscious may have been released under hypnosis, and intends to follow the trail.

Psychokinesis

Psychokinesis (PK) is the power of the mind alone to move or alter a physical object. It may seem a modern phenomenon, yet Michael Faraday (1791-1867), the chemist and physicist who devised so many great electrical experiments, set up the earliest known English attempt to test PK as long ago as 1853.

A number of American mediums were at that time working in England, giving displays of table-turning. Faraday was extremely suspicious of their often dramatic results, and with good reason: although they all willingly took part in his experiments, he found them to be exerting physical pressure on the moving tables.

Some years later, Marie Curie (1867-1934), who with her husband Pierre (1859-1906) discovered radium, tested Eusapia Palladino (see p.24), a then famous Italian medium who claimed that her spirit guide, "John King", could move objects about a table. Mr King failed the test.

There was then a gap of some years, until Joseph B. Rhine, an American, set out in 1934 to discover whether the fall of a die could be affected by the thrower fixing his or her mind on a particular number. He did not publish the results, but much later, in his *Reach of the Mind* (1949), he claimed some rather eccentric results: that subjects were better at influencing several dice at one time, that metal dice were more easily affected than wooden ones, that lead dice gave better results than aluminium ones. The actual results obtained were not spectacular, but were somewhat above chance. Other investigators have used coins and various objects, but their results have not been convincing.

A more interesting aspect of psychokinesis has been the attempt to move objects by thought-power. Sir William Crookes (1832-1919), a physicist who discovered thallium and invented the radiometer and spinthariscope, once attempted by the power of thought to alter a delicate chemical balance, but failed. H. Forwald of the Swiss Federal Institute of Technology at Zurich, half a century later, claimed that his subjects could cause objects to move sideways, although his results have been questioned; other experiments have given good results, but are open to criticism because they were not properly controlled.

However, in Russia, – where, it is said, 40 million roubles a year were being spent on research in parapsychology in the 1970s – considerable time was given to checking the claim of a housewife, Nina Kulagina, that she could move small objects such as matchsticks and pens, without touching them; she even appeared to affect the movement of a compass needle. No-one could show that she was cheating. A New Yorker, Felicia Parise, saw a film of Kulagina and subsequently moved small objects herself in experiments held at the Maimonides Center.

By far the most famous modern practitioner of psychokinesis is Uri Geller (see also page 80). He has repeatedly

Forcing a computer to malfunction (left) *is one of the weapons in Uri Geller's PK armoury. On a visit in November 1986 to Axel Springer Verlag, one of Germany's largest publishing houses, he succeeded in stopping the mainframe's tape drive, producing a screen message* (below) *that read "MAGTAPE FAILURE". The tape contained issue 43 of* HOR ZU, *Germany's largest radio television magazine.*

Michael Faraday (left, top) *tested PK in 1853.* ***Nina Kulagina*** (left, bottom) *has undergone more than 100 PK sessions, many under rigidly controlled laboratory conditions. She has moved objects, and once placed her hand on the arm of researcher Benson Herbert, creating intense pain and leaving a mark like a burn that took days to heal. She appears to work in a state of self-induced stress; her pulse rate sometimes reaches more than 200 beats a minute, the activity at the rear of her brain is four times the normal amount, and there is one report of a magnetic field surrounding her body. Soviet scientists call the force she generates "bioenergetics". She became aware of her powers when, angry and upset, she caused a pitcher to fall from a shelf.* ***J. B. Rhine*** (bottom) *is seen testing for PK with a dice tumbler.*

demonstrated his apparent power to cause metal to bend, and to alter the time on watches by merely concentrating on them, and has performed various similar feats under test conditions at Stanford University and elsewhere. There have been innumerable attempts to prove him a cheat. His chief antagonist is a magician, James Randi, a leading member of the America Society for the Investigation of Claims of the Paranormal, whose journal, *The Skeptical Inquirer*, is devoted to examining the claims of psychical investigators. Randi has duplicated some of Geller's accomplishments, but neither he nor SICOP seem to realize that all this means is that Randi is an accomplished conjurer – not, necessarily, that Geller is a pretender: Indeed, Randi's attitude is that of Houdini (p. 176), who made the same philosophical error 50 years previously. Geller has never yet been detected in fraud.

The nature of psychokinesis, if it is a real power, is clearly very mysterious and full of anomalies. It appears to depend very much on the state of mind of the subject concerned; he or she needs to be very fresh, for the powers decrease in proportion to the number of repetitions demanded. Tranquillity of mind does not seem necessary: Felicia Parise first succeeded in moving a small object after the severe emotional shock of a death in the family.

It is clearly also difficult to control the PK faculty: students tested by Dr Helmut Schmidt at the Parapsychological Laboratory at Durham, North Carolina, succeeded in making the indicator of a light meter move anti-clockwise – but were aiming to make it move clockwise!

This is yet another area in which scientists, instead of devising controlled experiments with subtle instruments, have concentrated on attempting to prove that psychokinesis is a mere circus trick – and have even enrolled stage magicians to duplicate the effects. If there is not sufficient scientific proof of the existence of psychokinetic power there is also insufficient evidence that it does not exist.

LEARNING PSYCHOKINESIS

Most researchers agree that anyone, given the will, can learn to move objects by the power of thought; but the learning process is seriously affected by your attitude of mind – and particularly by doubt. This applies to other "paranormal" skills such as dowsing: be sure that you cannot find water with a dowsing rod, and the one sure thing is that you will not!

To test your own powers of psychokinesis, choose a lightweight object with which you feel in sympathy – something for which you have positive feelings; a personal belonging such as a thimble.

Place it upon a smooth surface which is moderately slippery – a piece of glass or a polished wood surface, perhaps.

Now concentrate on moving the object simply by power of thought. Do not become frenetic about it; do not be over-anxious; try to concentrate steadily. Do not give up too easily or too quickly. If you detect the slightest movement (although make sure it is not the product of vibration, or caused by some other physical intervention), stop, and do not attempt any further experiment that day.

If you are clearly becoming successful, make the experiment more telling by marking the object's initial position with a piece of chalk, and measure its movement carefully.

When you feel ready, invite someone to witness an experiment. But choose carefully: whoever you ask should be broadly sympathetic (although not necessarily a "believer").

If you fail, the probability is that you have the wrong mental attitude: you do not have sufficient confidence in your powers. Try not to analyse the situation (especially if you find you begin to succeed!) The "paranormal" is in fact simply an extension of the normal: think of it as in some way weird or unnatural and you will start to destroy it.

Extra-sensory Perception

Extra-sensory perception, or ESP, identifies the strange sense by which some people can apparently transmit simple messages to others without any physical contact.

The number of ESP experiments in modern times is enormous. Relatively few have been conducted under proper supervision, and it must be admitted that some have been found to have involved cheating. For example, one of the first properly recorded tests was arranged in 1882, soon after the formation of the British Society for Psychical Research, when its first President, Henry Sidgwick, announced that the five young daughters of an English clergyman had convinced independent investigators of their telepathic abilities. However, six years later they were caught using a code to communicate with each other.

A more successful experiment in telepathy was conducted in 1937 by Harold Sherman and Sir Hubert Wilkins, when Wilkins, an Australian explorer, was hired by the Russians to find a pilot who had disappeared in the Arctic. Sherman suggested to Wilkins that during his trip they should try to communicate by telepathy. Three days each week Wilkins sat down and reviewed the day's events; in New York, Sherman sat in near-darkness and wrote down anything that came into his head. Among other incidents, Sherman learned of a fire at a place called Aklavik before the news came by radio.

There have been some spectacular results under strictly controlled conditions. One of the most famous was reported in 1937 by Professor Riess of Hunter College, New York. On a number of evenings, Riess turned face-upward a series of cards from a newly shuffled pack on his desk, and his subject wrote down the cards that came to mind. Two packs of 25 cards were used each day. Gradually, the subject became more accurate; and on the last nine days of the experiment her score of successes was 17, 18, 19, 20, 20, 19, 20, 21 and 21 – so far above chance as to be astonishing, and by far the highest score ever recorded in a series of ESP experiments.

Hubert E. Pearce, a divinity student, took part in a similar, better-controlled test in 1933-4, also in America, under Joseph Banks Rhine (1895–1980), founder of modern parapsychological research, and his assistant J. G. Pratt. Pearce performed 1,850 runs over an eight-month period and achieved so many hits that the odds against his score were calculated as 10 followed by 21 zeros to one. Only cheating or genuine ESP could have achieved such results. Rhine published the results of this and more than 100,000 other tests in a monograph entitled *Extra-Sensory Perception*, thereby coining the phrase.

***Australian explorer**, Sir Hubert Wilkins* (above, right) *seems to have communicated news telephathically from the Arctic to journalist Harold Sherman* (above, left) *in New York, during an experiment in 1937.*

Zener cards (left) *are often used in controlled ESP experiments* *(see p. 64)*.

More recently, under test conditions at Stanford, a small object was placed in one of eight aluminium cans, and the well known Uri Geller (see pp.61-2), brought into the room, was asked to indicate the can containing the object. He was correct 12 times out of 14.

As in general scientists have tended to scorn the possibility of ESP, they have been strongly critical of what they see as improperly or carelessly controlled experiments. But several have been forced to conclude that even when the results were somewhat suspect, something was going on which was not scientifically explicable. Some sympathetic scientists have asked what possible motive could persuade otherwise respectable men and women to fake results, especially when the cheating would have to be very carefully planned and executed.

There is an intangible factor that affects ESP experiments as it affects many other attempts to observe or control "supernatural" phenomena: an antipathetic atmosphere appears to reduce extra-sensory powers.

Time and again, someone who has formerly scored highly finds the success rate dropping when unsympathetic observers are present – although those observers have not been able to detect any change of behaviour in the experimenters they observe. This phenomenon, common to several related paranormal sciences (for example, see pp.25-26) is unfortunate, for it suggests to sceptical observers that ESP is entirely subjective, and can therefore be dismissed as "purely" mental, even hysterical.

It cannot be claimed that, so far, really conclusive results have been obtained under the most stringent controls; but there are enough loose ends to persuade some scientists to continue their experiments.

ESP EXPERIMENTS

ESP cards are readily obtainable in occult stores. The best known are Zener cards, on one side of which are simple symbols: a cross, a star, a circle, a square, and a set of wavy lines (see. p.63). You can also use numbers from 0 to 9, letters of the alphabet, or alternatively, you can invent your own set of symbols.

Usually, 25 Zener cards are used, five of each symbol. Shuffle the pack, and then turn up one card at a time, looking at it while your partner – who may be in a neighbouring room, or even some miles away – attempts to draw the symbol you are seeing. Record the symbols in order, then check your result.

According to probability, the result should be five "hits" in each run of 25 cards; the more runs that are made, the closer the average will be to five. Thus in a long run, say of 100 trials, a score higher than five or six is extraordinary; if it rises to eight or nine hits, something strange is happening.

Archeological finds *are examined psychically by Peter Nelson* (above left). *He then makes exact statements about their origin and use, and sometimes even gleans information about former owners.*

J.G. Pratt (left) *and Hubert Pearce during one of the long-distance ESP runs made at Duke University, North Caroline, in 1933-4. The tests were made with Zener cards (see above), developed by J.B. Rhine, and Karl Zener, a member of the University's psychology department.*

The Private Voice

Almost everyone has experienced moments some time in their lives when "something" has "told" them to do a certain thing, or not to do it. In some cases, it appears that this private voice has actually saved lives. "Don't get on that 'plane," the voice has said; and later it has crashed leaving no survivors.

This is an area of the supernatural which is full of pitfalls – there is a kind of poetry about the private voice that makes it almost irresistible to people of a certain temperament. For example, take the anecdote recorded by Sir Laurens van der Post (b.1907) about the death of his admired friend, the great psychologist C.G. Jung (1875-1961). Van der Post was returning by sea from a visit to Africa. One afternoon he had a sort of waking dream of Jung lifting a hand in farewell; the following morning he looked out through the porthole of his cabin:

"I saw a great, white, lone albatross gliding by it; the sun on fire on its wings. As it glided by it turned its head and looked straight at me. I had done that voyage countless times before and such a thing had never happened to me, and I had a feeling as if some tremendous ritual had been performed."

A moment later, he heard on the radio the news that Jung had died the previous day – at the precise moment, as far as he could determine, of his "vision."

A television news flash, *which* Lesley Brennan (left) *said interrupted a movie on the morning of June 1, 1974 told her of an explosion and fire at a chemical plant in Flixborough, England. She heard a male announcer say some people had been killed and many more injured. She passed the news on to two friends over lunch.* ***There was an explosion*** (above) *at Flixborough that day, but it did not happen until 4.53pm – nearly five hours after she had heard the news flash and more than four hours after she had told her friends. Twenty nine people were killed.*

Van der Post felt that somehow Jung had communicated with him at the moment of his death and the following day assumed the guise of the albatross in order to reassure him of his continued existence; although others might question the "vision", and set down the symbolic appearance of the albatross as a simple coincidence.

However, there have been many spectacular and independently recorded incidents of a similar nature – perhaps too many for us to be able to dismiss them so easily. A classic example was recorded by Henry Brougham (1778-1868), sometime Lord Chancellor of England, in his autobiography published in 1871. He had agreed with a friend, "G", that "whichever of us died first should appear to the other, and thus solve any doubts we had entertained about 'life after death'." The friend had gone to India, and they had lost touch. On December 18 1799, while on a visit to Scandinavia, Brougham was taking a bath:

"I turned my head around, looking towards the chair on which I had deposited my clothes, as I was about to get up out of the bath. In the chair sat G., looking calmly at me. How I

got out of the bath I know not, but on recovering my senses I found myself sprawling on the floor. The apparition, or whatever it was, that had taken the likeness of G. had disappeared."

Brougham later received a letter telling him that his friend had indeed died on the very day he had had his vision.

There are modern examples of such "visions" or "intuitions" which are as dramatic, if not more so. In his autobiography, the actor Sir Alec Guinness tells how in 1955, while in Hollywood, he was in a restaurant when an unknown young man came up and, introducing himself as James Dean, offered Sir Alec and his companion a place at his table. But before they sat down, Dean insisted on showing Sir Alec his new toy – a splendid sports car.

Sir Alec heard himself saying, "Please, never get in it. It is now ten o'clock, Friday the twenty-third of September, 1955. If you get in that car you will be found dead in it by this time next week." By four o'clock the following Friday, the younger actor had indeed been killed in a motor accident in his new car.

James Dean at the wheel of his car (far left) *before the crash foreseen by Sir Alec Guinness.*

The Perceptron (left, top) *was developed by NASA to sharpen astronauts' intuition.*

The Premonitions Bureau*, set up by* ***Peter Fairley*** (left, bottom)*, scored some successes. Karren Butler foretold a hurricane in Scotland* (below)

Any attempt to understand such phenomena as these must involve both new theories of time and an attempt to understand the nature of our private voices. Many would argue that they come from the unconscious – that somehow, at particular moments, some deep-seated instinct in humanity is triggered which enables us to break the bonds of time and space. If we were able to control and use these faculties, we might even be able to intervene in future events.

There is one very strange recorded incident in which such an intervention actually took place: it was reported to the author Arthur Koestler. It appears that a young man who attempted suicide by throwing himself in front of a London underground train was saved when the train pulled up just in time. But the brakes were applied not by the driver, but by a passenger who, apparently on instinct, pulled the emergency handle. London Transport confirmed the story. Coincidence, again? Surely too easy an explanation?

Almost every creative artist will admit that ideas, sometimes fully expressed, often drop into their minds unprompted. At their strongest, the voices seem to dictate whole works. For example, Siegfried Sassoon (1886-1967) claimed to have written *Everyone Sang* (probably his best-known poem) in a few moments, late one evening, without conscious thought and as though it was being dictated to him by someone else. It will be argued that the poem had been growing and taking form in his unconscious, perhaps for weeks or months. But that does not make the process any less mysterious – nor does it mean that it was not supernatural, in the sense that some process beyond nature, as we understand it was active.

Unidentified Flying Objects

Although for centuries man had been seeing strange sights in the skies, it was during the late 1940s and early 1950s that public interest in UFOs – unidentified flying objects – became something like an international mania. So much so that in 1953 the United States Government set up a Scientific Advisory Panel on the subject, which rather to its own surprise found that none of its members "were loath to accept that this earth might be visited by extraterrestrial intelligent beings of some sort" – although they did not find evidence that any "flying saucers" so far sighted were in fact connected with space travel.

Several million people all over the world believe that they have seen inexplicable shapes or lights in the sky; and a great number of them believe that these are spaceships controlled by intelligent beings from outside the solar system – probably even outside the galaxy. The hundreds of sightings or alleged sightings of UFOs cover an enormous range of experience – from coolly observed, simple phenomena reported by people who have no interest in the supernatural, to accounts by those who claim they have been captured by spacemen descending from space-capsules. Women have claimed to have been impregnated by spacemen; men have told of being forced to have intercourse with spacewomen, or of having sperm samples extracted by strange devices.

A great number of books have been published in which the writers have advanced their own theories about UFOs. Erich von Daniken, the most famous (or notorious) of these, attempts to show in his *Chariots of the Gods?* that spaceships were observed by the people of Mesopotamia thousands of years ago; C. G. Jung believed that "flying saucers" are a manifestation of the human desire for peace and harmony.

The most rational look at UFOs was taken by a team set up in 1966 by the University of Colorado under the direction of Dr Edward U. Condon, a former President of the American Association for the Advancement of Science, and financed by the American Air Force. The team had access to a very large file of alleged UFO sightings which had been collected since 1952 by the USAF in what was called Project Blue Book.

Similarities between a drawing (above, top) *and a photograph* (above, bottom) *excited UFO hunters in 1952. The drawing was made by a 13-year-old English schoolboy, Stephen Darbishire, before he had developed photographs of a saucer he had seen at Coniston. The photograph was taken by George Adamski in California and became the heart of Adamski's book* Flying Saucers Have Landed. *Adamski's co-author, Desmond Leslie, tested Stephen's story and Stephen was also questioned by Lord Dowding, Commander-in-Chief of Fighter Command during the Battle of Britain.*

The African Dogon tribe*, who live in Mali, decorate their houses* (right) *with motifs that have been interpreted as "the ladder to heaven". Robert K. G. Temple, in* The Sirius Mystery, *argues that the tribe was founded by spacemen from Sirius C, the companion of the dog-star Sirius, and links this theory with the Egyptian legend of Hermes, who landed on earth to teach men the art of civilization and then returned to his home amid the stars – presumably by spacecraft, although Temple does not believe that "modern" UFOs are craft from other planets.*

The UFO photographs *that have best survived rigorous examination were those taken in McMinnville, Oregon, on May 11 1950* (right). *Mrs Paul Trent was feeding her rabbits in the back yard of a farm when she saw a bright, silver-coloured disc-shaped object in the sky. She called her husband, and they photographed the UFO, which was moving slowly and noiselessly westward. The object seemed to hover for a while, change direction several times, then glide rapidly away and eventually pass out of sight.*

Both Mrs Trent and her husband described the UFO quite clearly (and independently). According to their description, it seemed to have a superstructure, and to be made partly of bright metal, partly of what looked like bronze. When it tilted away from them, they felt a distinct breeze; but they heard no noise, and saw neither smoke nor flame.

The photographs were developed and shown to a few friends before being picked up by the local paper, the McMinnville Telephone Register, *and published – the negatives having first been examined by photographic experts and declared free from any kind of chicanery.*

It is an undramatic story – but for that very reason more credible than many more colourful stories of people being abducted by spacemen, or shot at by megalomaniac robots. The Trents refused to elaborate their reports; they simply repeated the rather dull details again and again, not once being caught out in a mistake.

Mysterious circles *appeared in English fields in Hampshire* (above) *and Wiltshire* (right) *in the summer of 1988. Many other such circles have been reported, all apparently formed overnight with mechanical precision – the walls of the standing crops defining the circles are perfectly sharp. The evidence clearly excludes human agency. The scientific consensus is that the circles were formed by freak winds; others claim that they were formed by UFOs.*

The Scientific Study of Unidentified Flying Objects was submitted to the Secretary of the Air Force in 1968, and remains by far the most comprehensive examination of the subject. It concluded that there was no hard evidence to suggest the UFOs came from space; but admitted that there were some reports which remained impossible to explain in rational terms, and suggested that serious scientific study of the subject should continue. This has never happened, although President Jimmy Carter suggested it to NASA (having himself seen what he believed to be a "flying saucer" in Georgia, in 1969).

It is obviously impossible to evaluate sightings made in historical times: we have no means of knowing just what the ancients saw when they spoke of wheels of fire, fiery serpents, flaming crosses or simply "discs" – although there are some graphic descriptions in ancient literature of what seem very like some modern notions of inter-planetary space-ships. For example, take the prophet Ezekiel, who lived in exile in Babylon round *c.*586 BC, and right at the beginning of his Book, seems to describe a vehicle that corresponds to some of those reported more recently:

The pink, saucer-shaped UFO (below) *seen through a car windscreen is a simulation of a hypothetical sighting of a flying-saucer in the small town of Belleville, Wisconsin, USA. For several months in 1986-7, the town was plagued by many such UFO sightings, ranging from simple groups of lights, both stationary and moving, to cylindrical objects seen rising from forest clearings in broad daylight. Unfortunately, no good photographs were taken of these incidents which might establish them more clearly as definite UFO sightings. (Many such claimed sightings later turn out to be easily explicable as clouds or aircraft.)*

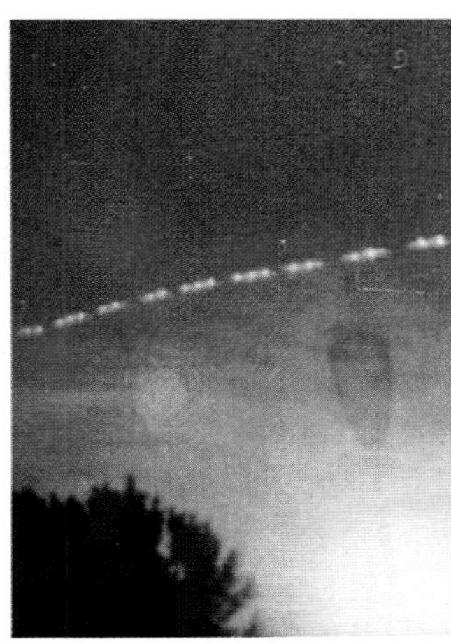

A string of lights (simulation, above) *was seen by 16 year-old Michel Imbeault in Montreal, Canada, moving silently and swiftly across the sky, following the St Lawrence river. It has never been explained.*

"I looked up and saw a storm coming from the north. Lightning was flashing from a huge cloud, and the sky round it was glowing. Where the lightning was flashing, something shone like bronze. . . . There was something that looked like a blazing torch, constantly moving. The fire would blaze up and shoot out flashes of lightning. . . . I saw four wheels touching the ground . . . each one had another wheel intersecting it at right angles, so that the wheels could move in any of the four directions. . . . There was something that looked like a dome made of dazzling crystal. . . ."

Modern writers such as Erich von Daniken and Robert K. G. Temple have constructed interesting theories based on ancient texts or drawings – the Biblical "pillar of fire" in Exodus, the star of Bethlehem, the "fiery chariots" and angels of the Bible have all been claimed as UFOs, as have reports of burning shields described by Pliny in 100 BC, and a spacecraft said (by Gervase of Tillbury) to have anchored itself to an English church steeple in 1270 (a spaceman emerged, but died in earth's atmosphere). The astronomer Edmond Halley

James A. McDivitt (far right), *was in the* Gemini 4 *space vehicle when he saw a cylindrical object with an apparent antenna in free flight over the Pacific Ocean on June 4 1965; it seemed to be closing in on the spacecraft, but vanished after the sun had temporarily blinded the astronaut.*

No manmade object known to be in orbit was in the area at the time. On another occasion, off the coast of China, McDivitt saw a light moving with Gemini 4*; he could not see any details.*

Later, after flying in Gemini 7, *Frank Borman* (near right), *on the right with the rest of the crew of* Apollo 8, *reported that in addition to the booster which was accompanying his craft in orbit, he saw another bright object among a cloud of illuminated particles. No satisfactory explanation has ever been advanced for these three sightings.*

The Hessdalen project (right) *in Norway used the latest instruments to measure objectively the many UFO reports in the area. Scrupulous tests, using the latest equipment, established that some UFO phenomena could indeed be measured, but failed to show what caused them.*

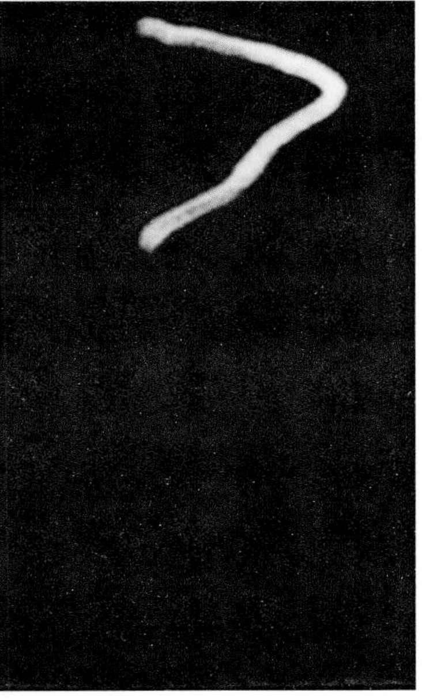

***These four strange lights** in the sky* (left) *were photographed for the* Columbus Evening Dispatch *after more than 150 calls had been reported from people in different parts of Ohio. Even Ohio governor John Gilligan said he had observed strange lights for 35 minutes while driving home.*

Artists' impressions of UFOs (left), *based on eyewitness accounts, show considerable similarities – but it is difficult to establish how reliable the eyewitnesses are and whether they might not, even if unconsciously, have been influenced by accounts of earlier sightings.*

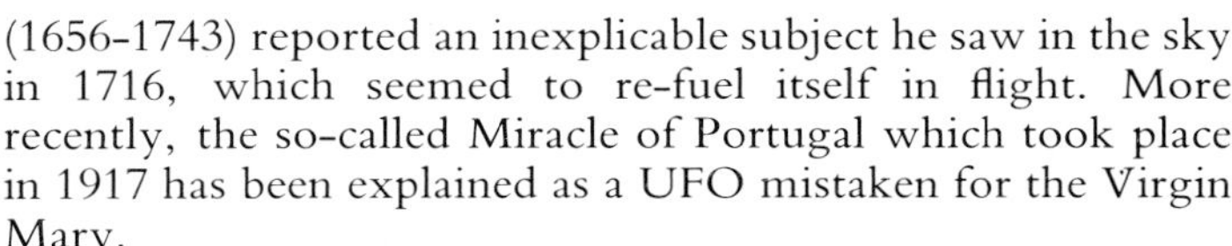

(1656-1743) reported an inexplicable subject he saw in the sky in 1716, which seemed to re-fuel itself in flight. More recently, the so-called Miracle of Portugal which took place in 1917 has been explained as a UFO mistaken for the Virgin Mary.

However, not all ancient sightings are clearly tall stories; nor are they necessarily simply cases of such phenomena as ball lightning. And not all modern reports are the products of hoaxes or hysteria – although there are many delightfully ingenious cases of fake photography – UFOs which have turned out to be models thrown into the air or suspended from wires, hand-held cut-outs illuminated by flashlights, drawings superimposed on photographic prints, reflections photographed through clear glass.

The McMinnville saucer (see p.72) was no model, and there was never any suggestion that Mr and Mrs Trent would have been capable of faking a photographic negative. A United States Air Force Committee examined the photographs in great technical detail, went to McMinnville, checked every aspect of the story and concluded firmly that "this is one of the few UFO reports in which all factors investigated – geometric, psychological and physical – appear to be consistent with the assertion that an extraordinary flying object, silvery, metallic, disk-shaped, tens of meters in diameter and evidently artificial, flew within sight of two witnesses. It cannot be said that the evidence positively rules out a fabrication, although there are some physical factors such as the accuracy of certain photometric measures of the original negatives which argue against a fabrication."

Since this conclusion was reached, the photographic negatives, computer-enhanced, have been re-examined, and their genuineness seems beyond question.

The McMinnville case is not the only convincing one – although the photographs are by far the most concrete evidence available. Many men and women who had much to lose by insisting that they had seen an object from outer space, have stuck to their stories despite enormous pressure and – sometimes – loss of promotion or even of their jobs. Both civil and military pilots have been among them – as have trained astronauts.

Although many scientists close their minds securely against any suggestion that UFOs may have come from outer space, it is now generally accepted that some very strange sights have been seen. In 1969 Cornell University held a symposium on UFO phenomena, organized by two astronomers, Thornton Page and Carl Sagan, under the auspices of the American Association for the Advancement of Science. One of the most interesting papers was given by a sociologist, Robert L. Hall, who having pointed out the possibility of "hysterical contagion" (which no doubt has been responsible for the wilder anecdotes of those who claim capture by little green men) concluded that it could not have been responsible for such a widespread world pattern of UFO sightings, and that if UFOs were not real, either social scientists or physicists had much to explain.

Carl Sagan himself appeared not to deny that something curious was going on; but did not believe that UFOs could come from other civilizations in the universe (although he conceded that there was probably intelligent life on a number of other planets). However, his argument depended on the supposition that earth's scientists know everything there is to be known about the possibility of inter-stellar travel, which may not be so.

The verdict on UFOs remains open. Although some scientists suggest that the great distance between our solar system and the nearest celestial objects which could possibly support life is too great for travel between them to be possible, others take the view that man may not yet be aware of every physical force in the universe, and that space-travel using some form of presently unknown energy might be possible. It is certainly true that a minority of properly recorded UFO sightings remains inexplicable.

VISITORS FROM SPACE?

UFO s (unidentified flying objects) have captured the imagination since earliest times. The list right includes reports by people who claim to have seen such vessels or interacted with their inhabitants.

CLOSE ENCOUNTERS OF THE FOURTH KIND – reports of personal contact with occupants, and temporary detainment

***1* Argentina**: *Ingeniero White, 1975, Carlos Alberto Diaz taken onto UFO*
***2* United States**: *White Mountains, New Hampshire, 1961, couple recalled details of UFO-boarding under hypnotherapy*
***3* Scotland**: *Lothian Region, 1957, Robert Taylor saw UFO, trousers torn by force as he was pulled towards craft*
***4* Brazil**: *Near Francisco de Sales, Minas Gerais, 1957, Antonio Villas Boas dragged onto UFO*

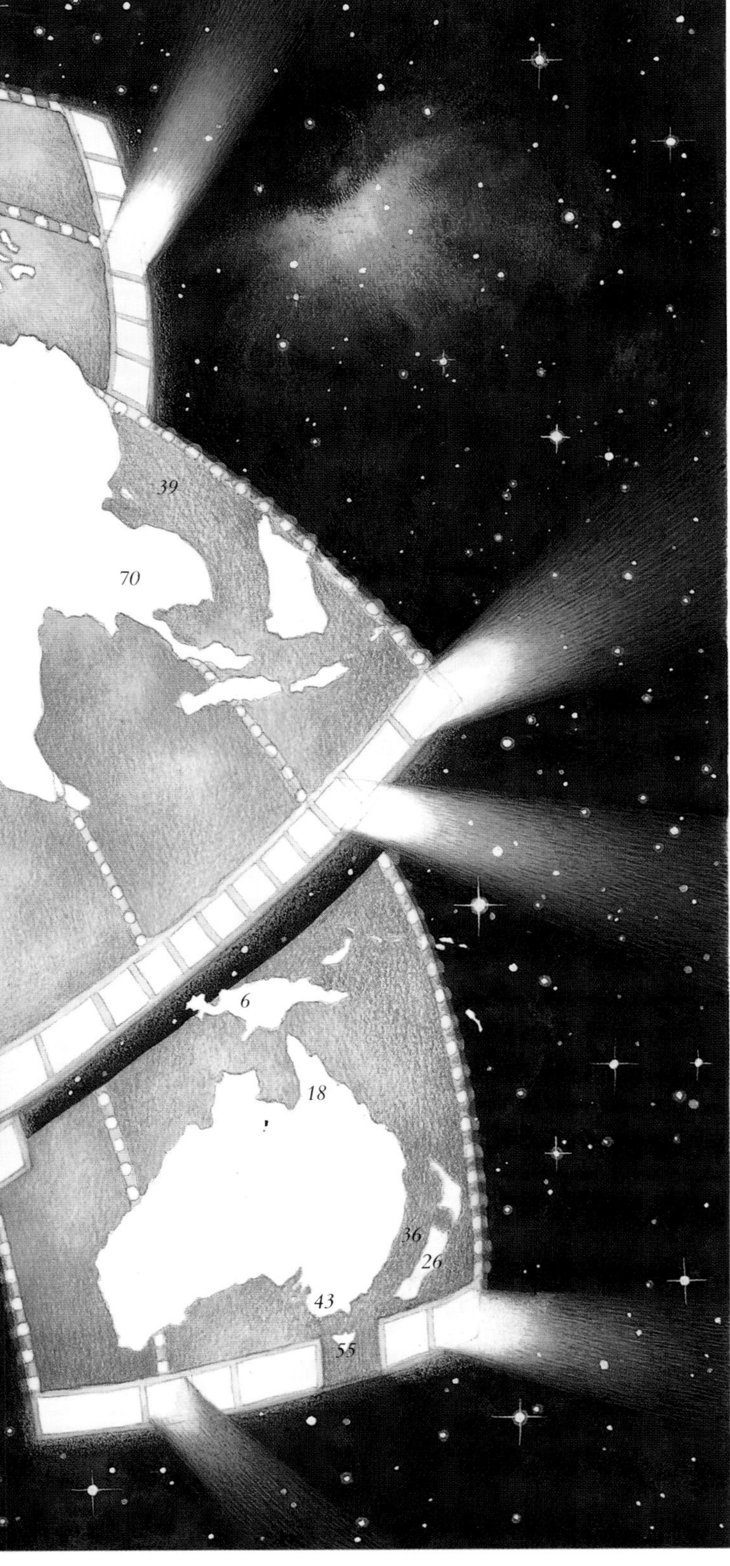

CLOSE ENCOUNTERS OF THE THIRD KIND – alleged sightings of UFO occupants from outer space
***5* United States**: *White Sands Missile Range, New Mexico, 1951, photographs taken of UFO; Socorro, New Mexico, 1964*
***6* New Guinea**: *Boinani, 1959, weeks of sky lights ended in UFO sighting*
***7* United States**: *Newark Valley, New York, 1964*
***8* United States**: *Eagle River, Wisconsin, 1961*
***9* England**: *Ranton, Shrewsbury, 1954*
***10* Venezuela**: *Caracas, 1954*
***11* United States**: *Flatwood, West Virginia, 1952*
***12* Brazil**: *Near Bauru, 1947*

CLOSE ENCOUNTERS OF THE SECOND KIND – some apparent interaction, such as interference with car ignition, burns on ground, physical effects on people or animals
***13* United States**: *Levelland, Texas, 1957; Denison, Texas, 1878*
***14* United States**: *Halfway between Columbus and Cleveland, Ohio, 1973, airforce crew came close to colliding with UFO; Ravenna, Ohio, 1966*
***15* Brazil**: *Near Catanduva, 1973*
***16* Romania**: *Transylvanian Alps, 1972*
***17* United States**: *Near Delphos, Kansas, 1971*
***18* Australia**: *Tully, North Queensland, 1966*
***19* United States**: *Florida, 1952*

CLOSE ENCOUNTERS OF THE FIRST KIND – no interaction between UFO and the environment
***20* Mid-Atlantic**: *Astronaut Borman claims to have seen UFO from Apollo, 1965*
***21* Denmark**: *Sonderborg, 1951*
***22* United States**: *Southern Michigan, 1966*
***23* France**: *Near Amiens, 1954*
***24* United States**: *Montgomery, Alabama, 1948*

RADAR VISUALS
***25* United States**: *Washington DC, 1952, Airforce Base spotted UFOs; Washington National Airport & Andrews Airforce Base, 1952, blips seen on radarscope; Washington DC, 1959, report of UFO sighting suppressed by CIA*
***26* New Zealand**: *East of South Island, 1978, UFOs tracked on radar, and tape recordings made*
***27* Mexico**: *Mexico City, 1975, UFO scraped underpart of Piper PA-24 aircraft*
***28* United States**: *Mississippi, Louisiana, Texas and into Oklahoma, 1957, Air Force RB-47 followed by UFO for over 700 miles (1,120 km)*
***29* France**: *Orly Airport, Paris, 1956*

DAYLIGHT SIGHTINGS
***30* United States**: *Carbondale, Illinois, 1973*
***31* United States**: *Over Hawaii, 1965*
***32* United States**: *Between Houston and Atlanta, 1948*
***33* United States**: *Over Fort Knox, Kentucky, 1947, Captain Mansell pursued UFO to his death*
***34* United States**: *Boise, Idaho, 1947*
***35* United States**: *Exeter, New Hampshire 1965*
***36* Tasman Sea**: *Between Lord Howe Island and Australia, 1931*
***37* China**: *Kukunor district, near the Humboldt Chain, 1926*
***38* Mexico**: *Zacatecas, 1883, Senor Jose Bonilla, director of the Zacatecas Observatory, saw small luminous bodies crossing the sun*
***39* China Sea**: *1909, giant luminous wheel, approx. 130 feet (39.5m) in diameter, allegedly spun over surface, then descended into water*
***40* Gulf of Oman**: *1906, giant luminous wheel*
***41* Persian Gulf**: *1879-1880 luminous wheel*
***42* Western Sahara**: *Rio de Oro, 1870*
***43* Australia**: *Bass Strait, 1978, Frederick Valentich was allegedly pursued in his aircraft by a UFO and never seen again*
***44* Sweden**: *Gotland, 1957*
***45* France**: *Oloron 1950; Gaillac 1950*
***46* United States**: *Oregon, 1950*

SIGHTINGS AT A DISTANCE OF MORE THAN 500 FEET (152.5 m)
***47* Canada**: *Coniston, 1952*
***48* United States**: *Hackensack, New Jersey 1973*
***49* United States**: *Bismark, North Dakota, 1973*
***50* Finland**: *Helsinki, 1946*
***51* United States**: *Kansas City, Missouri, 1897, 10,000 people said they saw UFO*
***52* United States**: *Tulare, California, 1896, alleged mass UFO sighting*
***53* France**: *Embrun, 1820*
***54* Iran**: *Teheran, 1976*
***55* Australia**: *Tasmania, 1974*
***56* United States**: *Leary, Georgia, 1969*
***57* Between Portugal and Spain**: *1957*
***58* Canada**: *Labrador, 1954*
***59* United States**: *Over Fargo, North Dakota, 1948; Lubbock, Texas, 1951, series of nocturnal lights*

ANCIENT AND HISTORICAL SIGHTINGS
***60* North Sea**: *1716*
***61* Ireland**: *Cloera, 1211, anchor of flying ship caught on arch above church door*
***62* Switzerland**: *Lausanne, 1762*
***63* France**: *Arras, 1461*
***64* England**: *Uxbridge 1322; London 1742; blazing ball seen moving from northwest to southeast, 1799*
***65* England**: *Byland Abbey, North Yorkshire Riding, 12th century, UFO flew over abbey; Leicestershire and Northamptonshire, 1387*
***66* Japan**: *Kii mountains, 1180, flying "earthenware vessel" seen; Tatsunokuchi 1271; bright object resembling full moon seen in sky, 1458; five "stars" circled moon, allegedly changed colour 3 times, then vanished, 1458; Mt. Masuga, 1468; Kyoto, 1606*
***67* Roman Italy**: *Arpi in Apulia, reports of ships seen in the sky, 216 BC; Tarquinia, flaming globe seen to travel across the sky, 99 BC; Spoletium in Umbria, 90 BC; sighting of a UFO formation, 393 BC*
***68* Chaldea** (now Iraq): *Near Chebar River, Ezekiel's vision of a wheel-machine with four occupants, 592 BC*
***69* Egypt**: *Papyrus written during reign of Thutmose III (c.1504-1450 BC) records fleet of flying saucers*
***70* China**: *Hunan province, rock carving, 47,000 years old, depicting cylindrical objects with occupants*

Messages from Space

It is now generally agreed that it is unlikely that man is the only intelligent creature to inhabit the universe. While (for no special reason) scientists are almost united in denying that creatures from other solar systems could have the technology to visit us, they cannot provide a reason why we should not be able to intercept any messages the inhabitants of other populated planets care to send out into the blackness of space. Indeed, these inhabitants may one day be able to intercept not only the TV and radio emissions which involuntarily escape from earth, but the messages we have purposely dispatched: the plaque we placed on the side of one of our spaceships, and radio messages.

The first of these messages was sent at 5pm on November 16 1974, when the 1,000-foot (304m) radio telescope at Arecibo, Puerto Rico, directed a three-minute signal towards a group of stars – the globular cluster M13 – 24,000 light-years away. It is said to be the strongest signal ever radiated by man. However, unless some speedier medium than radio is discovered it will clearly be some time before any reply can be expected.

A century earlier, man had thought of attempting to send out some message to whom it might concern. Charles Cros, a French inventor, suggested in 1861 the construction of a huge mirror which might flash a sun-powered semaphore message to Mars; the Victorian Canadians proposed the laying-out of an enormous illuminated cross suspended above Lake Michigan, to flash on and off every ten minutes.

None of this came to anything. But during the Second World War a more practical proposal was made by the Dutch astronomer Hendrick Christoffel van den Hulst. He suggested that as hydrogen atoms, changing their energy state, emitted a photon (a unit of electromagnetic radiation energy) with a frequency corresponding to a radio wavelength of 21 centimetres, and hydrogen is the main element in the universe, the microwave elements emitted by enormous quantities of hydrogen atoms might combine to a level observable many light-years away.

The American physicist Edward Mills Purcell in 1951 supported this theory: and it seemed likely that the scientists of any intelligent civilization would reach the same conclusion – that the 21-centimetre wavelength was one on which attempts to communicate with other planets should be made.

Eight years later, in 1959, it was suggested that as hydroxyl, the two-atom combination of hydrogen and oxygen, also emitted quantities of microwaves, the wave band should be widened to between 17 and 21 centimetres. In 1960, Project Ozma was organized: at 4am on April 8 a number of astronomers began – secretly, for they feared ridicule – listening intently to the 21-centimetre wavelength in the hope of hearing something that might be to their advantage. They continued for more than six days, but without results.

Two astronomers, Benjamin Zuckerman and Patrick Palmer, organized another experiment which started in 1976. From Green Bank Observatory they observed 659 stars between six and 76 light years away from the Sun, which in their view might support life. Their observations continued for four years, again without result.

But have we already come across such messages from other civilizations? If so, can they be regarded as supernatural? Certainly, if they have reached us, they are beyond nature as we comprehend it.

Nikola Tesla was the first scientist to suggest that he had heard messages from beyond our solar system. Attempting to discover a way to transmit energy by radio, he was working with equipment at Colorado Springs, in the United States, in 1899, when he began to perceive that his radio was registering signals in which there seemed to be "a clear suggestion of number and order not traceable to any cause then known to me." He believed he was hearing messages from space.

In the same year Gugliemo Marconi overheard similar "messages" which seemed to have a pattern to them – and which mysteriously contained within them the Morse letter V, which he had been using himself in test transmissions – as though some intelligence was including it as a sort of identifying factor.

In 1920, when Mars approached close to the earth, a British astronomer, David Todd, asked all radio stations to maintain silence while he used a basic radio camera to scan Mars for life. They did: and they, and a number of amateur radio operators, began to receive regular patterns of dots and dashes, which also showed up on Todd's radio camera.

Later, when the first reports of UFOs began to be

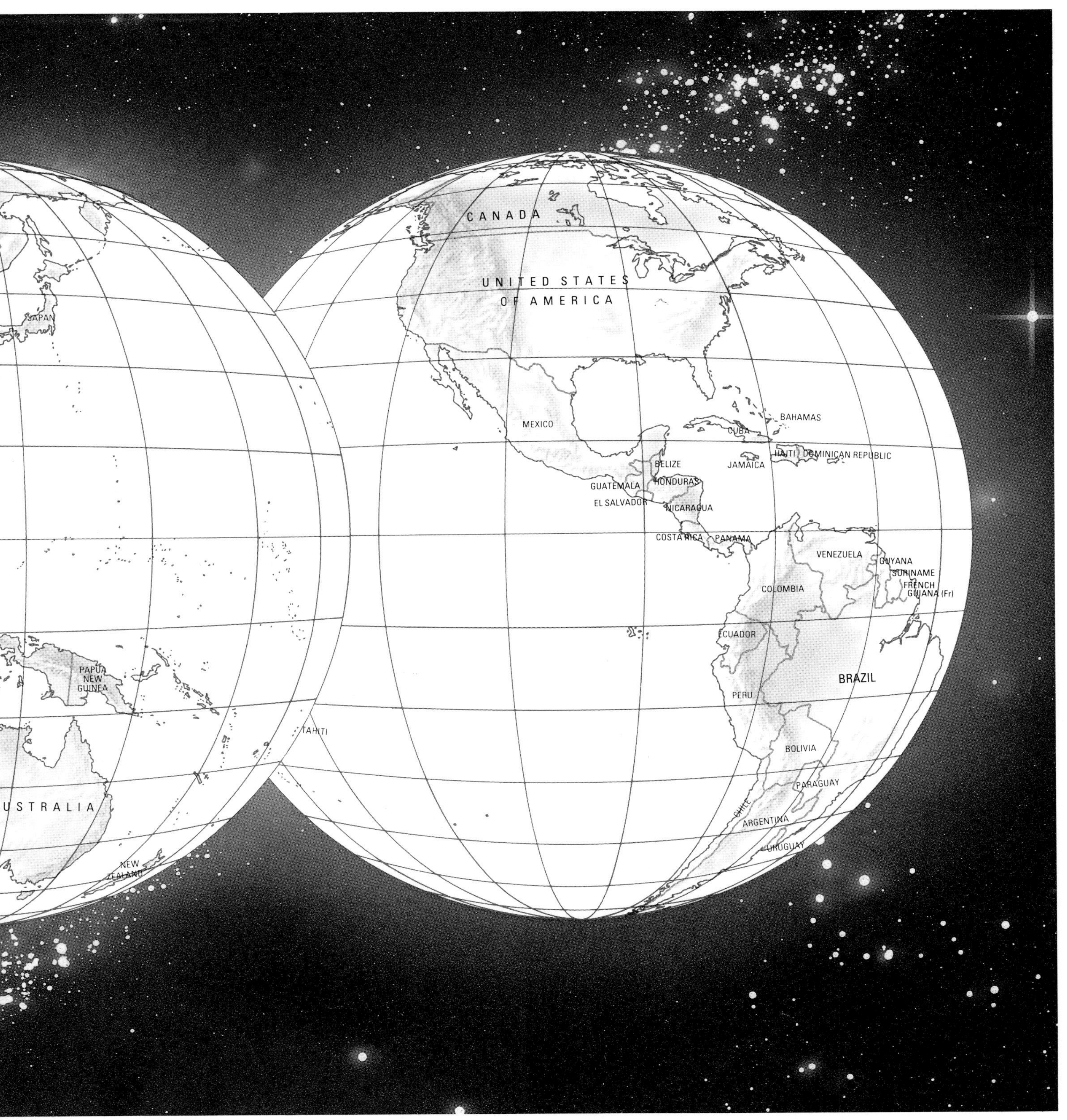
JAPAN
PAPUA NEW GUINEA
TAHITI
USTRALIA
NEW ZEALAND
CANADA
UNITED STATES OF AMERICA
MEXICO
BAHAMAS
CUBA
HAITI
DOMINICAN REPUBLIC
JAMAICA
BELIZE
GUATEMALA
HONDURAS
EL SALVADOR
NICARAGUA
COSTA RICA
PANAMA
VENEZUELA
GUYANA
SURINAME
FRENCH GUIANA (Fr)
COLOMBIA
ECUADOR
BRAZIL
PERU
BOLIVIA
PARAGUAY
CHILE
ARGENTINA
URUGUAY

AFRICA AND THE MIDDLE EAST

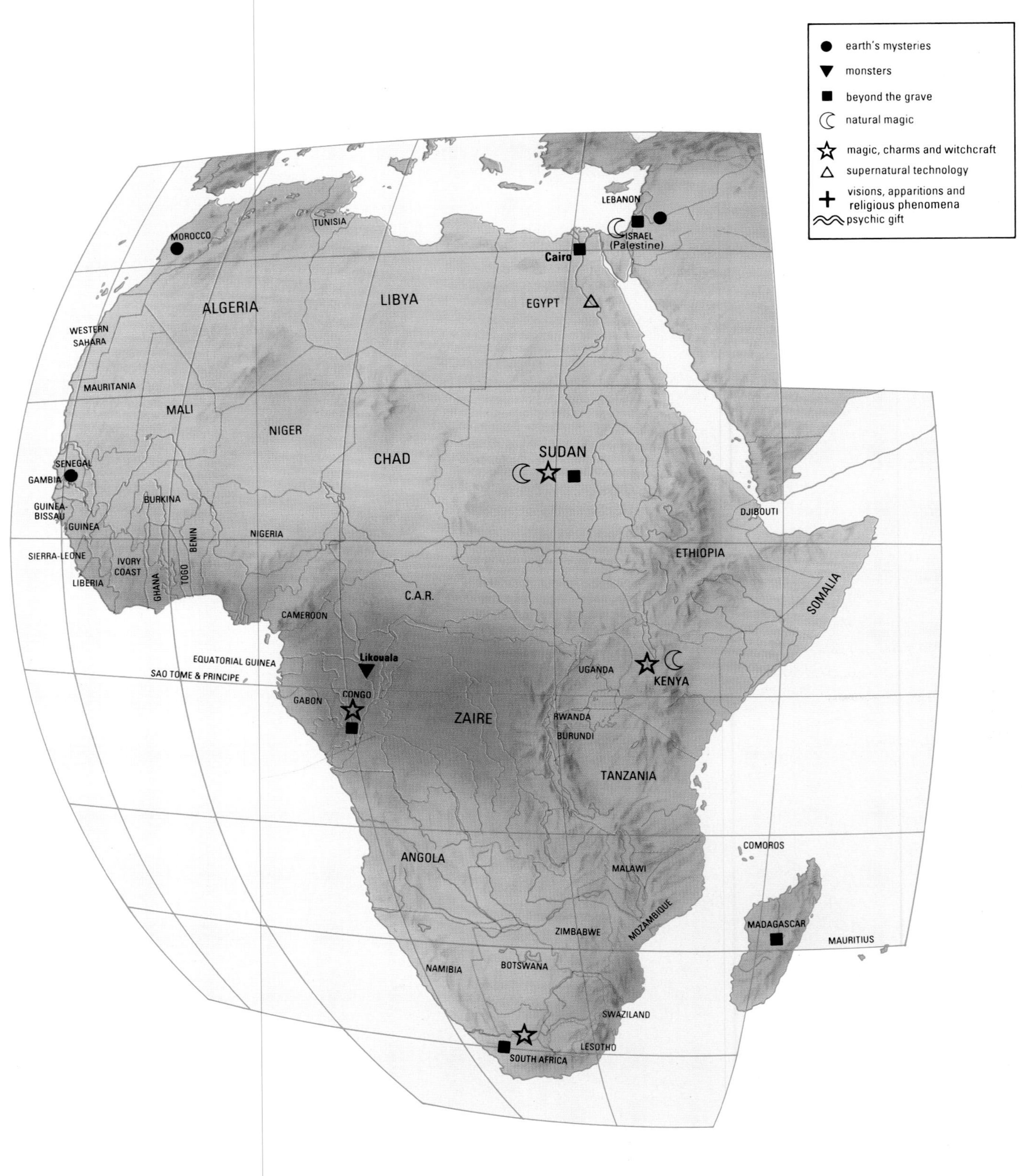

The most ancient and primitive societies worshipped the sun. At the temple of On, before Egypt was a kingdom, cattle were sacrificed to it. Various civilizations in Africa and around the Mediterranean had animal gods, such as the beasts of Anatolia. And in addition there were ancestral ghosts to be placated.

Concern with death brought about the building of the tombs of the kings at Ur, almost three thousand years before Christ, while in ancient Iraq the bodies of the dead were preserved in honey, and from c.*3500 BC in Egypt they were embalmed and buried, at first in mastabas and then in pyramids, the largest of which are among the wonders of the world. Later, other civilizations also built elaborate tombs: the rulers of Mycenae lay in circular vaults, the kings of ancient Ethiopia stood inside hollow crystal pillars.*

It is not surprising that an air of magic came to surround such remarkable edifices – nor that the idea that spirits had lives of their own became common. And from that idea to the appearance on earth of the gods themselves was not a great step. In Iraq, ladies of heaven, gods of vegetation, fish gods, moon gods, water gods, gods of wisdom, love and war were soon walking the earth and advising their earthly subjects.

The legends of these gods, and the physical remains of the tombs of the aristocracy, have contributed to an atmosphere of the supernatural which has attracted so many people to construct complex theories of magic connected with the Great Pyramid in Egypt, or to look curiously at the power claimed by African witch doctors to raise storms, bring rain, kill by curse or cure by spell.

Most African magic is perhaps no more mysterious than European magic, although it has undoubtedly had a longer history of "respectability" among the people on whom it is practised. The African magical tradition is remarkably tenacious: the best-educated African often refuses to dismiss as illogical the powers of witch doctors, and sometimes those powers seem so real that a curse placed even on a non-believer appears to work.

Egyptian magic is another matter: complex theories have been based on what are claimed to be magically inspired measurements used to construct the pyramids, which are still believed by some people to harness occult forces *(see pp.86-8)**. These are generally dismissed as nonsensical; yet they have been very seriously argued, and the mathematical construction of some pyramids and temples do seem to have a peculiarly interesting relationship with the universe.*

Lands which are so soaked in their own particular brand of magic have an air of their own, and it is as impossible to ignore it as it is to ignore their physical nature – their deserts or forests. It behoves Western man to treat them with respect.

EGYPT

THE PYRAMIDS

It is not surprising that the pyramids of Egypt should be regarded by some people as magical. The effort needed to build such imposing structures was so great that it might well be suggested that they are more than mere monuments to the monomania of Egyptian monarchs.

Interest has centred on the Great Pyramid at Giza, which, Napoleon calculated, contains enough stone to run a wall one foot thick (a third of a metre) right round the boundary of France, and within whose base could be contained the cathedrals of Florence and Milan, St Peter's in Rome and St Paul's in London.

It is argued that because no royal remains have been found in this pyramid, it must surely have been built for some other purpose than interment (this conveniently ignores the strong tradition that in AD 820 the Caliph Mamun found Cheops's mummy there, decked with gold and precious stones). Several theories have been advanced – the most common, that the pyramid represents a universal system of measurement devised by the ancient Egyptians. Victorian pyramidologists argued that the Great Pyramid, like Stonehenge and other giant man-made sites, was built as an astronomical observatory. More recently, it has been claimed that the very shape and proportions of the pyramid have given it magical properties – preserving food, sharpening razor-blades and even prolonging youth – so that extremists took to sleeping in tents made to the same proportions. (Aleister Crowley, the British magician, took things a step further by insisting on spending one night of his honeymoon inside the pyramid's innermost chamber. Mrs Crowley's comments are not recorded.)

The speculations of archaeologists about the origin of the pyramids are equally wide-ranging. Some see them as symbolizing stairways to heaven; others believe that the angles of their sides represent the rays of the sun. Mathematicians have speculated yet more wildly – for example, the 17th century British professor of geometry, John Greaves, believed that the ancient Egyptians possessed a knowledge of geometry long lost to the civilized world.

It was in the 1880s that serious – or manic – pyramidology really began, with John Taylor, the editor of the *London Magazine*. His major "discovery" was that if the perimeter of the Great Pyramid was divided by twice its height, the result was a figure almost identical to the value of *pi* – about 3.14159 – the constant that is multiplied by the diameter of a circle to give its circumference. The revelation that the ancient Egyptians knew about *pi* led to the supposition that the pyramid had been built in order to record the measurement of the earth itself. A highly religious man, Taylor concluded that God Himself had given the Egyptians primary wisdom.

After making his own studies, a friend and disciple of Taylor, Charles Piazzi Smyth, Astronomer-Royal of Scotland, came up with the pyramid inch, and claimed that the structure measured time as well as space – for the perimeter, in "pyramid inches", was equal to 365.2 multiplied by one thousand, so the ancients had also known the precise number of solar days in a year!

Astronomers took a hand, Richard Proctor confirming the theory that the pyramids were built on a foundation of astronomical knowledge: the motions of the planets could be observed and confirmed by sighting them through the pyramid's entrance, from within; while Livio Stecchini, an American professor, claimed that the Egyptians could have used the Great Pyramid to calculate the length of a degree of latitude and longitude to within a few hundred feet.

The idea of the Great Pyramid as a sort of giant refrigerator originated in the 1930s, when a Frenchman, Antoine Bovis,

Charles Piazzi Smyth *(1819-1900), Scotland's Astronomer Royal, claimed he could calculate all major dates in the earth's past – and its future – from the dimensions of the Great Pyramid. These ingenious calculations enabled him to lend the pyramid a significance of which its builders may not have been aware.*

claimed to find the remains of several cats and other animals which had died in the King's Chamber, and whose bodies were perfectly dehydrated and preserved. At home, he built a scale model of the pyramid and put a dead cat in it. The cat mummified in a few days. He then discovered that food placed in the pyramid seemed not to deteriorate.

A Czech, Karl Drbal, then built a cardboard pyramid, which had the same effect – and moreover he found he could use it to sharpen dulled razor blades. A Viennese gentleman, Oskar Jahnisch, who claimed to have used the same blade for five years, sharpening it by keeping it in a pyramid, took out a patent for Cheops Pyramid Razor Blade Sharpeners.

Pyramids have now been used for every purpose from calming the nerves and curing toothache, to conferring immortal youth. Michael Jackson has been said to sleep inside one, and a dog belonging to a Mr. G. Patrick Flanagan of California, a leading contemporary pyramidologist, became a vegetarian, apparently converted by the beneficial rays of pyramid power.

Although many people have been disappointed when trying pyramid power, others continue to confirm its efficacy. In his famous book *Supernature* (1973), Lyall Watson reported that he had been using the same razor blade for four months, keeping it in a pyramid (but it is not uncommon for some men to use blades that last as long without the supernatural aid of Cheops). Watson suggests that the pyramid, which he pointed out is shaped rather like a crystal of magnetite, might build up a magnetic field which could affect the blades' edges.

Whatever the truth, archaeologists have certainly confirmed the skill of the ancient builders: Flinders Petrie, the greatest of them, concluded that the errors in measurement were so slight that a thumb would cover them – the walls of the passageway descending for 350 feet (107m) into the heart of the pyramid deviated by less than a quarter of an inch (½cm) from the perfectly straight. The mystery of the pyramids may have more to do with the meticulousness of the Pharaohs' architects and builders than with unknown Egyptian magic.

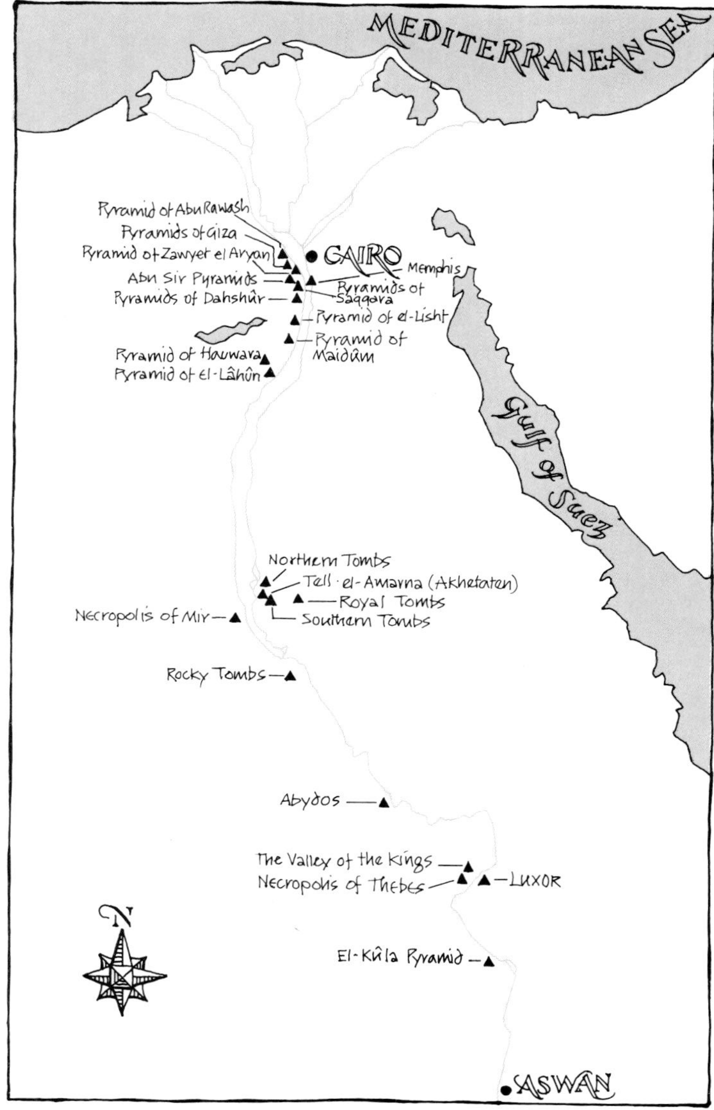

MAKING A PYRAMID

It is easy to try pyramid power for yourself: cut four pieces of cardboard, or perhaps plywood, into isosceles triangles with the proportion, base to sides, of 15.7 to 14.9 (a) – that is, for a pyramid six inches tall (15.2cm), the base should be 9⅜ inches (24cm), and the sides 8⅞ inches (22.8cm) each. Stick the sides together (b). Place the pyramid so that the base lines are square to magnetic north/south and east/west, away from electrical equipment or wires. (The best way to orientate it is to trace the base onto a piece of paper, draw two lines to divide it into quarters, then lay one of the lines north-south, using a compass.) Construct a little platform 3.33 units high (for the six-inch [15.2cm] pyramid, two inches [5cm] high), and put it inside the pyramid (c). This will mean that anything placed on the stand will have the same relation to the pyramid's surface as the pharoah's chamber in Cheops' pyramid. Your razor blade should face east/west.

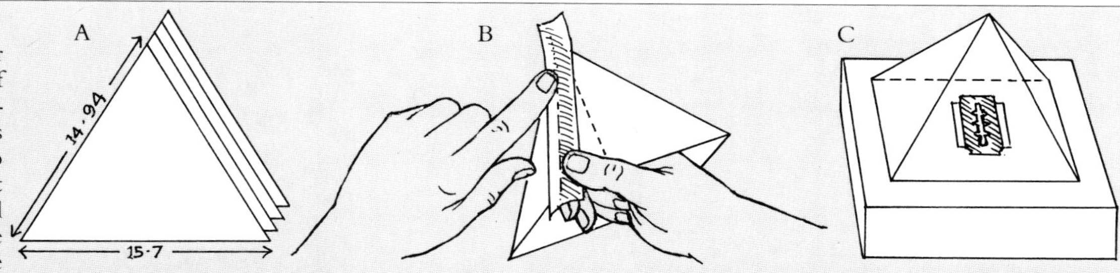

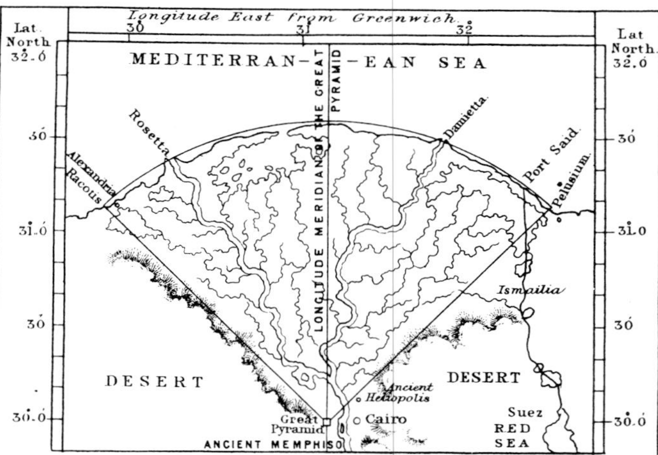

The Geographical location of the Great Pyramid (above) *has led to much conjecture. The Scottish astronomer Charles Piazzi Smyth (see p. 86) used this illustration in his book* Our Inheritance in the Great Pyramid, *to point out that the Pyramid is located at a latitude of 30° north, exactly one third of the distance from the Equator to the Pole, and orientated precisely to face the four points of the compass. He did not regard this as coincidental. Piazzi Smyth was also among those who suggested that the meridian line running due north-south apparently runs through more dry land – and less ocean – than any other such line. Thus, he declared, the centre of all the dry land habitable on earth "falls within the Great Pyramid's territory of Lower Egypt".*

The northern coastline of Egypt forms a fairly regular arc; in 1868 Henry Mitchell of the US Coast Survey discovered that the spot from which the arc is struck coincides exactly with the rock on which the Great Pyramid stands. It therefore stands at the centre of Egypt – or even the whole world, according to some calculations.

The pyramids at Giza (right) *are among the most awe-inspiring of all human creations, and are also some of the oldest, dating to before 2,500 BC. They were built on tombs, but it has been suggested that they may have also been used in astronomical calculations. Their proportions interest those who place mystical interpretations on mathematical relationships. It has been claimed that scale-model pyramids will preserve food, keep razor-blades sharp and cure many common ills (see p. 87).*

Omm Sety

One of the most remarkable of all reincarnation stories centres on the great temple of Sety I at Abydos.

In 1907, a three-year-old girl called Dorothy Louise Eady fell downstairs at her London home, and was pronounced dead by the family doctor – who was surprised, an hour or two later, to find her sitting up in bed, playing. But after her fall, she began to get dreams of a strange "home" which was not her own; and some years later, taken to the British Museum by her parents, she became fixated on the Egyptian galleries there, returning again and again to be with "her people." The Keeper of Egyptian Antiquities befriended her and taught her to read Egyptian hieroglyphics. She became more and more convinced, as she grew older, that she was the reincarnation of an ancient Egyptian girl, Bentreshyt, who had been seduced by the Pharaoh Sety I, and forced to commit suicide when the relationship was discovered.

Dorothy contrived to marry an Egyptian, and was taken to Cairo to live – where she said she was visited by the apparition of her former lover, Sety, and became entirely preoccupied by her studies of ancient Egypt. After an amicable divorce, she "married the Egyptian Antiquities Department," and devoted the rest of her life to Egyptology. She claimed not only to be visited regularly by Sety I, but to have travelled astrally, to have conversed with many of the ancient Pharaohs and their officials – and learned many facts from them about ancient buildings, which contributed to modern knowledge about their construction. She recorded her astral journeys and conversations in long diary entries.

But the story is more peculiar even than that, for on visiting Abydos for the first time she recognized it as her true home. In 1956, she went there permanently, to live in "her" temple until her death in 1981, calling herself Omm Sety ("Mother of Sety"). It was clear from the start that, however she had achieved it, she had an intimate knowledge of the temple buildings – without ever having studied them (they were at the time uncatalogued). Doubtful of her claims, the Chief Inspector of the Antiquities Department of the Cairo Museum took her to the temple in the dead of night, and told her to find her way to the Chapel of Amon. Without a light, she walked straight to it along the complicated corridors of the ruins. Then she went, in pitch darkness, to the Hall of the Sacred Boats.

Omm Sety became a healer, and there are records of many cases of injury or illness apparently cured by her. But she also became a learned Egyptologist, respected by the most eminent scholars – even when she insisted on speaking of historical figures as though they were friends ("such a *handsome* boy," she would say of Rameses II, and "the original rich bitch" of his mother, Queen Tuy).

Omm Sety died on April 21 1981 at Abydos. The local authorities refused to allow her to be buried in the tomb she had prepared for herself in the temple garden, but she lies not far away.

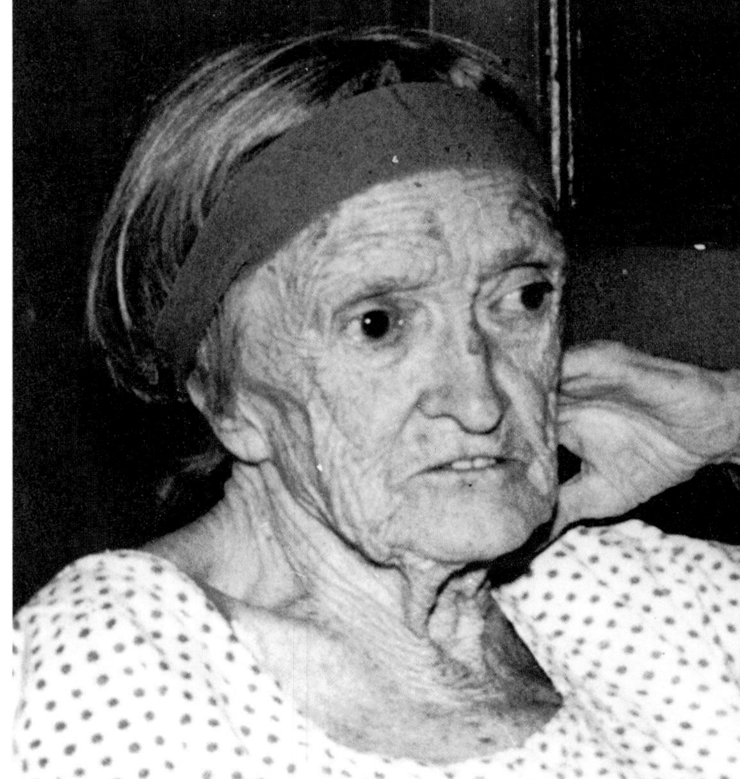

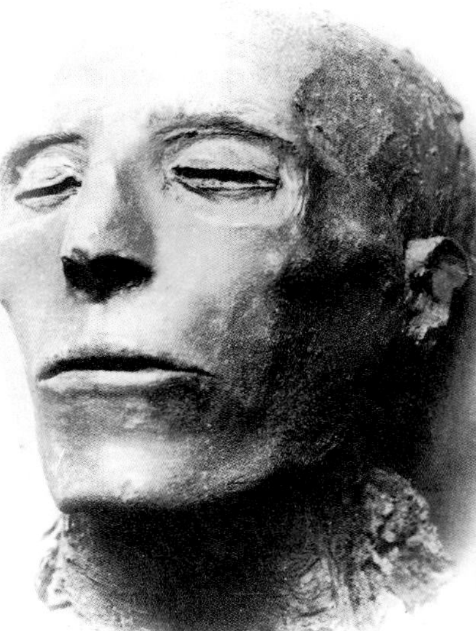

Dorothy Eady** (1904-81)* (above) *was an Englishwoman who claimed that **Pharaoh Sety I (right) *had seduced her during his reign from 1318-04 BC and, as a result, she had been forced to commit suicide. In her reincarnation as Miss Eady, she learned to read hieroglyphics, married an Egyptian and moved to Cairo – where she was visited regularly by the apparition of Sety. From astral visits to ancient Egypt, she learned much about the construction of its buildings and was able to make significant contributions to Egyptology. She eventually became a self-appointed guardian of, and guide to, the Temple of Sety.*

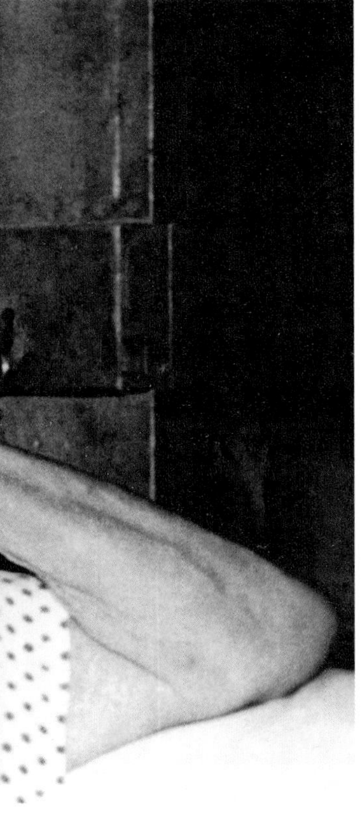

The stone sarcophagus *containing the mummy of Tutankhamun* (right), *with its discoverer Howard Carter and his assistant Callender (standing behind him), was a sensational archaeological discovery. But the opening of the tomb started what seemed a series of inexplicable linked deaths. Tutankhamun appeared to be striking back at those who had the impiety to open his grave – or even to admire it after it had been opened.*

The Curse of Tutankhamun

The most notable discovery of modern Egyptology – and one of the most remarkable of all 20th-century archaeological discoveries –was that of the tomb of the Pharaoh Tutankhamun, containing treasure of great beauty and value.

The ancient civilization of Egypt became the focus of such attention that it is not surprising that its religion was the source of much conjecture; and the fact that a tomb had been disturbed and – in the view of some people – desecrated, might have been expected to result in a certain amount of romantic story-telling. But the claim that those responsible for opening the tomb were subjected to a pharaohic curse is remarkably tenacious, and all attempts to produce rational explanations for the apparent results of the curse have failed to disprove the story.

The two men chiefly responsible for the find were the archaeologist Howard Carter – who had already made three major discoveries (of the tombs of Queen Hatshepsut, and of the Pharaohs Horemheb and Thutmose IV) – and Lord Carnarvon, an English peer. For five years Carnarvon financed Carter's investigation of the Valley of the Kings, where many pharaohs had been buried, and where it was supposed there might be tombs unpillaged by the robbers who had removed all the valuables from the known tombs.

In November 1922, Carter found a sealed doorway at the bottom of a flight of steps. He broke through it, to discover a second door, beyond which was a room crowded with the most astonishing grave-furnishings yet seen in Egypt: an apparently random pile of exquisite statues, chairs, chariots and jewelry – and in a chamber beyond, the multi-cased body of the young Tutankhamun himself.

It is claimed that in the antechamber Carter found a tablet bearing hieroglyphics reading: "DEATH WILL SLAY WITH HIS WINGS WHOEVER DISTURBS THE PHARAOH'S PEACE." However, such a tablet has never been seen and, according to rumour, Carter removed it before it could terrify his Egyptian workmen.

Lord Carnarvon never saw the Pharaoh's treasure properly displayed: before it could be removed, he fell ill, and died at his hotel – the Continental – in Cairo. At the moment of his death (2am) the whole city was plunged into darkness by a power failure. Coincidence, no doubt. At his home in England, at precisely the same moment, his fox terrier began to howl wildly; later, it died. Another coincidence?

Many others were to follow. Soon after Carnarvon's death, an American archaeologist who had been at the unsealing of the tomb fell into a coma at the Continental Hotel, and died

there. An American financier, George Jay Gould, asked Carter to show him the tomb. By the evening of the next day he had died of a fever. Joel Wool, a British industrialist, also visited the tomb, and died on the voyage back to England. Archibald Douglas Reid, a radiologist who x-rayed Tutankhamun's body, died on his return to England.

Over the next four years, 13 people who had been associated with the discovery had died; within seven years, 22. They included Lady Carnarvon, Carter's secretary, Richard Bethell, and Professor Douglas Derry and Alfred Lucas (two scientists who performed an autopsy on the Pharaoh's body).

It has been pointed out that a great number of the illnesses associated with these deaths have shown similar symptoms – including a curious numbness, lethargy and depression. Some writers have suggested that this might indicate that the ancient Egyptians knew of some poison which, millennia later, had affected some of the people who entered the ancient tombs (for, it is said, not only those connected with Tutankhamun's tomb have perished: over the last 200 years

The golden mask of death (main picture), *weighing 10.2 kilos (22½lb) of solid gold, was among the priceless relics found in the tomb of King Tutankhamun, an Egyptian Pharaoh of the 18th dynasty. The sensational discovery was marred by a growing belief in an ancient curse said to bring misfortune to those who tamper with graves of the Pharaohs.* ***A series of sudden, unexplained deaths*** *followed in the wake of the discovery and unveiling of the tomb. Lord Carnarvon* (right) *was the first apparent victim of the "curse of Tutankhamun", dying before he had even had a chance to see properly the discovery he himself had financed. Lady Carnarvon, beside her husband in the picture, died only a few years later, perhaps also from the curse,* ***George Gould*** (above right), *an American millionaire, was apparently another victim of the "curse", dying not long after Carter had shown him round the tomb.*

or so, many Egyptologists have died premature deaths – including the decoder of the Rosetta Stone, and perhaps the greatest Egyptologist of all, Giovanni Belzoni).

There may be no "Curse of the Pharaohs": it may be significant that the symptoms associated with those who died are somewhat similar to those of natives cursed by witch doctors, upon whose minds the curse probably works by convincing them that they are doomed. But despite the arguments of sceptics, it may be that too many people associated with the discovery and touristic development of Tutankhamun's tomb and its treasure have unexpectedly died for something curious not to have gone on.

It is of course possible that coincidence was the explanation. Gamal Mehrez, the 52-year-old Director-General of the Antiquities Department of the Cairo Museum responsible for sending some of the treasures on a spectacular world tour in the 1960s certainly thought so. "Look at me," he told one interviewer; "I've been involved with tombs and mummies of Pharaohs all my life. I'm living proof that it was all coincidence." Within a month, he was dead.

Gamal Mehrez (left) *died at the age of 52, within a month of his claim not to have been harmed by working with tombs and mummies.*

Carter's secretary, Richard Bethell (below, *on the left of the picture, with Carter) seemed to fall victim to the fatal illness that killed Carter and his other associates (see p.91). Viruses or bacteria, long dormant in the tomb, have been suggested as natural alternatives to supernatural causes.*

PALESTINE

MIRACLES

The miracles recounted in the Old and New Testament are major supernatural events in the history of Western man. Indeed, they are supernatural in the strictest sense of the word: events believed to have been imposed upon the natural order of things by a supernatural force – in this case, the Christian God.

For the person who believes that the Bible is literally true, there is little to be said about Biblical miracles: they are evidence of the divine power, and that is that. Others find it interesting to look at them from the standpoint of rationality, and to conjecture about their true nature.

The events of the Old Testament are so far removed from our own time that such conjecture must be fairly wild. They have become myths, and it is now impossible to discover their true nature. The Israelites no doubt in some way passed through the Red Sea on their escape from Egypt, but it is doubtful whether Moses parted the waters for them. It is much more likely that they crossed the Sea of Reeds, a papyrus lake which, before the Suez canal was constructed, was shallow enough to be fordable at certain times. There need have been no miracle.

Other cases may seem stronger: but with the strongest, the actual evidence is merely anecdotal. At the very least, it is impossible now to separate the genuine miracles (if such existed) from fairy-tales.

The miracles of the New Testament are a rather different matter. Again, these will be unquestioningly accepted by the fundamentalist Christian – though many church leaders now accept the view that they are not to be taken literally. But it must surely be true that at the very least Jesus was a skilful healer (though, if we set aside his divinity, it is impossible to say how he learned his skills).

Apart from his own resurrection, one of the most striking of Christ's miracles was the raising of Jairus' daughter from the dead. Almost every doctor working in a modern hospital will have performed what would have seemed, in Biblical times, a miracle: the simple stimulation of the heart which can now revive someone after a heart attack would then have seemed miraculous. But to suggest that Jesus' recovery of Jairus' daughter was not miraculous is to set it out of its own time, and also to misuse the word itself.

No amount of theoretical speculation or argument will shake the belief of those who look upon the miracle of the Resurrection of Christ as central to human existence itself. The most common of such speculations is that Jesus may have fallen – as the result of the fearful stress and pain of the crucifixion – into a cataleptic trance, from which he recovered after three days.

Alternatively, he may have learned from the Essenes – a mystical group of Jewish ascetics who had set up a quasi-monastic community in the desert – the techniques of breath-control and self-induced trance. These could have enabled him to stay in the tomb in a semi-inanimate state before rising apparently "from the dead". (There have been examples of Indian *fakirs* who have been buried for much longer periods than three days – see pp.110–1.)

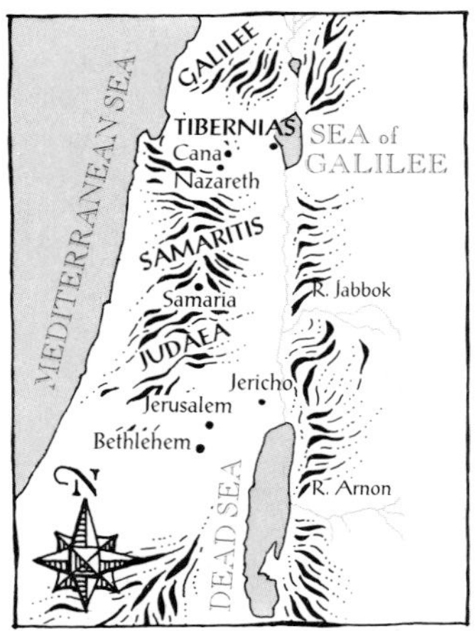

***Moses' parting of the waters** of the Red Sea* (right) *need not have been miraculous – scholars today believe that he may have led them across the nearby Sea of Reeds.*

About Christ's resurrection (opposite) *there is no agreement. For some it is central to their creed and to all history; others think Christ may simply have been in a cataleptic trance.*

ISRAEL

BALLS OF FIRE

In 363, at the instigation of the Roman Emperor Julian, an attempt was made to rebuild the Temple at Jerusalem. The project was started, but abandoned after the appearance of strange phenomena at the site, which resulted in several workmen being burned to death.

Julian, who although he did not persecute the Christians, was an opponent of that religion (for example, he forbade them to teach); and was sympathetic to the Jews, who were persecuted by the Christians. In particular he was perturbed by the Jews' lament that they could sacrifice only at the Temple of Jerusalem, which had been destroyed by Vespasian and Titus in AD 70. Motivated also partly by his wish to disprove Jesus' prophecy that not one stone of the Temple would be left upon another, Julian decided to restore the Temple at his own expense.

However, Eunapius, the Greek sophist and historian, in his *Lives of the Philosophers and Sophists* (*c.* AD 365) describes how "fearful balls of fire burst forth with continual eruptions close to the foundations, burning several of the workmen and making the spot altogether inaccessible. And thus the very elements, as if by some fate repelling the attempt, it [the restoration work] was laid aside."

The story was also told by St Gregory of Nyssa (*c.*331-396). He claimed that workmen "found themselves being driven one against another, as though by a furious blast of wind and sudden heaving of the earth", and that flames then issued from the earth and burned them.

There have been various attempts to explain the events: a random high wind, which frightened the workers; earthquake; fire bombs thrown by those who were against the rebuilding; to which we can add the possibility of fireballs (see p.162). But whatever the explanation, the Temple was not rebuilt, the Emperor Julian dying soon afterwards.

The Temple at Jerusalem (below) *where Christ confounded the doctors and from which he later drove out the moneychangers, was destroyed in AD 70, after a Jewish revolt was crushed by the Romans. Julian, the last pagan Emperor of Rome (361-3), decided to restore the Temple. But terrifying "balls of fire" disrupted the rebuilding and it was abandoned. Whether the fire was natural, human or supernatural in origin is unknown.*

In the 8th century Muslims built the ***Dome of the Rock*** (bottom) *on the site of the ruined Temple, without disruption.*

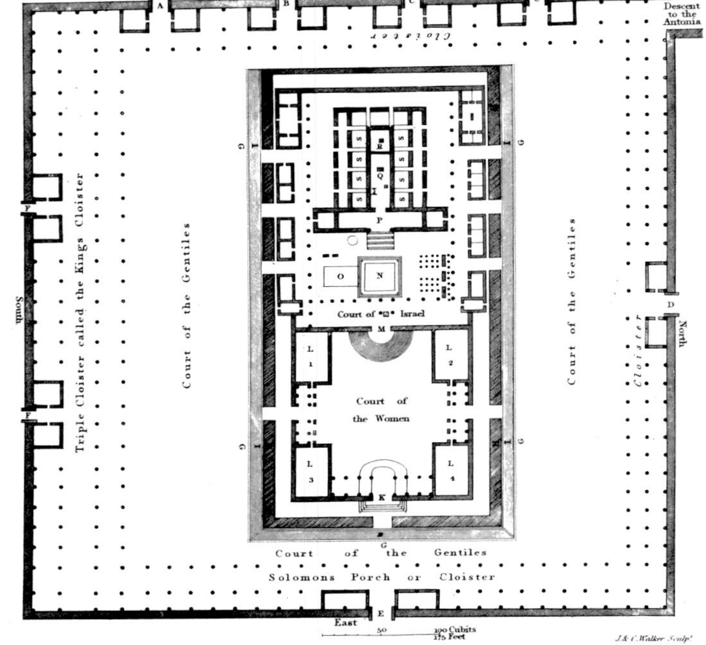

The Sudan

Zar Spirits

A Sudanese witch doctor (left) *casts a spell to help drive out a Zar – a spirit that causes illness – from a possessed person. Drums are often used to send the sufferer into a trance: then an animal is ritually sacrificed and the patient is smeared with its blood, which is believed to have magical qualities.*

The Sudan seems to be the last area of Africa where the ancient belief in *Zar* spirits still exists. These spirits are believed to cause illness (in Ethiopia they are known as Satans; in some other parts of Africa, Pepos). A *Zar* can sometimes be driven out of a patient; in other cases it may refuse to leave, and the best that can be done (as with personality defects in Western society) is to reconcile the two.

Possession by a *Zar* seems to take place when the subject is emotionally disturbed. The first thing that must be done is to discover what sort of *Zar* has taken possession – one form of diagnosis is to see what pattern of drum-beats most quickly sends the subject into trance. After much dancing, there is the ritual sacrifice of an animal, and the subject is smeared with its blood; this should result either in the *Zar's* expulsion or in the subject being reconciled to the possession.

One writer on the subject, William Sargent, reports that recordings of the drumming at a *Zar* ceremony in Khartoum "were effective in putting ordinary people into a trance when played in England."

Drumming in fact plays a very important role in witch doctors' ceremonies, powers and rituals, not only in the Sudan but also throughout the whole of sub-Saharan Africa and also in the Caribbean islands. Constant drumming not only generates excitement, it makes those attending the ceremony more susceptible to a witch doctor's powers.

Twigs play an important role *in Azande fortune-telling* (above). *They are arranged in a protective circle, and contemplating them, the witch doctor then sinks into a trance, hoping for visions of future events.*

In a purification ceremony *soon after birth, this baby of the Azande people in the Sudan* (above) *is ritually "smoked" to drive out evil spirits. The baby's father and maternal grandmother supervise the rite.*

Witch doctors, such as 90-year-old Githingi Maina (right) *are still eagerly sought by Kenyan Africans. A gourd is always a symbol of potent magic and often plays a part in the witch doctor's craft.*

KENYA

THE SAMBURU

Many primitive African tribes traditionally use trance-states in order to encourage the warlike spirit of their warriors, but also to relieve tension, and sometimes – it appears – as a means of depersonalization.

A nomadic tribe, the Samburu of northern Kenya, have priest-leaders whose authority is emphasized during the puberty rites of adolescence, when it is insisted that God will kill anyone who disobeys them. Circumcision and initiation apparently to some extent depersonalize young people, making them subservient to their leaders (rigorous drilling and the depersonalization which accompanies identical hair-cuts and uniforms have the same effect in the Western armed forces). Any deviance from accepted rules is treated by putting the disobedient young men into a trance, and reconditioning them ("re-education" is achieved by psychiatric means elsewhere in the world).

In Kenya, this is done by dancing ceremonies. The women begin these by dancing alone, accompanied by drumming. The men then join in, but keep themselves separate from the women. Finally, the two groups join. The women are not permitted to go into full trance-state, and if they do, they are led away: in a full trance-state uninhibited sexual behaviour can lead to jealousy when the trance is ended, especially when married women dance with unmarried men.

The men induce trance by the energy of their dancing – leaping repeatedly into the air and dropping heavily on their heels – and by hyperventilation (used also under other circumstances by both Arab and Christian groups). It seems that this behaviour stimulates a high degree of blood alkalosis, probably leading to brain alkalosis, which is known to provoke trance. The trances end in collapse; but not before the release of inhibitions which allows the leaders of the tribe to encourage fearlessness in its warriors, or renew the recognition of their own dominance.

All over Africa dancing also relieves the boredom which might lead to trouble during those periods when there is neither fighting nor hunting to preoccupy vigorous males. It seems to be very efficient in replacing alcohol or internecine violence.

CASTING OUT SPIRITS

In Europe, some priests will conduct ceremonies to cast out demons from those who are believed to be possessed. The expulsion of spirits among primitive African tribes, although having roughly the same purpose, is more obviously and openly associated with physical as well as mental illness.

In Kenya the witch doctors, the doctors of their tribes, no longer attempt to treat any illness which is the result of an obvious infection – malaria, say, or an infected wound. They simply refer the patient to a Westernized doctor. But in cases where the sickness resists diagnosis, or seems rooted in some psychological or spiritual malaise – for example, anxiety states and tension, with the usual accompanying headaches and general feeling of disability – they use methods passed down to them through the generations.

These involve a number of drummers who beat out a regular rhythm while the sick begin to dance in a circle, soon starting to twitch and jerk, and eventually falling to the ground in a totally relaxed state – although occasionally there are violent reactions similar to epileptic fits or a series of orgasms. It is at this point that there may be conversation between the doctors and the spirits inhabiting the sick bodies – ancestral voices may converse through the mouths of the entranced. These spirits seem benevolent, for before being expelled they often advise on the treatment of the sickness.

There seems little doubt that mild forms of emotional disturbance can be successfully treated in trance states; severe illnesses such as schizophrenia are more intractable.

The powers of witch doctors go far beyond the handing out of the paranormal equivalent of aspirin or bandages, or them acting as spiritual messengers or psychologists. What has been noticed is that not only do witch doctors claim powers to strike at enemies many miles distant, but those enemies accept such powers unquestioningly. For example, it has been observed that on being told a wasting spell has been cast on him, an African may indeed fall ill and waste away – to the point of death, without a suitable countervailing spell. This sounds reasonable; few nowadays would deny the psychosomatic powers of the mind of someone predisposed to believe in such spells. More disquietingly, some Westerners who have dismissed such magical powers have themselves appeared to become victims of spells, despite their scepticism. This suggests that witch doctors' powers could be acting on something akin to Jung's idea of the Collective Unconscious, manifesting itself in a sinister form.

Dance-induced trances (above) *are central to the nomadic Samburu tribe. During their dancing, the men hyperventilate and then eventually fall into a trance. This removes inhibitions in a more predictable manner than alcohol – something many leaders of religious cults around the world have discovered. It also reinforces the tribal elders' control over potentially rebellious young men.* ***For Samburu women*** (right) *such wild dancing with the men is forbidden, lest it triggers sexual licence, so their participation is restricted to singing.*

The Congo

Ancestral Spirits

At the heart of Africa, the Congo has long been a focus of magic; until the 15th century it was entirely untouched by civilization.

Unlike some other peoples, the Congolese do not worship their ancestors; highly superstitious, they simply seem to regard them as intermediaries between themselves and whatever force runs the world. However, there has always been a complete acceptance of ghosts and spirits, especially the *mizumu*, or spirits of the dead, who are as real as when they were alive: the Congolese people are convinced that the air about them is thick with such spirits – put your ear to the ground and you can hear their drums. They are talked with, asked for advice, fed and welcomed into the community. Almost everything that happens is at the behest of a spirit. They not only bring good luck or good hunting, but may be ill-disposed toward the living and have to be painfully propitiated. While they accept the idea of an all-powerful God, the concept is far too vague for them to be able to approach Him in person: witch doctors must be employed as interpreters between the living and the dead.

Witch Doctors

The Congolese witch doctor is known as a *mganga* or *mufumu* and is a kind of general factotum – doctor, veterinary surgeon, psychologist, magician, conjurer and herbalist. In common with many other witch doctors throughout the world, the *mganga* believes that illness is a product of possession – by a spirit which may be that of a dead person or of an animal (often a snake or a lion). Illness being inflicted by magic, he cures it by magic. Invoking a spell more powerful than that of the man who sent the sickness, he sends it back to plague the villain. It is fairly clear that when someone is cured by a witch doctor, the cure is the result of a sort of homespun psychology – all the more effective because of the patient's total belief in the doctor. In his capacity as judge and jury, the witch doctor will rely on a sort of trial by ordeal: a poisoned cup will be given to the accused to drink; if he survives, he is innocent. If he succumbs, he is guilty – not to say, dead.

The *mganga* also foretells future events, expels evil spirits from the possessed and makes sure that traditional laws are obeyed. No-one would dream of taking an important action without his advice: he consults the bones – generally the leg-bones of goats, frequently seen to stand on end, apparently of their own volition; from a trance, he gives his judgment. Seeing a lowering sky, he hastens to dress in his ceremonial robes and does a rain-dance; rain falls – seemingly as a result.

Some witch docors turn into sorcerers or *mlozi*, dangerous to society, with human teeth, bones, and cocks' feathers to help them weave their magic spells. These are hunted down and killed, sometimes by the members of secret societies formed for the purpose – but which are not as benevolent as they may seem. For example, the Banucapi or Atinga societies, disguised in animal masks and skins, travel from village to village ostensibly offering to cleanse them of sorcerers, but in reality extorting money and food by threats of either a physical or psychical nature.

A witch doctor consults the bones (left), *to determine what course of action should be taken; a ritual that is central to the Congolese way of life.*

AFRICAN STANDING STONES

When people think of standing stones, believed by some to have occult significance (see pp. 124-5), it is usually in connection with Europe – for example, Stonehenge in England and Carnac in Brittany, but there are significant groups of such stones in Africa. For example, at Msoura, in Morocco, there is a huge stone circle 180 feet (55m) in diameter, part of which is shown top left; in the Senegambian region of the west coast of Africa there are many megaliths – more than 800 stone circles, like those shown bottom left, have been recorded within an area of 15,000 square miles (39,000 sq km), and there are also more than 2,000 *menhirs*, or single upright stones. In Kenya, most of the standing stones form circles – one group near Lake Turkana is formed by stones marked with geometric and animal carvings. Some of the stones are consistently ranged either north-south or east-west – none of them appears to be placed at random, although the significance of the placements is not known.

Magic and the Arts

In the Western world, the arts have rarely been seen as magical, although to artists themselves they remain mysterious. However, in some primitive religions, art and magic are inextricably twinned. The Bakwele, Kuyu, Bateke, Babwende and Balumbo tribes of the Congo are famous for their wood-carvings – the product of fetishism, the use of magical figures through which to channel harm to enemies, or control natural forces; the Bambute pygmies of the Ituri forest channel magic through poetry and music; the beautiful small ivory masks and figures carved by the Warega people for "magical" religious purposes are among the most prized art objects of the Congo.

The Congolese attitude to sculpture and music is believed to reflect that of earliest primitive man, who drew on the walls of his cave pictures of the animals he hunted for food: it is perhaps there that we can find the origins of the artistic instinct – the desire or need to tame and control paranormal instincts and put them to practical use.

South Africa

Poltergeists

Although individuals in South Africa have an interest in the occult, there does not seem ever to have been a considerable body of evidence involving the white community there; the experience of the black South Africans runs parallel to that elsewhere in the Continent with witch doctors having a prominent role.

However, I. D. du Plessis, a South African author, collected a few anecdotes of paranormal events in the country, many involving active poltergeists. One of the best known cases occurred in 1921 in a Christian girls' hostel at Blaauwvlei, near Wellington, in the Western Province of the Cape. A particular small cupboard began to move about in a remarkable manner, both when in a dormitory of girls, and when in a room guarded by a number of interested people. It hurled itself to the floor; even when whipped with a *shjambok* by one irritated investigator, it continued to misbehave. A dog on the premises would usually bark violently just before the box began its movements. The phenomena continued for two months, and then ceased.

In 1937 the Afrikaans newspaper *Die Burger* investigated a poltergeist in the town of Lansdowne, where a house was plagued by crockery and cushions flying about. The children of the house had been severely beaten on the grounds that they were responsible; however, a neighbour, Mrs Strong, saw the bedclothes moving about without any human agency. She threw a cushion at the bed, which rebounded and struck her, followed by two cups and a plate.

Spiritualists visited the house, a local farmer attempted to *shjambok* the poltergeist, and the family dog was castrated on the advice of a clergyman who believed him possessed by an evil spirit, but all efforts were to no avail. The phenomena ceased, after a while, as suddenly as they had started.

A rather more original event occurred in 1918, in a town on the border of Basutoland. A witch doctor had been found guilty of burglary. A fortnight later, distinct sounds were heard at night, of a large animal moving about in the burgled house; these were followed by an uproar in the kitchen as though everything was being thrown about and broken – yet when the door was open, everything was neatly in its place. Local natives asserted that the house was being visited by Old Man Baboon, a spirit sent by the jailed witch doctor. However, the noises never recurred after that one night.

Perhaps the most assertive ghost ever reported in South Africa appeared over a number of years on a farm at Schweitzer-Reneke. This phantom had the habit of trying to pull people out of bed by their big toes, of moving pots and pans about, and emptying ash-buckets. It often attempted to join people in bed, sometimes lying heavily upon the occupants; it was occasionally heard to groan, and was identified as an old coloured woman whose name had been Old Griet. It was often heard moving about, and occasionally seen: "bent forward, taking long strides with big feet. It wore a large broadbrimmed hat and its clothes were in rags." Shots passed straight through the ghost, and it was not affected even when guns were loaded with salt – reputedly the way to deal with such phantoms.

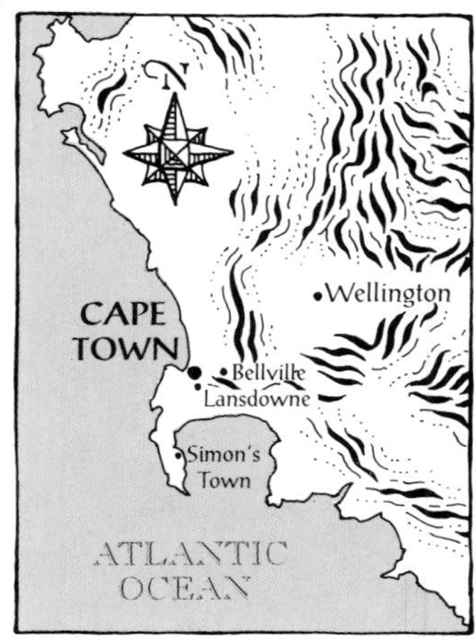

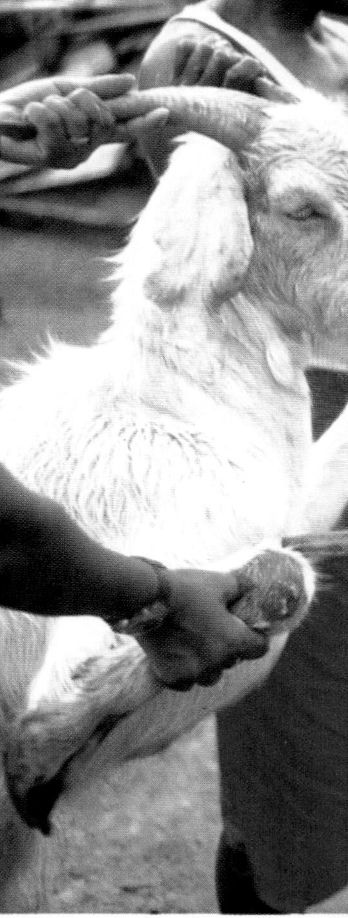

***The only fully trained** and practising white* sangoma *(witch doctor) in South Africa, Gert Pretorius* (below). *Once a policeman, then a gold-miner, Pretorius first consulted a witch doctor after his third wife had left him. The witch doctor told him that a bad luck spell hung over his lovelife and treated him with foul-smelling potions. Pretorius was so impressed that he decided to learn the witch doctor's craft himself.*

To do this, he moved to a mud hut in Zululand to live with three old sangomas. He emerged two years later as a qualified witch doctor, with the honorary name of Nyaka Chaka, meaning One Who Has Become Great Through Strong-Hearted Effort.

At first, black people in Krugersdorp were wary of this former policeman who had adopted Zulu "dreadlocks" (the Zulu hair style) and opened a dispensary in their main street. But today he is fully accepted and his shop contains a wide range of roots, dead animal skins, claws, teeth, snakes' glands, love potions and "special business luck powder". His diary and his waiting room alike are filled with engagements – to heal the sick, to bury the dead and to marry couples.

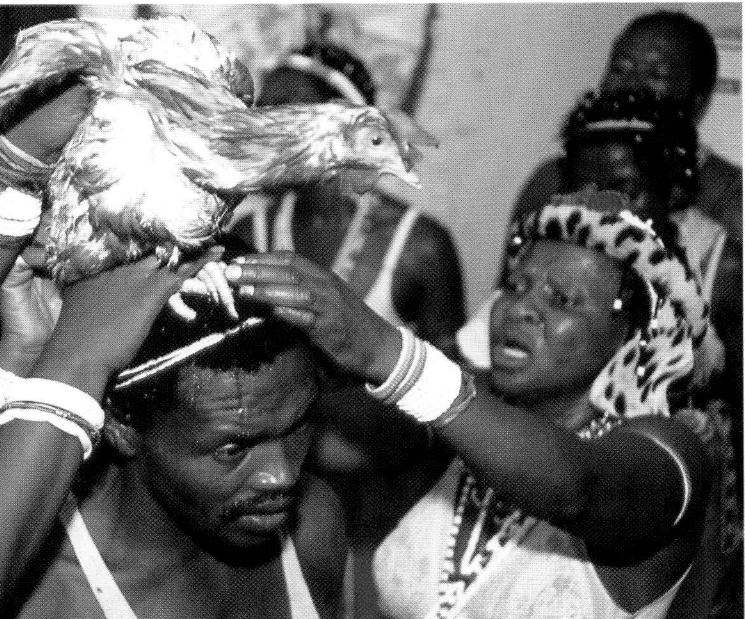

***Ritual sacrifice of a goat** is part of the ceremony of initiation into the Bantu ancester cult* (left, top). *The apprentice priests then drink the goat's blood and the contents of its bladder. Songs and dances signal the end of the ceremony and the apprentice is declared a fully qualified Sangoma (witch doctor).*

***Chickens and cocks** are often used by witch doctors as sacrifices, and as instruments in other cult ceremonies* (left, bottom).

Central Africa

Mokele-Mbembe: A Central African Nessie?

Unlike the celebrated monster often spotted in Loch Ness, *Mokele-mbembe*, the creature reputed to haunt the Likouala swamps and Lake Tele in Central Africa is little known and even less recorded. No photographs of it exist, for Central Africa, unlike the Scottish Highlands, is not on the tourist trail.

The first sighting was made in 1913 by Captain von Stein zu Lausnitz, who had led an expedition to the Likouala swamp region. He heard tales of a brownish grey animal with a smooth skin, perhaps as big as an elephant, with a long, flexible neck and possibly a long muscular tail. Any canoe that went near it was said to be doomed, the creature always attacking and killing its crew. The monster was reputed to live in caves along the shore of the river and to be vegetarian.

Due to the region's inaccessibility, no further efforts were made to find *Mokele-mbembe* until 1980. A crocodile expert, James H. Powell, accompanied by Dr Roy Mackal went deep into the wildest parts of Likouala country round Lake Tele to gather reports. As they hacked and squelched their way through appalling swamps and forests, they heard many reports. One of the oldest witnesses was Firman Mosomole, who said that 45 years earlier he had seen a snake-like creature while in a canoe near the town of Epéna. When shown an illustrated book, Mosomele unhesitatingly identified a sauropod dinosaur as the creature he had seen.

Mambombo Daniel, a local school-teacher, told of a more recent encounter he had had in 1977. He said he had seen a creature from only 30 feet (9.1m) away, describing it as grey-coloured, with a thick neck but a separate body – not therefore a huge snake. Another story came from a fisherman who said that a *Mokele-mbembe* had been killed in around 1959; all those who ate its meat subsequently died.

In 1983, the Congolese zoologist Marcellin Agnagna led an expedition to the Likouala region and said he had seen the monster himself. He was with two villagers near Lake Tele when one of them spotted a strange animal in the water. Wading out into the shallow water, they found themselves facing a creature with "a wide back, a long neck, and a small head", totalling about 15 feet (4.5m) in length. Unfortunately, they had run out of film for their cameras.

In his book *A Living Dinosaur* Dr Mackal suggested that, with its long neck and tail, four legs, vegetarian diet and length of 15-30 feet (4.5-9.1m), the *mokele-mbembe* sounded very similar to a small sauropod dinosaur. Certainly its description would not fit the range of known living animals.

Nor does another creature, the *Ngumama-monene*, reputedly a giant snake 130-195 feet (39.5-59.3m) long. First reported in 1961 by a woman who had bathed in the Mataba river, its reptilian head and neck emerged from the water close to her and was observed by local villagers for 30 minutes until it dived.

However, the most recent traveller to return from the area, the British explorer and writer Redmond O'Hanlon, found no trace of dinosaurs and dismissed the whole concept: Others remain convinced that the jungles of Central Africa may indeed shelter survivors from the distant past.

MADAGASCAR

ANCESTRAL SPIRITS

With their mixed African and Asian origins (the first people to settle in Madagascar probably arrived from Indonesia about 1,500 years ago, colonists from Africa following them later), the people of Madagascar have a rich mixture of customs and beliefs, among them traces of voodoo and tabu, called *fady*.

Most powerful of these is *razana*, their belief in the power of their dead ancestors, to whom frequent sacrifices are still made. The Malagasy claim this is actually a celebration of life: dead ancestors are thought to be powerful forces in the life of the living; if properly remembered and treated, the dead will guard and provide for the living. These ancestors are immensely powerful, their "wishes", as perceived in dreams or omens, or as interpreted by witch doctors, govern the behaviour of a family or community. Even their former property is respected, so a great-grandfather's field may not be sold or even sown with different crops. Disasters are blamed on the wrath of the ancestors concerned, and a zebu bull may be sacrificed to placate them. Huge herds of such cattle are kept as a "bank" of potential sacrificial offerings. In return for such sacrifices, the dead protect the living. But first this requires the living to perform the rites of second burial or "bone turning" for their forebears.

REBURIAL

Famadihana, as second burials are called in some upland regions, is a vital part of the Malagasy way of life and death. At death man abandons his mortal and perishable form to become a vastly more powerful and important ancestor. To make this possible, in the ceremony of bone turning, an ancestor's rotten flesh must be stripped off the imperishable bones, which are the real "house" of the ancestor. All Malagasy tribes consider a fresh or decomposing corpse unclean, and have to purify themselves with water after coming into contact with one – or even its possessions. (In one case, patients in a hospital incinerated all the bedding and equipment in the ward where a patient had died.)

Having buried an ancestor, the family wait until the time is right for *famadihana*. (The exact time for this can be signalled by a prophetic dream or the death of another ancestor.) Then, amid general rejoicing among assembled relatives, the now safely fleshless body is exhumed, wrapped in a fresh shroud and paraded around the village before being being taken back to the family tomb. During its excursion, the corpse is treated as though still alive, being talked to and involved in the family celebrations. Once returned to the family tomb, the skeleton is added to the other ancestors grouped together in the tomb. This posthumous sociability is thought to increase the ancestral powers so important for *razana*.

Razana is not restricted to backward rural tribes, nor even to pagan families. It has been reported among devoutly Christian families in the capital, Antananarivo. Nor is it just a privately practised rite. At the inaugural flight of Madagascar's first jumbo jet, a zebu bull was sacrificed to the relevant ancestors to avert any catastrophe. The airline boasts an excellent safety record!

The Mokele-mbembe *is represented in this drawing* (opposite page) *as a moderately sized sauropod dinosaur, whose size and diet correspond to the descriptions of the monster obtained from several reports of its sighting.*

Second burial, or bone turning *is common in Madagascar: the body is exhumed* (above) *before being taken to its final resting place in the family tomb.*

ASIA

Tsugara
Peking
JAPAN
Isu Islands
C H I N A
Shanghai
TIBET
NEPAL
INDIA
THAILAND
PHILIPPINES
SRI LANKA
BORNEO
NEW GUIN

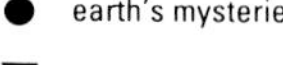

- ● earth's mysteries
- ▼ monsters
- ■ beyond the grave
- ☾ natural magic
- ☆ magic, charms and witchcraft
- △ supernatural technology
- + visions, apparitions and religious phenomena
- ≈ psychic gift

All over the world, men sought out and trained by their seniors to become shamans or witch doctors have had to undergo a severe training which has involved fasting and physical pain and deprivation. This was true of Christ no less than of the fakirs *of India or the* yamabushi *or* miko *of Japan. But from country to country, the emphasis differs somewhat.*

In Japan – as one might expect in a country whose tradition emphasizes the imperviousness of the hero to physical pain – the privations sought out by anyone who wishes to become any kind of wizard or prophet are considerable; in India, the privations are not perhaps as rigorous, but they continue after the fakir *has reached maturity in his art, and seem to be necessary to enable him to perform his most remarkable feats (such as levitation or burial alive). This tradition has spread to the West, where it is usually suggested that to get the best out of meditation or yoga, for example, careful attention to diet is necessary.*

Another difference is in the attitude of the "magician" to sex: in Japan, Tibet and China sexual abstinence seems to be a part of the necessary training; in India such abstinence is not always necessary, and indeed in Tantra – a form of yoga – the power of sexuality is nurtured and positively employed.

All over Asia, it is still taken for granted that what other cultures would call "magic" is in fact a natural phenomenon which can be learned and used. It occurs to practically no-one to question the powers of those who are learned in such matters. Perhaps in no other part of the world is it considered so natural that men (and, in some areas, women) should be able to demonstrate and use powers which in the West seem remarkable in the extreme.

In post-revolutionary China, as in the USSR, there was for a long time consistent denigration of anything which seemed supernatural or paranormal and its study was discouraged. Now, alas, it seems possible that there will be another attempt to stifle Chinese interest in the supernatural. But quite apart from traditional beliefs in certain forces which can be harnessed – for example, by the use of ley-lines – there has more recently been strong scientific interest in "sightless reading", which often seemed related to ESP. Acupuncture, now more and more widely recognized in the West, probably originated in China, and was certainly perfected there.

It is sometimes suggested that confidence in unseen powers is in some way a mark of mental inferiority. Asia demonstrates this to be untrue: India and China, to name only two countries, have extremely ancient cultures which have never lacked intellectual repute – the I Ching, *the ancient Chinese divinatory system, is one of the most remarkable collections of natural wisdom the world has yet devised.*

That the East has much to teach the West is indisputable; much may be learned from their ready acceptance of the mysterious as a natural part of life.

INDIA

THE NATURAL SUPERNATURAL

Indians often find it ludicrous that Westerners should be disturbed by the apparently supernatural feats of *fakirs* or holy men, which seem to them to be perfectly "natural".

For example, in 1941 a Forest Adviser to the government of Nepal, E.A. Smythies, claims to have seen one of his servants, a young man called Krishna, rise into the air in a seated position and hover there before returning to earth. The boy's fellow servants were not in the least surprised: Krishna, they explained, was being punished for not making proper sacrifices to the local gods.

Another well-documented observation was made by the Marquess of Halifax, when Viceroy of India. The Resident (British official) at Udaipur, Rajputana, summoned a sorcerer to perform for the Viceroy, who watched while an Indian boy was roped up in a blanket, put into a trance, and raised into the air for half a minute without visible means of support.

Somewhat similar is the famous Indian rope trick, when a rope is raised into the air by its own invisible means, a boy is prompted to climb it and he then disappears. There are not many reliable accounts of this trick; one, given by a journalist, John Taussig, who saw it performed at Premnagar near Dehra Dun, suggests that its effect may be produced by some form of hypnosis involving the "patter" of the *fakir* – for while Taussig, who spoke Hindustani, saw the boy climb the rope and vanish, a colleague, who did not know the language, saw nothing.

More interesting and reliable are accounts of the extraordinary physical feats of some *fakirs* or ascetics themselves. These are recorded in many anecdotes, and are sometimes well-documented.

In 1835 the Maharaja of Lahore heard of a famous *fakir* called Haridas, who had reputedly survived four months of being buried alive. He commissioned a similar demonstration. Doctors who examined the *fakir* found that he had cut the muscles under his tongue so that it could be folded back to seal off the nasal passages. They noted also that for some days before he was due to be buried he consumed only milk and yoghurt; for the last two days he fasted completely and used the usual yoga techniques to clean out his alimentary canal (among other things swallowing a thirty-yard (27.4m) strip of linen and regurgitating it).

He then closed his nose and ears with wax (apparently so that insects should not enter them) and sat with his legs crossed. Within seconds his pulse had become undetectable. He was wrapped in linen and placed in a chest which was closed with the Maharajah's seal, and padlocked. The box was then buried, and barley seed was sown above it. A wall was built around the site, and guards were posted.

Forty days later the wall was broken down, and barley was found growing above the grave. The box was dug up, and the lock and seals found to be intact. Inside it, Haridas was discovered in his original pose. Within an hour, he had recovered, and was in good – if frail – health.

He was never found to have cheated but was eventually discovered to be a regular seducer of his female disciples and on moral grounds was rejected by his followers.

Some other *fakirs* performed similar feats at about the same time. The ruler of the Punjab, Runjeet Singh, organized one performance, reported in the *Indian Journal of Medical and Physical Science* by an English observer. The *fakir* was locked inside a pavilion in the ruler's garden. The closed pavilion was guarded by the ruler's private army for six weeks. When it was opened, the *fakir* was discovered sitting inside a wooden box four feet by three (1.2 × 1m), itself standing in a three-foot (1m) deep pit. Lifted out, the *fakir* was examined by a doctor, who could find no discernible heartbeat, although the body was warm. After several wheaten pancakes had been placed upon his head, the *fakir* seemed to undergo some kind of convulsion, and began to breathe regularly. In half an hour, he was able to walk away. It was again generally agreed that there was no possibility of cheating.

Such displays seem to have become unfashionable, although there are many other demonstrations of the power of yoga to suspend or inhibit the body's normal behaviour or reactions (see p.112).

***For Indian* fakirs,** *feats such as burial alive* (main picture), *often for many weeks without food or water, are merely advanced yoga-like techniques to be learned like any other, and involving no magic.*

The last recorded burial seems to have taken place in February 1950, when, according to The Lancet, *a yogi called Shri Ramdasji was sealed in a concrete underground chamber for more than 550 hours. Then 1,400 gallons (6,363l) of water were poured in. A few hours later Ramdasji was found sitting underwater, in perfect health.*

The pulse rate of buried fakirs or sadhus often drops to near zero, yet they revive remarkably fast when exhumed. The same principle – of mind over matter – seems to apply to fakirs on their ***beds of nails*** (below) *who suffer hardly a scratch. Most eyecatching of all are the levitators, such as this* ***Hindu reclining on air*** (left).

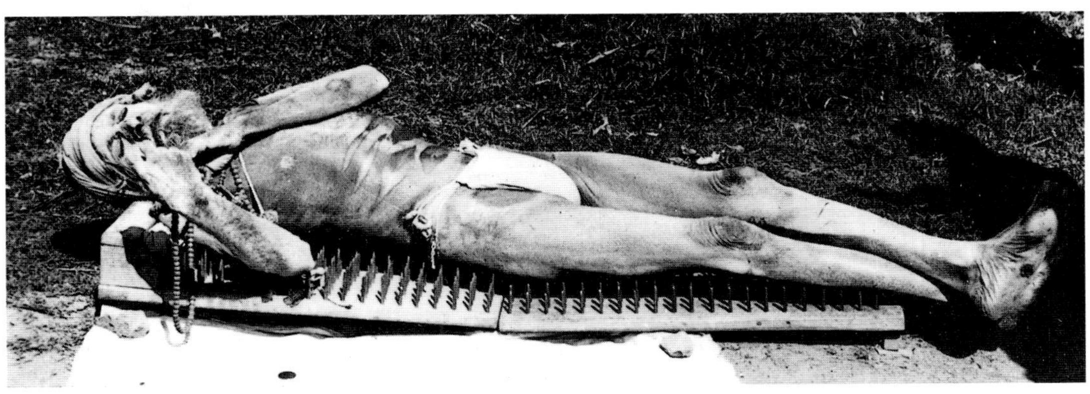

Yoga

In the West yoga is still regarded as something magical, a philosophy which it has on the whole – at least until very recently – denigrated, presenting it as merely a possible answer to emotional or mental disturbance, a short cut to self-realization, a cure for headaches or tensions. It is much more than this – and indeed there is more than one yoga. There are in the first place *bhakti* yoga, showing the religious path to God, *dhyana* yoga, the contemplative system involving meditation leading to a trance state, and *hatha* yoga – the best known in the West – which is the yoga of physical culture. *Karma* yoga encourages good deeds, charity, fasting; *kriya* yoga is primarily religious; *jnana* yoga is concerned with the study of sacred books; *mantra* yoga with sacred spells. The most sublime is *raja* yoga, which deals entirely with mental and psychic development leading to spiritual fulfilment.

A long and arduous course of *hatha* yoga is necessary before the body can be brought under the complete control of the mind. Anger and desire must be conquered, for they are signs of self-absorption and pride; so placidity must be cultivated. *Brahmacharya*, or abstinence from sex, must be practised by those who are really serious.

The *asanas* or bodily positions are practised, breath control is extremely important, as is meditation and concentration; finally, the successful aspirant may achieve *samadhi*, or a state of bliss, the unification of the individual soul and the Universal Soul.

This has little to do with the trance state assumed by those who have chosen to use yoga as a sort of transcendent form of conjuring – such trickery is denounced by the true *yogi*. However, it is the extraordinary subjugation of the body which has interested Western doctors and scientists, and there is no doubt that as a result of the study of yoga some astonishing feats have been achieved.

Some *fakirs* or *sadhus* have lain on beds of nails, with heavy weights placed upon their bodies; others have stood on one leg for several months – or have remained on the same spot for years. Some have submerged themselves in water for weeks, or sat in the Indian sun at the height of the hottest season, with fires blazing nearby to give additional heat.

But if these are conjuring tricks, no orthodox *yogi* would deny that his study enables him to gain astonishing control of his body, suspending breathing almost entirely, producing a change of pulse rate on demand (sometimes in different wrists at the same time); that he can ignore extreme heat or cold, go without food and water for an abnormal amount of time, and apparently enter into an exceptional degree of understanding with wild animals. Science has so far failed to explain how any of these feats are achieved.

It is said that yoga increases the IQ, sharpens powers of ESP, confers exceptional sexual vigour, and prolongs life. Sadly, there is no proof that any of these claims is true. What is undoubtedly true is that by the study of yoga some men have been able to teach their bodies to ignore some of what we have come to regard as the basic rules of nature. That is astonishing enough.

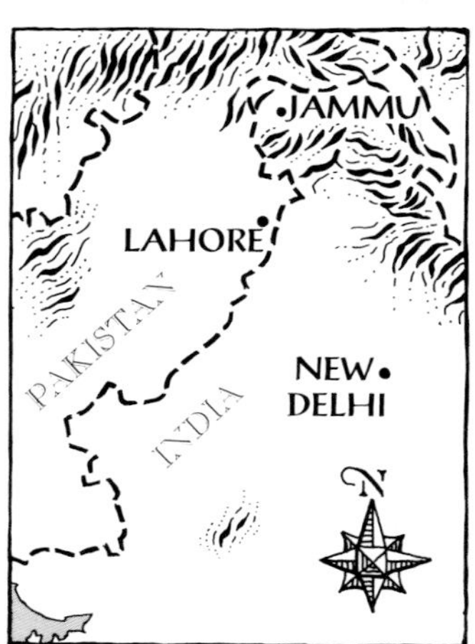

***Not all fakirs are thin**, as this plump practitioner* (above) *of the celebrated art of standing on one leg – for hours, days or even months on end – reveals. He is balancing a holy book as he stands.*

NEPAL

THE ABOMINABLE SNOWMAN

Of all the creatures who must be regarded as mythical because there is no absolute proof of their existence, none is more famous than the Yeti, or Abominable Snowman. Its modern history, as distinct from vague references in ancient Indian epics, seems to have begun in 1889, when a British army major found enormous footprints in the snow near the peak of a mountain northwest of Sikkim, in Nepal. Local people assured him that they had been made by the *yeh-teh*, "the hairy wild man" believed to live among the eternal snows.

But interest became almost universal in 1921, when members of a British climbing expedition saw some dark creatures moving about not far from them and later found the prints of huge, bare feet in the snow.

As is so often the case, once the creature had received worldwide publicity, sightings began to proliferate. But if they were either mistakes or deliberate fabrications, there were remarkable consistencies – for example, the shape of the footprints, of which many photographs and casts were made.

The expedition to Everest led in 1951 by Eric Shipton was among the first post-war expeditions to find new footprints, measuring 13 inches (33cm) long and eight (20cm) across. Writing in *The Times*, Shipton admitted that "the tracks were mostly distorted by melting into oval impressions, slightly larger and a good deal broader than those made by our large mountain boots."

Several subsequent expeditions mounted especially to hunt the yeti found nothing except a few questionable "footprints". But there is still a strong belief in the creature's existence – not least among the Sherpas, who suppose there are several types, among them one which customarily travels on all fours, and another which is said to have a pointed head, long arms and red fur.

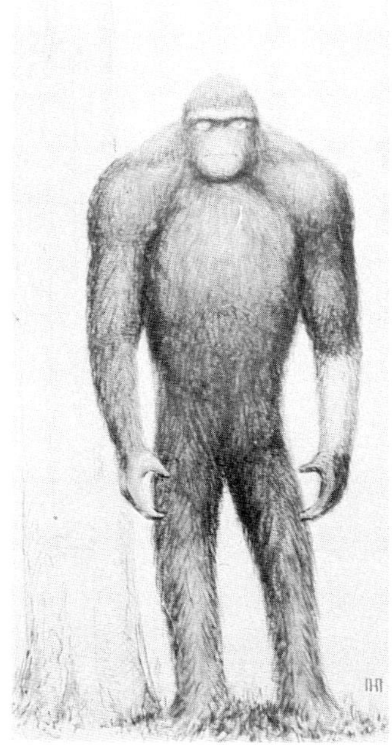

The yeti *in this artist's impression* (right) *is a gigantic hairy ape.* ***Mysterious footprints*** (above), *found on a glacier high up in the Menlung Basin in Nepal, appear to support the idea that the yeti is ape-like. But some mountaineers have cast doubts on their authenticity.*

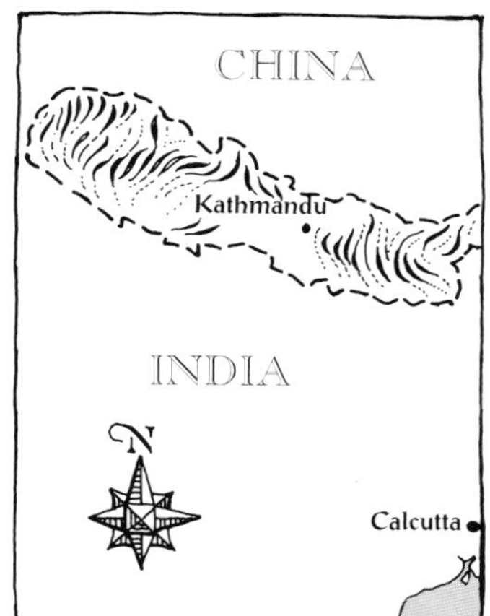

If this scalp (below) *belongs to a yeti, it accords with folklore and stories to be found across the Himalayas. Yet no complete and undisputed yeti, alive or dead – or even a skeleton of one – has yet been discovered.*

TIBET

REINCARNATION

Tibetans are among the firmest believers in reincarnation (see pp.57-9), and for many generations not only the *Dalai* and *Tashi Lamas* but the head *Lamas* of many monasteries, as well as some other grades of monks, have been chosen on that basis.

The Tibetan theory of reincarnation is basically Buddhist, although with some elements of the Hindu: it is believed that saintly men who might otherwise have earned liberation from the travails of the world can choose to be reborn in order to help lead others to salvation. These are known as *bodhisattvas*, and the earliest manifestation of one such was *Ge-hdun-grub-pa*, the first *Dalai Lama* of the Gelugpa Church, the most important Tibetan Buddhist sect. He died in 1475, but was believed to have been reborn as a child, and became the second *Dalai Lama*.

Rules were gradually evolved for the infallible recognition of a reincarnated *bodhisattva*: a dying *lama* might give instructions as to where his reincarnated self might be found; or a follower might be given the information in a dream. More often, a young child would suddenly announce his own status, and insist on being taken to the monastery which he recognized as his true home. There he would be tested – for example, asked to recognize various objects belonging to his predecessor, placed among a number of others. The present (14th) *Dalai Lama*, Pamo Tsiring, was the son of a peasant couple. When he was four, he was identified by *Lama* emissaries from Lhasa as the new incarnation of Chenrezi, God of Mercy, who had departed from the body of the thirteenth *Dalai Lama* some years previously. Taken to the *Potala*, or chief palace, of Lhasa he successfully recognized several objects belonging to his predecessor – including a box containing his false teeth.

THE *TULPA*

While ghosts, in the Western sense, are not much considered in Tibet, it is believed that by sheer willpower one can create a *tulpa*, or imaginary being who becomes real, and can be seen not only by oneself but by others.

There is one case of a *tulpa* being "created" by a Westerner, Alexandra David-Neel, a French journalist who became fascinated by Tibet and its customs, and using meditation and ceremonial rituals succeeded in manifesting the figure of a plump monk who became an amiable companion about the house. Eventually he became a nuisance, and it was only after six months' concentration that Mlle David-Neel managed to dematerialize him.

***Tibetans test reincarnation** of a Lama by his ability to recognize objects from his former life: the very young Head* Lama *of Nalanda Monastery* (left)*, passed the test when he was first brought into the monastery. Tibetans are firm believers in reincarnation, not only for their* Lamas *but for every living creature.*

China

Dragon Paths

The Chinese *tended to consider the whole landscape, both fields and mountains* (below) *almost as one giant creature; the* lung-mei *lines are similar in concept to the lines known in acupuncture, another ancient Chinese science. In each case, the aim is to focus and harness the energies carried by the respective lines of energy.*

Pagodas (right) *and other important structures were traditionally built on points where the* lung mei *(lines of the dragon forces) running through the earth were particularly powerful. These are similar, perhaps identical, to western ley-lines but are integrated into the old Chinese philosophy of* feng-shui, *"the science of wind and water".*

A feng-shui *expert* (opposite) *consults his books. The goal of much traditional Chinse thought and action – in medicine as in politics – has been to discover and establish latent harmonies between man and man, man and nature and earth and Heaven.*

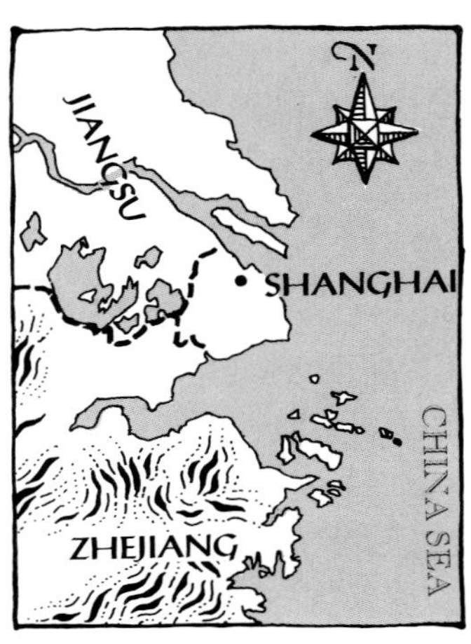

The existence of ley-lines (see pp.42-3) has been recognized in China for centuries. The *lung meis* which ran from hilltop to hilltop were supposed to mark the flight-paths of dragons, and certain alignments were significant as marking specially auspicious points on the earth's surface, where the "dragon pulse" (which produced lines of magnetic force) beat particularly evenly.

It has been suggested that the landscape of much of China was composed to mirror the tenets of the ancient philosophy of *feng-shui*, "the science of wind and water", which concerns itself with the balance between man and nature. The German theorist Ernst Borschmann believed that the temples and pagodas which crowned certain hills in some way harmonized the forces which ran in the ground beneath them, and marked points where the forces were particularly strong.

Feng-shui proposes that the surface of the earth "mirrors the powers of heaven" – that is, conforms in some way to the positions of the stars and the movements of the planets. The scientist Joseph Needham suggested that the forces running along the *lung meis* were governed by planetary positions. Like the ley-lines recorded in England, the Chinese lines for some time run straight, but then curl and whorl as they reach certain epicentres, as though to concentrate their force.

The nature of that force is not understood, although the *lung meis* lines are still marked on some modern maps. In the days of the Emperors, only they or members of their family were allowed to be buried on a dragon's path; the lines were believed to convey force and energy towards the Chinese Emperor in his capital, Peking.

The Concubine's Ghost

In 1954 Dr Wong Wen-hao, Chief Secretary for the Government in Nanking, was driving from Nanking to Wukong, when he was seriously injured in a motor accident.

Unconscious for more than six weeks, he muttered, sometimes incoherently, complaining that "a woman" was troubling him, and he wanted her driven away. One day, with great difficulty, he wrote the three Chinese characters *Sze*. His son-in-law in Shanghai consulted a planchette board and received the message "deceased concubine" and "make the grave early," apparently sent by Dr Wong's mother. He discovered that the sick man's grandfather had started a business in Shanghai with money lent to him by a young concubine called Sze. After the businessman's death, his family failed to recognize Sze, who died shortly after entering a nunnery; she was given perfunctory burial, and no memorial. Several members of the Wong family, on their deathbed, had announced that Sze had appeared to them to demand re-burial and a memorial tablet in the family hall.

Dr Wong's father consulted a medium who told him that Sze had caused the accident in which Wong had been injured, and that he would die unless her demands were met. He was sceptical, but had Sze's coffin exhumed and reburied with proper ceremony, setting up a memorial tablet. Three days after the funeral, Wong (whose recovery was thought impossible by his British doctor) came out of his coma.

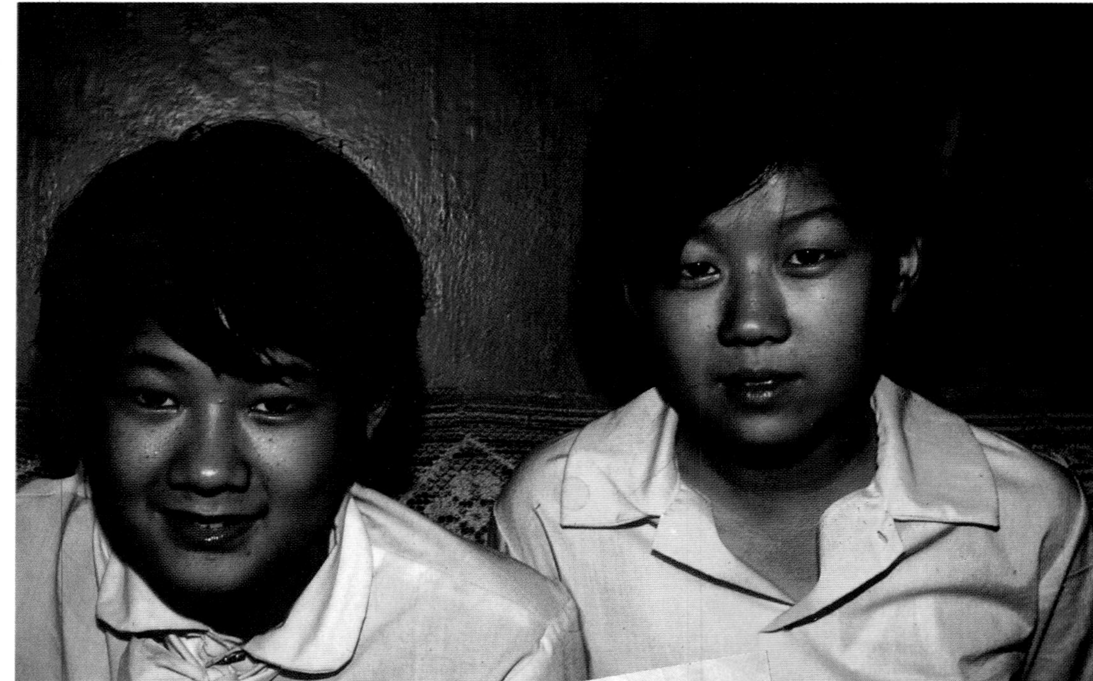

Xiong Jie and Li Hong-Wu (right), *are two of the "wonder" children", recently discovered in China, who have managed to reproduce accurately simple drawings and messages* (below) *placed under their arms or elbows, "reading" without using their eyes. Initial scepticism has been dispelled by the results from closely observed tests. The boys managed to reproduce these messages accurately, as a comparison of the two columns reveals.*

Seeing with the Elbow

One of the most interesting areas of research into the paranormal has been explored in China during recent years.

In March, 1979, the *Sichuan Daily* published an article claiming that a 12-year-old Chinese boy was able to "read" printed or written material hidden in people's pockets by placing his ear against the pocket concerned. The story was at first treated as ridiculous; young Yang Yu was clearly cheating. But then came reports of similar talents in other children: they could, it was claimed, "read" by using almost any part of their body. Reports came in of children reading with their feet, hands, pigtails, even buttocks.

Fortunately, the matter was raised during a period of intellectual tolerance in China, and historians announced that they had found allusions to similar talents in records written 2,000 years ago. The Shanghai scientific journal *Nature* published a learned article on the matter, and arranged scientific tests of 14 subjects aged between nine and 12; more than 2,000 scientists, doctors, teachers and journalists were invited to open demonstrations. During these the subjects successfully "read" material placed in heavy paper bags or opaque plastic boxes. One of the first of them, Jiang Yan, successfully "saw" a drawing of a cluster of bananas on a green background, simply by placing a single fingertip on the concealing cloth. Two sisters from Peking, Wang Qiang and Wang Bin, were not only able to "read" messages placed under their armpits, but proved to be able to communicate the messages telepathically to each other.

A number of respected scientists, at first intensely sceptical, finally had to concede that some faculty was at work which they could not understand. The Chinese-American physician

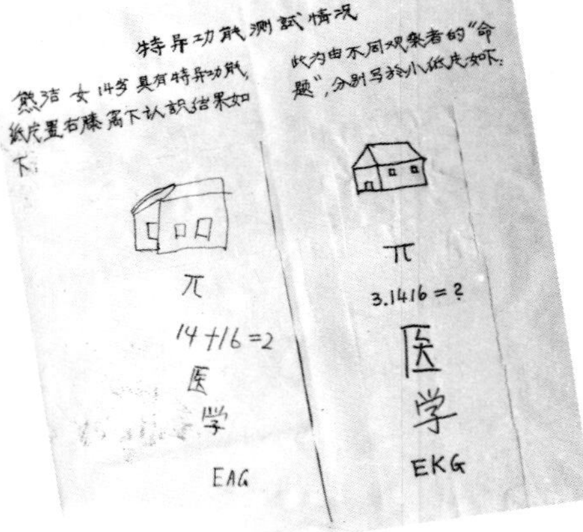
特异功能测試情况
熊洁 女 14岁 具有特异功能,纸片置右膝窝下认识结果如下:
此为由不同观察者的"命题",分别写於小纸片如下:
π
14+16=2
医
学
EAG
π
3.1416=?
医
学
EKG

Dr Chih Kung Jen led a team of specialists who conducted tests on 12 psychic children in the autumn of 1980, and found that they achieved a 98 percent success rate.

Some newspapers in China have denigrated the carefully organized tests, perhaps for political reasons: the *Shanghai Wenhuibao* quoted the National Science Committee in 1981 as stating that the strange talents of the children were merely "ridiculous propaganda"; on the other hand, Zheng Rong-liang, visiting professor of biophysics at the Johns Hopkins University in Baltimore, claimed to have actually witnessed many of the described phenomena, and was sure they were real. Similar phenomena have been found in Russia – for example, in 1962 Rosa Kuleshova, of Takin in the Urals, impressed local doctors by her ability to "read" colours with her fingertips. Later, after some practice, she could interpret written and printed messages in the same way.

JAPAN

Japanese society has always had a place for "magic", revered by peasants and aristocrats alike, though in 1873 the Meiji Government – eager that Japan should join the modern world – suppressed many of the "superstitious" aspects of religion, and ordered the prosecution of (for example) any *miko*, or medium, who professed to deliver messages from the dead.

Interestingly enough, it was the Americans who were responsible for encouraging the return of magic to Japan: in 1945, General MacArthur's Religious Bodies Law allowed the Japanese people for the first time for 70 years, the freedom to worship as they pleased, form religious bodies, and carry on religious activities.

It had always been difficult to separate spells from prayers, and in 20th-century Japan most people are still influenced by "luck" – there are lucky and unlucky days, many taboos, and innumerable superstitions, sometimes varying from district to district. The erosion of formal religion seems to have resulted in a strengthening of unofficial cults, and while, for example, only 18 percent of the population believes in personal survival after death, the general attitude towards the supernatural, is at least permissive and often positive.

Magical Cults and Charms

One of the strongest of recent magical cults arose in 1960, when the True-Light Supra-Religious Organisation, or *Sukyo Mahikara*, was founded by Okada Yoshikazu. Almost two hundred *dojos*, or temples, exist in modern Japan as local centres of the cult, whose followers claim to be able to halt disease, repair broken appliances, improve the taste of food, open the eyes of the dead – and resurrect dead goldfish – simply by lifting their hands and exerting *okiyome*, or the force of purification.

A Western researcher, Winston Davis, conducted a survey of the Organization in the 1970s and recorded many apparent "miracles" experienced by its members, sometimes as the result of the possession of a special amulet which allegedly transmits the "spirit rays" of *okiyome*. Fifty percent of the people he questioned said that should their car break down they would employ *okiyome* to repair it before thinking of sending for a mechanic.

The possession of the amulet is specially important, and the claim that it works miracles for its possessors is made with far greater conviction than a similar claim for "lucky charms" in the West. Instructions for the care of the amulet are very

The Ghost of Sogoro haunting Kozuke (above) *illustrates how dramatically ghosts are believed to intervene in Japanese life. The picture shows a revenge haunting by the good peasant Sogoro, unjustly put to death by his evil landlord Kozuke.*

complete: it must be taken off only when the owner is naked; it must not be hung on a nail with any other amulet, lest their wavelengths be confused; if it is dropped, "immediately notify the head office in Tokyo", for the fall will probably have caused it to become "disconnected".

Ludicrous though this may sound, Davis recorded many cases of misfortune occurring to those who failed to maintain their amulets in good condition: though his was an unscientific survey, and the evidence is less than convincing.

The *Miko*

In ancient Japan, the *miko* or shaman played an enormously important part in religion and daily life. Today, women predominate in this calling, and practise in four ways: blind mediums called *itako* recite the words both of ghosts and of *kami*, or sacred beings; other *mikos* work with ascetics to summon *kami* to local religious ceremonies (particularly in the villages of the northern part of the main island). Then there are those, particularly found in the seven Isu islands, who go into seizures or trances, and act as clairvoyants. And finally, there are the *kyoso*, or founders of new religious sects like the *Sukyo Mahikara*.

Most of the *mikos*, as well as the *yamabushi*, or ascetics, undergo initiations which are far from comfortable: Mrs Chichii Yae, a well-known *itako*, lived for a week in the bitter cold of deep winter in a small hut near a well, eating no meat, no fish, no vegetables and no salt; seven times every day she had to go to the well and pour three buckets-full of cold water over each shoulder while reciting mantras. Mrs Nara Naka, of Tsugara district, had during her initiation to pour 33 buckets of cold water over each shoulder. In some cases, a total of 33,333 buckets of water are poured during an initiation.

As in the case of shamans elsewhere in the world, these privations apparently resulted in the purification of the people concerned: reaching the point of collapse, they then experience new strength and a transformation of their whole beings.

The ascetic *yamabushi* are somewhat different from the *itako*. They sprang originally from Buddhism, and are first recorded in Japan in the 8th century; having taken Buddhist vows, they retire to particular monasteries, live without cereals or meat, and devote themselves to the constant recitation of particular religious texts. Some men, some women, they also perform rituals and occult exercises which give them power over spirits; they are frequently healers and exorcists, and can summon the spirits of the dead.

These can be "new ghosts" (of people who have died within a hundred days) or "old ghosts" (who died earlier). In general, ghosts should be summoned on the third or fifth day after the coffin has left the house. When a ghost comes, it greets in turn all its relations, in a rite which can last for eight or nine hours, after which it is dispatched to its own world, its Ancestor invited to show it the way back.

These ceremonies still take place. Sakurai Tokutaro, one Japanese parapsychologist, was present in 1966 at a rite during which the ghost of a family's eldest son, killed in a fall from a bridge a hundred days earlier, addressed all its relatives, neighbours and friends individually, through a medium, making 73 speeches in all.

In addition to their religious commitments, the ascetics can and do perform certain "tricks" such as fire-walking and bathing in boiling water. An American scholar, Dr Carmen Blacker, saw one Shinshukyo priest shower himself with boiling water without injury, and later herself followed a *yamabushi* of the Tanukidani sect across a path of red-hot stones, feeling only "a mild warmth."

In Japan ghosts are accepted as an ever-present aspect of everyday life and are not necessarily regarded as sinister: they may even exert a beneficial influence over practical everyday matters. These prayers, attached to small wooden plaques (above), *have been offered by Japanese students hoping for exam success.*

The Philippines

Psychic Surgery

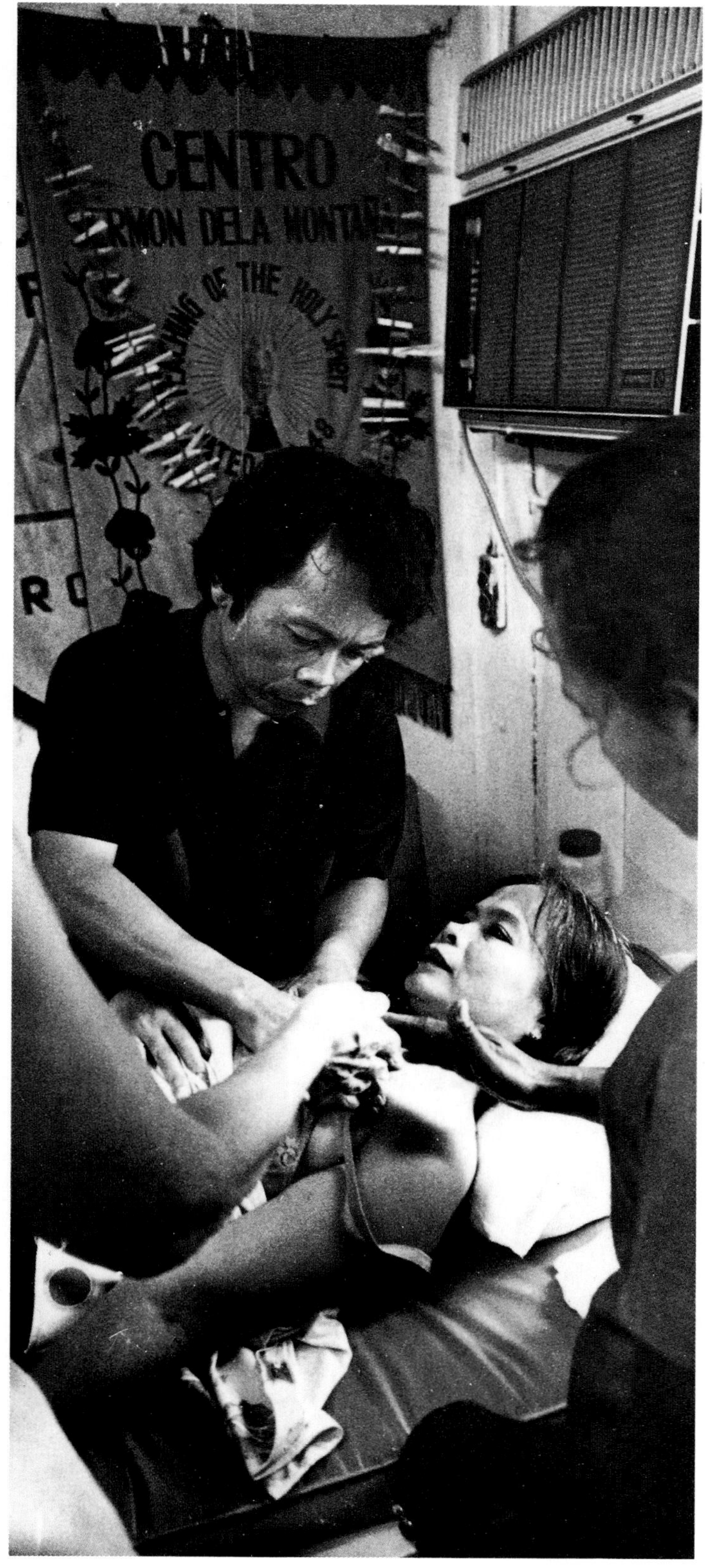

Healing with hands *is common in the Philippines. Some seemingly miraculous cures have been recorded, including "surgery with bare hands". Mrs Marcos, wife of the former president, witnessed an operation performed by Brother Virgilio Gutierrez* (left), *one of the Philippines' best known faith healers, and was much impressed. Medically better-informed observers were not convinced.*

Psychic surgery – surgical operations carried out by the bare hands, without anaesthetic, by "surgeons" with no medical training – has been common in the Philippines for many years.

These surgeons claim a divine right to perform such operations, and are often associated with the fundamentalist Espiritista Church. The first Filipino psychic surgeon seems to have been a man named Terte, who began working in the 1940s; he was followed by Tony Agpaoa, who during the 1970s treated up to 200 patients a month, and founded his own church, the Church of Science and Revelation. Within the past 20 years many other healers have appeared.

The most reliable account of psychic surgery in action in the Philippines is given in his book *Healing* (1974) by Dr William A. Nolen, a practising American surgeon and a wellknown medical journalist. He describes an operation performed by David Oligani upon a man with blood clots in his legs. Oligani first, without touching the patient, produced a scratch on one of his legs, then setting fire to cotton wool in a glass, placed it over the scratch. After a while, a substance which appeared to be a blood clot appeared through the skin inside the glass. (Dr Nolen points out that this appears to be a replication of the "cupping" known to Western doctors for centuries.)

He then observed an operation on another patient's abdomen, during which Oligani apparently thrust his fingers into the stomach and pulled out bloodsoaked tissue. The stomach, afterwards, displayed no sign of a scar, and Dr Nolen noted that the substance supposedly removed from the stomach was quickly disposed of, and was unavailable for analysis. His experience of genuine operations convinced him that red dye rather than blood had coloured it, and that sleight of hand had been employed.

Later, Dr Nolen himself was operated on by Joe Mercado, and clearly saw him palm a blob of fat which was later produced as the tumour which had been removed from his stomach. There seems little doubt that the psychic surgery he observed was faked. Nevertheless, sick people from Europe and the United States continue to travel to the Philippines in search of help – although in decreasing numbers.

GREAT BRITAIN AND IRELAND

Britain is said to have more haunted houses than any other country in the world. Speak to most people about "the supernatural", and they take it for granted that you mean ghosts (although they sometimes have different ideas about what they mean by this). The British certainly appear to have a particular affection for these nebulous beings. Almost every house more than 100 years old seems to have a ghost story of some sort attached to it, while castles and mansions invariably have their haunted rooms or corridors, along which chains are said to clank or headless figures to glide. Places with particularly unpleasant associations breed ghosts: the Tower of London has scarcely a corner without its attendant phantom.

The reason for this is intangible; certainly European culture has always had room for ghosts – the Greek and Roman worlds were full of them. The phenomenon may have something to do with the general European attitude to death which has always been less fatalistic than that of people in the East, or those of the Americas. Europeans seem in general to have regarded the afterlife as something very close to "real life"; not in the way that the African tribes do, with the dead continually requiring attention, but in the sense that one may continually overhear them, as though they are close by, and able to make their feelings known. John Donne, the 17th-century poet and preacher, suggested that it was as though when one died one simply went into another room; and the door, Europeans have always felt, has been left ajar.

Efforts to put a foot in that door, so that the room beyond can be seen and examined, have been many; and in the past 100 years have been conducted mainly by the British Society for Psychical Research. This organization has in general been run by serious-minded men and women who have frequently been excellent researchers, careful to keep fact separate from fiction, and to present the results of their enquiries in a manner which could not easily be disproven by science.

The trouble with ghosts is that it is very difficult to rationalize about them. They are often seen when we are in a state of some tension, because of special circumstances or the general atmosphere; and this tends to make for rather scrambled reports. Then again, it is very difficult when describing such emotive events as the appearance of someone we loved, not to embroider, not to be overconfident about what we saw or thought we saw. And yet, too many people are confident that they have seen them – for anyone to dismiss them out of hand.

Where poltergeists are concerned, it is another matter: the evidence for them is surely incontrovertible. Poltergeist activity takes place in every part of the world, but it has been most eagerly explored in Europe – perhaps because Europeans tend to regard them as a particular affront to rationalism. Yet this rationalism has had to retreat before the evidence.

Looking at ghost stories in general – those which seem likely, or even proven, and those which seem unlikely and perhaps merely anecdotal – one finds they have one thing in common: someone at some time believed them, and believed them passionately. This does not of course mean that they are true; but it may mean that they are worth investigation, and should certainly not be dismissed out of hand.

***Glastonbury Tor** (left), crowned by its ruined tower, is thought by many to be one of the principal centres for the ley-lines which are said to run through the British landscape. These lines link ancient structures (notably Stonehenge) – natural features such as hilltops and church spires or towers. Glastonbury Tor is rich in such associations: as well as a church, built on ground consecrated in c.1100, there are traces of Stone Age buildings beneath the nearby ruined Abbey. Joseph of Arimathea is said to have hidden the Holy Grail in the Chalice Well at the foot of the Tor, and according to legend, Glastonbury is also the burial place of King Arthur.*

ENGLAND

STONEHENGE AND THE LEY-LINES

The question of whether Stonehenge was an ancient astronomical observatory or the centre of the Druid religion need not concern us here: its significance to those interested in the paranormal is as the largest of the monuments standing on the ley-lines which crisscross the British countryside, and as the centre of mysterious forces connected with them.

For at least 60 years it has been argued that Stonehenge and similar megalithic monuments mark out channels along which flow strange forces, whose nature is unknown. The existence of these channels, or ley-lines, was first suggested in the 1920s in a theory set out by a British businessman, Alfred Watkins. He believed that certain sites – hills, standing stones, cairns, holy wells, earthworks, castles and churches marked out pathways, perhaps up to 6,000 years old, carefully laid out by prehistoric man.

Watkins named these tracks ley-lines, and published his theory in a book, *The Old Straight Track*, in 1925. Archaeologists and historians rejected it; but it started a sort of craze for discovering ley-lines. Within a few years ley-line hunting had become a hobby with a number of ramblers, and the theory was more and more developed as many of them advanced further speculations about the alignment of ancient sites. Soon, the whole map of England was covered with circles, triangles and lines marking alleged ancient tracks.

The interest for occultists came somewhat later, in the 1940s when two British dowsers, Captain F.L.M. Boothby and Reginald Allender Smith, following the pioneering work of French dowsers, discovered that beneath the sites allegedly joined by ley-lines ran mysterious currents of magnetic force, which seemed guided by the lines. The presence of animal tracks suggested that animals recognized this force, and in some way used it. Another dowser, Guy Underwood, in a posthumous book (*The Pattern of the Past*, 1969), argued that the force seemed to focus on certain ancient sites, such as Stonehenge, and other artificial landscape features – where it settled into giant whorls or spirals, "blind springs" hidden in the earth but marked on its surface by animal activity and plant growth out of character with the area.

One prevalent theory is that ancient man understood geomancy, and was able to harness it by channelling it along ley-lines – rather as the Chinese used the "dragons' paths" (see pp.116-7). The most important points along the lines are marked by standing stones or other structures which act as nodal points where the energy can be tapped; more minor points – such as holy wells – were often used for healing. (Non-European people have often believed that earth forces could be channelled through stones: for example, the Sioux Indians used a standing rock in South Dakota to renew their psychic powers, by standing with their backs against it.)

There have been various speculations about the nature of the energy focused on the stones. Dr E.T. Stringer, a geographer, proposed in the early 1970s that a "telluric force" is induced by electric currents within the earth; others have suggested that the presence of quartz in the earth may help to channel the energy: quartz being one of the most common of

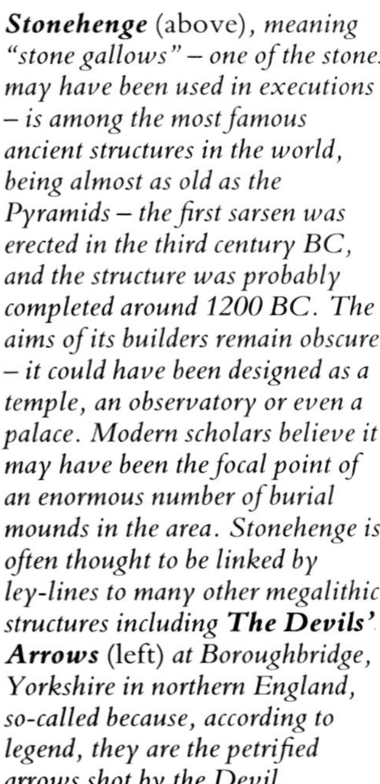

Stonehenge (above), *meaning "stone gallows" – one of the stones may have been used in executions – is among the most famous ancient structures in the world, being almost as old as the Pyramids – the first sarsen was erected in the third century BC, and the structure was probably completed around 1200 BC. The aims of its builders remain obscure – it could have been designed as a temple, an observatory or even a palace. Modern scholars believe it may have been the focal point of an enormous number of burial mounds in the area. Stonehenge is often thought to be linked by ley-lines to many other megalithic structures including* ***The Devils' Arrows*** (left) *at Boroughbridge, Yorkshire in northern England, so-called because, according to legend, they are the petrified arrows shot by the Devil.*

all crystals, this would be difficult to disprove (but see p.34). It has also been suggested that there is some relationship between the lines of power and planetary movements, hence the astronomical alignment of Stonehenge and other sites.

During an experiment in the mid-70s centred on a 12-feet-high (3.6m) standing stone near the river Usk at Crickhowell in South Wales, a physicist, Dr Eduardo Balanovski (of Imperial College, London) measured the magnetic field around the stone with a gaussmeter and found a variation far above average. John Taylor, of King's College, London, was so intrigued by this that he conducted his own experiment and found that around a spiral marked out on the stone by a dowser, the gaussmeter indicated a magnetic force double the measurement elsewhere.

It has recently been suggested that the theory of lines of energy running not far below the earth's surface is connected with James Lovelock's Gaia theory – a scientific vision of the earth itself as a living being. Just as lines of energy run through the human body (those lines which, at certain junctions, are intercepted by the acupuncturist's needle), so, it is suggested, similar lines run through the earth. The ancients, unconsciously recognizing their significance, made a connection between them and fertility.

The strange behaviour of compasses and electrical and radio equipment at or near some of the ancient monuments certainly suggests that some unknown force is at work there, and in 1977-8 the Dragon Project was established to look at the energy aspects of these and other sites.

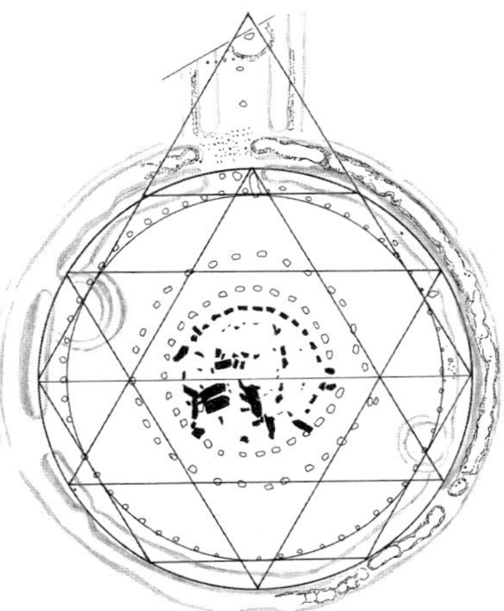

One of the many theories *about Stonehenge suggests that the mathematical relationships in the groundplan* (above) *of the stones and surrounding earthworks relate to ancient principles of cosmology. They derive from the "square of the sun" – a magic grid of numbers that supposedly could be exploited to control solar energy. By extension, this is thought to be the purpose for which the henge was used.*

HAUNTED BRITAIN AND IRELAND

Britain abounds in reports of haunted houses, of skulls that seem to resist burial, and of curious ghostly figures. Sometimes the phantoms have been traced to historical characters who came to an unfortunate end.

CASTLES, GREAT HOUSES AND INSTITUTIONS
1 Tower of London; University College; Broadcasting House; Bank of England
2 Blenkinsopp Castle
3 Windsor Castle
4 Lancaster Castle
5 Hastings Castle
6 Scarborough Castle
7 Berry Pomeroy Castle
8 Rochester Castle
9 Ludlow Castle
10 Hampton Court Palace
11 Arundel Castle
12 Bellister Castle
13 Featherstone Castle
14 Lorton Hall
15 Levens Hall
16 Samlesbury Hall
17 Speke Hall
18 Rufford Old Hall
19 Rolling Hall & East Riddleston Hall
20 Wilkington Mill
21 Chambercombe Manor
22 Bisham Abbey
23 Raynham Hall
24 Renishaw Hall
25 Littlecote House
26 Greta Hall
27 Wycoller Hall
28 York Museum
29 Broughton Hall
30 Killaloe
31 Kilkenny
32 Claydon House
33 Woburn Abbey
34 Testwood House
35 Sandford Orcas
36 Puttenden Manor
37 Salisbury Hall
38 Old Castle Inn
39 Glamis Castle

SCREAMING SKULLS
40 Higher Chiltern Farm: houses the skull of Theophilus Brome, attempts to move it have resulted in "horrid noises"
41 Brougham Hall; Threlkeld Place
42 Calgarth Hall
43 Burton Agnes Hall: the burial of a lady of the hall was followed by poltergeist activity, until her skull was bricked up in the walls of the hall
44 Bury St Edmunds
45 Bettiscombe Manor: allegedly haunted by the skull of a prehistoric woman
46 Tunstead Farm; Flagg Hall
47 Warbleton Priory Farm: two skulls were unearthed, thought to be those of a murderer and his victim
48 Skull House; Wardley Hall
49 Turton Tower; near the old Timberbottom farmhouse, where two skulls apparently resisted all attempts to move them
50 Hatherton Hall: the skull of Sir Hugh de Hatherton was allegedly reclaimed by his ghost after being used as a drinking vessel
51 Browsholm Hall; Whalley Abbey

GHOSTLY MONKS AND NUNS
52 Abbeyshule
53 Chingle Hall: allegedly haunted by a Franciscan monk and a monk in a black cape and cowl
54 Bolton Priory: tourists frequently claim to have seen the ghost of the "Black Canon"
55 Bury St Edmunds Abbey: several phantom monks have allegedly been seen here
56 Beaulieu Abbey
57 Buriton (village): haunted by the ghost of a wandering friar
58 St Dunstan's Church, St Giles Church, St Magnus the Martyr & Westminster Abbey
59 Little Abbey Hotel (Missenden Abbey)
60 Checkley Church
61 Lindisfarne
62 Elm Vicarage: a phantom bell sounds a knell before the death of a parishioner
63 Farnham parish church: visitors claim to have witnessed a ghostly celebration of Mass
64 Newstead Abbey: the ghost of a monk waits at the bedside of dying members of the family
65 Watton Abbey
66 Holy Trinity Church; Theatre Royal
67 Borley Rectory: described as "the world's most haunted house"
68 School in St Helens, Lancashire

HIGHWAYMEN, HORSEMEN AND GHOSTS OF THE ROAD
69 William Nevison: haunts "Hanging Wood"
70 Tom Hoggett: the ghost of the "King of the High Tobymen of the Great North Road"
71 Ned King: his ghost is said to have been seen at the Punch Bowl Inn
72 Horrocks: the ghostly figure is probably that of Grimshaw who found Horrock's ill-gained booty and in selling it was accused of having stolen it himself; he hanged for his alleged crime
73 John Whitfield: his cries haunt the Carlisle-Penrith road
74 Criselle Cochrane
75 Lady Katherine Ferrers
76 George Weston
77, 78 & 79 Dick Turpin: haunts several stretches of road
80 Major Smalman
81 Bronze Age rider: dates back 2,500 years – perhaps the oldest ghost in Europe
82 A pair of disembodied hairy hands terrify victims on Dartmoor
83 Nance: her ghost is said to help travellers in distress
84 Cromwell family coach
85 Clonmel

Screaming Skulls

In many cultures and countries skeletons have, perhaps understandably, been associated with death and haunting. However, a peculiarly English preoccupation, in terms of ghosts and hauntings, has been with the skulls alone – skulls which bitterly resent any indignity offered them.

Stories of "screaming skulls" have been recorded in Somerset, Cumbria, Yorkshire, Suffolk, Dorset, Derbyshire, Sussex, Lancashire – indeed, in most counties of England. They usually relate to skulls which appear to cause poltergeist activity, or scream like banshees, often because someone has attempted to remove them from some place to which they have become accustomed, but sometimes simply because they have been separated from their bodies.

One story is attached to William Corder, whose murder of his mistress, Maria Marten, in the Red Barn at Polstead in Suffolk in 1828 caused a sensation in the first half of the 19th century. It appears that after his hanging, Corder's body was dissected (as was the custom), and a Bury St Edmunds' doctor, John Kilner (who had the macabre hobby of collecting skulls), stole the head, polished the skull, and mounted it in an ebony box. His household was immediately terrified by poltergeist disturbances; Kilner gave the skull away, and the new owner now had his own share of haunting and misfortunes until he gave the skull a Christian burial.

In other cases burial was no solution, for the skulls concerned allegedly dug themselves out of their graves and reappeared in the homes of their reluctant owner. Some of them may still be found in the houses which they appear so unwilling to leave. But it must be admitted that there is not one single case of a "screaming skull" which has stood up to the examination of ghost-hunters.

***Some skulls "refuse" to be buried**, like that of Theophilus Broome* (previous page), *who died in 1670. Attempts to bury the skull, despite Broome's request that it be kept in the farm, were thwarted by spades breaking and other strange mishaps.*

***Pentagon power** was perhaps revealed in the Scilly Islands* (left) *when the mere tracing of the pentagon shape raised the temperature by five or six degrees.*

***The Cerne Abbas Giant** in Dorset* (bottom, opposite) *is still thought to encourage fertility in any childless couple who make love within it.*

The Power of the Pentagon

The economy of the Isles of Scilly, off the shores of southwest of England, largely depends on the cultivation of early-flowering *Soleils d'Or*, a variety of narcissus. During the early 1980s the crop began to flower up to two months late, with disastrous economic results.

After much investigation, the only reason for the change of flowering pattern seemed to be connected with the cessation of an old custom by which, on midsummer's day, a six-inch (15cm) layer of straw was spread over the bulb fields and burned. It was decided to counterfeit the effect; and when the earth was briefly scorched with a propane burner the *Soleils d'Or* flowered as early as mid-November, although research revealed that the heat generated never actually reached the bulbs themselves. There are various possible explanations for this, including the fact that the scorching may stimulate nitrates which encourage growth.

However, Peter Tabraham, station foreman of the Ministry of Agriculture Centre on the islands, discovered that the burnt ground remained throughout the year up to six degrees warmer than the surrounding land. An amateur dowser, he could trace the perimeters of the burned land up to two years later (although ploughing removed the traces).

There then proved to be a connection with the form of the pentagon. Mr Tabraham discovered that simply by tracing a pentagon on the ground – even marking one simply by planting five sticks in the earth – a two-degree temperature rise could be induced within it. By marking out the pentagon two or three times, the ground could be warmed progressively by five or six degrees.

The practical result of his experiment was the rescue of the Islands' economy. The Ministry of Agriculture recorded the facts – although they did not publicize the mysterious way in which the rescue had been achieved, "or we would have lost credulity."

Giants and Horses

The Celts who ruled Britain before the Romans had dozens of gods and goddesses: each tribe looked for protection and prosperity to its own deities – most of whom have vanished without trace. One or two can still be seen, portrayed on a grand scale as giant figures cut in the chalk or soil of the

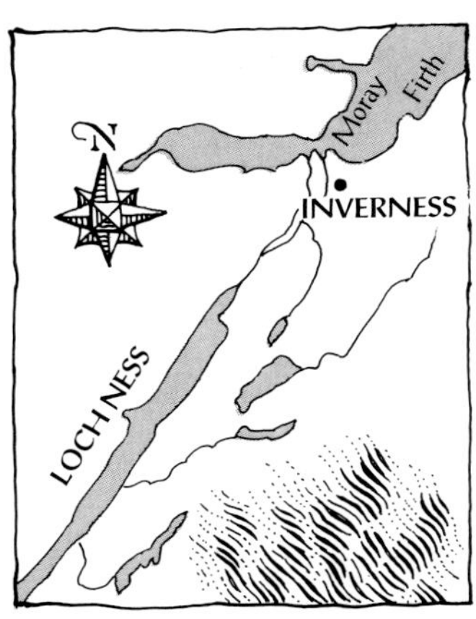

Glamis Castle (below) *in Angus, near Dundee in Scotland, has a long history of ghostly visitations: according to tradition, it is haunted by Macbeth, who allegedly murdered Duncan there. Another ghostly inhabitant is "Earl Beardie", who is said to have played cards with the Devil and lost. The ghostly forms of a negro servant boy, a gibbering madman and a tongueless woman are also said to have been seen in the castle or its grounds. In recent years there have been several reported sightings of the so-called White or Grey Lady, whom several witnesses claim to have seen kneeling in a pew in the chapel.*

A Scottish Poltergeist

A poltergeist that enjoyed considerable newspaper and television publicity was heard and seen in action in the small town of Sauchie, Clackmannanshire, Scotland in November 1960.

An 11-year-old girl, Virginia Campbell, was staying with her brother Thomas, a miner, in Sauchie, sharing a bedroom with her nine-year-old niece Margaret. On November 23 the family was at tea when Mr and Mrs Campbell saw a heavy sideboard move, by itself, about five inches (12.5cm) away from the wall against which it stood, and then return. That night, loud knocks were heard coming from Virginia's room, while she was in bed.

The family prudently summoned the local minister, the Rev T. W. Lund, who evidently suspected Virginia of trickery, and carefully saw to it that she could not make any noise by rapping the bedstead or wall. However, the knocking continued. Mr Lund then saw a large chest in the bedroom, full of linen and weighing about 50 pounds (22.5kg), rock, lift itself, and move 18 inches (46cm) along the floor.

On November 25 Mr Lund was present in Virginia's room when her pillow twisted itself beneath her head, without her touching it with her hands. He called in a physician, Dr W. H. Nisbet, who heard knockings and "a mysterious sawing noise", and saw Virginia's bed-linen make strange movements which clearly had nothing to do with any physical action of hers.

The poltergeist now followed Virginia from the house, and on that same day (November 25) her schoolmistress, Miss Stewart, saw the girl with her hands flat on her desk-top, apparently trying to close it against some force which was pressing it open. She claimed that she then saw the desk behind Virginia raise itself into the air and settle down some way from its original position. She immediately examined it: there were no means by which Virginia or anyone else could have moved it. Later, a blackboard pointer allegedly began to vibrate, before throwing itself from a table; the table in turn started vibrating beneath Miss Stewart's hands and then began to move.

The phenomena continued for some weeks; some of the knockings were recorded on a tape-recorder. After a religious service in the Campbells' house, things were somewhat quieter, although there were still noises, and both Virginia and Margaret claimed that someone invisible from time to time pinched them. On January 23 1961, Virginia placed a bowl of bulbs on her teacher's desk: the flowers immediately rearranged themselves. When Virginia left the town, shortly afterwards, the phenomena failed to follow her and there were no further reports of disturbances.

IRELAND

HAUNTED HOUSES

Few Western countries are as soaked in traditional stories of the supernatural as Ireland, although stories of "the little people" and their activities remain simply stories. This is in spite of the efforts of such sympathetic investigators as the poet W. B. Yeats (1865-1939), who spent many hours in rural Ireland talking to those who had allegedly seen supernatural beings.

Many houses throughout Ireland have the reputation of being haunted – more usually by conventional-sounding ghosts, both visible and invisible, than by poltergeists. Very characteristic is the description of the haunting of an old house in County Kilkenny, formerly a barracks built to house some of Cromwell's men. Two ladies staying in this house in 1880 independently heard during the night the sound of coals being raked, and of loud coughing; in the following year one of them returned, and in the middle of the night again heard coughing, and also marching feet.

Waking in the dark, the visitor later saw a figure standing, apparently reading her Bible, by moonlight; the figure then moved towards a drawer where the visitor kept her jewellery, and she thought it was perhaps a thief. However, nothing was missing in the morning; when she told a servant, she heard that an army colonel had once cut his throat in the room in which she had slept. The Society for Psychical Research investigated the case, and could find nothing inconsistent in the tale, which was characteristic of many similar anecdotes of other places around the country.

As well as houses, some particular places in Ireland have the reputation of being haunted – near Clonmel, the figure of a young girl is often seen walking in a particular lane; the grounds of Rathfarnham Castle, in County Dublin, and the road between the castle gate and Dodder Bridge seem to be haunted by the ghost of a retriever dog which drowned attempting to rescue its master, who fell through ice and drowned in the winter of 1840-1.

BANSHEES

One of the strongest Irish traditions is of the banshee or boheentha, said to foretell an imminent death. The famous banshees of Craglea, near Killaloe (in 1014) and of the Fanshawe family (in 1642) are the two best-known. However, during the early years of this century there were many reports of wailing women seen and heard before a death.

Sometimes the noise of weeping alone is heard or the spectral figure of a woman is seen. Particular families have their individual banshees – not always human: one Irish family is haunted by the figure of a small dog. Whenever it is seen, news of a death follows. The family crest of the Gormanstown family is a running fox, and it is said that whenever the head of the house is dying, real foxes gather in groups in the grounds of the castle. When the 12th Viscount, Jenico, was dying in 1860, pairs of foxes were seen beneath the castle windows, sitting and howling. Twenty years later, foxes barked beneath the window of the dying 13th Viscount, and on the evening of October 28 1907, a coachman and gardener at the castle saw several foxes nearby. That night the 14th Viscount died, miles away in Dublin.

Two days later the Hon Richard Preston was watching by his father's body in the castle chapel when, at 3am, he heard a noise. He opened the chapel door. A few feet away sat a full-grown fox; nearby were several more. He went to the other door, near the altar; outside, were two more foxes.

What seems on the face of it just a pretty legend apparently had, at that time at least, more substance than some.

THE VISION AT KNOCK
In the small village of Knock, in County Mayo, on the evening of August 21 1879, a number of people saw a vision on the gable end of their little church (right), of an altar, with the figures of St John the Evangelist, the Blessed Virgin, and St Joseph surrounded by angels in a brilliant golden light. They were entirely convinced of the truth of the vision, and suggestions that some joker had projected the figures onto the whitewashed end of the church by means of a magic lantern are still scornfully dismissed by the community, which has profited from the regular pilgrimages of more than a million people a year, and a visit – in 1979 – by Pope John Paul II.

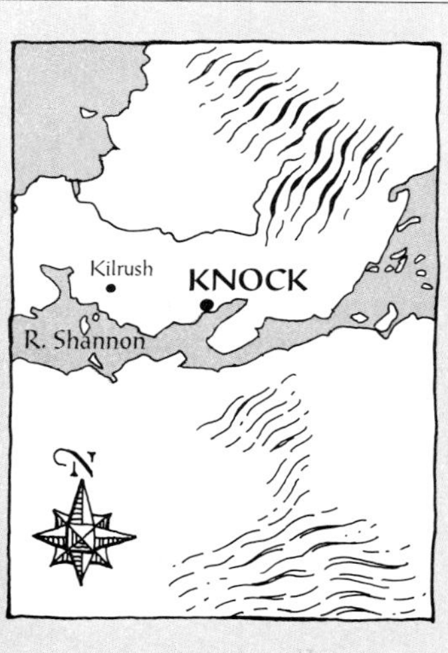

WALES

THE VIRGIN AT LLANTHONY

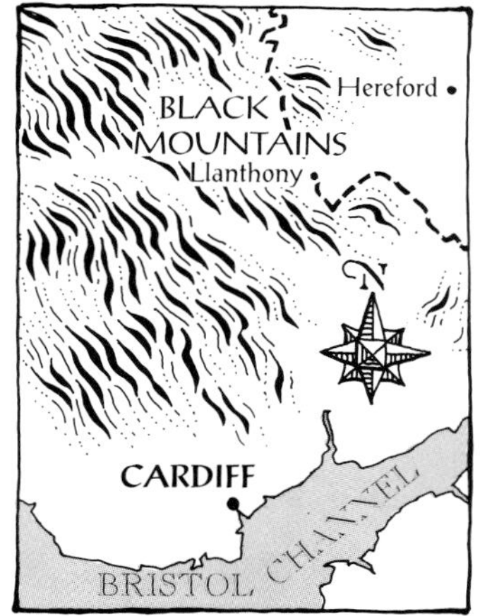

Reports of the appearance of the Virgin Mary in the British Isles are few and far between. The best-attested vision occurred in 1880 near the beautiful ruins of Llanthony Abbey, at Capel-y-Fin, in the Black Montains of Wales.

Capel-y-Fin housed a monastery at the time, led by Father Ignatius, a somewhat eccentric religious leader and a friend of the sculptor Eric Gill. On the evening of August 30, four boys aged between nine and 15 claimed to have seen the Virgin, who walked towards them and then disappeared into a hedge. On September 4 some members of the community congregated at the same hedge and sang *Ave Maria*, when the Virgin once again appeared, together with "a man unclothed save for a cloth round the loins." The couple then vanished. Eleven days later, four different people saw "the whole heavens and mountains break forth in bulging circles of light, circles pushing out from circles – the light poured upon our faces and the buildings where we stood, and in the central circle stood a most Majestic Heavenly Form, robed in flowing drapery."

It must be admitted that the accounts read like those of classic religious ecstasies rather than actual events; but those reporting the visions were serious people who clearly believed what they said. Subsequently, a potion was prepared from leaves of a Holy Bush growing at the point in the hedge where the second vision appeared. The plant was wild rhubarb, and the potion efficacious in the cure of certain disorders, notably constipation.

***The Egryn lights** made inexplicable appearances around preacher Mrs Mary Jones* (right, top) *at Egryn Chapel* (right, bottom) *and other places near Barmouth in Wales in 1904-5, during the Welsh Methodist Revival. Mary Jones claimed to have seen visions and to have received messages from "The Saviour in bodily form." Believing herself to be the medium for the spreading of the Revival, she led a nightly mission in her local chapel. Before long, other people claimed to see the lights and "stars", which appeared to rest over the roof of the chapel and above particular houses. Journalists who witnessed the lights reported that converts invariably came to the next meeting that took place at a house singled out in this way.*

WESTERN EUROPE

- ● earth's mysteries
- ▼ monsters
- ■ beyond the grave
- ☾ natural magic
- ☆ magic, charms and witchcraft
- △ supernatural technology
- ✚ visions, apparitions and religious phenomena
- 〰 psychic gift

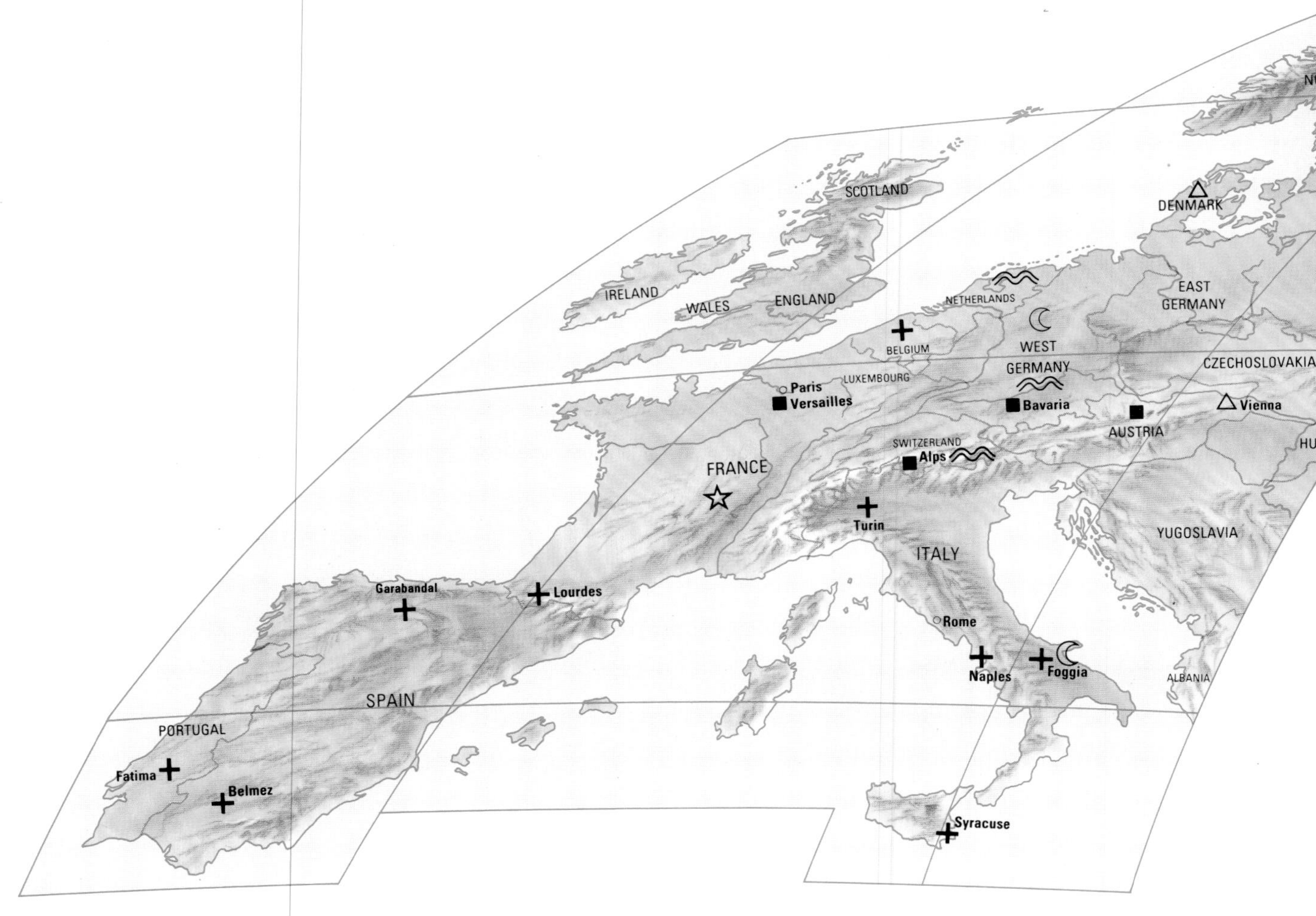

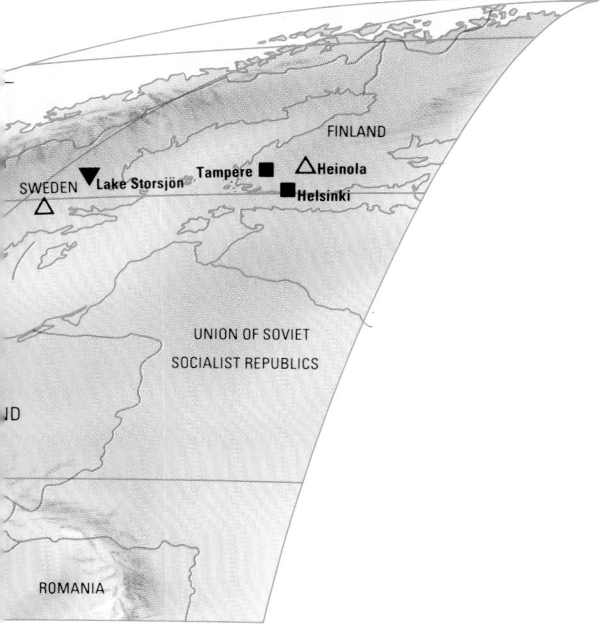

Western man's interest in the supernatural began in Europe, as elsewhere, as a simple desire to discover how the universe works: when there seemed no rational explanation for a particular phenomenon, an irrational one was taken for granted. Irrationality, 2,000 years ago, no doubt seemed less reprehensible than it does now.

The problem has been, over the past millennia, that an increasingly large proportion of people in the enlightened West has become reluctant to "believe" in occult forces (and we must remember that the word does not imply "magic", but simply describes what is so far inexplicable to us). The Western churches – especially those furthest removed from Roman Catholicism – have begun to deny their own biblical origins, which have much to do with the supernatural; their attitude today is to continue (although with some exceptions) to accept their own "magic" while denying the "natural magic" increasingly sympathetic to the thinking of the New Age.

So the appearances of the Holy Virgin throughout Europe are acceptable to many conventional Christian worshippers, while the appearances of ghosts are taken by most to be imaginary, the product of emotional instability. Healers who subscribe to the Christian or other faiths are acceptable; those who rely on natural healing techniques practised for centuries by countryfolk (once called witches) are regarded with considerable suspicion.

Science, since the Age of Enlightenment, has taken much the same attitude. As there was no reason why one person could "put someone to sleep" and influence them, simply by suggestion, hypnosis had to be fraudulent; as there was no evidence that sticking a pin into a particular point of the human body could reduce pain, acupuncture could not possibly work. Yet both hypnosis and acupuncture are now accepted as helpful medical techniques. Rather similarly, priests and ministers, who would once have regarded ghosts as nonexistent, have been forced to consult historical traditions for methods of exorcising them.

As one looks around Western Europe at events which most people would regard as supernatural, no-one could fail to be impressed by the sheer number of people who have been in contact with it. Rationalists search for natural explanations – for example, stigmata are said to be psychologically self-inflicted; the appearances of the Virgin to be self-induced hallucinations. Even if this is the case, there are well-recorded incidents which defy reason: for example, no amount of rationalization has so far explained the case of the Icelandic medium Indridi Indridason (p.138), or of the Weimar poltergeist (p.150).

The particular interest of Western supernatural phenomena, indeed, is not that they form discernible patterns of occult events, but that in the face of constant investigation and suspicion so many of them resist explanation, and maintain a firm hold on the imagination of ordinary people.

Iceland

Indridi Indridason

A little-known and spectacular case of mediumship, investigated in Iceland at the beginning of the present century, still stands as one of the best-attested of its kind and resists all attempts at rational explanation. The medium was a young man called Indridi Indridason.

Indridason was born in 1883 in the west of Iceland, the son of a farmer. When he was 22, and still more or less uneducated, he went to Reykjavik to learn typography. Previously, there had been no sign that he was in any way psychic – but early in 1905 he attended a circle which was attempting to investigate table-tapping. The moment he touched the table it began to move violently.

Indridason was frightened and wanted nothing more to do with the experiment, but was persuaded to continue to take part. Within a short time he was speaking in various voices, performing seemingly miraculous medical cures, and producing automatic writing. He became famous throughout Iceland – denounced by some people as a fake, regarded by others as having remarkable psychic powers. The Professor of Theology at the University of Iceland, the Rev. Haraldur Nielsson, investigated the case, and was convinced of the medium's sincerity. Then, in 1908, a very distinguished Icelandic scientist, Gudmunder Hannesson, decided to examine Indridason under carefully controlled circumstances.

Particularly known for his integrity and impartiality, Hannesson set up conditions under which it would have been very difficult indeed for Indridason to have got away with any deception. Assisted by the Rev. Nielsson and a reputable ophthalmic surgeon, Bjorn Olafsson, Hannesson arranged a series of seances in a locked room which had been carefully searched. A strong, small-meshed net was nailed from floor to ceiling to confine Indridason and the "watchers" to a small space; Hannesson sat outside this cage. Indridason was made to strip and was carefully searched before going into a trance.

Despite all these preparations, not only did Indridason speak in various voices, but heavy objects were thrown about and a weighty music-box rose into the air and started playing while Nielsson was holding both of Indridason's hands. The spirits then began to attack Indridason, who started levitating with a force so strong that Nielsson could scarcely hold him down; finally both men were thrown into the air and then dashed to the floor. A large wooden pulpit, firmly fixed to the wall, was wrenched from its position, its woodwork torn from the wall and floor with considerable force.

Hannesson entirely failed to discover any way in which Indridason could have caused these manifestations. Although the events took place in darkness (the one weak spot in the otherwise meticulously controlled experiment), the objects were marked with fluorescent tape, and could be clearly seen to move while Nielsson – of whose probity there was never any question, continued to hold the medium's hands. Try as he might, Hannesson could find no rational explanation for the results of the experiments.

Indridi Indridason (above, top, seated) *the son of a farmer, claimed to show amazing psychic powers early in life. Investigated by* ***Gudmunder Hannesson*** (above left) *and* ***Haraldur Nielsson*** (above right), *he managed to confound all critics and sceptics by exhibiting his paranormal skills during the most rigorous tests. He held his last seance in 1909, and died three years later of tuberculosis.*

FINLAND

THE YLOJARVI POLTERGEIST

In 1885, an elderly retired elementary school-teacher, Efraim Martin, and his wife, employed a 13-year-old girl, Emma Lindroos, to help them in their three-roomed cottage at Ylojarvi, near Tampere in Finland.

On January 12, the front door of the house burst open with such force that plaster fell from the walls. Locked drawers sprang open and the contents were scattered. A hymn book was thrown against the wall. On subsequent days such phenomena were repeated, accompanied by even stranger, senseless ones: a sheep was found in a cowstall with its legs tied together, a cow's harness was turned inside out.

When the girl became ill and was sent away, the strange events ceased. But there was much talk in the neighbourhood, and in March 1885, the Martins and Emma were accused of having deceived the public in order to make a profit by selling brandy to the many visitors who flocked to the house. Fifteen eye-witnesses described phenomena they had seen there, many of them went out of their way to explain why they thought Emma or the Martins could not have faked them.

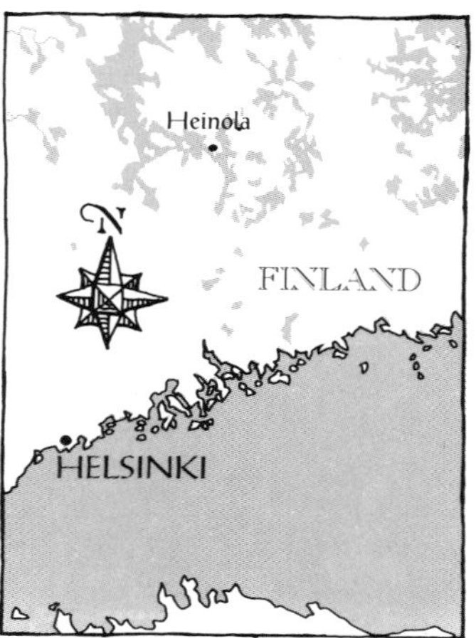

***As two women** prepared to enter an elevator in a block of flats in Helsinki on April 19 1957, a man standing nearby said, "After you, please," and followed them in. They recognized him as Dr Juho Kusti Paasikivi* (below), *Prime Minister of Finland until his death four months earlier. Although no-one pressed the button, the lift stopped. As "Passikivi" left the lift, he said, "Ladies, you will certainly wonder why I am here when I should be in a grave," but he offered no explanation.*

THE IMJARVI UFO

UFO and allied experiences vary greatly; those which include visitations by strange creatures or humanoids are usually treated with considerable derision. However, a description of an encounter reported from Imjarvi, 9½ miles (15km) from Heinola, in southern Finland, in 1970 does include certain interesting circumstantial details.

The report came from a woodman, Aarno Heinonen, and a farmer, Esko Viljo, who were skiing, and were resting in a clearing in woods when they heard a buzzing noise and saw a strong light moving in the sky. It approached the clearing, and descended, surrounded by a luminous red-grey mist. They eventually saw a round metallic object about 10 foot (3m) in circumference and flat at the bottom, at the centre of the cloud of light.

A disc now descended from the craft, and stopped at a height of about 10 foot (3m) from the ground, a strong beam of light shining from a tube at the centre of its bottom. In this light the two men saw a creature standing, holding a black box in its arms from which a yellow pulsating light shone. The spaceman was about 30 feet (9m) tall, human in shape but with very thin arms and legs. It had a hook-like nose, and small pointed ears. It wore light green clothing, boots of darker green and white gauntlets. Viljo remembered a conical helmet. The creature now directed the light from the box at the two men, who found themselves enveloped in a mist thick enough to hide them from each other. The fog eventually vanished – "torn apart," was how the men put it – and the UFO itself could no longer be seen.

The men were intensely uneasy, the more so when Heinonen, attempting to move, collapsed and found that his right leg was apparently paralysed. Viljo half-carried him to his home, 2 miles (3km) away.

Heinonen now suffered from violent headaches and pains in the head and neck; his urine was black, and continued to be so for over two months. A local physician, Dr Pauli Kajanoja, who examined both men, believed they were severely shocked, and the symptoms seemed to him characteristic of exposure to radioactivity, although he could not prove this.

On the day – January 7 – on which the men had their experience, there were independent reports of a light in the sky from the area around Imjarvi. Heinonen subsequently claimed several more encounters with UFOs. Independent investigators tend to believe that he was suffering from a psychological disorder; but prior to the first encounter both men had been extremely rational, even somewhat unimaginative, and their circumstantial account carries considerable weight. A local boy later confessed that in February 1969 he had seen a bright light, like that of a welding-torch, in the sky very near the spot where Viljo and Heinonen had had their encounter. He had said nothing about it for fear of being ridiculed.

SCANDINAVIA

NORWAY: SEA SNAKES

The existence of giant *Lindorns*, or sea snakes, in the lakes of Norway was probably first proposed in prehistoric times – Bronze-age razors have been found with carvings of a strange snake with a horse-like head, while in the 19th century, Klovevatn, a tiny lake on Hareidland, a mountainous island off the west coast, was said to contain a large *Nykk*, or water spirit, which had made a huge gap in one of the island's crags.

The *Lindorn* has from time to time been particularly described: it has a crown or ridge on its head, a ring about its neck, pointed ears and a horse-like mane. It can lurk beneath mountains – or even climb over them (according to tradition, there is a mountain range on the north shore of an enormous *Lindorn* which has coiled itself there to protect the lost treasure of Norway).

Lindorns usually live in lakes – one had its lair in Lake Varejell, near Molde, whence it emerged to pounce on the local cows, which it swallowed whole. More ordinary sea serpents have been seen from time to time off the coasts of Norway.

The Bride & The Lindorm

There has generally been a strong belief in Norway that sea serpents originate inland; in 1752 Erik Pontoppidan, Bishop of Bergen, published a treatise in which he argued that "sea serpents are not generated in the sea, but on land, and when they are grown so big that they cannot move about on the rocks, they then go into the sea and afterwards attain their full growth."

The bishop had personally spoken to many farmers about their sightings of land snakes several fathoms in length, "which they call the *Lindornen*, or great snakes", and also about "water snakes many fathoms long, particularly in Lake Mjosen or Mjosa in Hedemarken, which are strong enough to upset a boat."

The Swedish folklorist Gunnar Olaf Hylten-Cavallius organized a hunt for a specimen during the last half of the 19th century, but without result (despite the offer of a large reward). There have been random sightings since – the most recent ones during the 1930s at Lake Storsjon; but no photographs have ever been taken, nor a monster caught.

SWEDEN: VOICES FROM THE AIR

In 1962, Dr Hans Bender of the University of Freiburg, in Germany, led a team of scientists in investigating a strange phenomenon – the appearance on recording tape of voices apparently from nowhere, unconnected with the recordings being made.

Jochem Sotscheck of the Central Office for Telegraphic Technology at Berlin, analysed several tapes which allegedly bore "psychic voices", and, together with other notable scientists, reached the conclusion that there was no rational explanation for their presence on the recordings.

LAKE MONSTERS

Lake Storsjön (right) in Sweden may harbour a monster comparable to that of Loch Ness, but with a longer history. In the 1890s Dr Peter Olsen, a zoologist, collected 22 reports of sightings since 1820. At the same time, a company built a trap for the monster, baited it with live piglets, and hired a Norwegian harpoonist to shoot the monster on appearance. There was no such appearance, but sightings are still being reported. According to legend, the rune stone (far right) on Froson Island in Lake Storsjön binds the monster in the lake until someone is able to decipher the inscription.

Similar phenomena were first reported in 1959 by Friedrich Jurgenson, a Swedish painter and film producer, when a tape on which he had recorded bird-song suddenly produced strange voices, speaking in Norwegian. In 1964 Dr Bender led a team of psychologists to meet Jurgenson and attempt to capture more voices from the air. Tape-recorders were set up in the usual way, using new tape. During recording no sounds were heard – and the participants were careful not even to move their own lips while the machines were running. When the tapes were replayed, faint voices were heard against the white noise background.

The words spoken by the voices appeared usually to have some connection with the people present. For example, on one occasion the word "Rasmus" was clearly heard – and Dr Bender later stated that at the time he had been thinking of a friend of his, Brigette Rasmus (unknown to anyone else present). Voice analysis showed that the voice pronouncing her name had no resemblance to Bender's. When, on a later occasion, the team got lost on its way to Jurgenson's family house, one of the scientists – called Gisela – developed bad toothache. At his home, Jurgenson had himself set up a recording session, and was startled (on playing the tape back) to hear the words "*Sie kommen bald. Zahnarzt. Zahnarzt*" ("They will arrive soon. Dentist. Dentist.") On its arrival, the team heard the tape and certified it.

Thoughts may be transferred to tape, *according to a number of scientists, such as Dr Hans Bender* (right), *who led a team in 1964 to discover the source of inexplicable voices captured while recording other matter entirely.*

The image of a giant sea snake *or* Lindorn *has become firmly embedded in the Norwegian consciousness. Although it has never been photographed, many artists have depicted it* (opposite page), *often inspired by witnesses' descriptions.*

Experimenters have of course examined the possibility that the recording machines might have been picking up radio transmissions, and have been able to dismiss it. Such experiments were mounted in England in March 1971, at the laboratories of Belling & Lee Ltd, which test British electronic defence equipment. The physicist and electronics engineer Peter Hale concluded "I cannot explain what happened in normal physical terms."

The messages on the tapes seem almost invariably to record the thoughts of the people engaged in the experiment – although often in an ungrammatical mixture of languages. Dr Konstantin Raudive, a Latvian living in Bad Krozingen, has recorded more than 100,000 phrases in a mixture of Swedish, Russian, German and his native dialect of Latvian. Similar words and phrases have been recorded in various parts of the world – and in aircraft far above the earth's surface.

Denmark: UFO Sightings

One of the more convincing recent sightings of a UFO in Europe was reported by a police officer in Denmark in 1970.

On Thursday evening, August 13, Evald Hansen Maarup was driving home in his police car when a strange light surrounded it, and all its electrics (including the police radio) ceased to work. The officer stopped his car. He then noticed the temperature inside it was rising steeply, although not uncomfortably.

The light outside, which was bright but cold (like that of neon lights) was dazzling, and Maarup now saw that it seemed to emanate from "a big grey thing" about 33 feet (10m) in diameter and about 66 feet (20m) above him. The officer got out of his car and saw the last of the light disappear into a hole about 3 feet (1m) in diameter. The object then began to rise, and accelerating swiftly, vanished within a few seconds. The radio now worked normally, and he reported the incident to his station at 10.50pm.

Maarup had taken several photographs with the police car's fixed cameras. When these were developed and analysed by the police laboratories, they showed a cone of light consistent with his description. The Defence Command at Vedbaek announced that what Maarup had seen had been the landing of a T-33 jet trainer. Maarup retorted that he had seen the lights of an aircraft 10 minutes after the phenomenon had occurred, and the two were not to be confused.

An Air Force Press Officer, confessed that while the Air Force did not recognize the existence of UFOs, a number of reports had been received over the years, which could not be explained. Some time later, the wife of an Air Force radar operator told the press that on the night of the sighting, a UFO had been officially tracked over a very long period.

The Netherlands

The Psychic Detectives

In various parts of the world, psychics have attempted to help the police detect criminals. Two of the best-known "psychic detectives" were Dutch.

Gerard Croiset was born in 1909, and had a deprived childhood and a disturbed adolescence. During the 1930s he discovered a talent for clairvoyance, and after the Second World War he was taken up by Willem Tenhaeff, a lecturer in parapsychology at the University of Utrecht, and later Director of its Parapsychology Institute. Croiset's talents were considerable, and his reputation led to his being invited by several police departments to help with insoluble crimes.

Several of his successes seem questionable, and it has been alleged that Tenhaeff exaggerated; but some are impressive to the most critical observer. For example, in 1961 he was asked by an official of KLM, the Dutch airline, to look into the disappearance in Brooklyn, New York, of a four-year-old child. Immediately, on the telephone from Holland, Croiset asserted that the child was dead, and began to describe a building in which her body would be found. He also described her murderer. When he received a photograph of the child and a piece of her clothing, he added some more details. Some hours after this, the police (not acting on his advice) found the little girl's body and arrested and charged a man who was subsequently convicted of her murder. There were several parallels between the actual events and Croiset's words. In general, despite his getting several facts wrong, he was more often accurate than not in his descriptions of the place where a body would be hidden, and of the murderer.

Peter Hurkos was a building worker whose psychic abilities apparently surfaced after he fell from the fourth storey of a building. In 1947, he allegedly helped Dutch police to identify a murderer in Limburg. He offered advice on the identity of the Boston strangler – tracing him, psychically, to a man whom the police arrested, but who voluntarily committed himself to a mental institution, so making it impossible to try him for murder. His appearance, home and behaviour precisely matched Hurkos' description. Later another man confessed to the Boston murders, although Hurkos always insisted that he had pointed to the real killer.

Gerard Croiset (above) *has been called the "psychic detective" for his allegedly amazing clairvoyant powers. Since his first successful "discovery" of the whereabouts of the missing daughter of a Kansas professor in 1959, Croiset has often helped the police with their inquiries by utilizing his psychic powers.*

For the Dutch magician Chandou (left), *riding a bicycle blindfold through city streets was easy. After spending years with Indonesian yogis, Chandou appeared able to impress even the most sceptical Westerners with his "radar fingers", which could apparently read letters or documents when he was blindfolded. But he could not "see" with them in the dark, claiming he needed light like ordinary people.*

FRANCE

LOURDES

It was on Thursday, February 11 1858 that a simple 14-year-old peasant girl, Bernadette Soubirous, went to collect firewood in open countryside just outside the small village of Lourdes, in the foothills of the Pyrenees.

The two children who accompanied her went on ahead; and shortly after they had parted, Bernadette saw a vision of a young woman, veiled, in a white gown with a blue edge, her hair falling about her shoulders. Bernadette's companions, looking back, saw the child on her knees but did not see the vision. She told them about it, and later told her confessor. She claimed to have seen the same woman again, no less than 18 times; and asking who she was, was told "I am the Immaculate Conception" – a phrase unfamiliar to the young girl, but which impressed investigating priests. Clearly, Bernadette had seen the Virgin Mary.

The miracles said to have accompanied the vision were impressive: a stream of clear water sprang from the ground where Bernadette was told to scratch the earth; a candle-flame failed to injure her hand. Later, when news of the vision had spread, a farmer brought his paralytic son to the stream; plunged into it, the boy stood up and walked.

Lourdes became the most famous healing-place in the Christian world; a commission of clerics set up by the Bishop of Tarbes claimed that "the Apparition bears every mark of truth and that the faithful are justified in believing it as certain." A bath-house was built at the spring, and special trains were shortly bringing invalids who believed that the water could cure them.

There can be little doubt that certain illnesses have been cured at Lourdes. The question is, are the cures miraculous? The water, when analysed, proves to have no special qualities. Some cures are so clearly psychosomatic (they are no less cures for that, of course) that supernatural intervention need not be considered. However, some seem on the face of it to meet the rigorous conditions, laid down by Pope Benedict XIV, which must be satisfied in such cases before a cure can

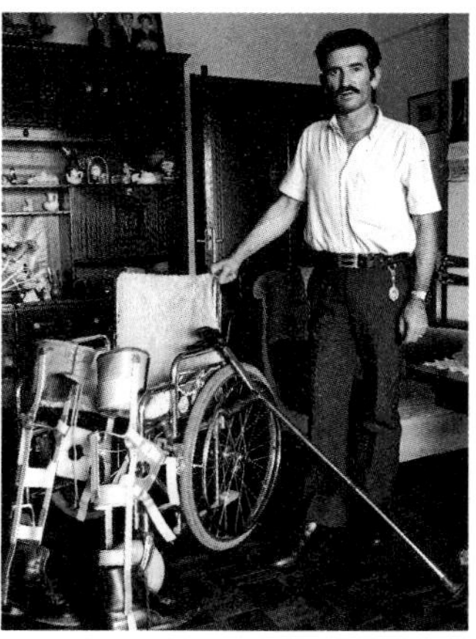

qualify as miraculous: the illness cured must be serious, and impossible, or at least very difficult, to cure; it should not already be on the decline when the cure takes place; no medication should have been given; the cure should be sudden – instantaneous – and complete, and should not correspond to a crisis brought about by natural causes; and the illness should not recur.

In 1957 Dr D. J. West made a study of 11 cures effected between 1946 and 1955 that seemed to fulfil the criteria. He concluded that it was impossible to establish that they were truly miraculous: in particular, the case-histories were all inadequate, there was no experimental control of the situation and all the illnesses described had, in other circumstances and in other subjects, responded at least temporarily to psychosomatic suggestion.

No cure recorded at Lourdes will satisfy the strict criteria of unbelievers. However, the place is still regarded as holy by many Christians, and pilgrimages continue to bring the sick from all over Europe to take the waters there. That Bernadette existed is beyond question. She had no other visions. But after all, one had been enough.

The *Grimoires*

Three French *Grimoires*, or books of magic, sum up the knowledge of the subject gathered together by magicians between the 16th and 18th centuries. The *Grand Grimoire* was printed in the 17th century, and contains "the Infernal Devices of the great Agrippa for the Discovery of all Hidden Treasures and the Subjugation of every Denomination of Spirits, together with an Abridgement of all the Magical Arts." From it, one can learn how to make a pact with the Devil, and how to control minor devils by using the Dreadful Blasting Rod. *The Grimoire of Honorius the Great*, dating from the late 16th century, is full of prayers to raise the Devil; *The Arbatel of Magic* (1575) tells how to summon the seven Olympic Spirits which rule the planets, how to gain a fortune, and how to prolong life.

These books are almost all based on *The Key of Solomon*, a book which took its title from the words of Jesus to St Peter: "I will give you the keys of the kingdom of Heaven, and whatever you bind on earth shall be bound in heaven." This book exists in manuscript in various parts of the world but it is very rare in printed form.

King Solomon was reputedly a great magician – the *Key* dating from AD 200 or thereabouts) gives a long list of demons which were under his control, and it is from them that he gained some of his knowledge of magic.

The *Grimoires* were not popular with the Catholic Church; Pope Innocent VI was only one of its leaders who attempted to suppress them, ordering the 1350 edition of *The Key of Solomon* to be burned. But there were too many manuscript copies about for the Church to be able to burn them all.

The Ghosts of Versailles

The strange adventure experienced by two tourists who visited Versailles in 1901 is one of the most gripping of all ghost stories.

It concerns two Englishwomen, Miss C. A. E. Moberly, daughter of a Bishop of Salisbury and later principal of St Hugh's College, Oxford, and Miss Jourdain, daughter of a Derbyshire vicar, who succeeded her friend at St Hugh's. They were on holiday in Paris and, having decided to spend a

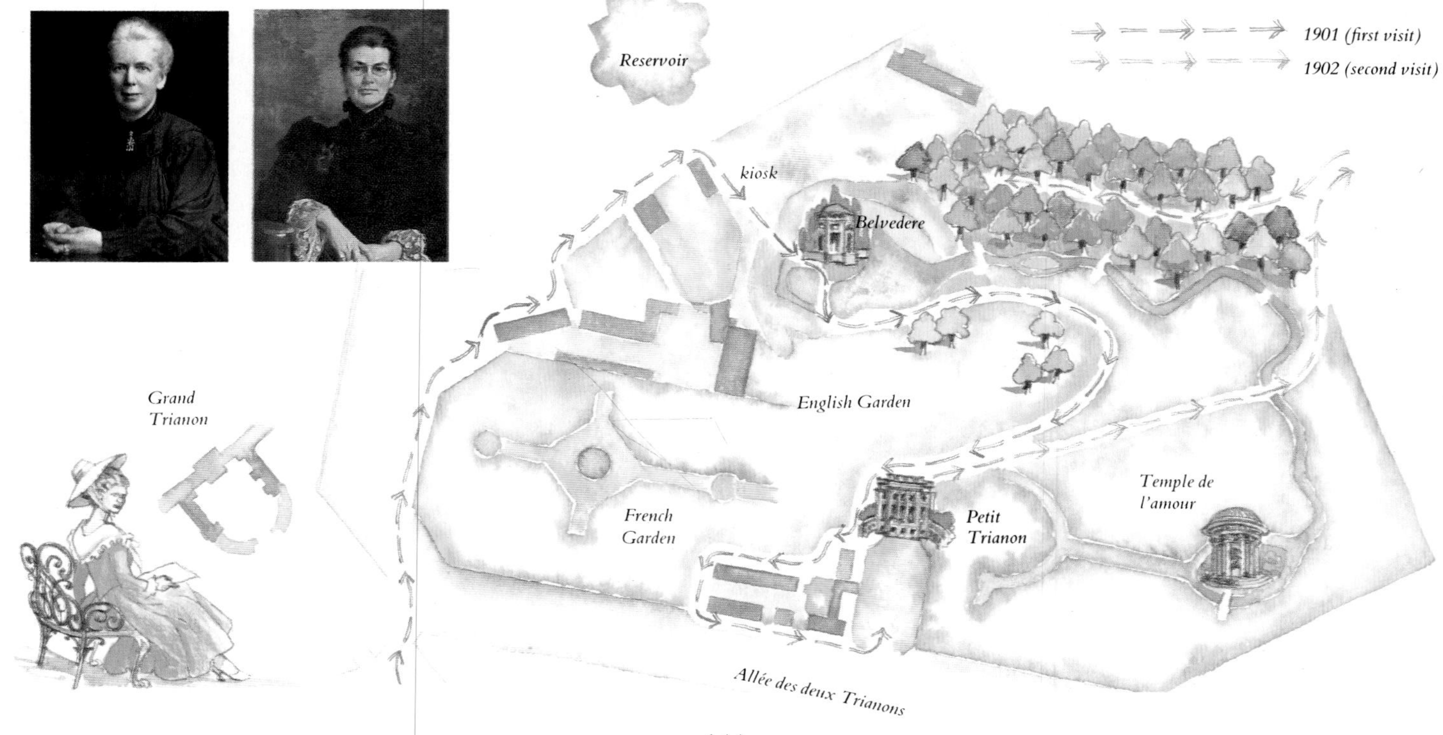

Jose Gabriel (*page 143*, above) *discarded his wheelchair after visiting Lourdes, half-cured by its miraculous atmosphere. Lourdes attracts* ***many chronic invalids,*** (*page 143*, below) *hoping for a cure.*

A view from the orangery *at Versailles* (below), *as it was in the 18th century, shown here in an original engraving.*

On the map of the Trianons (opposite) *the path of Miss Jourdain, left, and Miss Moberley, right, on their 1901 visit, when they might have seen 18th century figures, is marked in red; that by Miss Jourdain alone in 1902, in mauve.*

They became convinced that they had travelled back in time and visited Versailles not as it was in 1901, but as it had been in a previous century. After ten years of research, they published (under noms-de-plume) a book (*An Adventure*, 1911) about their experiences, identifying some of the characters they saw as persons well-known about the court, not doubting that the woman in the *fichu* was Queen Marie Antoinette.

Mapping out the route they claimed to have taken, it was found that it would have meant their passing through a

day at Versailles, set out to visit the Petit Trianon. The date was August 10: the anniversary of the sacking of the Tuileries in 1792. When they reached the Grand Trianon they did not turn right along the Allée des deux Trianons but, in error, crossed it and entered the gardens. Lost, they asked the way of two men in what seemed rather old-fashioned dress, including tricorn hats. These men, apparently gardeners, told them to go straight on across the French Garden. Had they done so they would have reached the Petit Trianon, but they bore to the left. A short time later they passed a repulsive-looking man in a slouch hat and cloak sitting on the balustrade of a circular kiosk, were given direction by a man who insisted they should go to the right, and crossed a little rustic bridge. On a seat on the edge of the English Garden, Miss Moberly saw a woman in a pale green fichu bodice. Ater receiving further directions, they reached the Petit Trianon.

The two women felt that something strange had happened to them. On two subsequent visits to Versailles they saw both people and things which seemed insubstantial, and vanished when approached. Buildings which they had seen on the first occasion had now disappeared, and the landscape was often different (where the woman in the *fichu* had been sitting there was now a large rhododendron bush). They said they had actually conversed with some of the men in old-fashioned clothes, and were struck by their curious accents.

number of solid brick walls (erected since the 18th century). But the landscape conformed to accounts of the gardens of Versailles as they were in earlier centuries.

The women's account of their adventure has been examined time and time again, not only by parapsychologists but by historians with detailed knowledge of Versailles in that period. There seem to be elements which are inexplicable except in terms of the paranormal. Comparing their descriptions of the grounds with historical records, it has been concluded that their time-visit took them to Versailles as it was in about 1770: the small kiosk which they described was discovered on an old map, but had been demolished by 1800. No less than 20 other features described by the ladies were found to apply to the Versailles of 1770, but not to the modern buildings or grounds.

Other people have had somewhat similar experiences at Versailles: a Mr and Mrs Crooke and their son Stephen, saw the supposed Marie Antoinette at about the same time as Miss Jourdain and Miss Moberly. In 1928, Miss Clare M. Burrow, a teacher in a girls' school in Haslemere, and her companion, saw a number of people in old-fashioned dress, and later, reading *An Adventure*, realized they had shared the authors' experience. There have been other accounts.

No one has yet succeeded in explaining away the whole experience.

Germany

Willy Schneider

Germany, and especially Munich, was an important centre for the investigation of mediums and other parapsychological phenomena. One of the most notable mediums of the years between the two World Wars was the Austrian-born Willy Schneider, who began to make an impression on parapsychologists in 1922, when he was 18.

Schneider was discovered as a medium in 1921 by Baron Albert von Schrenck-Notzing, a particularly thorough investigator of the paranormal, who in 1922 invited Erik J. Dingwall, a member of the English Society for Psychical Research, to travel to Munich to observe some of his tests.

Dingwall was impressed: tables tilted and levitated, and handkerchiefs appeared to be manipulated by invisible hands. "However monstrous these phenomena may appear to those persons who are not acquainted with the mass of evidence now adduced in support of their reality," he wrote in a report, "to ignore them is impossible for the scientific man."

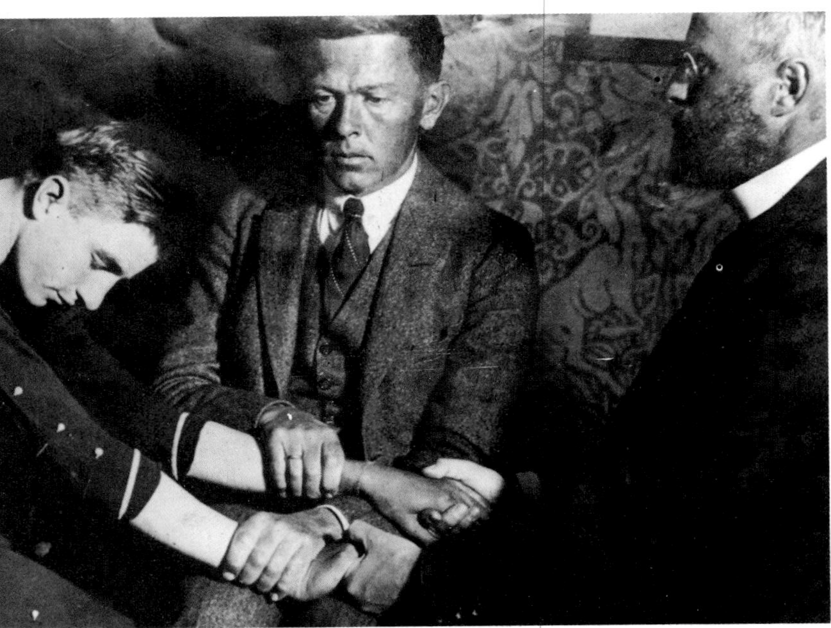

Willy Schneider (above) *often performed seemingly amazing feats of telekinesis while his hands were firmly held by witnesses.*

A thorough investigator of the paranormal, *Baron Albert von Schrenck-Notzing,* (left, bearded) *found no reason to suspect Schneider of deception. Schrenck-Notzing is shown here with Charles Richet, a parapsychologist who also investigated cases of apparently paranormal incidents.*

A vivid description of Schneider is given by a more distinguished observer – prize-winning writer Thomas Mann. Mann was invited to a seance with Schneider, and on the following day sent Schrenck his account of it, published many years later in the English magazine *Encounter*.

Schneider was stripped to the skin before being dressed in tights and then held hand and foot. Mann clearly saw a handkerchief lift itself into the air, violently manipulated from within by a concealed hand – then "an indefinable something, which had not been among the objects on the floor, arose from the same place as the handkerchief. More or less shapeless, it seemed to be some 20 inches (51cm) long and might have been taken for part of a forearm with the prehensile organ belonging to it (the suggestion of a closed hand)." Then a bell rose from the floor and violently rang itself before being flung to the ground beneath the chair of one of the witnesses.

"Any thought of a swindle in the sense of a conjuring trick is absurd," Mann concluded. "There was simply no one there who could have rung the bell. Willy [Schneider] could not have done it, because his extremities were being held, and besides, he was five feet away, sunk in magnetic sleep. Who, or what, lifted the handkerchief and squeezed it from inside?"

Willy Schneider was never detected in fraud; Schrenck-Notzing was generally agreed to be beyond suspicion.

Witchcraft

Witchcraft trials took place in most European countries during the 16th and 17th centuries, and so-called witches – often harmless old men and women merely practising country skills of healing – were persecuted and burned. In Germany the persecution of witches assumed giant proportions: more than 100,000 men and women were tortured and burned.

In some countries, the law – although forced by fear to conform to inquisitors' demands that witches should be hunted out – modified the cruel treatment laid down; but in Germany it was rigorously applied: suspected witches were tortured by every recommended means (including the gouging out of eyes, cutting off of ears and hands, flogging, and finally disembowelling and burning) in order to make them confess.

One very common means to discover a witch was by thrusting a pin into the flesh: if the person felt no pain, then witchcraft was likely. Witch-hunters soon became adept at seeking out those parts of the body – well known to modern acupunturists – where the senses are not very acute.

Witch trials took all too predictable a form. The victims, sometimes betrayed by members of their family, under duress signed a formal confession, the terms of which were laid down by the inquisitors. Children were particularly active in denouncing their seniors (as at Salem, in the United States); they accused each other, too, and seemed to derive much enjoyment from the trials which followed.

Fear of the supernatural (like unquestioning faith in it) is always dangerous, and some people were quick to realize that a considerable profit could be made by playing upon it. Jakob Bithner, an official of the Austrian province of Styria in the 17th century, collected witches on a wholesale basis, and then handed them over to the official inquisitors – for payment in cash. Another official, at Lindenheim, offered the same service until outraged public opinion was turned against him, forcing him to flee.

It was remarkably difficult to stem the tide of violent hysteria which flowed through Germany in the troubled 17th century. High officials who showed any leniency were denounced and hounded from office – such as Vice-Chancellor Hahn of Bamber, forced to resign because he was too merciful to the victims of persecution and attempted to protect some of the accused.

FAITH HEALING

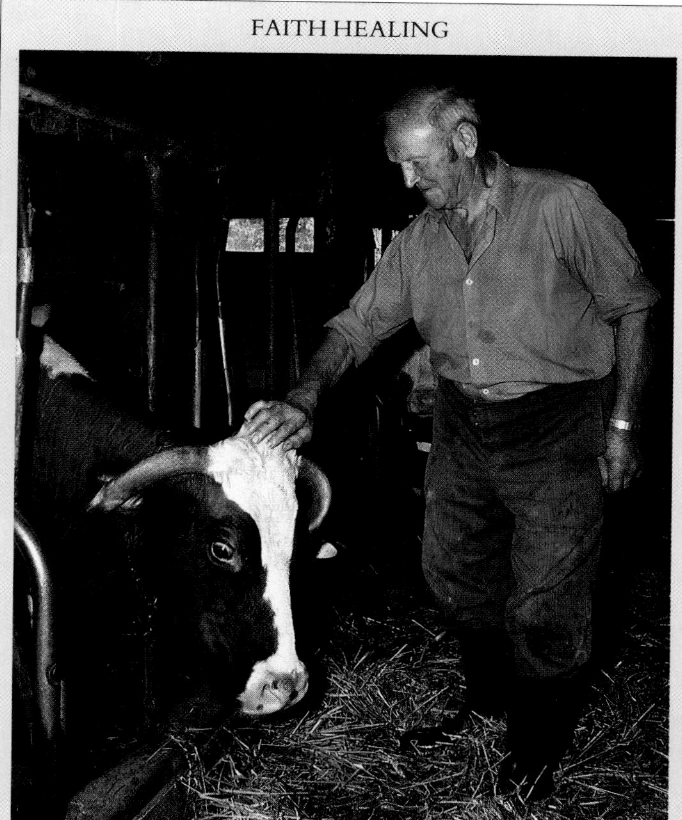

Faith-healing flourishes in modern Germany. Animals as well as humans can be treated, as Herr H. demonstrates with a cow afflicted with a growth (above). From his human patients, suffering from warts, ringworm or other skin complaints, Herr H. demands real faith. He recites the Lord's Prayer up to 18 or 21 times each time he lays hands on the sick person. Two or three visits are usually needed and they must be at the right time for the illness concerned. Between 11 and 12 o'clock in the morning for warts, but only on Fridays, ideally when the moon is waning. Such "white magic" seems to depend on a positive response from the patient. Herr H. will not treat sceptics or scoffers.

If the tide was stemmed by any one man, it was by the Jesuit Father Friedrich von Spee, who became convinced that the wholesale persecution was unjust, and went so far as to publish a book denouncing it. But it was too late to help the 100,000 men and women who had perished by 1775, when the last witch was executed.

The Lauter Poltergeist

At the end of the Second World War, Carola Schrey and her husband fostered two orphans, the 13-year-old Irma and a younger girl, Edith. The family lived in a small flat in the Bavarian village of Lauter.

In the summer of 1946 the formerly placid Edith showed signs of violent temper, and when taxed with her tantrums attributed them to "Ditti". Ditti was her own nickname. She began to fall into trance states. Shortly afterwards, Irma – hitherto withdrawn and quiet – showed the same signs of disturbance. Excrement and urine, not traceable to the girls, next started to manifest themselves in the apartment, and objects began to fly about and self-destruct; food sprang out of cooking pans; Mrs Schrey's typewriter typed incomprehensible messages to itself while locked in its case.

When Irma was attacked by invisible agencies, her hair hacked and her skull injured, Hans Bender, of the Institute for Border Areas of Psychology and Mental Hygiene (see p.140) was summoned. He was convinced that the disturbances were real and thought that they originated in Irma's jealousy of Edith. But there was no evidence at all that Irma had been physically responsible for the poltergeist activity, which eventually ceased of its own accord. Shortly afterwards, the Plachs, an elderly couple in the village of Vachendorf, not far away, were playing cards with their 14-year-old adopted daughter Mitzi when the cards began vanishing from their hands. By the end of the evening, only 19 remained in the pack. Later that night all sorts of household things apparently threw themselves about. When the Plachs tried to leave their bedroom, they found the door locked on the outside. Neighbours who broke down the door found the key hanging from a clock in the neighbouring room.

The phenomena continued: even when objects which had been flying about were captured and locked in a box, the box flew open and the aerial flights continued. Hans Bender also examined this case. In his presence, a heavy wooden shoe kept inside a glass case flew across the room and struck Franz Plach on the head.

In this case an adolescent girl again lived in the family, but here there was no evidence that Mitzi was at all unhappy or disturbed. Once more, the phenomena ceased in due course.

Switzerland

Carl G. Jung

Switzerland, that most sensible and prosaic of countries, produced the man whose adventurous mind and infinite capacity for exploring the strangeness of human existence opened many doors that his peers might have wished to remain closed.

Carl Gustav Jung (1875-1961) was a Swiss psychiatrist who, with his colleague (later his rival) the Austrian Sigmund Freud (1856-1939), pioneered the 20th-century exploration of the human mind. Interestingly, Jung came to psychiatry through what seems to have been an inherited interest in the paranormal – both his mother and grandmother were deeply interested in the subject, and the ability of a cousin to enter trances during which she apparently conversed with spirits interested Jung so much that he engaged in a study of her and her circle which ultimately led him to a career in psychiatry.

Freud publicly disagreed with Jung on the subject, but secretly he too was interested. He is said to have exclaimed, late in life, that were he to have his life over again, he would devote it to a study of the psychic.

Freud's interest may perhaps have dated from the day in 1909 when the two men were discussing the paranormal, and Freud was, as usual, debunking it. Jung suddenly felt a premonition that something strange was going to happen: and indeed, there was suddenly a loud and unexplained sound from a bookcase next to them. Jung claimed it was a psychic manifestation. "Nonsense", said Freud. "Not at all", said Jung – and moreover, it would happen again: upon which there was a second detonation.

Freud was shaken but not converted; Jung persisted in his interest, although he was at first cautious in expressing it. ("There are things," he said, "which are simply incomprehensible to the tough brains of our race and time. One simply risks being taken for crazy and insincere, and I have received so much of the other that I have learned to be careful in keeping quiet.") Nevertheless, ten years later he sent a paper on the psychological background to a belief in spirits to a meeting of the Society for Psychical Research in England. In his autobiographical *Memories, Dreams, Reflections* he refers to his experiences of the paranormal – including the strange case of a knife which suddenly exploded in his kitchen.

Jung's work – especially in his theory of the collective unconscious – is essential reading for anyone interested in the paranormal. It was his conviction that many paranormal phenomena (not only psychical events, but predictive techniques such as the Tarot cards and the I Ching) could be explained by reference to the great well of human experience and knowledge which had built up over millennia, where the chief preoccupations of humanity were expressed in symbols that occur again and again in folklore and myth.

This, he thought, probably explained the "flying- saucer" craze: among the universal images or archetypes most influential on the mind of man is the mandala, a round disc particularly important in Buddhist and Hindu art, symbolizing the wholeness of the self. Jung believed that the "flying saucers" seen in the skies were really mandalas visualized by people with a deep inner longing for spirituality and peace.

Incident in the Alps

In the early 1920s two Englishmen, David and Eddie, attempted an assault on the 14,000 foot (4,270m) Finsteraarhorn, in the Bernese Alps, accompanied by a Swiss guide. Eddie disappeared during the night, and no trace could be found of him. David was forced to return to England, but promised to return to seek for his friend's body.

Almost a year later, the guide who had accompanied them was in the area where the incident had taken place. He clearly saw David, not far from the hut where they had spent the night, gesturing towards a crevasse. Next day, the crevasse was explored, and Eddie's body was found in it. Later, the guide heard that David had died, of blood poisoning, three days before Eddie's body was recovered.

Carl Gustav Jung (opposite), *the great psychologist, in the study of his tower at Bollingen, was the first important 20th-century scientist to examine the paranormal extensively. He created entirely new intellectual concepts for defining and understanding the supernatural; his theories of the Collective Unconscious, of Archetypes, of individuation and of synchronicity* *(see p.149)* *are invaluable to all who attempt to interpret or examine the supernatural. Jung himself had many personal experiences of the paranormal throughout his life.*

The Finsteraarhorn in the Bernese Oberland (left) *was the scene of a sighting of an Alpinist who had died only three days previously in England. Significantly, he was sighted by a Swiss guide just before the body of his companion, who had disappeared a year earlier while they were both attempting the 14,000 foot (4,270m) climb, was recovered from a crevasse.*

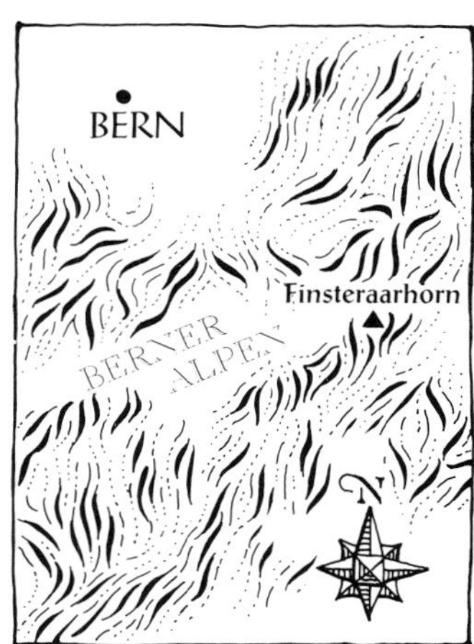

AUSTRIA

THE ORGONE BOX

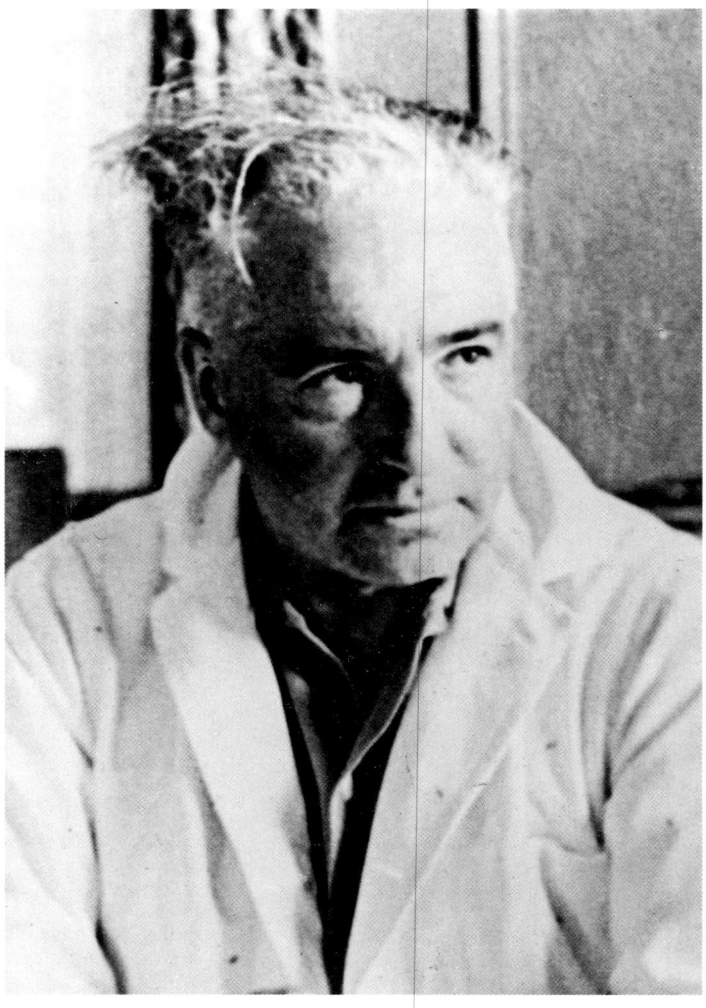

Wilhelm Reich (above) *was the century's greatest practitioner of sexual magic – although he termed it "orgone energy". Suppressing this natural energy could, he claimed, lead to all manner of ills, such as neurosis in individuals and social tensions and breakdowns in society. To release these psychosexual energies, he encouraged patients to sit in "orgone energy accumulators" – large upright boxes made of wood and metal. Reich's theories of "orgone energy" endeared him to some who saw him as a successor to the alchemists, but serious scientists regarded them as too weird to be taken seriously.*

One of the very few modern men to claim to have created life was the Austrian-born Wilhelm Reich (1897-1957), a conventionally trained scientist who studied medicine at Vienna University.

His main theme was that sexual energy was of vital importance not only to the creation of life but to its complete fulfilment and that sexuality was "the centre around which revolves the whole of social life as well as the inner life of the individual." He eventually concluded that almost all sickness – including psychological ailments such as schizophrenia and depression – was the result of failing to achieve "true orgasm": complete sexual satisfaction.

He was an important member of Freud's Psychoanalytic Society in Vienna, but later broke with Freud. In 1939, forced to leave Austria because of Nazi activity, he settled in New York. In 1935 he had announced that he had succeeded in producing what he called *bions* from certain substances (such as coal), and that these were capable of developing into protozoa (single-cell organisms). Biologists rejected this, but Reich worked on, and in 1939 announced that the radiation given out by bions produced from sterilized sea sand was a hitherto unknown form of energy, which he called *orgone*, and described as "the basic life-stuff of the universe."

In 1942 he founded the Orgone Institute, a centre for development of his theory that the lack of repeated discharge of this energy through "true orgasm" led to both individual and social neuroses. Reich claimed that orgone could be measured, collected in an "orgone box", and used for the treatment of serious diseases, including cancer. However, the United States Food and Drug Administration declared it a fraud and in 1956 he was sentenced to two years imprisonment for contempt of court and violation of the Food and Drug Act: he died in prison a year later.

THE WEIMAR POLTERGEIST

Poltergeist phenomena recorded at Hopfgarten near Weimar in 1921 are of special interest because the person in whose presence they centred was too weak, because of illness, to have been capable of producing them by other than psychic means.

Minna Sauerbrey was the second wife of a clockmaker, Ernst Sauerbrey, and in February 1921 was dying of cancer. She lay on a couch in the family kitchen so weak that she could not move or be moved. Suddenly, loud raps began to make themselves heard in the kitchen. Sometimes the noises were heard in several directions at once, and objects were seen to move away from Frau Sauerbrey – although they were already beyond her reach. The police were called in and saw several objects move, including a wash-basin. A clock stopped ticking and a dog in the room was terrified.

The police learned that Sauerbrey's son Otto, a hypnotist, had hypnotized his stepmother some time before, in order to alleviate the pain of her illness. They charged him with shortening her life by hypnosis (she died on March 27). He was acquitted. The poltergeists ceased their activity after Frau Sauerbrey's death.

ITALY

STIGMATA

***Stigmata 1-inch (2½cm) wide appeared on the hands** of 80-year-old former Roman florist Antonio Ruffini* (right). *He has been the focus of other paranormal events: on August 12 1951 he had a vision of the Virgin Mary. He has also experienced being in two places at once during sleep – for example, he has described the details of a journey he claims to have undertaken with missionaries to remote African regions. One of the missionaries confirmed that Ruffini always knew what had happened on their trips.*

Of all the examples of stigmata, or the replication on a living body of the wounds of Christ, those borne by the Italian priest Padre Pio are the best-known in modern times.

Padre Pio was born Francesco Forgione, in Pietrelcina, on May 25 1887. Naturally religious, he entered a monastery when he was 15, and became extremely ill because of his tenacious observation of long fasts. In 1910 he was ordained and entered the monastery of San Giovanni Rotondo in Foggia, where he remained for most of his life.

It was in 1918, after he had said mass at the monastery, that Christ is alleged to have appeared to him. Immediately afterwards Pio's hands, feet and chest began to bleed copiously. He attempted to conceal the wounds, but when they were noticed his superiors summoned a local doctor – the first of many to examine him, including Dr Luigi Romanelli, the chief of staff of the City Hospital of Barletta.

The agnostic theory about the formation of stigmatic wounds is that they are psychosomatic, and this is perhaps confirmed by the fact that the wounds generally conform to the vision of the crucified Christ as seen in religious paintings – that is, the wounds are in the palms of the hands and the soles of the feet, rather than in the wrists and ankles, as they were under the Roman form of crucifixion.

However, it is certainly true that in Padre Pio's case the wounds seem to have been particularly peculiar. For one thing, doctors agreed that they were not simply surface wounds – the hands were actually pierced; one could see through the wounds. (Dr Giorgio Festa, a Roman physician, testified in 1919 that "If I were to be interrogated by superior authorities on this particular question I would have to answer and confirm under oath, so much is the certitude of the impression received, that I would be able to read something or to see an object if it were placed behind the hand.") The feet also appeared to be completely pierced, although because of the thickness of the foot and the acute pain suffered, it was not possible to confirm this.

Many psychologists would argue that stigmata are produced as the result of trauma triggered by the contrast between the ideal religious life and the "sinful" life lived by the subject – the inability to conform to an idea of perfection. But even if this is the case, the physical manifestation of such cruel wounds remains unexplained.

Padre Pio's stigmata persisted until his death in 1968. It is also asserted that there are many examples of his bilocation – appearing in one place when he was clearly, physically, in

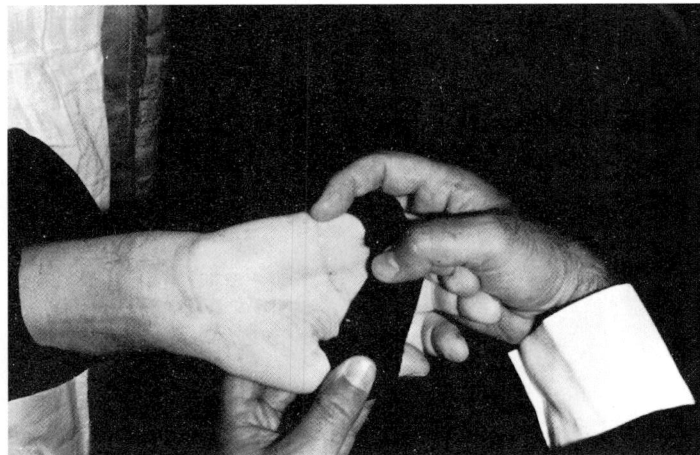

Padre Pio (near right) *remains the most famous of the men and women whose hands displayed the stigmata or marks similar to those traditionally made by the nails driven through the hands and feet of Christ. The bleeding was certainly genuine, if unexplained.* ***After his death the wounds*** (far right) *equally mysteriously disappeared, leaving no trace.*

another. One example of many on file at his monastery was the occasion in 1942 when Bishop Alfredo Viola of Salto celebrated his silver sacerdotal jubilee in Uruguay. On the night of the celebrations, the Archbishop of Montevideo, who attended, was awakened by a figure which knocked on his door and said "Go to the room of Monsignor Damiani; he is dying." When the Archbishop reached the priest's room he found him extremely ill (he later died, of angina pectoris). On his bedside table was a note in Damiani's handwriting: "Padre Pio came." In 1949, the Archbishop travelled to Foggia and had an audience with Padre Pio, who tacitly confirmed his visit to Uruguay, although in fact he never corporeally left his native Italy.

The Blood of St Januarius

St Januarius was Bishop of Benevento 300 years after the death of Christ and was martyred by the Romans. Early in the 5th century, the cathedral of Naples obtained his relics – his skull, and two phials supposedly containing his blood. The blood is claimed to liquefy every year at the time of his feasts (on September 19 and December 16) – sometimes positively foaming in the glass.

This phenomenon has been very thoroughly investigated in recent years, and there is no doubt that it does sometimes occur, although intermittently. When liquefaction does not take place the failure is invariably viewed by the faithful as the sign of divine wrath: in 1976, a severe earthquake struck the area after non-liquefaction. Sometimes the blood is already liquid when the case containing the phial is taken from its vault; sometimes liquefaction takes place in full view of a congregation, the clotted blood suddenly turning bright red and shining, with bubbles of gas appearing.

It has been claimed that the blood contains wax which reacts to heat, thus presenting the illusion of liquefaction: but there appears to be no correlation between the temperature in the cathedral and the speed of liquefaction (although both the bulk and weight of the blood in the phial seem to vary).

The relics are all contained in a silver and glass case which could not be opened without destroying them.

The Weeping Madonna

In Syracuse in 1953, Antonietta Januso, a pregnant woman, had a series of fainting fits after which she noticed that a plaster statue of the Madonna in her bedroom was weeping. The weeping Madonna became famous, and attracted pilgrims from all over the country.

Scientists analysed the liquid, and discovered that it was indistinguishable from human tears; the Vatican recognized the event as a genuine miracle and a shrine was set up to contain the statue, which is still venerated. No rational explanation has been found for the phenomenon.

The Shroud of Turin

In 1989, following carbon-dating tests, it was announced that the Shroud of Turin – the cloth appearing to bear the image of a crucified corpse – had been found not to be contemporary with the beginning of the Christian era, and could therefore not, as had been claimed, be the shroud in which Jesus Christ had been wrapped after his death. But the shroud is still one of the most mysterious objects in the world.

It was first put on display in 1353 as "the true burial sheet of Christ." It was a piece of linen, about 14 feet (4.26m) long and 3 feet (1m) wide, on which were two sketchy, brown images of a male body – as though a corpse had been laid on its back on the bottom half of the sheet which had then been folded over to cover its front, and the linen had somehow "photographed" the likeness of the body. The shroud attracted a great deal of attention, and some condemnation as a forgery. But it was preserved as a holy relic, and in 1578 was purchased by the Duke of Savoy and placed in Turin Cathedral.

In 1898 a photographer, Seconda Pia, was invited to photograph the shroud for the Cathedral records. On developing his plates, he found what seemed to be a portrait of a man – the image on the cloth had been a negative image, and his own negative turned it into a positive.

Was he looking at a photograph of Christ? Many people believed so. It had been possible, before, to believe that the shroud was a fake; but what 14th-century forger could have counterfeited a photographic negative? There were other

Photographic negatives of the image mysteriously displayed on the Turin shroud (left) *suggested that this was indeed the shroud that had enwrapped Christ. It has been revered as such since the 14th century. Serious tests on the cloth in the 1970s seemed to confirm its antiquity, but the results of carbon-dating tests announced in 1989 showed that it dated only from the 14th century. How the image became so deeply imprinted on the cloth remains a mystery. There is no evidence to suggest that it was painted, and artists claim that the kind of image shown would be extremely difficult to counterfeit.*

arguments for the shroud being genuine: not least that the marks of crucifixion were not – as many stigmata are – simply wounds at the centres of the feet and hands, but at the wrists and ankles, where the bodies of victims of Roman crucifixions were actually pierced by nails.

Photographers and students of anatomy were on the whole convinced that the shroud must be genuine. The closest examination could reveal no traces of paint on the linen, and the positions of apparent bloodstains and the characteristics of the wounds shown seemed absolutely accurate.

It was in the mid-1970s that serious tests began. Seventeen small samples of the shroud were removed for scientific examination. This revealed that the stains composing the figure were on one side of the cloth only: even separate threads were affected only on one side, so the cloth had not been soaked by body fluids or blood, or even by paint. Dust on the linen was analysed, and, amid much excitement, was found to contain grains of pollen which came from plants not only common to Jerusalem but to Istanbul and Urfa, suggesting that the shroud might indeed have originated in the Holy Land and travelled to Italy via what is now Turkey.

In 1976 two American scientists, a physicist (John Jackson) and a United States Air Force captain (Dr Eric Jumper), used image-enhancement to produce a three-dimensional image of the head portrayed on the shroud, and claimed not only to show that coins had been placed on the eyes in the tradition of biblical times, but that the coins had been leptons – those described in the New Testament as "the widow's mite."

Although there have been suggestions that anti-clerical scientists faked the carbon-dating results, it is now generally accepted that the shroud dates from long after the time of the crucifixion – probably from about the 14th century. What has not been determined is how the image was produced: the shroud still keeps its secret.

VISIONS OF THE VIRGIN MARY

There have been countless reports of visions of the Virgin Mary; some of the most famous are plotted below. Some people claim to have talked with her, others describe miraculous events supposed to have taken place in her presence.

Key

1 Bakerfield, California, USA, from 1984
2 Guadalupe, Mexico, 1560
3 Isabel, Texas, USA 1927
4 Cincinnati, Ohio, USA, from 1956
5 Robinsonville, Wisconsin, USA, 1859
6 Bayside, New York, USA, from 1968
7 Havana, Cuba, late 1970s
8 Saut d'Eau, Haiti, from c.1850
9 Knock, Co Mayo, Ireland, 1879
10 Llanthony, Wales, 1880
11 Walsingham, Norfolk, England, 1061
12 Fatima, Portugal, 1917
13 Garabandal, Spain 1961-5
14 Lourdes, France, 1858
15 Paris, France, 1830
16 Vorstenbosch, The Netherlands, 1947
17 Pontmain, France, 1871
18 Beauraing, Belgium, 1932
19 Kayl, Luxembourg, 1947
20 Neuholz, Alsace, 1871
21 Herodsbach-Thurn, Bavaria, 1949-52
22 Heede, West Germany, 1937-40
23 Grenoble, French Alps, 1664
24 Montichiari, Italy, 1947, 1951
25 Cefala Diana, Sicily, May 1967
26 Citluk, Yugoslavia, 1981
27 Hasnos, Hungary, 1949
28 Cluj, Romania, 1948
29 Rwanda, Africa, 1980-5
30 Cairo, Egypt, 1968-70
31 Grinkalnes, Lithuania, 1943
32 Grushevo, Ukraine, 1987
33 Beit Sahour, Jordan, 1983
34 Siberia, location unknown, 1958
35 Manila, Philippines, 1988

SPAIN

THE GARABANDAL VIRGIN

On Sunday, June 18 1961, after morning mass had been said in the small Spanish town of Garabandal, two children, Conchita, aged 12, and Mari Cruz Gonzalez, 11, were found by two friends, Loli Mazon and Jacinta Gonzalez (who were both 12) stealing apples from the schoolmaster's garden.

Having collected a good supply, they all left the garden, and then began picking up stones and throwing them toward their left-hand side (the side on which the devil is said to be found). Getting tired of this, they were sitting on the ground playing with pebbles, when Conchita saw "a very beautiful figure . . . shining brilliantly." She drew the other girls' attention to the figure, when they too saw it. According to Conchita, it wore a long, seamless blue robe, had fairly big pink wings, and looked about nine years old.

The children returned to the same spot the following day, when the figure reappeared. In church, they began to fall into trances, and on July 1 the angel told them that the Virgin would appear to them on the following day. Conchita recorded the Virgin's visit in her diary; an angel stood on each side of her, and on her right was a very large eye, which Conchita took to be the eye of God. The Virgin was very beautiful and she seemed to be about 18 years old.

The crowds which soon gathered at Garabandal were in no doubt of the reality of the girls' experience: they seemed to be able to communicate with each other even when separated by the press of people, and they walked backwards, arm in arm, along dangerous tracks where they might have been expected to fall. On July 18, Conchita fell to her knees in the street, and a luminous white host or communion wafer appeared out of thin air and placed itself on her tongue. This event was, by chance, filmed, and has remained inexplicable.

The girls are said to have had 2,000 visions. The Catholic church was unimpressed, and declined to give any weight to the manifestations. On June 18, the Virgin allegedly announced to Conchita that many cardinals, bishops and priests were "on the road to perdition", and, apparently piqued, vanished. A miracle has been promised, following a worldwide divine warning, which will convince mankind of the truth of the vision.

BELGIUM

There are two cases of visions of the Virgin Mary appearing in Belgium. The first occurred at Beauraing, 60 miles (96km) southeast of Brussels. The vision was seen by four girls and a boy, aged between nine and 15, who were members of the Voisin and Degeimbre families. On November 29 1932, Albert and Fernande Voisin and Andree and Gilberte Degeimbre went to collect Gilberte Voisin from her convent school. On the way, they visited a grotto set up by the convent nuns. Albert Voisin then claimed he saw the Blessed Virgin, dressed in white, walking along a viaduct above the grotto.

The news spread and 15,000 visitors gathered at Beauraing. Although the children claimed that the Virgin appeared, none of the crowd saw her. On January 2 Gilberte Voisin reported that the Blessed Virgin had said, "I am the Mother of God, the Queen of Heaven, Pray always, farewell." She was never seen again.

Twelve days later, a 12-year old girl, Mariette Beco, had a vision in Banneux, 50 miles (80 km) away. She saw a woman's figure moving about the garden of her house, beckoning to her. Formerly a truant from school and not especially religious, Mariette now began regular attendance at lessons and at church. She described seeing a figure wearing a halo standing on a cloud a little way above the ground who led Mariette to a spring near the house, which she said was "reserved for her". Mariette described the vision several more times, "seeing" it in the presence of a number of observers to whom the figure remained invisible.

FACES IN CONCRETE

One of the strangest occult manifestations in Europe during the past half-century took place in the 1970s in the small Spanish village of Belmez de la Moraleda.

One morning in August 1971, Maria Gomez Pereira went into her kitchen to find the likeness of a strange male face looking up at her from her concrete kitchen floor. It looked as though it was painted, but nothing would scratch the paint, which seemed an integral part of the concrete. A few other people saw the image, in the house in Rodriguez Acosta Street, before Senora Periera's son Miguel broke the floor up with a pickaxe – the family found the image disturbing. Fresh concrete was laid.

One week later, on September 8, the image was back, in exactly the same place. The news spread, and pilgrims began to travel to the village and the house – despite the fact that the face appeared to have no especially religious characteristics. This time, the family decided that the image must be

The strange faces (previous page) *that appeared on the concrete floor of a small Spanish village house defied both rational explanation and the most determined efforts to scrub them off. There were ultimately 18 of them. They slowly faded, reappeared and ultimately vanished. The house was built on the site of a disused cemetry.*

Despite careful examination by experts, *there has been no explanation as to the nature of the mysterious face which appeared upside down on the concrete floor of a small house in a little Spanish village* (right). *The face looked startled; then slowly faded away.*

preserved, and in November it was cut from the floor and mounted behind glass. When this had been done, the floor was excavated, and nine feet (2.7m) down some human bones were found (it was already known that the house, and others nearby, had been built on the site of a disused cemetry).

Professor Camon Aznar, an art expert from Madrid, examined the image, and described it as the portrait of a startled man, his lips slightly open; it was, he thought, a most delicate and subtle piece of portraiture.

To everyone's further astonishment the image's expression seemed to alter, subtly, from week to week – and then slowly began to decay. Meanwhile, another face had appeared on the floor, and a fortnight later, yet another. The parapsychologist German de Argumosa considered the faces excellent examples of paranormally produced art.

Within two years, no less than 18 faces were seen on the floor, some much smaller than others. One parapsychologist, a Professor Argumosa, claimed to have seen a face gradually appear – on April 9 1972 – and his statement was confirmed by two well-known Spanish journalists who were present. The face was photographed before it disappeared, later the same day. Argumosa, disturbed by growing rumours that the whole phenomenon was somehow faked, invited Professor Hans Bender, of Freiburg Institute in Germany, to visit Belmez de la Moraleda. In May 1972, after many interviews, Bender concluded that the faces were genuinely paranormal – and noted that the phenomena appeared to look different to different people. He attempted to remove the images by various means, including scrubbing with detergents, but failed. Many parapsychologists from all over Europe visited the house, and some recorded on tape strange cries and voices, and sobbing.

The images had more or less vanished by the end of the 1970s, reappearing in the mid-eighties, then vanishing again. No "rational" explanation appears to have been forthcoming.

Portugal

The Fatima Virgin

On May 13 1917 ten-year-old Lucia dos Santos and two younger cousins, Francisco and Jacinta, were looking after a flock of sheep in the Cova da Iria, a valley not far from the village of Fatima in central Portugal, when there was a flash of light and "a pretty little lady" was seen – by the two girls, but not by the boy – standing in the air above a tree.

She told the girls she came from heaven, and that they could meet her again in the same place on the 13th of every month. She eventually promised them a miracle on October 13 and on that day Lucia, in the presence of about 70,000 people, was told that the First World War would end that day. It did not. However, something else happened, which was witnessed by everyone present, including a large anti-clerical faction headed by Avelino de Almeida, editor of the atheistic journal *O Seculo*. The crowd saw the sun describe a series of small circles in the sky, spiralling down towards the earth; the phenomenon lasted for about eight minutes, after which the sun resumed its conventional position.

No explanation has ever been found for the sight, which caused a panic in the crowd. De Almeida, who had hoped to expose a fraud, wrote of the "sun's macabre dance". An independent witness, Alfonso Vieira, another writer, described it as he saw it from 20 miles (32 km) away – so he would not have been affected by any crowd hysteria or mass hallucination. Anti-clericals were furious with the children, who were treated with considerable cruelty by an atheistic local administrator.

During Salazar's dictatorship the climate changed: Lucia became a nun. In 1936 and 1941 she divulged details of other prophesies made by the Lady, but these were such that anyone might have made them. At her death she left an envelope allegedly containing another prophesy, but the Church has not revealed any clue as to its contents.

The events at Fatima are still regarded as miraculous: although why Our Lady should have relied upon a solar conjuring trick to convince a crowd of her reality has never been explained.

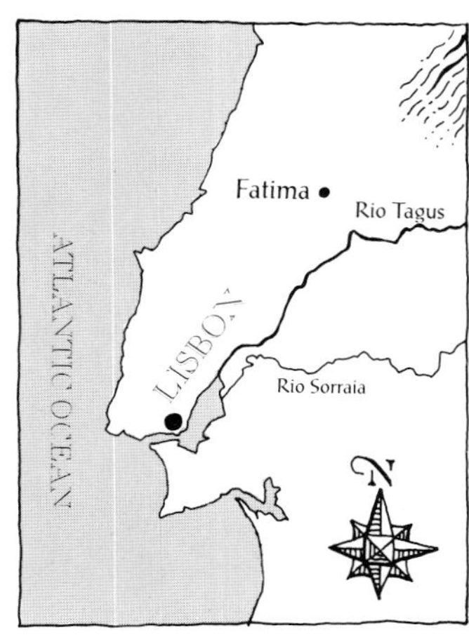

***Two young Portuguese children**, Lucia dos Santos and her cousin* (above), *claimed to have seen several visions of the Virgin in 1917, sometimes before huge crowds. Their village of Fatima has since become one of the greatest centres of Catholic pilgrimage.*

EASTERN EUROPE

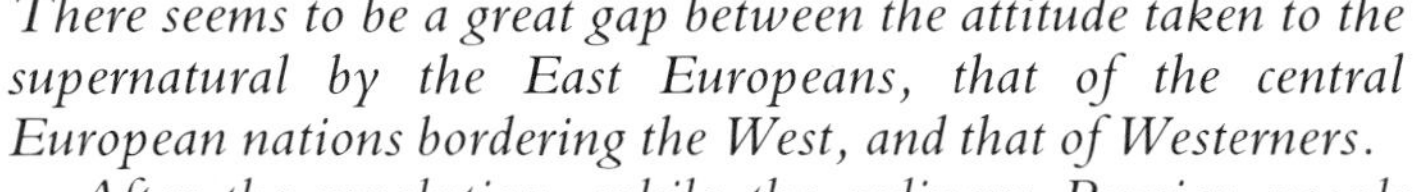

There seems to be a great gap between the attitude taken to the supernatural by the East Europeans, that of the central European nations bordering the West, and that of Westerners.

After the revolution, while the ordinary Russian people were content to treat the supernatural as a normal part of life, something which it is best to keep at a discreet distance; their scientists entirely neglected to examine it or even recognize that it existed. Although during the 1920s and 30s there were small pockets of scientific enquiry, these were unrecognized by official bodies, and some similar attempts to explore the unknown were positively repressed.

In the country mystery was still respected: there was a particularly strong tradition of charms and spells, and men and women with a talent for the dramatic had no difficulty in passing themselves off as healers. Sometimes, of course, they indeed had genuine healing talent; even where they did not, the belief of their "patients" often enabled them to heal themselves, the "healer" claiming the credit.

Some countries of central Europe have led the way in paranormal investigation: in Czechoslovakia, formal investigation into ESP was well under way in the early 1920s. Poland produced more successful mediums, between the two World Wars, than perhaps any other country in the world, and carefully examined their claims.

By contrast, the Soviets (at least until the last few years) have left "magic" to itself. This may be because the USSR has always been highly authoritarian, and the supernatural is by its nature not easily controlled: hypnosis, psychokinesis, or any means of influencing the mind, can be used against authority as well as by it and there is little doubt that one reason why those who experiment with the supernatural have not received official backing in the USSR is that its rulers are highly nervous of it. Other areas of the supernatural have been neglected for political reasons: the very idea that unidentified flying objects could have penetrated USSR defence systems was ludicrous; therefore they could not exist and there was no point in examining reported sightings.

Within the past few years the situation has been slowly changing. Although the official attitude to the supernatural and paranormal has remained the same, there has been an unmistakable if slow movement in the direction of toleration, or even genuine interest. Astrology has been examined (although less emotively described as cosmobiology); there have been quiet explorations of the land that lies between psychology and the occult; demonstrations of PK have been treated seriously, and the results of controlled experiments published (if, in the main, in somewhat obscure publications).

The rapid liberalization which has overtaken many areas of life in the Communist countries promises well for those interested in the occult: it seems very likely that much material until now severely restricted will, during the next few years, be made available for examination and discussion.

USSR

RASPUTIN

Russia has a rich tradition of legends and miracles. What might be called the superstitious tradition probably reached its apogee in the remarkable Gregory Efimovich Rasputin (1871-1916), an illiterate Siberian monk who claimed (without very much supporting evidence) supernatural powers. He attained a position of considerable power about the Russian court, chiefly because the Czarina (the wife of Nicholas II) believed he could cure her son of haemophilia. Politically ambitious and sexually insatiable, he was murdered by a group of nobles who found his political activities distasteful. He seems to have had hypnotic powers, and was considered a magician of sorts. He probably did more than any other single man to discredit serious study of the paranormal in Russia.

ESP

As early as 1926 a body was formed to look into extrasensory perception. Two years later its head, L. L. Vasiliev, travelled to France and Germany to talk with parapsychologists there; in 1932 he was encouraged to undertake an experiment in telepathy.

Among other tests, Vasiliev attempted to hypnotize people over a distance, and claimed to have put subjects into a trance, or awakened them from one, when he and they were more than 1000 miles apart. However, enthusiasm for Vasiliev's work was not forthcoming and his experiments were not particularly carefully monitored, nor as far as can be discovered were they ever followed up.

Since his death in 1966 there has been no news of formal Russian experiments in parapsychology, although Western literature on the subject is carefully studied in the USSR – and there have from time to time been eccentric episodes: in 1978 the exiled Russian chess master Victor Korchnoi claimed that Anatoly Karpov (against whom he was playing in the World Chess Championship) was using a hypnotist to damage his concentration. British observers believed that Russian chess masters were indeed instructed in ESP and hypnosis.

In the 1960s the Soviet astrophysicist Dr Nikolai Kozyrev originated a theory of time which he believed would begin to explain the nature of ESP. It involves a previously unknown form of energy which Kozyrev postulates as being denser near the receiver of (say) a psychically transmitted message, and thinner near the sender. He believes that this energy *is* time, and that the power of thought can physically affect it: his equipment has recorded changes which relate more strongly to emotional than to calculated thought, for example.

Telepathy, he hypothesizes, depends on the physical density of time, and those people who are particularly good at sending telepathic messages seem to have some way of (unconsciously) making time thin around themselves, and denser around the recipients of the messages. Kozyrev's theory is complex and speculative – but he is not alone in proposing it: the American theoretical physicist Dr Charles A. Muses suggested in 1963 that time, "although subjective, has quantitatively measurable characteristics", and "may be defined as the ultimate causal pattern of all energy release."

TELEPATHY AND ANIMALS

In the 1920s, a number of experiments were mounted in Russia to test the theory that animals, as well as men, possess extrasensory powers. The most famous of these animals was an alsation called Mars, a circus performer controlled by his owner, Vladimir Durov, who seems to have been more showman than scientist, and trained a variety of animals.

Nevertheless, some of the demonstrations were impressive, and proved impossible to discredit. Two acadamicians, Vladimir M. Bekhterev and Alexander Leontovitch, mounted a controlled experiment in which Bekhterev passed Durov a note inviting him to instruct Mars to perform a task. Durov stared into the dog's eyes without speaking or gesturing; the dog then searched the untidy room and from a mess of papers and books brought the scientists a telephone book – the article they had requested.

Bekhterev, impressed, worked with Durov, devising experiments which he believed made it impossible for the trainer to communicate with his animals other than psychically, and concluded that "mental suggestion can directly affect the behaviour of trained dogs." Later, an electrical engineer, Dr Bernard Kajinsky, made careful studies of Durov at work, and claimed to detect high-frequency electromagnetic waves, 1.8mm (1/8in) in length, originating in Durov's brain (although more recently scientists have claimed that Kajinsky's equipment was too primitive to have been able to measure such waves, even if they existed).

Yevgenia Davitashvili (left)*, a Russian healer, was born in a small village in Kuban, where she learned secrets handed down by her family about curing headaches, backaches and other minor complaints. She works at a distance, "massaging" her clients without physically touching them, sometimes via television.*

Nanuli Kenchadze (below)*, a Caucasian, works by traditional "laying on of hands", curing sick people such as Valeria Petrova, who was suffering from blurred vision and sleeplessness.*

Faith Healing

In May 1989 the Foreign Ministry press centre in Moscow was given over to a meeting demonstrating the present state of faith-healing in the USSR. Alan Chumak presented his system of hypnotic massage, successful (he claimed) in treating 93 percent of conditions. Nokolai Levashov, a radiologist, suggested that he found it possible to "see" the condition of the interior of the body (without the aid of x-rays). Valery Avdeyev, a mystic with powers of telekinesis, explained how his theory of cosmic energy, which could change the state of human consciousness, could cure illnesses.

Practitioners of unconventional medicine in the Soviet Union have created the USSR Folk Medicine Fund which plans to build a spa near Moscow with 1,500 beds, where the best practitioners of alternative medicine will work. The Russian correspondent of the *Independent* wrote that "paramedicine's modern relevance is growing. It touches an inchoate popular belief that mankind is hurtling towards apocalypse – ecological, military or otherwise – that our only hope of salvation lies in our tapping internal psychic forces."

***Madame Blavatsky** (1831-91)* (opposite, top)*, founded the Theosophical Society. Of Russian origin, she lived in many countries, finally choosing Madras, India, as the centre for her mystical society. Her teachings merged Eastern and Western mysticisms in a way that proved immensely popular. After her death, the movement fell apart.*

The monk Grigori Rasputin (opposite, bottom) *(1871-1917), with the Czarina and her haemophiliac son, whose illness the monk seemed able to cure. Such seemingly supernatural powers gave him great influence at the imperial court, and aroused the jealousy that led to his assassination by nobles.*

The Aura

Surprisingly, some of the most interesting work which has been done on the human aura – the field of energy which mediums claim to be able to see, surrounding the human body – has been done in Russia during the past 50 years.

This began in 1939, when an electrician, Semyon Kirlian, found it possible to photograph parts of the human body under treatment by electrotherapy, by means of an electric spark apparently generated by the body itself. He invented a machine and began to take colour photographs which showed an astonishing display of colourful flares and sparks.

He went further, and photographed plants in the same way, noticing that there would be a difference in the pattern of light emanating from a healthy leaf and an unhealthy one from the same plant. This tied in with the discovery that the aura of a human being differs according to health.

Despite wide interest in the work of Kirlian and his wife, it was not until 1960 that state money was made available, and they were able to set up their own laboratory. Among other things, it has been found that "phantom" parts of vegetable matter can be seen – that is, the aura of part of a leaf which is cut away still appears in a photograph taken immediately afterwards: there is believed to be some connection with the

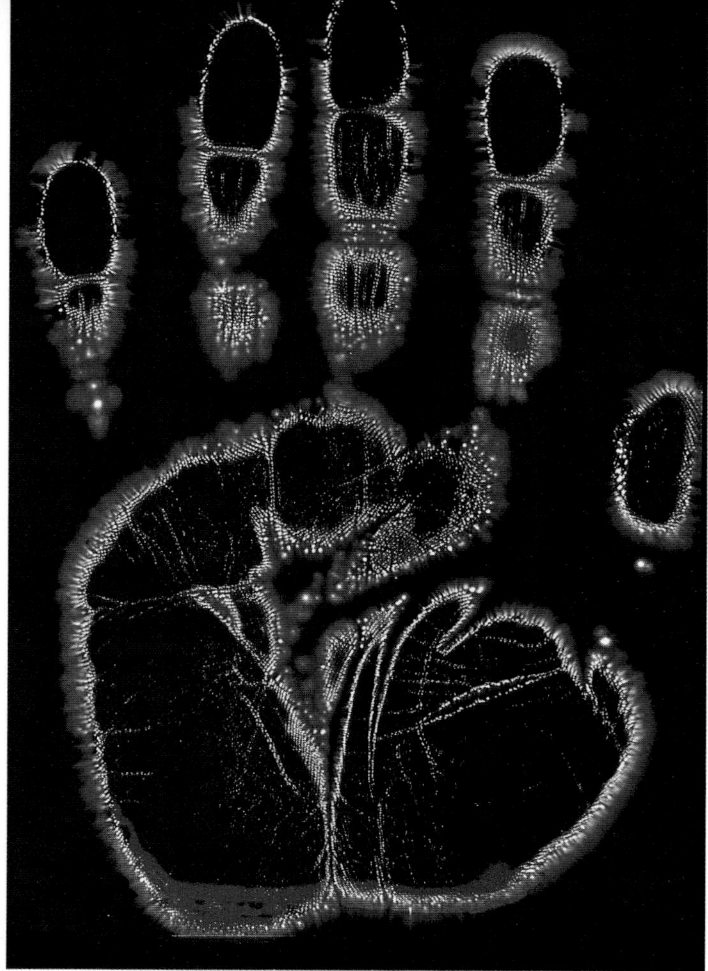

"ghost limbs" which amputees can still feel after they have been removed.

During the 1960s, biophysicists and biochemists at the Kirov State University in Alma-Ata were studying the revealed energy field with an electron microscope, and had named it the Biological Plasma Body. (There is no connection with the "plasma" beloved of spiritualists; the reference is to an ionized gas, the nuclei of whose atoms have been stripped of electrons.) A connection has been discovered between the points of the aura from which flares originate, and the main acupuncture points.

Ball Lightning

In August 1978, five Russian mountaineers, encamped in the Caucasian mountains, were sleeping in their tents when – according to an account in *Soviet News* – a bright yellow blob of light entered their tent. One of the mountaineers, Victor Kravunenko, saw it nudge his companion's sleeping-bag, after which there was a scream of pain; it emerged, and proceeded to examine the sleeping-bags of the others, in turn. When Kravunenko's turn came, he felt as though he had been burned by a welding torch, and fainted.

He recovered in time to see his companions being attacked, and he was again badly burned; when he and the others were hospitalized, it was found that pieces of muscle had actually been torn from their bones. One man, Oleg Korovin, was killed by the inanimate attacker.

It was assumed that the yellow object was that rarely-seen phenomenon, ball-lightning, which for many years was believed by scientists to be a figment of the imagination. Some of the accounts of it are indeed unusual: lightning balls have been seen to pass through closed windows and keyholes, follow people about, enter aeroplanes in flight – in 1958, "a large orange ball of something" entered the cockpit of an Aer Lingus aircraft flying between Shannon and Newfoundland. It made its way into the passenger compartment, chasing a frightened air hostess down the gangway, but fortunately left the plane without doing serious damage.

The phenomenon is infrequently seen, but there is now no question that it exists. It takes the form of a ball of electricity, sometimes as small as one inch (2.5cm) in diameter, sometimes as large as five feet (1.5m), and generally yellow or white with a blue tinge. There seems little way of guarding against these balls, which can pass through many solid barriers. They do not always attack human beings, but sometimes damage metal fittings: the Rev J. H. Lehn, of York, Pennsylvania, was in his bathroom in 1921 when a lightning ball entered it, rolled past his feet, climbed into the washbasin and melted the chain holding the sink-stopper in two. Several weeks later, a similar ball melted the chain of the bath-stopper.

Such balls vanish as mysteriously as they appear, sometimes with a small explosion, sometimes silently. Science has little to say on the subject, partly because, the occurrence of ball lightning being so rare, it is extremely difficult to study.

__A Kirlian photograph__ of the palm of a human hand (above) *is produced by interaction between the subject and an applied electric field. It is claimed that the subject's health can be measured by studying such photographs and examining the distribution of sweat on the skin.*

__An artist's impression__ (right) *__of ball lightning__. For many years the phenomenon was thought by scientists to be fiction, but there have been enough sightings recorded from all over the world to confirm its existence.*

POLAND

MEDIUMS

Between the two World Wars, more successful mediums appeared in Poland than in any other country in the world. There had been mediums there before World War I, of course. Stanislawa Tomczyk impressed parapsychologists in the first decade of the century, Warsaw scientists confirming that she could move a celluloid ball by the sheer force of her mind. She levitated objects and imposed a weight of 2oz (60g) on a letter-weight machine without physically touching it; poltergeists followed her around like attentive pets.

Between the wars, Madame Przybylska successfully forecast events in the Polish war in the Ukraine, and Franek Kluski produced flying lights and provoked spirits into kissing observers – "with luminous and rather cold lips", while the detached hands of little children materialized (and were even moulded in plaster).

Stefan Ossowiecki, another Polish psychic, who had always been plagued by poltergeists, was able almost infallibly to recite messages handed to him in sealed envelopes, and was tested (as a kind of party entertainer) by most members of Polish society, including the President, Marshal Pilsudski, who sent a chess formula to him in an envelope sealed with the official seal of the Minister of War, who himself carried it to Ossowiecki. The latter correctly recited the formula; the still sealed envelope was returned unopened to the President, who, impressed, authorized the psychic to use the anecdote for publicity.

Ossowiecki also claimed that he saw people's auras clearly enough to be able to paint them, and that he could employ psychokinetic powers to move small objects at will.

Stefan Ossowiecki (left) *was probably the most famous clairvoyant in Poland between the two World Wars. Many important people came to believe Ossowiecki's strange talents to be genuine after they had had occasion to test them personally. It proved impossible to catch Ossowiecki out in any form of cheating, and the fact that he resolutely refused to perform for money suggests that he was honest. The general feeling was that his feats were performed in some way by an exquisite sense of touch – his fingers could "read" the messages even through the envelopes containing them.*

OUR LADY OF CZECHOSTOWA

The picture of Our Lady of Czechostowa (left) in Poland is perhaps the most famous of the portraits of the Madonna thought to possess miraculous powers. It is also claimed to be among the oldest, for it is said to have been painted by St Luke, from the life, on the top of a cypress wood table used by the Holy Family at Nazareth. According to tradition it was removed to Constantinople (Istanbul) by St Helena, mother of the first Christian emperor Constantine, about 330, where it was honoured for about 500 years before being given as a gift by the Byzantine emperor to a Ruthenian prince. Removed to Kiev in the Ukraine, where it remained in the Royal Palace of Belz for 579 years, it was damaged by an arrow during a Tartar raid in 1382, which left a still visible scar. The Prince of Belz then decided to move it to safety in one of his territories in Upper Silesia. The horses drawing the cart containing it stopped at a little village called Czestochawa and refused to go any further, despite all coaxing. Taking this as a sign from heaven, the Prince founded a fortress-monastery there to house the Madonna. Ever since then, it has been miraculously linked with the defence of Catholic Poland against its many enemies.

In 1430, during an unsuccessful attempt by plundering Hussites to remove it, the face was slashed with sabres. When artists tried to patch the scars, they found that after every attempt the scars reappeared and ultimately they gave up, proclaiming a miracle; the scars are clearly visible on the right cheek of the Madonna.

In 1909 vandals tore off the gold crown and overdress of pearls. Pope Pius X provided a new crown and granted spiritual favours to those who made a pilgrimage to the shrine. A picture of Our Lady hangs in the Pope's chapel at Castel Gandolfo in Italy.

Czechoslovakia

ESP

There is a long tradition of interest in the paranormal in 20th-century Czechoslovakia. Neurologists, psychiatrists, engineers, chemists, doctors and biologists all collaborated on PSI research at the University of Prague between 1920 and the Second World War, and the claims of prominent Czechoslovakian mediums were very thoroughly examined.

The Czech military used clairvoyants during the First World War, and some soldiers were taught clairvoyance and dowsing techniques in order that they could discover buried mines; in 1925 the military commissioned a handbook on ESP, which the army published.

It is claimed that not only do the modern Czech army and the population in general persist in their interest in ESP but the world of scientific scholarship also shows a keen interest in reincarnation, ESP, PK, telepathy and mediumship.

Perhaps the most interesting of all Czechoslovakian psychic experimenters was the sculptor Bretislac Kafka, who set up an experimental centre for the study of parapsychology near Prague, where he trained a number of people in ESP, and had several well-publicized and spectacular successes – as when in Krasno and Becva, on June 18 1925, he ordered his psychics to discover what was happening on Roald Amundsen's expedition to the North Pole. They announced that there was impenetrable fog and high winds at the pole – conditions which, it was reported two days later, had indeed prevented Amundsen from reaching his goal.

Kafka also experimented with hypnosis, and on one occasion kept a man under his influence without food for three weeks, merely instructing him from time to time to eat a nonexistent apple from a mythical tree. At the end of the period the man was perfectly healthy.

Among his conclusions was the view that psychics had a much thinner aura around them than less "sensitive" people, and were more open to the unseen world of inexplicable energies.

During the 1960s, when Milan Ryzl was researching the possibility of using hypnosis to train people to sharpen their ability for ESP, he tested a volunteer, a bank clerk, Pavel Stepanek, who proved a remarkably efficient exponent of ESP, and in early experiments in which he was asked to "guess" whether the black or white side of a number of cards was uppermost, he succeeded in 57 percent of cases – odds of well over ten million to one.

The long series of tests which followed confirmed Stepanek's consistent ESP ability. His reputation spread, unassailable by critics, and his most successful result in carefully controlled experiments was achieved against odds of 112 million million to one.

The Balkans

Romania: Dracula and other Vampires

Hypnosis (left) *has long been practiced and held in high regard in Czechoslovakia – perhaps unsurprisingly, as it is part of the central European milieu that gave birth to the ideas of both Jung and Freud (see p.149).*

The Original Count Dracula *was Vlad the Impaler* (right), *notorious for his many cruelties. These did not include drinking the blood of his victims although 15th-century prints show him enjoying a meal among piles of impaled corpses, and he was said to carry the odour of blood with him. Films such as the 1931* **Dracula** (above, *with Bela Lugosi and Helen Chandler) were based on Bram Stoker's famous 1897 novel, which created the human vampire legend.*

The legend of the vampire Dracula became well known throughout Europe after the publication in 1897 of the famous novel by Bram Stoker. Stoker dreamed one night of a vampire king rising from his grave. In the British Museum library he found gruesome accounts of the life of Vlad Tepes, "Vlad the Impaler" – a Prince of Wallachia who was also known as Dracula. Accordingly, he set his story in Transylvania, "the land beyond the forest", a former province of Hungary, now a region of Romania.

Stoker's novel became a best-seller almost overnight, with its vivid account of a young solicitor visiting a weird castle where, in a ruined chapel, he finds 50 great boxes full of churchyard earth, in one of which lies the un-dead Count, gorged with blood.

Traditionally, Romania does not have a strong belief in vampirism, although it has naturally played up to tourism by pretending it does. However, there does seem to have been a habit of piercing corpses with a stake in order to prevent their ghosts from walking – and garlic has always been used to

***Legends of strange hairy half-human beasts**, such as men with tails or unicorn's horns,* (right) *still circulate in Romania even in the 20th century but they originated many centuries ago in the remote wooded valleys of Transylvania. Such legends may have helped give Bram Stoker the idea for his famous novel* Dracula.

keep them away should they do so.

At the height of the vampire scare the bodies of those said to have risen from the dead to drink the blood of the living were exhumed. In one or two cases, they were found with blood on their faces, and in such a condition as to suggest that they had left their graves. However, the consensus is that these were unfortunates who, perhaps in an epileptic fit or some trance state, had been buried alive and, recovering, had tried to claw their way out of their coffins.

There are a few Romanian cases in which a sturdy belief in metamorphosis has been recorded. Dr Corneliu Barbulescu, of the Institute for Ethnological and Dialectological Research in Bucharest, interviewed an old man, Toma Neghina, who claimed that he knew someone who turned himself into a wolf at night. Another man implored his friends to tie him to the wheel of a cart at night lest he go off to join the wolves heard howling in the forest.

An old woman told Dr Barbulescu that when she was very young two of her friends had seen another girl strip naked and go into the woods to become a she-wolf. They did not take her clothes, for otherwise she would not have been able to turn back into a human. (The proposition that she might have gone unclothed into the woods for some other purpose was not examined.) Barbulescu overheard one woman telling another about a third who, while travelling, had been attacked by a wolf which bit off a piece of her skirt. When she returned home she was greeted by her husband, who had a bit of material between his teeth. . . .

Psychologists have studied a specific condition – lycanthropy – in which patients identify themselves with wolves. In April 1975 *The Guardian* of London printed a report of an inquest on a 17-year-old man who believed he was becoming a werewolf; that his hands and feet were turning into paws; he began growling, then stabbed himself to death. The phenomenon is not unknown in North America, where, of course, there is a large wolf population.

One of the most tenacious beliefs in Romania is of young men and girls born with tails, and therefore, traditionally, bound to become ghosts, witches or vampires. Vestigial tails are not, in fact, particularly uncommon in humans – they are merely extensions of the coccyx, which normally consists of four vertebrae but can have more, in which case there will be a protrusion: a Chinese boy was recorded with a tail a foot (30 cm) long; a Greek soldier had one two inches (5cm) long, and in 1881 a student at West Point military academy in the United States had a tail that interfered with his riding.

Bulgaria: Suggestology

During the 1960s and 70s the Bulgarian Institute of Suggestology and Parapsychology headed by Dr Georgi Lozanov attempted strictly controlled examinations of yoga, PK, the alleged impact of cosmic influences on telepathy, and the possibility that the human mind could influence plant growth.

The term "suggestology" was coined by the Institute to embrace the inexplicable powers of the human mind, often seen in parapsychology. Dr Lozanov was particularly interested in healing, and the way in which "suggestion", through the psyche, could accelerate a patient's recovery. He related this to *prana*, the vital energy released in yoga, which enables a yogi to anaesthetize himself, staunch a flow of blood and slow the heart-beat almost to cessation.

Having devised a system of anaesthesia dependent not on hypnosis but on "suggestivity", and succeeding in using it to enable surgeons to perform minor operations on subjects without conventional anaesthetics, in 1965 Lozanov supervised an operation for a large inguinal hernia, which was televised to a large number of students. Without hypnotizing the patient, who was fully conscious throughout, Lozanov merely suggested that he would feel no pain; they chatted throughout the hour-long operation, performed by two surgeons, and the patient was – at Lozanov's suggestion – able to decrease the blood supply to the operative area; the bleeding was consequently much reduced. The surgeons found that the wound healed much more quickly than usual.

Although the film of the operation has been widely seen – for example, it was presented at an international medical congress in Rome in 1967 – Lozanov's technique has not been followed up, and is still regarded much as Western doctors regarded acupuncture when it was first demonstrated: that is, with superior condescension. However, Lozanov has gone on experimenting, working, among other things, on teaching children, blind from birth, to "see" through their skin, and on "suggestopedia" as a medium of education.

Powers of Flight?

Levitation is one thing, the ability to fly another. In the 16th Century, Sigismund Callimachi of Silistra, claimed to be able to fly, and was seen to do so by a number of townspeople, whose testimony was so persuasive that he was summoned to give an exhibition before Michael, son of Petrusko, the ban of Craiova. Callimachi took off from the tower of church at Ruschuk, and succeeded in gliding for almost half a mile using only his arms. He failed to survive the experiment, but was considered to have performed a miraculous feat.

Yugoslavia: Visions of the Virgin

Visions of the Virgin Mary, relatively common in historical times, have become less prevalent during recent years. However, less than a decade ago one was reported from the village of Medjugorje, near Citluk, in Yugoslavia, causing embarrassment to the atheistic Communist authorities.

The visionaries were six children aged between 10 and 17, who on June 24 1981 claimed to have seen the Virgin standing on a hill near the village, holding the infant Jesus. The children returned to the same spot day after day, and the vision recurred almost daily for five months. She told the children five "secrets", which were confided by them to the Pope, and invited them to enter religious orders.

On some occasions as many as 30,000 people met at the place where the vision occurred, and several spontaneous cures were reported. The Virgin also apparently espoused the cause of Croatian nationalism. In November, the authorities forbade access to the place where the vision occurred, and the Virgin apparently then began to appear at the children's homes. There have been no recent reports of the vision.

The Weeping Virgin

In October 1920, at Tuzla, in Bosnia-Hercegovina. Stjeman Bratic, a worker in the salt mines, carved in an underground cavern a statue of the Virgin upon whose cheeks, each morning, fresh crystalline tears were alleged to have been seen, which, although solid to the touch, vanished after an hour or two. When her head, which had been knocked off and placed at some distance from her body, was overnight miraculously restored to her shoulders, no evidence could be found that anyone had entered the mine, which had been closed overnight. The Virgin mysteriously disappeared – on the very night when Stjeman Bratic died.

A vision of the Virgin Mary *drew huge crowds in the Yugoslavian village of Medjugorje* (above) *to celebrate a vision of the virgin seen there in 1981 by six children. This message from the Virgin sounded ominous, for she said it was the last place on earth she would visit – before its end?*

GREECE

THE GREAT HEALER

Although Greece has played little part in the modern history of the paranormal, there is nevertheless a sense in which that country fathered the whole modern preoccupation with alternative medicine and "miracle cures."

The curing of sickness by psychical or psychological means had been known in almost every primitive prehistorical society, but it was formalized when Asclepius, whose cult, which was centred in Epidaurus, but spread to Crete, Cos and Athens, became a god.

Sick people travelled to Epidaurus from all parts of the Greek world to have their illnesses cured by incubation: after three days of ritual purity followed by various sacrifices, a gift of money and an offering of three cakes (to success, recollection and right order) they slept in a chamber in Asclepius' temple, wearing a laurel wreath. Sometimes their dreams revealed the treatment they should undergo; sometimes they simply woke to find themselves cured.

Many inscriptions found at Epidaurus and at Athens tell of successful cures, sometimes brought about by faith, sometimes by more conventional medical treatment. The illnesses which were cured by reference to the god were those which are now recognized as psychosomatic. Sometimes they were spectacular – patients were said to have dreamed that operations were performed upon them, and woke to find that the ulcers or growths of which they had complained had vanished.

Many other gods subsequently became associated with healing: Apollo, Paieon, Isis and Serapis were all believed to have performed cures. But despite the intervention of others, Asclepius remained the most popular and influential of the healing gods, and was respected in Greece until the Christian era – and even afterwards, for although he was looked upon as a rival to Jesus, the early Christians were nevertheless forced to acknowledge his healing power, contenting themselves merely by insisting that even so, he was not as powerful as Christ.

Elaborate buildings at Epidaurus (left) *marked the centre of the cult of Asclepius, to which sick people from all over the Greek world travelled to be made well. Often this healing was primarily psychosomatic or psychological in approach.*

Asclepius, a legendary healer (left) *who was later deified for his medical services to mankind, established Epidaurus as a centre of healing. Few, if any drugs were used. Instead, the invalid would sleep in the* ***temple confines*** *and be visited in a dream by a god, who might take the form of a snake* (right)*; on waking, he could find himself cured. (This snake was a symbol of Asclepius' healing powers.) Other cures relied on rest, listening to music and relaxing in idyllic surroundings, combined with accepted medical techniques such as lancing boils.*

THE AMERICAS

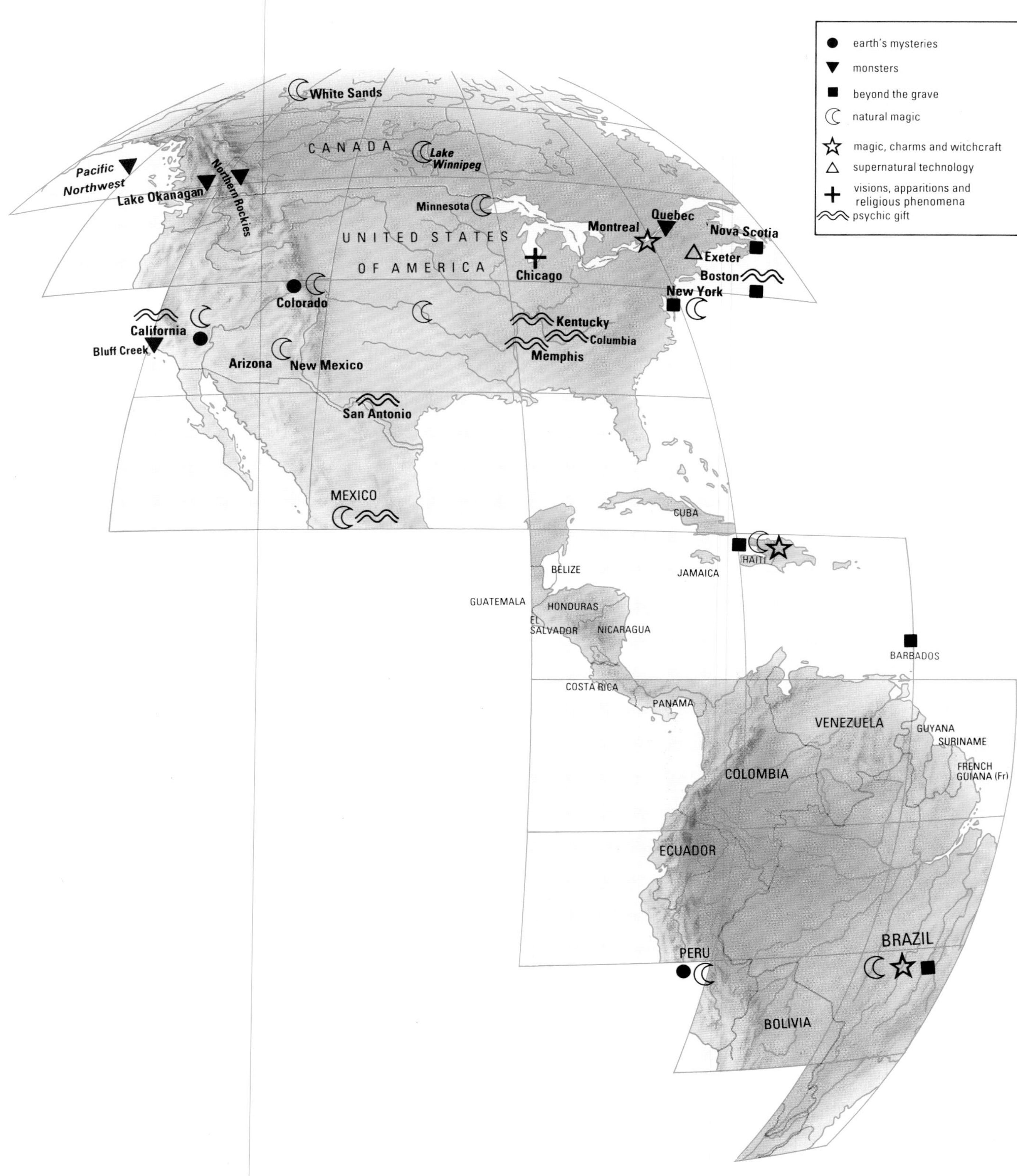

Of all the areas of the world, North and South America perhaps embrace the widest – and wildest – boundaries of the supernatural. On the one hand, the most careful examinations of PSI phenomena have been made under meticulously controlled conditions. On the other, there has been perhaps a greater concentration of tricksters and fraudulent mediums and others in California than anywhere else in the world. The new vogue for "channelling" (see pp.50-2) – a more fashionable name for mediumship – has undoubtedly attracted a number of people eager to make a quick buck; more traditional mediums have often been outraged by their claims.

American mediums have in the past undoubtedly done much to alleviate suffering and to heal the sick. At the other extreme, drug traffickers have used witchcraft in a nauseating way to attempt to protect themselves against the police, sacrificing animals and even humans in blood rites. Voodoo, in its origin relatively innocent, has been distorted by cruelty and vice.

America has also provided, over the past 60 years or so, admirable examples of the supernatural being taken seriously – from Cayce and the psychologist William James to the serious investigators of our own time, such as those of the Society for Research into Rapport and Telekinesis. The existence of UFOs has been widely denied – yet the United States Government has been forced to set up several bodies to examine the innumerable reports on file.

The diverse attitudes taken by most modern Americans to the supernatural must have something to do with the heterogeneous nature of the nation: not only people, but legends and beliefs, from all over the world have gathered here – from Europe, Asia, the Far East. . . . It is no wonder that such a wide variety of paranormal interests exists.

Before North America was colonized, the indigenous inhabitants had their own belief systems: the American and Canadian Indians had their own gods, their own shamans, their own occult laws. These exist only patchily today – yet within living memory Indian witch doctors were able to release remarkable powers. In South America, the coming of white missionaries had an equally dampening effect on local magic: yet here too, local patterns of the paranormal persist.

So, too, do some pre-Christian ideas which have been given a thin veneer of Christianity: psychic surgeons have founded their own churches – although voodooism, certainly in Haiti and in other parts of the Caribbean and South America, has very little to do with any other form of worship or magic.

The most extraordinary physical manifestation of religion in the Americas is certainly seen in the enormous symbols of birds, animals and abstract patterns marked out upon the ground as signals to the gods: there have been attempts to connect these with beings from other planets – but it seems most likely that they are of earthly origin, even if the means by which they were drawn remains a mystery.

The United States

The Boston Poltergeist

A poltergeist experience in Boston, Massachusetts, in the middle of the 19th century is notable because it is recorded by a man who was particularly concerned to investigate it fairly. In fact, H. A. Willis made strong attempts to persuade two Harvard university professors to help him examine the events which seemed to be taking place – but suspicious of anything remotely supernatural, they declined his invitation.

The phenomena began in May 1867, when a young Irish girl, Mary Carrick, arrived at Mr Willis' house to work as a servant. Suddenly, on July 3, the bells which hung in the kitchen and were used to summon service to the various rooms of the house all began to ring violently together for no apparent reason. Mr Willis detached the wires connected to the bells, but they continued to ring about every half-hour despite the fact that they hung ten feet (3m) from the floor.

Mr Willis soon noticed that there seemed to be some connection with Mary, for the bells "never rang unless the girl was in the room or the adjoining one, but were often seen and heard to ring when different members of the family were present in the room with the girl." Within a day or two, other noises were heard: for example, there were loud knockings which followed Mary from room to room.

The girl was terrified – and when, towards the end of July, chairs began to upset themselves, crockery to throw itself about, tables to move and kitchen utensils to hurtle about the rooms, she became hysterical, and was sent to an asylum for treatment. During the three weeks she was away, all was quiet. She returned temporarily, but began sleepwalking, and after a while was returned to the asylum. The untoward noises and events did not follow her. Nor did they ever occur again in Mr Willis' house.

He was never able to account for the goings on. At one time he believed the phenomena had something to do with electric currents, and placed the bedposts of Mary's bed on glass; the noises that had occurred during the night then stopped. Similarly, when she was seated on a chair placed on glass, the crockery remained inert. But nothing he could do prevented the phenomena altogether.

Snake-handling

Certain evangelistic churches in middle America, still hold snake-handling services. They are apparently based on two scriptural passages in which immunity from serpents is promised to the faithful: "if they pick up snakes . . . they will not be harmed" (Mark XVI:18), "you can walk on snakes and scorpions . . . and nothing will hurt you" (Luke X:19).

At these services a box containing rattlesnakes, copperheads and other poisonous snakes is usually placed on the platform. When members of the congregation show "exercise of the spirit" – a state very similar to that of the trances experienced in primitive African religions, and involving the same sort of twitching and shivering – the box is opened and the snakes handed around.

Handling the snakes often induces hysterical collapse, known as "wiping the slate clean for God". Relatively few

Jimmy Swaggart (right) *the American tele-evangelist, preaching at Nassau Coliseum, New York. Until his disgrace for sexual and financial lapses, his impassioned sermons, using every cliché of heaven and hell, had an almost magical effect even on television viewers, who donated huge sums of money to him, sometimes after being "cured" by touching their television screens. This is a new variant of faith-healing.*

Poisonous snakes *are handled by members of a chapel in Cartersville, Georgia,* (below) *who interpret literally the Bible passage saying "They shall take up serpents". The local preacher says that "when people get right enough with the Lord they come up and handle them". Very few cases of snake bites have been recorded.*

cases have been recorded of fatal accidents; when, occasionally, people are bitten, and die, they are invariably condemned for having lived sinful lives, and are said to have been punished by God. The extraordinary thing is that the highly poisonous snakes are for the most part somehow inhibited from attacking the worhippers who handle them.

The atmosphere generated at snake-handling ceremonies is often hysterical and clearly has a sexual element; it is said that the less religious young men of the neighbourhoods where they are regularly held have learned that young women leaving the services are frequently in a state of excited sexual tension, and take advantage of the fact.

Religious Trance States

The rhythmic clapping and music which accompany some American revivalist religious meetings, together with the carefully rehearsed cries of the preachers and the whipped-up reactions of the congregation, have much the same effect as the drumming and chanting with which African witch doctors induce trance-states. Such a strong focusing of emotion can result in the most intense "religious" experience, with a corresponding heightening of the worshippers' sense of worship. There are dangers, however: what amounts to mass hypnotism – similar to that used by the Nazis at their rallies in Germany in the 1920s and 30s – produces an atmosphere either of guilt or celebration (and they are not mutually exclusive).

Such activity is of course deeply disturbing to the emotionally insecure; mental hospitals have recorded an increase in the number of patients admitted after revivalist meetings in their neighbourhood. It is perhaps significant that the effects of the meetings are on the whole depressing rather than enlightening.

The televising of meetings of this sort – during which millions of dollars have been extracted from viewers, and mass hallucinations has resulted in the virtual deification of, for the most part, entirely unworthy religious leaders – has been insufficiently studied. This may be the most common use of "religious magic" in our time.

The Navaho Sand Paintings

The Navaho Indians, who now live on a reservation along the Arizona-New Mexico border, use an age-old familiarity with the powers of nature to inform their magical rites. Even today tribal life is full of ritual, and every action is accompanied by its good-luck song or chant, to ward off evil or disease, to bring rain. . . .

But it is the "curing ceremonies" which are most impressive. The Navaho believe that sickness is inflicted by supernatural means, and can therefore be cured by supernatural means. So, if an illness is sufficiently grave, the whole tribe will gather for a curing ceremony, presided over by a medicine man. He is not in any sense a magician – he does not go into a trance, but simply ensures that everything is properly done, according to tradition.

The ceremonies can last for one or two nights, or for as many as nine, and the participant must be pure. Baths, sexual abstinence, great care about where one lies down to sleep or sits to eat – all combine to create a proper state of readiness. Herbal medicines, music and magical objects all play their part in the ceremony, but most important are the paintings drawn in sand, often by as many as 20 artists working over as many hours.

At last, after all the preparations, and when prayer-sticks and paintings, chanting and song have ensured the absence of evil spirits, the sick person is brought to the main sand painting, and some of the sand is scattered on his or her body to draw the gods' attention to it. More purification chants, often extremely long and complex, are sung – and the

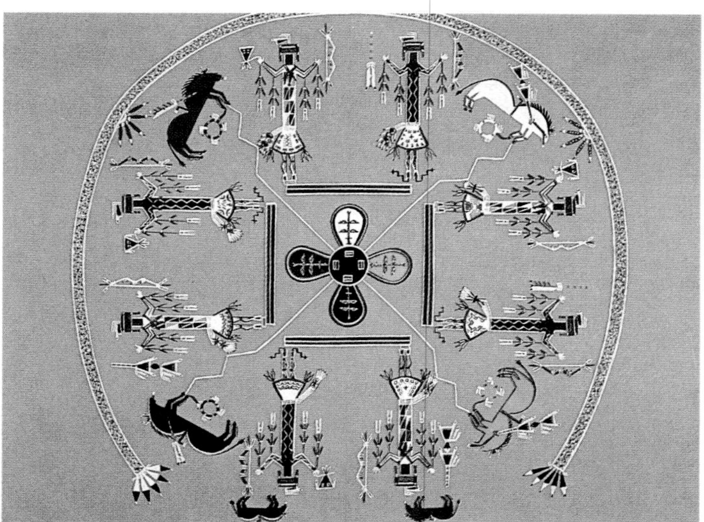

***The Navaho Indians** use often elaborate and intricate sand paintings* (above) *to help cure many sorts of illness. The Navaho, living along the New Mexico-Arizona border, retain an unusually large number of traditional rites and rituals.*

***Enormous pictures of men and animals** are found in many parts of America – as here* (right), *near Blyth, in California. They were probably inscribed by Indians, who could not have known that men, as well as gods, would be able to see them from the air.*

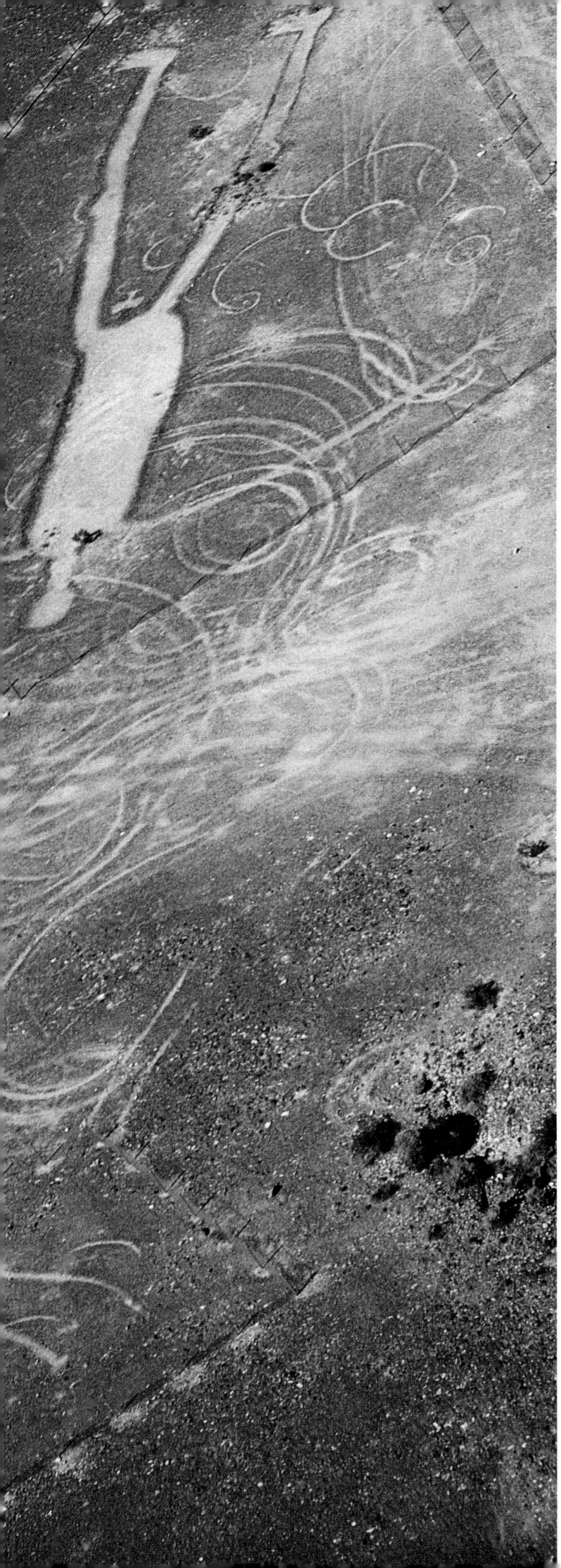

participants must be word-perfect. At the end of the ceremony the accumulation of spiritual power is considerable: as with the faith-healing with which we are more familiar, complete belief is often said to result in a cure.

The Colorado Giants

Within the past 20 years, almost 300 large-scale "drawings" have been found, scrawled across the face of the Mojave desert along the valley of the Colorado river, of animals and humans, horses and lions, rattlesnakes and fish. . . .

The figures are as difficult to explain as the more ambitious ones on the Nazka plateau of southern Peru (see p.188); they seem to have been made in much the same way – lightly scribbled, the surface of the rock not deeply incised, the figures only fully understandable if seen from the air.

It seems clear that the figures were magical in origin, perhaps meant to appease the gods – or maybe to illustrate their power. The rattlesnake was believed by some Indian tribes to have magical powers; a large drawing of a fisherman spearing two fish with a spear tipped with shining quartz may have been designed to bring good fortune to hunters. It has been suggested that some of the figures are astronomically aligned. The oldest ones have been dated to around 3000 BC; the most recent to the 16th century, for a horse is shown – an animal unknown in the area until the Europeans arrived there in the middle of that century.

A Prophetic Dream

There are several examples of prophetic dreams in American history – including that of President Lincoln, who dreamed that he stood at the foot of a coffin and, asking whose it was, was told it was that of the president, who had been assassinated. A short while afterwards, that fate befell him.

But one of the best-documented prophetic dreams was that of Samuel Clemens, a young apprentice river-boat pilot working in 1858 on the Mississippi steamboat *Pennsylvania.* His younger brother Henry was a clerk on the same boat. One night Sam, sleeping onshore, had a vivid dream of his brother lying in a metal coffin resting on two chairs, with a bouquet of white flowers, one single red flower at its centre,

Edgar Cayce (left), *the famous psychic, clairvoyant and healer; an uneducated country boy who devoted his life to curing the sick.*

Harry Houdini (right), *although sceptical, was fascinated by spiritualism.*

William James (opposite), *the distinguished philosopher and psychologist, was drawn into an investigation of psychic phenomena, although he felt a personal distaste for such things.*

resting on his breast. He told no-one about the dream.

A week or so later, Sam was transferred to another boat, the *Lacey*, which remained at Greenville, Mississippi. Near Memphis, the boilers of the *Pennsylvania* blew up, with the enormous loss of life. Reaching Memphis, Sam found his brother alive, but fatally scalded. He stayed with him until he died. After a night's sleep he went to see the body. It lay with many others – but while they were all enclosed in pine coffins, the people of Memphis, touched by Henry's youth and beauty, had subscribed for a metal coffin. It lay across two chairs, and on the dead boy's breast lay just the bouquet Sam had seen in his dream.

Later, Sam left the riverboats, and became America's best known 19th-century novelist, Mark Twain.

Edgar Cayce

More than 40 years after his death, Edgar Cayce (1877-1945) is probably still America's most famous psychic, clairvoyant and healer.

Cayce was an uneducated country boy from the heart of Kentucky who, at the age of 13, was sitting in a wood reading his Bible when he received a visit from a beautiful woman who promised to grant him a wish. He asked to be able to help others, especially sick children. Two nights later the boy, previously extremely bad at lessons, found he had been suddenly granted the capacity to spell perfectly – and what is more, to spell words before they had left the lips of those who tested him, and to "see", psychically, the pages from which they were being quoted.

Cayce did not at first exploit his psychic gifts, but in 1901, after an experience during which, in trance, he cured himself of a voice ailment, he began healing – not only healing those who came to see him, but thousands with whom his only contact was by letter.

Although some people suspected Cayce of fraud, there seems no room for doubt that he did achieve many cures (although he also had his failures) – nor that he was a transparently honest man, whose gift was in some ways a great burden to him: he was painfully shy and insecure – and until late middle age he declined to accept any fees for his work.

Sadly, he deeply mistrusted scientists. However, he did so with reason, for when in 1906 he agreed to give a reading before some doctors, they were suspicious of the nature of his trance and badly injured him by thrusting needles through parts of his body, and by partly cutting off a fingernail in an attempt to prove that he was faking. He felt no pain while in trance, but considerable pain when he came out of it. His reluctance to take part in any further "scientific" tests means that there is little objective evidence as to the efficacy of his diagnoses (they have been claimed as being 85 percent accurate) or his cures (often the result of extremely eccentric concoctions, which nevertheless seem to have worked).

Later in his life, Cayce apparently developed an ability to read the unconscious minds of his subjects, and when he died left almost 15,000 verbatim records of his work, either in diagnosis and healing, or detailing the lives of the people who consulted him.

He was, in a way, the precursor of the contemporary American interest in what is known as the New Age, seeing life as a combination of the physical and spiritual, a perfect amalgam of which should include psychic powers which, properly cultivated, can be used in daily life.

Harry Houdini

Harry Houdini (1874-1926), still perhaps the most famous escapologist and stage magician of modern times, had a keen interest in spiritualism, and was the first conjurer to fall into the trap of believing that because he could reproduce by purely mechanical means the effects seen at many seances, all seances must be "rigged".

He became interested in spiritualism after the death of his mother in 1913, longing to establish contact with her; but disappointed in this, he made no further experiments. However, in 1920, Sir Arthur Conan Doyle – the creator of Sherlock Holmes – took him to a seance held by Martha Beraud, known as "Eva". He found this fascinating. But his attitude in public remained one of extreme scepticism, and in 1924 he published a book entitled *A Magician among the Spirits* in which he was so eager to discredit spiritualism that he distorted and invented facts.

Houdini's battle with one medium became notorious: Mina Crandon, known as "Margery", who became perhaps the best-known medium in America between the wars. Her "control" was her dead elder brother Walter. She was investigated by the *Scientific American*, which had offered a prize of $2,500 to any medium "who could produce a visible psychic phenomenon." The journal's team had seen "Margery" at the centre of phosphorescent lights, moving objects, ringing electric bells, and a disembodied arm. James Malcom Bird, its associate editor, was impressed, and said so.

Houdini was determined to expose "Margery" as a fraud. He had a box built, in which she was locked, her hands passing through two holes in its side so that they could be held. When the seance began, the top of the box burst open. Houdini insisted Margery must have been responsible. The box was closed again, at which "Walter" made his feelings known in no uncertain terms, banging and shaking the box. A piece of rubber was wedged into a box containing an electric bell, making it difficult for it to ring. Houdini disclaimed any knowledge of this, and himself had checked the box before the seance.

Other sessions followed but no-one succeeded in exposing "Margery". Houdini – who had been claiming that he had done so – was approached again to test her, but died before the test could be set up. Although, he certainly succeeded in counterfeiting on stage the feats of some psychics, he cannot be said to have "exposed" a single one of them.

New York Ghosts

Any great city has its anthology of ghost stories; New York is no exception, despite its relatively short history.

One of the most tenacious hauntings took place in Greenwich Village, at a building at 51 West 10th Street which was demolished in 1956, but formerly contained a number of artists' studios. The ghost was that of John La Farge, an artist who died in 1910, and painted, among other canvases, the *Ascension* which hangs over the altar of the Church of the Ascension not far away. The painting incidentally, fell from the wall of the church at the moment of La Farge's death.

Another artist, Feodor Rimsky, and his wife claimed to have first seen La Farge's ghost in studio 22 – formerly inhabited by La Farge – in 1944. Three years later, a dinner guest of Rimsky's saw the same figure, and described it. Now came a period of poltergeist activity – windows opening by themselves, curtains moving. In 1948 La Farge was seen again, this time in another studio one floor up – where, it turned out, there had once been a rest room used by him during his lifetime. John Adam Maxwell, an illustrator, saw not only La Farge but an unidentified woman, both dressed in the costume of the 1880s. Believing them to be intruders, he hit out, but damaged his hand on a filing cabinet when it went straight through the male figure.

Several other people said they saw the ghost; in February 1954 a seance was held at the studios. Little emerged about La Farge, but the medium expressed the fear that in trance she might throw herself from a window. It was later discovered that in the 1870s a young model had thrown herself from a window of the room in which the seance was held.

William James

William James (1842-1910), the brother of the novelist Henry James, was arguably the greatest American philosopher and psychologist of his time.

He became interested in psychical research by accident. There were many mediums at work in Boston during his youth. When his mother and sister had sittings with a Mrs L. E. Piper, he was at first scornful; but, persuaded to attend them, discovered that from a deep trance Mrs Piper was able to relate facts about the James family that were completely unknown outside it.

He was convinced that it was his duty to investigate such a remarkable phenomenon, and after organizing several sessions with Mrs Piper, decided that she was genuine. He took a leading role in examining her in a series of sessions held over some years, during which she purported to transmit messages from the spirit world – many of them in "cross-correspondence": that is, messages which made no sense by themselves, but were significant when combined with other messages received by other mediums.

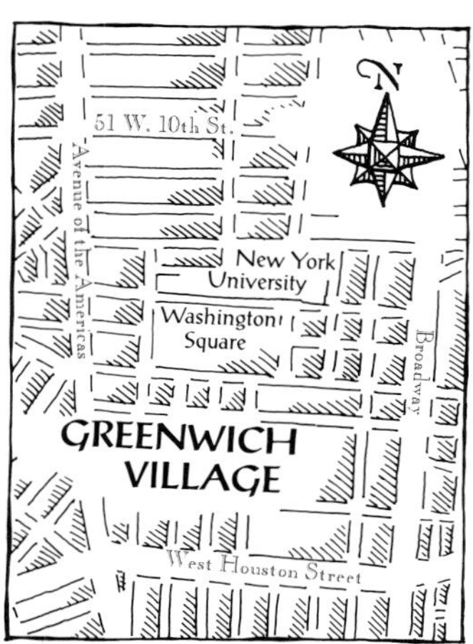

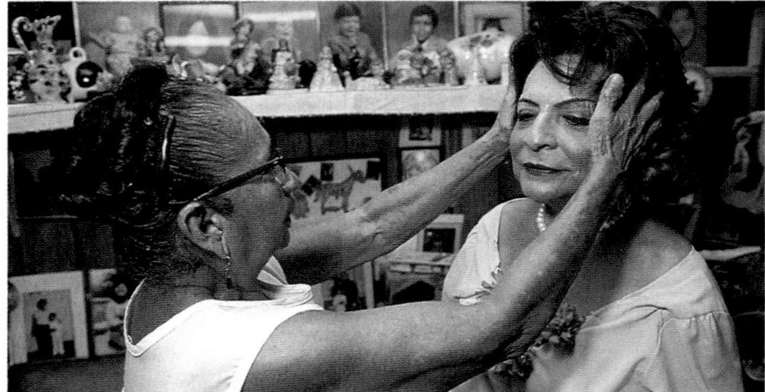

At the end of his life, and despite severe attacks from colleagues, James was unrepentant. He admitted that while "the phenomena are as massive and widespread as is anything in nature", the study of them "is tedious, repellent and undignified". But nevertheless, that study must be carried on, for the reasons he outlined:

"The first difference between the psychical researcher and the inexpert person is that the former realizes the commonness and typicality of the phenomenon here, while the latter, less informed, thinks it so rare as to be unworthy of attention. I wish to go on record for the commonness. The next thing I wish to go on record for is the presence, in the midst of all the humbug, of really supernormal knowledge. . . ."

The American Society for Psychical Research

The American Society for Psychical Research was founded in 1884, prompted by the existence of the English Society.

William James worked at the heart of the Society, and brought into it a number of distinguished scientists. From the start the ASPR was more scientifically orientated than its English counterpart, and the attitude of its members was broadly sceptical – although they all agreed that physical phenomena seemed to exist and deserved careful scientific study. Committees were organized to examine thought-transference, hypnosis, and so on, and the Society received much publicity as "the first organized scientific body in the country devoted to experimental psychology."

After five years, funds ran out, and the ASPR became merely a branch of the English society. Between 1904 and 1906, J. H. Hyslop established an independent American Society for Psychical Research; but this too petered out.

In 1907 the ASPR was revived as a separate body, although perhaps at first as a more credulous organization, not as interested as formerly in scientific research into the supernatural. However, in the late 1930s its reputation was revived. Particularly under the guidance of Professor Gardner Murphy, its research director then president, it took an increasingly serious attitude to its work.

The most dramatic event in America's attitude to PSI occurred in 1930, when Duke University laboratories were opened to biologist Dr Joseph Banks Rhine. He concluded that clairvoyance and telepathy were basically similar and he combined them in the term "extra-sensory perception."

The apparent success of his experiments, conducted within admirably careful guidelines, scandalized many American scientists, and the American Psychological Association actually organized a symposium at its 1938 annual conference in Columbus, Ohio, to attack them although they were unable to explain away the findings.

In 1957, the Parapsychological Association was formed as a professional organization whose aim was eventually to incorporate the American Psychological Association; it has done its best to see that the highest standards of intellectual respectability have been maintained in parapsychological research, and its experiments have in general been impeccably conducted and supported by careful methodology.

America and PSI today

The American public today shows a considerable interest in the supernatural and the paranormal. This ranges from utter preoccupation at one end of the scale – by those who lean on psychics or mediums as others lean on priests or psychiatrists– to a humorous tolerance at the other. Scientists display the same range of attitude, but within much narrower limits: while some, with that openness of mind which has in the past led to the greatest scientific discoveries, concede that there are still things in heaven and earth which they may not understand, others are so determined to reject PSI that they are even capable of distorting evidence which seems to confirm it.

At Duke University, at several other universities (although usually in small pockets of research) and under the aegis of the ASPR, serious work has continued since the Second World War. A basic conclusion has been that while there have always been particular people with remarkable PSI powers, PSI exists everywhere and in everyone, and only ingrained attitudes of mind disguise or repress this.

This fact has resulted in an extraordinary variety of fascinating experiments. For example, Harold Puthoff and Russell Targ, at Stanford Research Institute in Palo Alto, California, have been working on remote viewing – the kind

Dr Ed Bardner (left) *uses rare minerals to make what he calls "harmonic orbs", harnessing and concentrating psychic powers.*
A Mexican healer (below left), *lays her hands on a patient in a mixture of prayer, incantation and physical contact. The cure also depends on the patient's receptivity.*

A message to W. E. Cox of SORRAT*, apparently written of its own accord by a pen in a sealed box* (right)*, is one of several phenomena recorded during the Organization's investigations into the paranormal.*

of clairvoyance which seems to enable an alternative body to leave our conventional selves, and to witness events far from our physical position. Helmut Schmidt, of the Mind Science Foundation in San Antonio, Texas, has developed random number generators and random event generators to test individuals' apparent capacity to influence physical events by mind-power alone. Ian Stevenson, a psychiatrist teaching at the University of Virginia Medical School, has collected an enormous dossier on reincarnation, studying cases among the Eskimos, the Lebanese and the Indians, as well as in the West.

In 1969, after much argument, the Parapsychological Association was accepted in affiliation with the American Association for the Advancement of Science. Although there is still antagonism from conservative scientists and psychologists (far less from the latter), there is a strong movement toward the recognition of PSI as a legitimate field of research: recognition of the effects of psychedelic drugs and of widely-practised meditation has strengthened the case of the PSI workers.

Those who have worked for years in the field have formerly taken the view that there is no point in trying to convince the scientists of the existence of PSI: for them, it so obviously did exist, that eventually it would be recognized; why waste energy in argument? Rather similarly, many scientists took the equal and opposite position: PSI could not exist because "it did not make sense."

Happily, the younger PSI experimenters and the younger scientists are beginning to come together: biologists, psychiatrists, physicians, philosophers are now more ready to listen than they were previously, and to concede that some of those forces which used to be called "supernatural" are not so far out of line with modern scientific and philosophical concepts as was once thought.

The Sorrat Experiments

Some of the most serious recent attempts to examine psychokinesis have taken place during the past decade in Missouri, where John G. Neihardt, Professor of English Literature at the University of Illinois at Columbia, formed the Society for Research into Rapport and Telekinesis, known as SORRAT.

It is a recognized fact that PSI and PK are difficult to achieve in the presence of sceptics. It seems also true that where a group of people is unanimous in the supposition that such powers are available, they readily manifest themselves. In the case of SORRAT, this was certainly so from the beginning. Some of the phenomena were unexpected and strange: for example, carefully checked thermometers revealed that areas of coldness developed around target objects. However, the earliest manifestations were of paranormal rapping. Then, in 1965 – four years after the formation of the group – a small oak table suddenly levitated; then a larger table (weighing more than 80 pounds/36kg). These objects raised themselves into the air when only lightly touched by the fingers of members of the group.

THE WEEPING ICON

The apparent weeping of an icon of the Virgin in St Nicholas Albanian Orthodox Church in Chicago (below) has attracted thousands of visitors. Moisture has been seen to emerge from the area of the canvas on which the eyes are painted, and has run like tears down the face.

Even stranger events followed: objects levitated untouched by human hands. Professor Neihardt and a PK specialist, William Cox, a colleague of the father of modern parapsychology, Dr J. B. Rhine, constructed a closed box so fixed that it could not be moved or tilted; inside the box, always carefully sealed so there could be no tampering with it, coffee grounds were spread to reveal the movements of dice and other objects placed in it; when carbon paper and a stylus were placed in the box, "direct writing" occurred – although none of the messages was particularly significant.

Cox was so impressed by the success of SORRAT's experiments that he left Rhine to concentrate on the group's work – discovering early on that PK effects occurred within the sealed box even when no-one was attempting to instigate them. This was the first recorded occasion on which it was shown that PK or PSI events could occur spontaneously.

The death of Professor Neihardt in 1973 somewhat disorientated the group, but two members, Joseph Manginii and Dr J. T. Richards, continued experiments with Cox.

Remarkable results continued to be recorded – if with the elaborately random and slightly comic effect which attends so many paranormal events. For example, on one occasion, a variety of objects was placed in the sealed "mini-lab." They included unmarked paper, a pencil, dried peas dyed white and blue, several pipecleaners, a small glass, leather rings firmly attached to the inside of the box, and a set of six spools strung on a wire.

Cox and Richards sat with several friends in darkness around the box while the sound of busy shuffling was heard. When the box was opened, it was found that one of the six spools had completely vanished, and the ring of wire on which they had been strung was re-twisted; 30 blue peas had climbed into the glass; two straight pipecleaners were twisted into linked rings, and the leather rings had been torn from their fixtures.

Similar events followed, some of them filmed by a cine-camera. It has been claimed that the films were in some way animated by Cox; but experts have declared this to be impossible outside a film laboratory.

Cox's laboratory became a virtual playground for spirits – or whatever causes the PK effects (occasionally, mediums have claimed that spirits were involved). At one time, a piece of blank paper was left in a typewriter placed outside a mini-lab, but as far as possible guarded from any possible human typist. Some time later, the following verses inexplicably appeared, neatly typed:

A clever man, W. E. Cox
Made a really remarkable box.
In it, we, with PK,
In the usual way,
Wrote, spite of bands, seals and locks!

The verse was, alas, unsigned.

Interestingly, SORRAT members "created" their own ghost, an entirely fictional 17th-century Englishman who, when summoned to a seance, would levitate tables and rap on furniture.

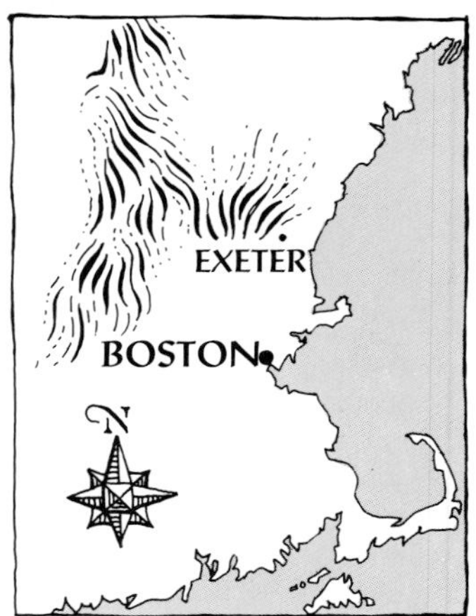

A UFO at Exeter

Among the reports of UFOs which remain unexplained, and are somewhat easier to credit than others, is that of a sighting at Exeter, New Hampshire, on September 3 1965.

This was reported by a hitchhiker, Norman J. Muscarello, and confirmed by two police patrolmen, Eugen Bertrand and David Hunt. Muscarello was walking three miles (5km) south of Exeter at two in the morning, when a group of five red lights appeared over a nearby house. They moved, in a group, over nearby fields, pulsating in turn, and always in the same pattern. They were bright enough to light up the area, but they did not seem to be emitted by a particular object – at least not one Moscarello could discern.

On the same night, patrolman Bertrand stopped at 1am to investigate a parked car, and found in it a distressed woman who said she had been followed by a light. The patrolman stayed with her for 15 minutes, but saw nothing. Meeting Muscarello, later, and hearing his story, Bertrand returned with the hitchhiker (who had reported his sighting at Exeter police station) and indeed saw the same red lights. They came so close that the patrolman fell to the ground and reached for his gun.

When the lights again approached, Bertrand and Muscarello took refuge in the police car, and the former radioed a colleague, Patrolman Hunt. Hunt received the call at 2.55, and drove to the site, where he too saw the lights. A little later, the duty officer at Exeter police station received a hysterical phone call from a man who claimed that strange lights had followed him to a call-box, and were now coming right at him. The call was suddenly broken off; the man was never traced.

The local Air Force Base had no record of any aircraft which could have been carrying the lights. John Fuller, a journalist, found more than 60 people in the area who had seen strange phenomena in the sky for several weeks around the same time. He examined the whole case at length in his book *Incident at Exeter*. No rational explanation has emerged: the Pentagon suggested that what the hiker and officers had seen was simply the stars and planets (which does not seem to explain why the lights were red).

CANADA

MEDICINE MEN

When "civilized" Western explorers first arrived there, Canada was inhabited by indigenous North American Indians; it was not long before it became clear that forces were at work among them whose nature was far from clear to the white man.

The most spectacular forces were commanded by the *pilotois* or medicine men attached to each tribe. Invited to foretell the future, especially in times of crisis, the *pilotois* built himself a wigwam, retired into it, and working himself into what seemed an hysterical frenzy, communed with spirits. Meanwhile observers seated outside the wigwam saw it shake, sometimes lifting itself clear off the ground, occasionally illuminated by strange lights. Strong winds often arose at the same time, and weird voices were heard wailing.

This phenomenon was reported as early as 1609. Many Catholic missionaries later reported the same sort of experience, and one of them, Fr Paul LeJeune, head of the Jesuit Mission to the Huron Indians in the 17th century, observed the phenomena very closely indeed. Despite his greatest efforts, he was unable to detect trickery, and concluded that the Devil must be at work.

Pilotois *or AmerIndian spirits have been credited with shaking Canadian Indian wigwams such as this* (above)*, sometimes lifting them right off the ground with the strength of their occult powers. No-one has ever been able to explain how (assuming the shaking to be trickery) the wigwams could have been moved about so violently by one unaided man.*

The phenomenon of the Shaking Tent was recorded well into the 20th century. In 1929, A. K. Black, an official of the Hudson's Bay Company working at White Sands, in the Mackenzie River Basin, watched carefully as young Indians built a wigwam. He assured himself that the poles supporting it were so firmly fixed into the ground as to be immovable except by the greatest force. He then sat with the Indians who surrounded the wigwam, a few feet from it, while the *pilotois* crawled into it through a small aperture.

As soon as he disappeared, the tent began to shake; the *pilotois'* voice was heard, at the bottom of the wigwam, apparently conversing with a spirit whose voice was heard at its top. After answering questions from members of the tribe, the *pilotois* announced that he was going to call the spirit of a bear into the wigwam and kill it. The wigwam subsequently shook even more, and the poles supporting it bent until they almost touched the ground. Eventually, the *pilotois* emerged. Black inspected the wigwam, and found that despite its continual movements, the tent-poles were as firmly fixed as they had originally been.

Much the same observations were made by a Professor Hollowell at Berens River, Lake Winnipeg, in 1930; Sister B. Coleman at Cass Lake, Minnesota, in 1937, and Regina Flannery at James Bay in 1939 but no-one was able to discover any signs of cheating.

THE AMHERST POLTERGEIST

Poltergeists are not unknown in the country. The most famous case arose in Amherst, Nova Scotia, in 1878, in the small cottage of a shoemaker, Daniel Teed, when bedclothes and furniture began to move about, and there were loud reports like pistol-shots. A local doctor was called to examine Teed's sister-in-law, Esther, who began showing alarming symptoms of blowing up like a balloon. While he was there, her bedclothes moved about, writing appeared on a wall, and a piece of plaster flew around a corner and struck him.

Dr Caritte observed the household closely, and succeeded in contacting spirits, which answered simple questions by rapping on the bedroom wall. When the Rev A. Temple, a Baptist minister, arrived, a bucket of water boiled itself in front of him. When Esther left the house, all was quiet; when she returned, the manifestations began again, even more acutely than before. There was in particular an attempt to set the house on fire by the use of lighted matches which appeared in mid-air, setting fire to clothes and furnishings.

Unsurprisingly, it was now suggested that Esther should leave permanently. A neighbour took her in, at first quietly – but soon he began to be disturbed by noises, and Esther was hit on the head by a flying scrubbing-brush. She then went to work in a restaurant. The Inspector of Fisheries for Nova

Scotia, W. H. Rogers, was visiting the restaurant one day when the door of a kitchen stove refused to be shut by Esther, and finally jumped off its hinges and crashed to the floor.

Esther for a while became a circus exhibit – a boy's pocket knife leaped from his hand and stabbed her, iron spikes which she handled grew too hot to hold, and so on. Walter Hubbell, an actor and stage magician, convinced that she was a fake, tried for some time to expose her, but was completely unable to do so. Within a few months she was not only exhausted by the manifestations which continually occurred around her but was in prison, having been found guilty of arson when a barn (according to her) spontaneously burst into flame.

Hubbell wrote a famous book on the Amherst affair, which has been evaluated again and again by psychical investigators. The consensus is, that while Esther cannot be completely cleared of trickery, if she did organize all the events that occurred, and were witnessed, she was one of the greatest conjurers the world has known.

The Hunt for Bigfoot

Such a wild country as Canada naturally attracted many stories of mysterious beings who lived in the hills and forests – man-eating giants and monsters who accounted for the frequent mysterious disappearance of explorers (who were doubtless prey to the natural perils of the country). The very names of the Loup-Garou, or werewolf, and the Susquatch man (a large, hairy personage not unlike the legendary Green man of the English forests) were still used, within living memory, to frighten naughty children. Most monsters have by now been consigned to the pages of fiction; but one or two stories resolutely decline to die – among them, the Abominable Snowman or Yeti (see p.113) and Bigfoot.

Bigfoot lives in North America, and has done so from time immemorial (the Salish Indian tribe of British Columbia has a legend of the great hairy beast Sasquatch; the Huppas of California speak of Omah). One of the earliest sightings by a white man took place in 1811, when a Canadian trader found footprints measuring 14 by eight inches (35.5 × 20.5cm) in the snows of the northern Rockies, near Jasper, Alberta.

But it was in the 1950s, perhaps stimulated by speculation about the Yeti, that sightings began to be reported on an almost regular basis. Various witnesses came forward with tales of abnormally big, humanoid but hairy creatures – rather like enormous apes – which had appeared in various areas of Canada. Photographs of tracks began to appear, some of them clearly faked, but others more difficult to explain.

A notorious piece of cine-film shot in 1967 at Bluff Creek, in north California, near the Oregon Border, appears to show Bigfoot. The creature had allegedly been active in the area ten years previously, plaguing a team of road-builders not only by leaving convincing footprints, but by playfully moving heavy equipment about.

In October, 1967, two men – Roger Patterson and Bob Gimlin – were on a Bigfoot expedition in the area when they suddenly came across one, standing by a creek. Patterson seized his cine-camera and shot several feet before the film ran out. There have been claims that the creature was impersonated by a confederate in an animal skin; but Patterson and Gimlin stuck to their story, which has never been convincingly demolished.

There have been literally thousands of other sightings, of various degrees of credibility, and some of them recorded by police officers. One of the most recent was reported in a local newspaper (the *Concord Monitor*) in November 1987: a Mr Walter Bowers was shooting pheasant at Salisbury, New Hampshire, when he saw the nine-foot (2.7m) tall creature: "His whole body was covered with hair, I would say a kind of greyish colour . . . The hands were like yours or mine, only three times bigger, with pads on the front paws, like a dog – long legs, long arms. It was just like a gorilla but this here wasn't a gorilla."

Although there are some weird stories – of ESP communication between Bigfoot and its observers, or of Bigfeet who have vanished into thin air when shot at – it seems unlikely that everyone who has reported seeing such a creature is deranged or lying. Janet and Colin Bord, two British experts on the subject, have suggested the possibility that the creature may be a descendant of *Gigantopithecus*, which lived in China 500,000 years ago. A more convincing explanation must await the capture of a living Bigfoot, or at least one recently deceased.

Ogopogo

The Canadian equivalent of the Loch Ness monster (p.132) is Ogopogo, which is said to inhabit Lake Okanagan in British Columbia. It is presumably related to Naitaka, the Indian snake of the water, a demon-god to whom pigs and chicken were sacrificed. A number of sightings of Ogopogo were reported during the 1920s, and a local tourist body capitalized on the matter by offering a million dollars for proof of the monster's existence. This was never claimed, although a Canadian woman swimming in the lake in 1987 described being bumped, in a friendly sort of way, by a 30-foot long (9m) water-creature like a giant worm.

The Champ

In the 1980s the state legislatures of Vermont and New York passed resolutions to protect the health of a monster allegedly inhabiting Lake Champlain, the waterway which runs between New York and Vermont and up into Quebec.

Known as Champ, this monster was first sighted in 1819 by a boatman: his description might be that of the Loch Ness or Okanagan monsters – long, worm-like, with several "humps". During the rest of the 19th century there were many more sightings, and the showman P. T. Barnum offered a large reward for Champ, dead or alive.

Reliable recent sightings have been rarer, but in July 1977 Sandra Mansi produced a remarkably clear and graphic photograph of Champ. Although experts could not fault the photograph itself, the negative unaccountably went missing before it could be examined. Such accidents too often result in the disappearance of evidence of the supernatural.

Bob Gimlin (left) *is one of many witnesses who claim to have seen Bigfoot, the American equivalent of the Yeti or Abominable Snowman in the Pacific Northwest, in Canada, commonly called by the Indian name Sasquatch. Gimlin, a half-Indian cowboy, shot a famous but disputed piece of 8mm film of a female Bigfoot in northern California.*

Frank and Jim Rieger (below left) *and **Lilian Vogelgesang and her daughter Jamie*** (below right) *all claim to have seen Ogopogo, a monster said to inhabit Okanagan Lake in British Columbia. They say it was olive-green, with a long neck, smooth shiny skin and flippers, was chasing fish, and was about 50 feet (15m) long and at least five feet (1.5m) in diameter.*

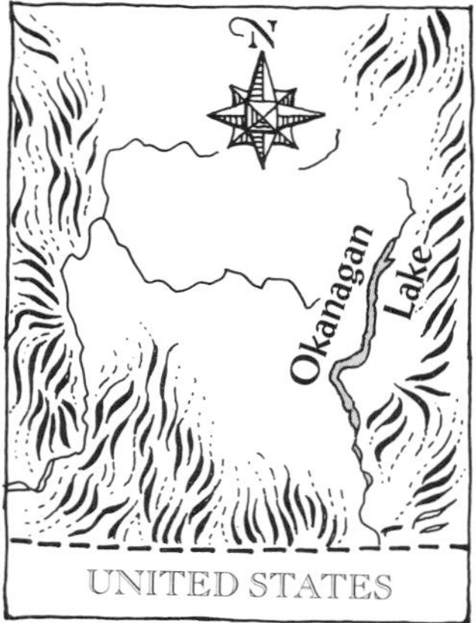

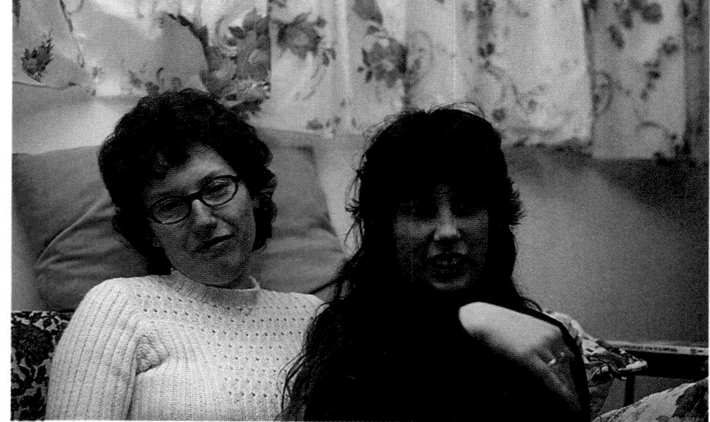

MEXICO

PSYCHIC SURGERY

Mexico has for many years been one of the two world centres of psychic surgery – of alleged surgical operations conducted by the bare hands of the "surgeon". Although Filipino psychic surgeons have been detected in frauds (see p.121), several Mexicans have better reputations. Jose Arigo, perhaps the most famous "surgeon" of the 1960s, was observed by several European researchers, and not detected in fraud.

The methods of Mexican "surgeons" very much resemble those of the Filipino "surgeons", although they seem if anything even more casual. Lourival de Freitas has been seen to operate on a young girl suffering from saturation of the lungs simply by plunging a pair of scissors down her throat. "Maria" was seen by an American doctor, Guy Lyon Playfair, to make a large hole in a patient's neck with a pair of scissors and then to pull tissue of some kind from it with a pair of workman's pincers.

The operations sound horrific: Dr Playfair saw Edivaldo Oliveira Silvo apparently rip open a man's abdomen, and several times saw patients with their eyes hanging out of their sockets as sight problems were treated. Playfair was himself "operated on" for a digestive problem, and was convinced that Edivaldo's fingers had actually penetrated his stomach. His symptoms were at least temporarily alleviated (he agrees that in most cases, psychic operations seem only temporarily to resolve medical conditions).

In his book *The Flying Cow*, Dr Playfair relates psychic surgery to the ingenious and complex theories of Hernani Guimaraes Andrade, a Brazilian engineer and founder of the Brazilian Institute for Psycho-Biophysical Research, whose conception of time allows for a number of dimensions, so that the physical reality we recognize is only one of several; the interventions of the psychic surgeons – and indeed of more conventional healers – is on one of these planes, and makes use of Biological Organizing Models (BOMs) to reconstruct the body after (for example) the removal of tumours.

Dr Playfair's own belief is that psychic surgeons make use of a force unknown to man but apparently known to certain plants and animals, which enables diseased tissues to heal themselves. Their knowledge is instinctive, and has nothing (he believes) to do with their fundamental Christianity. He points out that their failure to eradicate disease is no greater than that of conventional surgeons, who often fail to cure the conditions causing, for example, a cancerous growth.

Many questions remain to be answered about psychic surgery. It is true that tricks have sometimes been used, and it may be that those who have been convinced have simply not worked under sufficiently rigorous test conditions.

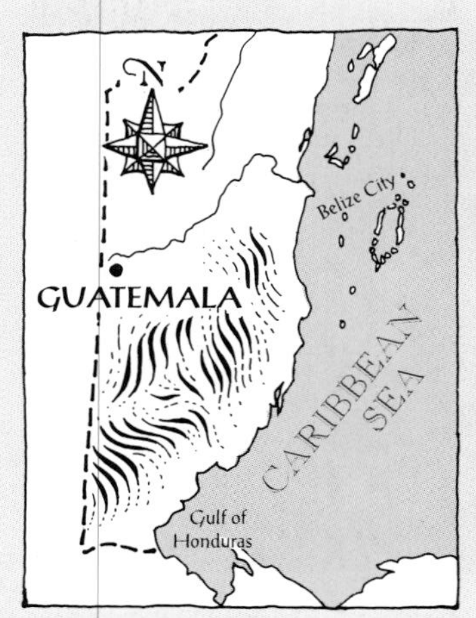

THE MAYANS

Forms of the Mayan language are spoken by Indians living in Mexico, Belize, Guatemala and Honduras, descendants of a people with an obscure history. Only the ruins of their great cities in the Yucatan, Guatemala and Chiapas, with their elaborate royal and religious buildings, including vertiginous pyramids (right), today testify to their former greatness.

Mayan civilization was clearly strongly religious, worshipping an androgynous creator. All nature, including the sun, was considered to be alive and constantly renewing itself. They also believed in ghosts and even in 1881, the native guides who accompanied the British Mayanist Alfred Maudsley on his trip to the city of Tikal, refused to sleep there for fear of ancestral spirits believed still to inhabit the ruins of the former city.

Mayan artists and mathematicians were convinced of the order of the universe, as shown in the skies, and constructed a complex calender in which each day had its characteristic "fortune" and each 20-day period had an overall theme of either good or ill fortune. Numerology, astronomy and astrology all combined in a fascinating system of divination, now lost. Mayan priests were able to accurately predict eclipses, the transits of Venus and the return of comets enabling them to predict the best time for every human enterprise, although they never realized that the earth went round the sun.

Mayan civilization had a darker side. Human sacrifices were made to their gods at the tops of the pyramids by magnificently robed priests, the victims' bones being cast into pit holes dug in the rock. After the gods had been placated by this ceremony, their attention was drawn to human prayers by smoke signals.

***Voodoo** is popularly considered a religion concerned almost entirely with the promotion of evil. This is by no means the case: voodoo has a positive side as well, providing emotional support and comfort, which oppressed black people in the Caribbean feel more conventional religions have failed to offer. During carefully prepared and mounted ceremonies* (left), *men and women make ready for possession by* loa, *or god-spirits, which came to Haiti from Africa with the original slave ships. Because they wished to help the slaves, they are usually benevolent, helping the poor and sick to forget their poverty or illness.*

However, there is no denying that Voodoo in Haiti sometimes has another dimension: ceremonies usually involve a certain amount of lascivious sexual behaviour, and Voodoo priests make use of sexual magic (see pp.32-3) to their own advantage to strengthen their control over the members of their congregations.

HAITI

VOODOO

In Port-au-Prince, a Voodoo drummer (far right) *and priestess invoke a spirit,* Azaka, *inviting it to attend a ceremony. Drums are very important for voodoo ceremonies, almost hypnotizing the participants with their incessant rhythms.*

Clerveus Narcissa (near right) *was buried in an Haitian cemetery in 1962, but here stands beside the grave from which, encouraged by a Voodoo priest, he rose, as a zombie. There are only a very few well-authenticated cases of people who have recognized the "walking dead" as relatives whose funerals they had attended.*

Voodoo and Haiti are inseparably associated, although it is clear that Voodoo's roots lie somewhere in West Africa (the word derives from *vodun* – a god or spirit). It has various meanings – embracing black magic of one kind or another, but also a more conventional religion, based on the belief that the gods can help their followers in their daily lives.

Initiation into Voodoo may take place for any one of a number of reasons – a run of bad luck which needs correction, for instance, or because religious observances have been neglected, or because of persecution by dead enemies.

During a week of preparation the postulant is assured that the spirit will be set free from the body, and that evil will be vanquished. On the last evening the candidate is washed, and then for a further week prepared for possession by the *loa* – the spirit of someone who once lived on earth, but is now a god. The *loas* are usually benevolent – although a few are evil. While someone is possessed, they are not responsible for their actions, and other people at the ceremony are under obligation not to reveal to them how they behaved while possessed.

The final preparation for possession involves a soup in which pieces of sacrificed chicken are mixed with the candidate's hair and nail clippings, and a fire ceremony during which purifying flames are passed over the arms and legs. Finally, he or she emerges into the sunlight barefoot, dressed in white, is baptised with a leaf dipped into water, and given a new Voodoo name. The *loa* now possesses the postulant, who for 40 days must not wash or change clothes. This magical preparation results in a certain amount of dissassociation: the candidates often feel faint and nauseated, "hear" strange noises, go into trance, stagger about, speak in strange voices; when ritual dancing and chanting starts, they can fall completely under the control of the Voodoo priests.

The psychologist Dr William Sargent, points out in his book *The Mind Possessed* that "the various possession states provide an outlet for every type of normal and abnormal behaviour among people whose lives are one long struggle against poverty and despair"; the behaviour of the possessed, he noted, resembled that of the *loa* presumed to possess them – for example, occupied by the spirit of Ghede, the god of the phallus, a man's behaviour would be overtly sexual.

It is clear that it is possible for the evil side of a personality to be released, and it would be silly to deny that acts of cruelty or masochism have sometimes taken place during Voodoo ceremonies. But its propensity to evil seems to have been wildly overstated.

ZOMBIES

It is generally believed that Voodoo priests can raise people from the dead to become zombies – one story is of a young woman who in 1950 refused to sleep with a Voodoo priest; he dug her up after her death and used her as a zombie until rebuked by the Catholic Church.

The mentally retarded are often suspected of being zombies, and this is usually the explanation when anecdotes are followed up. However, there are one or two more interesting cases – one of them, well-attested, of a zombie arrested in a Haitian village whose aunt identified him as the nephew she had seen dead and buried four years earlier. A Catholic priest learned from the man that he was one of a band of zombies raised and set to work by a Voodoo priest.

In his book *The Magic Island* (London, 1935), W. B. Seabrook tells of a number of zombies owned by a Voodoo priest called Joseph, who one morning put his wife in charge of them. She gave them salt biscuits to eat, not realizing that salt is the one thing that brings zombies to the knowledge of what they are. The zombies immediately woke from trance and made for the cemetery and their untenanted graves, where they attempted to dig themselves back into the ground, turning to rotting corpses as they did so.

Barbados

The Disturbed Tomb

Coffins placed in orderly positions (near right) *were mysteriously rearranged* (far right) *on a number of occasions. No explanation has been found.*

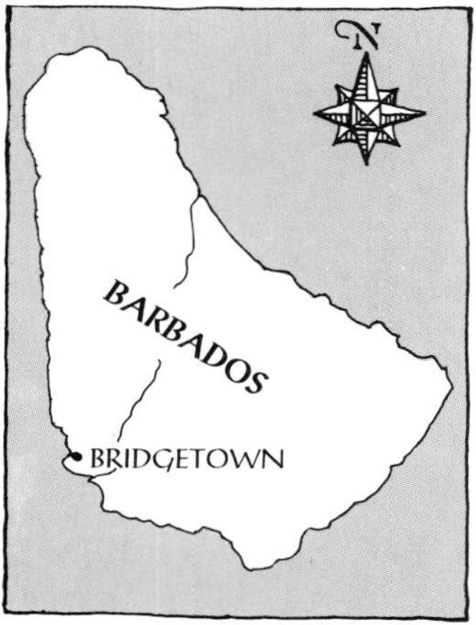

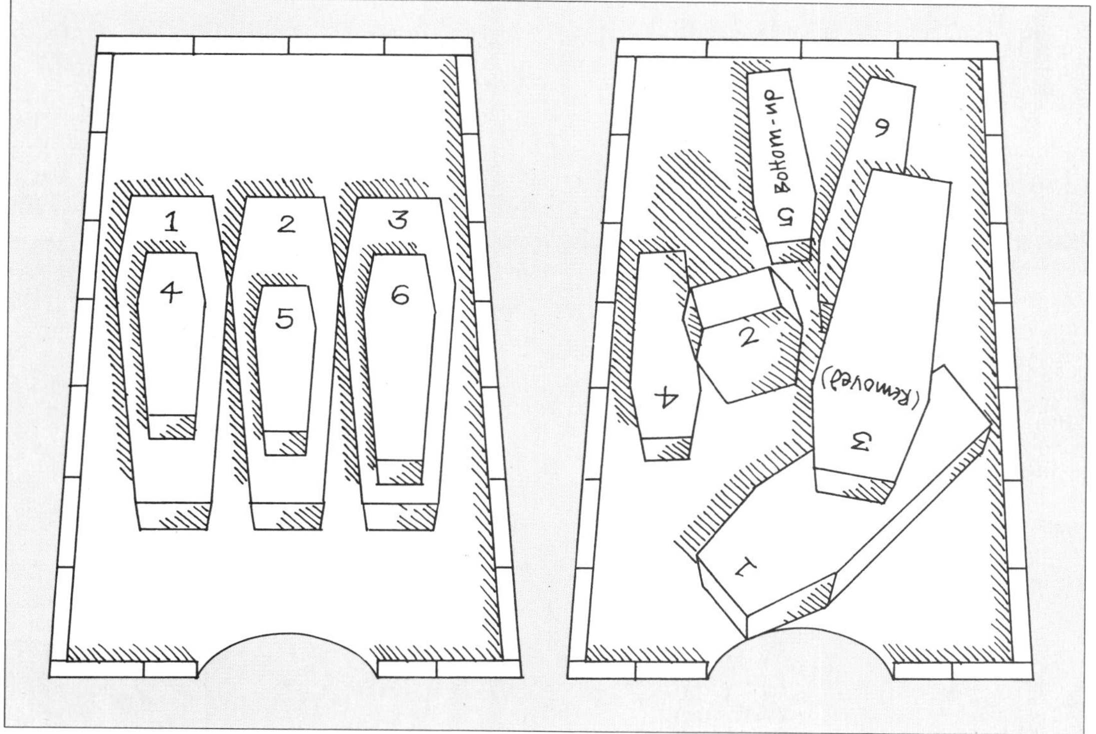

The Chase family of Barbados used to bury its dead in a large and very solid tomb in the graveyard of Christ Church, overlooking Oistins Bay. The tomb was sealed by a monumental marble slab, and it was generally agreed that only a concerted effort by a number of workmen could open it.

In 1807/8, two burials were held: that of Mrs Thomasina Goddard (on July 31), and that of a child, Mary Anna Maria Chase, on the following February 22. On July 6 1812, the funeral party of Dorcas Chase, the elder sister of Mary Anna Maria, arrived at the tomb, and when the marble slab was lifted aside, it was found that the heavy lead coffins of Mary Anna Maria and of Mrs Goddard had been moved across the floor of the tomb. They were replaced in their original positions, and Dorcas' coffin was placed next to them. However, there was considerable discussion as to how the coffins could possibly have been moved.

Thomas Chase, the then head of the family, died within the month, and on August 9 the marble slab was once more lifted aside; this time the coffins were undisturbed. But the next time the tomb was opened – on September 25 1816, for the burial of a child – they were again no longer in their original positions.

At future burials crowds naturally gathered to see whether the coffins had been disturbed: they were not disappointed. On one occasion, in 1819, Viscount Combermere, the Governor of Barbados, himself attended a funeral and saw how every coffin in the tomb had been moved, and one shattered. This time a layer of sand was scattered in the tomb, on which anyone entering it – by whatever means – would leave footprints. When the tomb was reopened nine months later, not only were seals previously placed on it found intact, not only had concrete sealing the marble slab to be chipped away before it could be moved – but inside, the coffins had again been shuffled around – one hurled across the tomb with such violence that it had damaged the wall.

The Hon. Nathan Lucas, a witness with the Governor, wrote: "I confess myself at a loss . . . thieves certainly had no hand in it; and as for any practical wit or hoax, too many were requisite to be trusted with the secret for it to remain unknown; and as for negroes having anything to do with it, their superstitious fear of the dead and everything belonging to them precludes any idea of the kind. All I know is that it happened and that I was an eye-witness of the fact!!!"

The coffins were removed from the tomb, which have remained open and empty. Investigations since 1820 have failed to come up with a satisfactory solution to events that are particularly well-attested. One observer examining drawings of the coffins' positions before and after a disturbance, pointed out that they had all moved in the same way, "exactly as if caught when rotating at a snail's pace around their centres of gravity . . . The picture they present is that of a swirl, or a spiral effect, like so many metal shapes, heavier at one end than the other, spun around by some force gravitational, gyroscopic, electro-magnetic, or goodness knows what." Earth-movement is unlikely to have produced the result.

PERU

THE NAZCA PLATEAU

The Nazca plateau of Peru looks, from the air, like a slate on which some giant has scrawled childlike but remarkably sensitive pictures.

Figure after figure – 18 birds, a spider, a giant candelabra and various abstract patterns – lie on the surface of the desert and the surrounding hillsides, covering almost five hundred square miles (1290 sq km) between the Andes and the coast. Some of the lines making up the patterns stretch for as much as five miles (8 km) across the earth's surface. It is only from the air that they can be fully seen and comprehended.

They are fragile, the outlines scratched thinly into the earth – only the particularly still, dry climate of the area has enabled them to survive for something like 1,500 years (the pyramids and surviving ceramics of the ancient civilization of the area are dated to around 300 BC-AD 540).

Maria Reiche, a German who specialized in studying the Nazca drawings, produced the first tenable theories about how they were made – including the discovery that they were first plotted on a small scale, then "squared up" and reproduced at their full size. She believed that the drawings involved complex mathematical calculations, amounting to a code relating to planetary movements – for some of them appeared to be astronomically aligned. The drawings are almost all made in one continuous line, and it has been suggested that among other things they may have been used as ceremonial religious pathways.

The most spectacular theory about the origin of the drawings was advanced by the Swiss writer Erich von Daniken, who in his book *Chariots of the Gods?* (1970), proposed that they marked the landing places of flying saucers bringing astronauts from civilizations based in other galaxies. On a number of grounds – including the unsuitability of the sandy Nazca soil as a landing-site, and the unlikelihood of astronauts needing to lay out markers for take-off (quite apart from the general improbability of his theory) – von Daniken's book, although very popular, is extremely unconvincing.

Some theories have been dismissed by scientists: computers have examined the alignment of the drawings and failed to find any astronomical correlation. It is probable that the truth about these astonishing sketches will never be known. The best guess is that they were indeed designed to be seen from the sky – but by the gods, as part of the rituals of worship, offered to them in appeasement, celebration or praise.

The Nazca lines – *mysterious markings such as this spiral* (left) *– were inscribed in the dusty earth of Peru about 1,500 years ago, by an Indian people of whom little is known. There have been many explanations – including Von Daniken's weird suggestion that they were made for visiting spacemen. It seems likely that the vast drawings were designed to be seen from the air. Two Americans, Jim Woodman and Bill Spohrer (in 1975) actually constructed a hot-air balloon made of cloth (which could in theory have been made by ancient Nazca aeronauts) and flew in it over the desert.*

Brazil

The Macumbas

The Macumba religion is practised by a large number of Brazilians, and involves the apparent possession of worshippers by their gods; in a process that in some respects resembles that of Voodoo ceremonies (see pp.186–7). There is an initiation ceremony before anyone can become a member of one of the numerous Macumba cults. The initiate having gone into a trance, the priest must decide which god has taken possession, in order to prescribe the appropriate ceremony. This involves animal sacrifice after which blood is smeared on the initiate; during deep trance, suggestions are made for changes in behaviour and for obedience to the cult.

During worship, drumming and dancing encourage worshippers to go into trance-states in which their faces often violently change expression, and they sometimes become totally exhausted. On coming out of their trance, they usually know nothing of what has happened during the ceremony, but their behaviour is often changed.

Shamanism

Shamanism has always been a major feature of the supernatural in Brazil. A Brazilian shaman is a man, or sometimes a woman, who while in a trance can talk to spirits and with their help see into the future, cure illness, and diagnose diseases before a conventional doctor can do so.

Shamanism in Brazil is often hereditary. However, sometimes the power is suddenly recognized in a person, and a local shaman will undertake to train such a man to recognize his own individual spirit – usually a bird or animal – and to open himself to it so that he can be possessed. The most prestigious spirit of Brazilian shaman is that of the jaguar.

The shaman uses certain tools – a ground rattle or a maraca – to gain the spirit's attention, and takes drugs to help him into a trance-state. The trance-states are like theatrical performances, usually seen by firelight and at night. To cure an illness, the shaman will blow tobacco smoke on the part of the body affected, and then apparently suck out the illness.

Brazilian Indians are careful of their souls – and with reason, for these are often stolen away. A shaman is sometimes hired to search for the missing souls of relatives, and to see that they are returned to their bodies. A soul can fly from its body at the sight of a ghost, or on an encounter with the *Tupi Anyang*, a terrifying spirit with long hair and a boneless body which engages in erotic activity.

The *Tupi* shaman was often as important as the chief of a tribe: some powerful shaman persuaded whole tribes to follow them from one part of the country to another – often in search of the land of Maira, a sort of Mexican Eldorado. At the end of the journey they would build a house and dance in it day or night without sleep or food, in the conviction that it would eventually rise into the sky and endow the dancers with magical properties.

After death, most shamans turn into jaguar spirits; so they are usually buried as far from the tribe as convenient, thorn bushes planted around the grave to keep their ghosts from haunting.

Drugs, be they strong tobacco (above) *or mushrooms, have traditionally been used by seers or shamans to help them enter hypnotic trances in which they can give instruction or advice to their followers. Brazilians frequently consult shamans who are in such states of trance.*

AUSTRALASIA AND OCEANIA

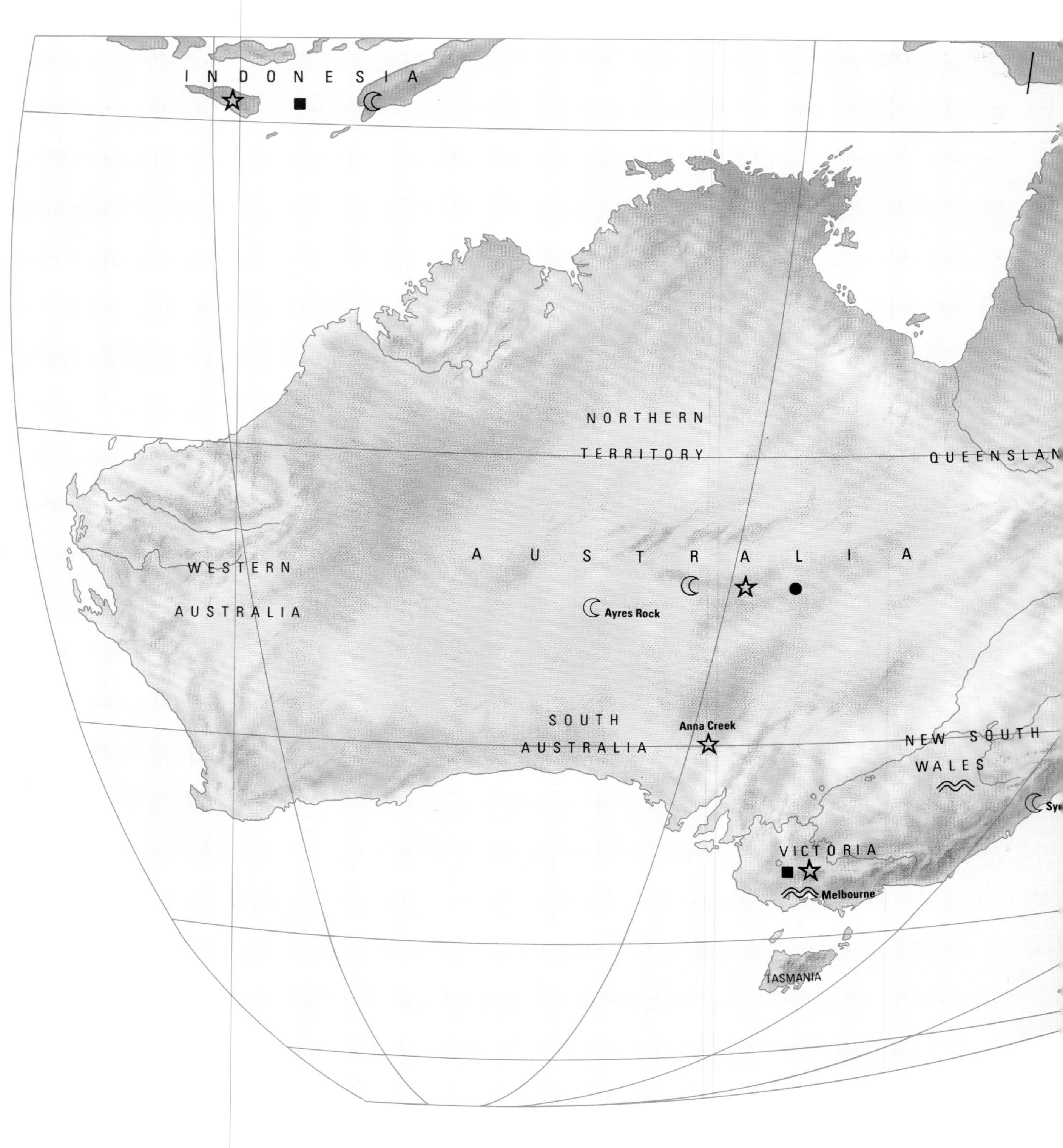

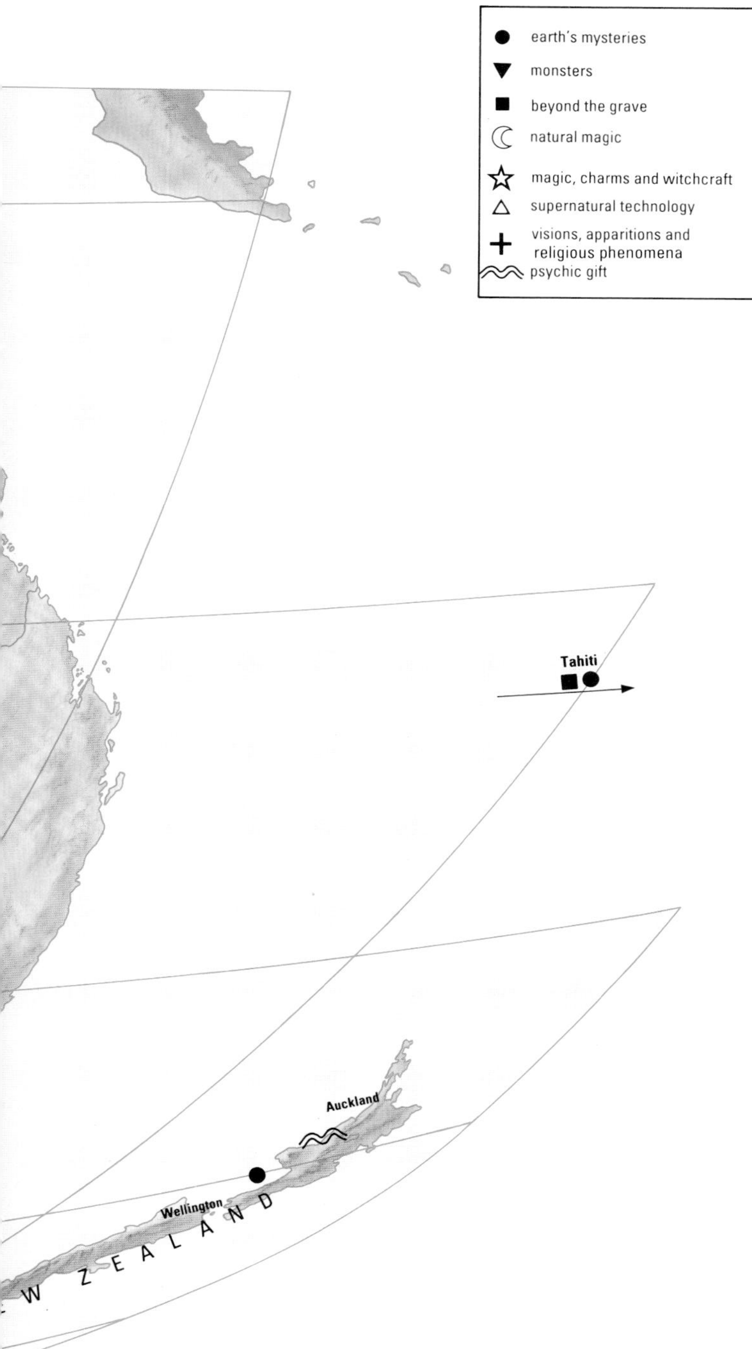

Australia is a single, vast religious site to the Aboriginal people who were the Continent's sole original inhabitants. A vast narrative that makes such epics as the Iliad *or the* Mahabharata *look like short stories, chronicles the history of the Dreamings, or ancestral beings, who formed the world from chaos and filled it with animals, stones, earth, insects, plants, water, fish, birds – and humans. There is a Dreaming for everything which lives: a Honey Ant Dreaming, a Gum-tree Dreaming, a Bush-fire Dreaming: and the Aboriginal view of their country (much simplified) is not unlike the view of the earth taken by some modern physicists – that perhaps it is itself a vast living organism.*

This seems a strange idea to modern Western man; but within its context it is understandable enough – and explains the Aborigine talent for being at one with the landscape, for having a remarkable ability to find water, seek out hunted prey, foresee evil events; where everything is mystery, mystery is ordinary and everyday. The Maori people of New Zealand have a culture not entirely dissimilar, although perhaps less keenly developed – perhaps because they were "in-comers", probably from Pacific islands; their country is "new" to them, in terms of millennia. Yet they, too, have shown strange powers of ESP and divination – and both people share with native Africans the power to kill or cure by the simple act of suggestion.

The idea of the landscape itself as a living entity certainly suggests a solution to some of earth's mysteries: there do seem to be particular places where natural laws are suspended – for example, the so-called Bermuda Triangle. These may simply be vortexes of natural energy – the equivalent of the nodules of power where ley-lines meet, or those points on the human body where acupuncture needles can interfere with the energy flow.

The "green movement", with its concern for the damage man is doing to his environment, is almost the large-scale image of a healer concerned with the health of a patient – although it has yet to be suggested except by a very few people that the power of thought, a focusing of the minds of a great number of people, may have an effect not only on the actions of other humans but perhaps on the behaviour of earth itself.

Yet if it is the case that the earth reacts to symbolic signs upon its surface, that it has a "nervous system" of its own, of which ley-lines and perhaps magnetic forces (allegedly seen at work in the Bermuda Triangle) are a part, who can be certain that man may not be able to intervene in it by the so far underdeveloped force of sheer imagination and will-power?

The symbolic art of the Aborigines has for 30,000 years suggested just this: that everything which exists is a necessary part of earth and life on earth, and reacts upon every other part. It is an increasingly sympathetic view, and outward manifestations of it may include just those forces of the occult about which modern man is most confused.

AUSTRALIA

THE ABORIGINES

Descendants of the original inhabitants of Australia, who probably established themselves on the Continent 30,000 years ago after travelling from south-east Asia, nurse strong and extremely complex beliefs about the supernatural powers of their remote ancestors; they also have the strongest conception of the one-ness of creation, established many centuries ago during Dream-time, when spirit beings set the Sun, Moon and stars in their courses and created all things.

The aborigines are fiercely defensive of their spirit centres and paths, and pass down from generation to generation their knowledge of the Dream-time heroes who personified creatures or plants. Local groups or lodges memorize chants and rituals and care for sacred relics, which are anointed annually with blood or red ochre and fat, and ensure the propagation of the species they represent.

An individual stands in a particularly strong relationship with the animal, plant or object which is his or her totem, and will neither kill nor eat it except in the utmost necessity; people who share the same totem are brother and sister, and may not marry. The totem strengthens in sickness, and may warn, in dreams, of approaching danger.

Ritual chanting induces a trance-like state during which the members of a totem-lodge become the heroes of the Dreaming; various ceremonies – *corroborees* – involve the drawing of blood, ritual "blooding", and the reverent handling of the sacred relics. The aborigine myths are rehearsed by the recitation of long narrative poems. These vary enormously from tribe to tribe, as do the spirit-beings who care for or sometimes attack individuals. There are a few ultra-powerful ones – the Sky-beings, such as *Baiame* in New South Wales and *Bunjil* in Victoria – and innumerable lesser ones such as the Lightning Brothers, the Red Kangaroo Men and the Mountain-devil woman. Most of these are good.

There is a strong belief in magic and, despite the encroachment of modern Australian civilization and therefore of modern medicine, it is still suspected that someone who for no apparent reason becomes seriously ill or dies must be subject to black magic. This can be directed in various ways: by performing a magical rite over a footstep, or making an image and stabbing it with a pin (as in European witchcraft). One of the strongest rites is that of bone-pointing, when a pointed bone or stick with a piece of wax at one end is jerked in the direction of the victim by a magician who stands with the sun or moon at his back, taking care that no water is in front of him. The pointing-bone releases an invisible splinter which penetrates the very being of the victim.

The *Sydney Sun* reported in April 1957 the case of Charlie Lya Wulumu, a 19-year-old native admitted to Darwin Hospital, apparently fatally ill. He claimed that one of his tribesmen had "sung him to death", since when creeping paralysis had affected his arms, legs, chest and throat. He recovered after some time in an iron lung, but only after he had been assured that the curse on him had been lifted. Another widely-reported case concerned the whole family of a native girl who, in Anna Creek, South Australia, contrary to custom, married an aboriginal sheep-shearer. Subsequently she, her husband, their baby, the bride's parents and her 14-year-old nephew were condemned to death by the *kurdaitcha* or witch doctor. The baby died, apparently of suffocation; the nephew was next admitted to hospital, extremely ill. The *kurdaitcha* was arrested, but the terrified young woman refused to testify that he had "pointed the bone" at her, and as a result the curse was lifted.

Kurdaitcha can act benevolently; one with an expert command of the necessary ceremonies can extract a faulty heart or kidney without leaving so much as a scar. But a victim convinced that he has been cursed will invariably die. A victim may be saved by an equally clever medicine-man by extracting the "badness" which has been imposed on him.

Medicine-men are chosen from those young men who show a particular ease in going into trances and having visions; they are initiated in special rituals after long fasting – after which they have the power to "fly through the air" (in out-of-body experiences), possess x-ray vision and special healing powers.

Some attention has been paid to the ESP abilities allegedly possessed by aborigines. Their rumoured accomplishments are great: they are said to be able to identify small objects at distance, to transmit messages by telepathy, to hear sounds inaudible to other human ears. In 1949 members of the New South Wales Parapsychological Institute set up an ESP test with the usual cards (see p.64) and produced what were described as "highly significant" results: one old woman, Lizzie Williams, proved to be particularly adept – but it was admitted that cultural difficulties (the aborigines found the symbols on the cards difficult, and were emotionally con-

Aboriginal songmen (opposite) *keep modern aborigines in touch with the traditions and legends of their past by reciting them from memory. The Australian landscape is, for aborigines, effectively a vast song waiting to be sung, crossed by the "songlines" – paths on which aborigines travel.*

Aborigine women *at a* corroboree, (above) *at Mount Allen during which songmen recite traditional legends, and magical powers are invoked.*

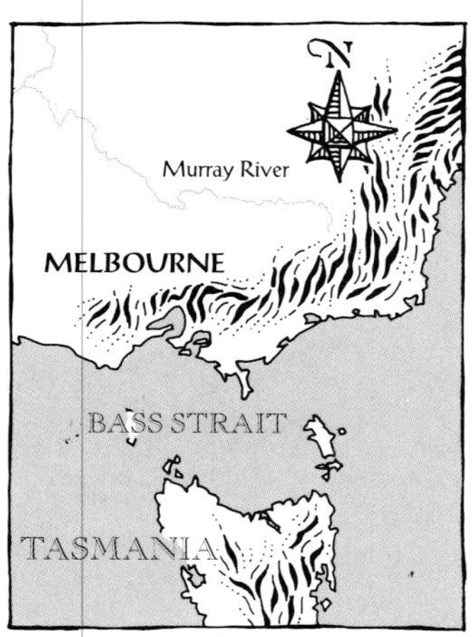

fused when others were substituted) made it impossible to be sure of their ESP achievements. However, the experiments convinced Dr A. C. Hardy, President of the British Association for the Advancement of Science, who was in no doubt that "no one who has examined the evidence for telepathy among these primitive people with an unbiased mind can reasonably reject it without intellectual dishonesty."

Charles Bailey

The major figure in Australian parapsychology was the medium Charles Bailey, who unlike many European mediums, positively welcomed investigation of his talents.

Bailey's early career was in a succession of indifferent jobs. But eventually, in 1889, he began to make his living as a professional medium, and later gained the patronage of an American-born Melbourne millionaire, T. W. Stanford. Accounts of the many seances held during that period were correlated and presented to Stanford University, California, together with a vast random collection of objects Bailey apparently managed to materialize during them: birds' nests, seaweed and sand, a fishing net, a live turtle, ivory, precious stones, a human skull, a leopard's skin and a large piece of tapestry.

This all sounds comic: but we should remember that many of the seances were held under rigorously controlled conditions, including a number conducted in 1904 by Dr Charles MacCarthy. MacCarthy vetted everyone present, searched Bailey before each session, and then sewed him into a canvas bag with only his arms and head free. The seance room was searched and locked during the sittings. In seven sessions under these conditions Bailey materialized (or "apported") 54 objects, including some mysterious cylinders and tablets purporting to have been inscribed by Babylonian spirits, half-cooked *chapattis*, a crab, and a small live shark.

MacCarthy came to the conclusion that the phenomena produced during the seances were definitely paranormal but was disappointed when the British Museum proclaimed the Babylonian script to be fake: which did not explain how Bailey had been able to produce the tablets. Occasionally accusations of trickery were brought against him, and although never caught cheating, his reputation suffered.

Picnic at Hanging Rock

The best-known supernatural event ever to have been reported from Australia is that of the picnic at Hanging Rock, celebrated in one of the best Australian films of recent years.

Hanging Rock is a volcanic outcrop rising to 500 feet (152.5m) from a plain not far from Melbourne; and on St Valentine's Day 1900 –a Saturday – 19 girls and two teachers set out to picnic at the rock.

In the afternoon, three of the senior girls were given permission by their French teacher, Mlle Diane de Poitiers to explore the rock. An hour later they had not reappeared – and Mlle de Poitiers noticed that the only other teacher in the group, Miss Greta McCraw, had also vanished. A search was made without result – but after another hour, the youngest of the girls, Edith Horton, suddenly appeared, in hysterics. She knew nothing of the other girls, or of Miss McGraw. They were never seen again.

Edith remembered nothing about the time she spent on the rock – although she recalled seeing Miss McCraw making her way towards it. The mistress did not reply to the girl's cries, and, surprisingly, was clad only in her drawers.

A week later, a search party found one of the three older girls, Irma Leopold; she was uninjured apart from minor scratches. Her corset was missing, but she had not been sexually assaulted. When revived, she could remember nothing. Some months later the Headmistress of Applegate College, Mrs Appleyard, drove to the rock and threw herself to her death.

There have been innumerable suggestions about what happened at Hanging Rock. Perhaps the girls simply got lost and died of exposure, and their bodies were eaten by animals? Perhaps they were kidnapped or murdered? Or were they taken by UFOs, or slipped into some time-warp? C. J. Niven, an American theologist, suggested that they were lifted to a heavenly plain from which Miss Leopold, perhaps for some sin, was later rejected.

None of these suggestions are true, for the simple reason that the events in the story never happened. Although there was a ladies' college at Woodend (called Clyde College) it did not open there until 1919. Incidentally, St Valentine's Day 1900 was a Wednesday, not a Saturday.

The source of the story seems to be a novel, *Picnic at Hanging Rock*, published as recently as 1967. Its author, Joan Lindsay, has always declined to say whether it is based on fact – although several elements are factual. That a very large number of people regard the story as fact is an instance of how much we need the supernatural, how uncritically we are prepared to accept it when it is sufficiently beguiling – and how carefully all investigators of the paranormal must be in checking alleged facts.

That having been said, Hanging Rock is a remarkable outcrop of curiously-shaped rocks, the formation of which often suggests weird faces. To visit it alone, at dusk, is to subject oneself to the kind of atmosphere which – together, perhaps, with the knowledge of curious legends associated with the place – might result in such inventions as the picnic story.

INDONESIA

The Kris

The *kris* is a short ceremononial sword worn on notable occasions by Indonesian men of good family. It is often of ivory or gold, and as elaborately decorated with jewels as the family fortunes allow. It is often heraldically designed, or its handle made in the shape of animals', birds', insects' or devils' heads.

However, it is the blade which is of real value, and must be treasured. There is always one *kris* which is at the heart of family tradition, kept in a place of honour, often daily decked with fresh flowers. It is believed to hold all the strength of its ancestors, guarded by their spirits.

This *kris* must be carefully handled if it is not to turn against one. For example, thieves will attempt to steal it in vain: there will inevitably be a nasty accident – the thief will trip and be badly injured or killed by the sacred blade. One, improperly acquired, was seen flying through the air in a menacing manner, and was quickly returned to its rightful owner.

The *kris* is said to possess all sorts of strange powers: during the Second World War an Indonesian doctor, arrested by the invading Japanese, managed to smuggle his family *kris* under

***Young men stab themselves** in the Balinese* Kris *dance* (above), *based on an episode from the ancient epic* Mahabharata. *But the magic of the Burung, the Balinese religous trance – or alternatively the powers of self-hypnosis – prevents injury, or even the appearance of blood. The* kris, *a short ceremonial sword, is worn throughout Indonesia and is often credited with being the repository of ancestors' spirits. Stealing someone else's* kris *is said to bring disaster to the thief.*

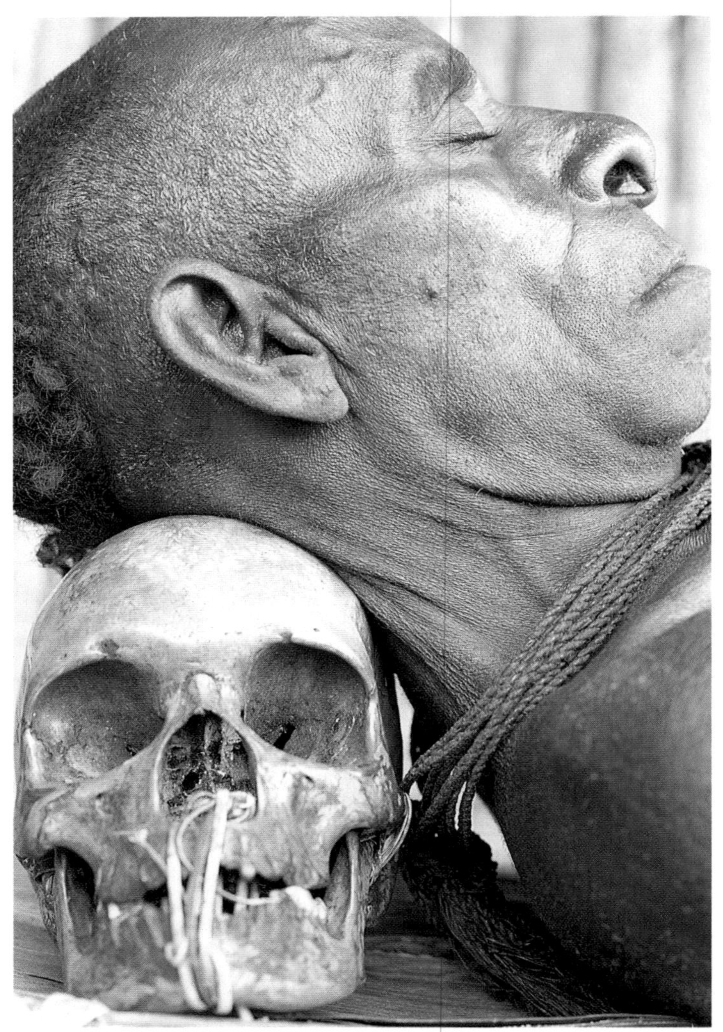

his clothing. The Japanese guards became unaccountably worried whenever they approached him; several refused to come anywhere near him; and for no particular reason he was rapidly released.

The Village of the Djajadiningrat

The Djajadiningrat family has for centuries been centred on a particular enclosed village, entry to which is confined to a small group. Those family members who leave the village are not permitted to return. Those who remain are careful not to have any worldly dealings with those outside the village walls – even insisting on paying considerably over the market price for anything they have to buy from outside, lest, in reselling it, they are tempted by the profit motive.

Those who have left the village are symbolized by 40 stone jars of water and 40 trees planted beside the jars – each representing a particular clan. Study of these by the elders will reveal any help needed by outsiders – whether this is supplied by herbal medicine, prayer or material assistance.

When they ruled Indonesia, the Dutch made several attempts to penetrate the village, but without success; one Dutch commissioner who entered without permission died quietly in his bath soon afterwards. Visits made by Japanese officials during the occupation had the same fatal results.

An Aznat tribesman *in Irian Jaya, Indonesia, sleeps with his head safely cradled on the skull of an ancestor* (above). *Regarding the skull as the literal resting place of an ancestor's spirits, the Aznat guard them jealously.*

A witch doctor prepares to cure a patient (right) *of a stomach complaint: first she dances to the sound of drums, and murmurs in an unknown language, and then she enters the house of the afflicted to spread some rice and medicinal plants on the patient, who will be expected to make a full recovery. Locally, the efficacy of such cures is widely accepted.*

The totem (opposite) *is a powerful magic symbol: Maoris believe it can bestow blessings and provide protection from evil.*

New Zealand

The Maoris

The magical powers once associated with the Maori people have been notably diminished by integration with the white population; but older people retain some knowledge, especially of health cures. Illnesses are generally believed to be the result of violating a *tapu*. *Tapu*, which translates as "sacred", with connotations of "forbidden", was the force that governed the whole of pre-European Maori life, taking the place of law as well as of religion. Elaborate ceremonies (*whakanoa*) were needed to remove it. The higher a Maori's position, the more he was subject to *tapu*: *tohungas*, or priests, were so *tapu*, especially after taking part in a religious ceremony, that food had to be served to them on stalks to avoid physical contact.

Charms, or *karakia*, ranged from childish jingles to full-blown spells cast by a *tohunga*. An important *karakia* had to be recited at dawn or dusk and in a single breath: if a mistake was made, or words were forgotten, the person chanting it was likely to lose his life at the hands of the gods. Special poses were sometimes adopted when reciting them. As in European witchcraft, the power of the spell was greater if the shaman was naked. *Karakia* were used for a great variety of purposes: to ensure safety during childbirth, to win battles, to cure sickness, to bring rain, to ensure good hunting, to cause a flood to subside, a kite to fly well, rats and birds to enter snares, or even to bring ocean monsters to the rescue of distressed sailors.

Black magic was contained in the *kete tuatahi*, the "basket of knowledge" of evil, brought to earth by the god Tane; its techniques were passed from generation to generation. As in other cultures, the young man who wanted to become a *tohunga makutu*, or sorcerer, had to undergo various ordeals and would then have to prove his knowledge and skill by destroying – at a distance – plants, animals and even human beings: favourite subjects were relatives and sometimes even his instructor.

Makutu, or black magic, was usually practised at the *tuaahu*, a sacred place often located close to the village latrine, which was itself sacred. The sorcerer needed a piece of hair or portion of the spittle of the victim in order to operate on a human being – but a kite could be sent into the air to drift over the enemy, trailing a cord which, if it touched him, would destroy his courage.

There was also white magic, in which a sacred fire would be used to cook food which, carried by a traveller, would protect him against evil. Single hairs, blessed, could be used to cause wells of water to spring up from dry ground; love charms were produced which would win brides.

Tohungas believed that all sickness emanated from the gods, and so would concentrate on trying to discover what was behind the affliction: was it caused by enemies, by the sinning of the sufferer, by another shaman? A *tohunga* would recite a number of words to the sick person, and from the patient's reaction to them discover the source of the illness (this is interestingly similar to the word-association tests given by Western psychiatrists).

Maoris were also subject to an endless number of omens (*aitua*), most of them unlucky. In warfare, the outcome might depend on the position or shape of a rainbow, the direction of a flash of lightning, or the performance of a war dance (*peruperu*). New Zealand's international rugby team, the All Blacks, have carried on this tradition for many years, in their *haka taparahi* (a war dance without weapons) before matches.

Divination was taken very seriously. It would be used for various purposes – foreseeing the future of the tribe and individuals, discovering whether illness would be fatal, and so on. A leaf might be thrown into the air and its flight observed; kites might be flown, songs chanted which embodied prophesies. To find whether a person had died as a result of witchcraft a *tohunga* would recite a prayer over a fern stalk and plant it on the grave. If after a time it sank into the ground, this was a sign that a sorcerer had been at work.

A *tohunga* would prepare by fasting before attempting to foretell the future. Sometimes mechanical means were used: two sticks would be stuck in the ground, for instance, and a third tied across them. A lock of hair of a Maori chief would then be waved above the sticks, and auguries drawn from the movements of the hair, and whether it struck the horizontal bar.

There are few recognized practitioners of magic among modern Maoris, but there is still a strong tradition of divination. The Maori has great confidence in meanings drawn from dreams, and from the behaviour of animals. There have always been serious seers – usually male – and these still appeal to the gods to answer questions during the hours of sleep. It is said that recent disasters have been forecast by Maoris using this method; but on examination hard evidence is impossible to find. New Zealand magazines carried stories of how Maori seers had predicted a calamity during the royal tour by Queen Elizabeth and Prince Philip in 1953. Sure enough, at the height of the tour on Christmas Eve, New Zealand suffered its worst rail disaster – and at a place called Tangiwai (in Maori, "wailing waters"). But there is no evidence that anyone foresaw the extraordinary nature of the accident – the collapse of an ice wall in a volcanic crater lake which unleashed a flash flood upon a railway bridge just as the North Island express reached it. Coincidence deepened when, on the very next royal tour, a bus carrying Maoris home from welcome ceremonies hurtled over a bank after its brakes failed.

One form of divination occasionally still practised (although, it seems, mainly by children) is *niu kowhatu*, performed on the bank of a river, pond or lake. Three stones are thrown by the seer – one into the water, one behind him, and one directly upward. Auguries are drawn from the sound caused by the stones thrown into the water: the greater the noise, the better the augury. The stone thrown backwards indicates bad luck if it falls to the left, good fortune if to the right. If the stone thrown upward falls in front of the thrower, the auguries are good; bad, if it falls behind.

The disastrous railway accident (below) *in New Zealand on Christmas Eve 1953, when the front carriages of an express train from Wellington to Auckland dived into the flooded Wangaehu River, killing 144 people, was said to have been predicted by a Maori* tohunga *or priest. Divination has always been considered important by the Maoris and used for many different purposes – foretelling the fates of individuals or of the tribes, predicting the outcome of war or an illness. This tradition survives, divination through dreams being especially common.*

TAHITIAN GHOSTS AND TABUS

Perhaps because they are relatively rare, the animals, birds and insects of Tahiti are believed to be ghosts – even the large brown rat, if it comes into the house, is believed to have done so in order to climb into the dreams of sleepers with tales of ancient wars, or perhaps to announce a death.

Death is the message brought, too, by the *upoa*, a small sea-bird with a mournful cry, which is believed in particular to foretell the death of members of royal families. The Tahitian owl is an evil ghost, and the *toreau* or plover warns of the approach of strangling demons – the graceful *opea*, a swallow with black and purple feathers, is on the other hand a benevolent spirit. There are convincing records of these warnings proving accurate; it may of course be argued that tradition is sufficiently strong for the cry of a *upoa* to be fatal to a sick prince.

Likewise, the breaking of a tabu has often been fatal, whether for similar reasons or not. One notable case was that of a white man who in the second half of the 19th century acquired and planned to cut down a plantation of ironwood trees on the central cape of Papaoa. All large trees in Tahiti, but especially the ironwoods (below), are believed to be hiding-places for ghosts, and natives pleaded against the desecration. The white man went ahead – and a few weeks later died, screaming that he was being strangled by ghosts.

There have been other deaths ascribed to strange powers on the island: the German film director Fred W. Murnau died in a motor crash shortly after completing his film *Tabu*, during the shooting of which he had landed on the sacred island of Motu-Tapu and pitched camp on a sacred burial ground. Robert Keable, an English writer, built a house over the traditional grave of a famous warrior chief, and died in strange circumstances.

The strangest tabu is connected with the vault of the royal family of Vaitape, Bora-Bora, near Tahiti, which can be approached by no person or animal not connected with that family: people, rats, lizards who so much as step near the vault have their eyelids turned inside out, and die in pain.

GLOSSARY

ABOMINABLE SNOWMAN A large creature, not human but walking upright, allegedly living in the mountains of Tibet. Also known as the Yeti.
ALCHEMY A medieval form of chemistry whose ultimate goal was the elusive "philosopher's stone" which would turn base metal into gold and was also the Elixir of Life, curing illnesses and conferring eternal youth on those who drank it.
ALTERED STATE OF CONSCIOUSNESS (ASC) A state in which the usual balance between consciousness and unconsciousness is changed – for example, during hypnosis, or in a trance or dream state, when the conscious is subdued and the unconscious takes over. The operation of some phenomena is thought to depend on the subject being in an altered state of consciousness.
AMULET An object worn to protect its owner by warding off evil, or to bring good luck as a kind of mascot or lucky charm. See also TALISMAN.
APPARITION The inexplicable appearance, sound or feel of a person, animal or thing which does not inhabit the usual three dimensions or conform to reality as it is usually understood. See also GHOSTS.
ASC See ALTERED STATE OF CONSCIOUSNESS.
ASPR The American Society for Psychical Research, founded in 1884.
ASTRAL BODY The "soul" or "spirit", the intangible or non-material counterpart to the physical body.
ASTRAL PLANE A dimension beyond the physical world in which the ASTRAL BODY operates.
ASTRAL PROJECTION OR TRAVEL The movement outside the physical body of the ASTRAL BODY, while the former is asleep (see OUT OF BODY EXPERIENCES).
AURA The indefinable emanation, like coloured bands of light, that surrounds a person, animal or thing. The colours and form of each aura are believed to be characteristic of the person, animal or thing it surrounds and to change according to a particular state of mind or emotion.
AUTOMATISM Physical actions – for example, drawing, playing music, and so on – not controlled by the conscious intelligence of the person making them.
BALL LIGHTNING An orange-yellow ball of electricity, ranging in size from 1 inch (2.5cm) to five feet (1.5m). It has not often been seen and scientists have so far failed to explain its precise nature.
BIGFOOT A creature similar to the ABOMINABLE SNOWMAN; it inhabits the forests and wastelands of North America.
BILOCATION The apparent appearance of a person in two places at the same time.
BLACK MAGIC Supernatural skills used to evil ends – for example, to serve the Devil or harm an enemy.
BLACK MASS A ritual parody of the Christian Mass, performed by diabolists, or devil-worshippers.
CABALA See KABALLAH
CHAKRA According to Hindu theory, the energy centres that link the soul to the body.
CHANNELLING The transmission of information or advice to people in this world from spirit guides in another world.
CLAIRAUDIENCE The ability to "hear" voices inaudible to others, which are alleged to offer information about the "next world" or the future.
CLAIRVOYANCE The ability to see things beyond normal sight.
COSMIC CONSCIOUSNESS A sense of unity with the universe, usually described as a moment of extreme intensity and joy.
COVEN A group of witches (usually thirteen) gathering to practise occult skills.
CROSS-CORRESPONDENCES Communications conveyed by two or more mediums at the same time but not in the same place – the individual communications may seem nonsense, but are thought to be significant when considered in the light of the others.
DEMATERIALIZATION The dissolution of material existence, or more loosely, the vanishing of a spectre or ghost.
DEMON From the Greek *daimon*, meaning spirit, although the word is usually used to represent an evil force.
DEMONOLATRY The worship of demons, or devils.
DEMONOLOGY The study of demons, or devils.
DIVINATION The practice of discovering future or past events or of gaining unknown, possibly occult information through unconscious or supernatural means.
DOPPELGANGER The ghost of oneself; its appearance is thought to herald death.
DOWSING The discovery of water, oil, metal or other buried material usually by means of a forked stick, or sometimes a pendulum.
DRUID A member of a pre-Roman Celtic priestly order which worshipped nature and may have performed sacrifices. Modern druids have revived many of the ancient practices and added new mystical rituals of their own.
ECTOPLASM The substance said to emanate from the body of some mediums.
ELIXIR OF LIFE A liquid sought by the alchemists because it was believed to cure illness and confer eternal youth.
ESP Extra-sensory perception: the use of senses unrecognized by most people, in telepathy, clairvoyance and precognition.
EVIL EYE The belief that some practitioners of the supernatural can kill or bewitch with just a look. In many cultures the wearing of an ornamental eye is thought to avert this evil.
EXORCISM The expulsion, by a religious, usually Christian, ceremony, of a possessive demon or devil from its temporary home within the body of a human being.
EXTRA-TERRESTRIAL A creature or thing beyond or from beyond the earth's atmosphere.
FAITH HEALING The curing of an illness by the simple expression (by the subject or by a "healer" or other person) of faith that they will be cured.
GHOST A visual APPARITION without a material presence, recognizable as that of a person (or occasionally, an animal) deceased. Alternatively, it may be a head, or other part of the body. Some ghosts appear to friends or relatives, others seem to belong to, or haunt, a particular place.
GRIMOIRE A witch's or warlock's textbook, originally in manuscript form, passed from generation to generation. Its main preoccupation is with interaction with or dominance over demons.
HALLUCINATION A vision, apparition, ghost or other phenomenon which seems on examination to have been the result of hysteria or imagination rather than of any truly paranormal event.
HAUNTINGS The appearance or manifestation of GHOSTS that are seen, often more than once, in a specific place, usually one that had a special significance in the life of the deceased.
HERMETICA Ancient philosophical writings that explore the hidden mysteries of the universe – for example, alchemy and astrology.
HYPNOTISM The encouragement of a trance state during which the subject becomes suggestible, and may be REGRESSED or encouraged to attempt paranormal feats.
I CHING (Book of Changes) An ancient Chinese book of philosophy and divination.
INCUBUS A male demon which preys upon, or has intercourse with sleeping women. (See also SUCCUBUS.)
KABALLAH (Sometimes Cabala or Quabalah), meaning tradition. A Jewish system of philosophy and mysticism.
KIRLIAN PHOTOGRAPHY The photography of the AURA and other energies invisible to the eye; devised in the 1950s by the Russian Semyou Kirlian.
LAYING ON OF HANDS A method of faith healing which does not depend on traditional medicine but on a healer touching the afflicted area or limb.
LEVITATION The capacity for human beings (and objects) to rise unsupported into the air.
LEY-LINES Lines of energy allegedly running through the earth, connecting buildings, monuments and natural features, similar to those which in human beings are intercepted in acupuncture. Known in China as "dragon lines".
LOCH NESS MONSTER A creature thought to inhabit Loch Ness in Scotland, although its existence has never been proven.
LYCANTHROPY A condition whereby a person believes him or herself to be turning into a wolf.
MAGIC An allegedly indefinable and immeasurable occult force which can be commanded by magicians (including witches) and used for good (white magic) or evil (black magic); its effects cannot be reproduced by any known rational force.
MAGICIAN A practitioner of black or white magic.
MAGUS A title usually given to a master magician or head of an order of magicians.
MANIFESTATION The inexplicable appearance of objects, apparently from nowhere, usually during a seance, at the hands of a medium or other person alleged to have supernatural powers.
MANTRA A syllable, word or phrase chanted monotonously over a period of time, as a blessing, spell or invocation, or to free the spirit from the body.
MATERIALISATION See MANIFESTATION

MEDITATION One of the many techniques for blotting out an awareness of the known world and turning attention and thought inward; the goal is to achieve the negation of the self.
MEDIUM A person who claims to possess the means to communicate with spirits, generally of the dead, and to be able to communicate messages from "the other world" to the known one.
MESMERISM The term derives its name from Franz Anton Mesmer (c.1734–c.1815), a healer who believed that it is possible to use forces in the universe to cure illness and act as a beneficial influence on the body in general, through a kind of universal fluid known as animal magnetism.
METAL BENDING One of a range of psychokinetic phenomena whereby metal, even heavy objects, appears to bend without the exertion of physical force.
NATURAL MAGIC The application of supernatural powers or ESP, usually for healing purposes, without the use of incantantations, spells or other instruments.
NEAR-DEATH EXPERIENCE The separation of the "soul" from the body, in times of extreme danger or illness; usually described as a sensation of travelling down a tunnel to be greeted by dead friends or relatives, accompanied by a feeling of extreme joy.
NECROMANCY Word usually used interchangeably with magic, but more specifically, the conjuring up of the dead, sometimes for the purposes of divination.
NOSTRADAMUS Latinized name of Michel de Nostredame (1503–66), a doctor who performed remarkable cures. He became famous for his prophecies in the 1550s expressed in obscure quatrains, some of which are believed to have relevance even to 19th and 20th-century events.
OBEAH African sorcery which combines VOODOO with Christianity.
OCCULT Meaning unknown, secret or hidden; loosely used to refer to anything which cannot be rationally or scientifically explained.
OUIJA BOARD A board bearing the letters of the alphabet, used to spell out messages allegedly from spirits by means of an object (popularly a glass, but strictly a board on casters) activated by the fingers of mediums or experimenters sitting around it, in a form of AUTOMATISM.
OUT-OF-BODY EXPERIENCE (OBE) The temporary departure of the spirit from the physical body, as in ASTRAL PROJECTION, or sometimes during lucid dreams.
PARANORMAL Beyond normal experience – used of any phemonenon so far inexplicable by rational or scientific means.
PARAPSYCHOLOGY The study of paranormal phenomena by interested parties, either amateur or professional.
PK An abbreviation for PSYCHOKINESIS.
PLANCHETTE Similar to a OUIJA BOARD but uses a pencil to transcribe messages, rather than a pointer or other device to select words and letters.
POLTERGEIST A force that throws or moves objects which are clearly not in physical contact with any human agency.
POSSESSION The apparent occupation of the mind of a human being by a spirit, sometimes believed to be diabolical.
PRECOGNITION An inexplicable knowledge of future events.
PREDICTION The announcement of future events by someone with command of precognition.
PREMONITION The knowlege of a particular future event, often some kind of disaster.
PROPHECY The foretelling of future events, often religious in character, and sometimes alleged to be divinely inspired.
PSI A term used by parapsychologists to denote all apparently psychical abilities.
PSYCHIC SURGERY The alleged power to perform surgery with the bare hands and without anaesthetic.
PSYCHOKINESIS (PK) The ability to move physical objects solely through the power of concentration.
PSYCHOMETRY The ability, by handling an object, to discover its previous history, or sometimes events with which it has been associated in previous, even remote centuries. Also known as object reading.
REGRESSION The persuasion of a subject, under hypnosis, to "remember" previous lives, of which they apparently have no conscious knowledge when awake.
REINCARNATION The conviction that a human soul lives many times, returning after death to inhabit body after body; these past lives are allegedly revealed under REGRESSION.
SABBAT A meeting of witches, but more specifically those that take place on days sacred to them, such as Candlemas (February 2), and Lammas Day (August 1).
SATANISM The worship of Satan (the devil) and other evil forces.
SCRYING Crystal-gazing, or the use of a crystal as a means of "seeing" the future: in general, nothing is "seen" in the crystal – it is a means of focusing the powers of a seer.
SEANCE A meeting at which a MEDIUM attempts to contact spirits and sometimes to deliver messages from the "other world" to the known world.
SHAMAN A witch doctor.
SORCERY Black magic, or magic used to evil ends.
SPEAKING IN TONGUES Speech, usually not intelligible, believed by some Christians to be divinely inspired, using a person's voice as the means of communication. Such people often "deliver" the messages in a trance state, a form of AUTOMATISM.
SPIRITUALISM Belief in, and attempts to contact, spirits of the dead which are said to reside in the "next world"; generally through the use of mediums.
SPR The Society for Psychical Research, based in London, and founded in 1882 to examine claims of paranormal happenings. It is still in existence today.
STIGMATA The appearance of visible marks on the skin or body which correspond to the wounds suffered by Christ during the crucifixion.
SUCCUBUS A female demon which prays upon, or has intercourse with, sleeping men. (See also INCUBUS.)
SUPERNATURAL Any phenomenon for which there is no apparent rational explanation, and for which one seems unlikely to be found (in contrast to the paranormal, for which a scientific explanation seems possible, and may one day be found).
SYNCHRONICITY Separate events which seem to be linked, but between which there is no clear logical connection.
TABLE-TAPPING A practise often presided over by a medium, but sometimes conducted by amateurs, in which people sitting around a table with their hands resting on it, invite spirits to communicate with them by moving the table or making a noise.
TALISMAN A charm similar to an AMULET but made for a specific purpose.
TAROT A pack of cards with symbols such as the Hanged Man, the Fool, the Empress, and so on, used for divination and as a means of penetrating occult mysteries.
TELEKINESIS The movement of objects, apparently without human intervention, but through the exertion of PSYCHOKINESIS.
TELEPATHY The transference of thought from one person to another, sometimes at considerable distances apart, through inexplicable, psychic means.
TRANCE The departure from the normal waking state, sometimes with the help of hypnotism, into a subconscious state.
UFO An unidentified flying object, often supposed to be from another planet, but frequently the result of over-active imagination, fraud or natural occurrences. There are very few genuinely inexplicable UFOS on record.
VAMPIRE According to popular mythology, a human being, sometimes known as the "undead", who although believed to be deceased, remains in some sense alive, by emerging from the grave during the night to take sustenance from the blood of the living.
VOODOO Magical rites, in which people are believed to be temporarily possessed by spirits, practised in the Caribbean, particularly in Haiti.
WARLOCK Popularly, a male witch; properly, a practitioner of black magic.
WEREWOLF In mythology, a man or woman who, generally at full moon, metamorphoses into a wolf.
WITCH A person, male or female, who practises magic, particularly under the stimulus of fertility rites.
WITCH DOCTOR Also known as a shaman; a person, usually a man, thought to possess magical, especially curative, powers.
WIZARD A practitioner of magic or sorcery, usually a man.
YETI See ABOMINABLE SNOWMAN.
YOGA A Hindu philosophy, adopted by many people in the West, whose goal is the unification of the individual soul and the Universal soul. The best known form is the yoga of physical culture, but other types are concerned with the study of sacred texts, religion, and so on.
YOGI A practitioner, especially a master, of yoga.
ZENER CARDS A set of cards, usually 25, made up of five groups of simple symbols, used in conducting ESP experiments.
ZOMBIE A corpse believed to have risen or been raised from the grave.

BIBLIOGRAPHY

The following is a list of books which contain additional information about the subjects discussed in this book; many of them provided useful source material.

Agee, Doris, *Edgar Cayce on ESP*, New York, 1969.

Aldersmith, Herbert, and Davis Davidson, *The Great Pyramid: its divine message and original co-ordination of historical documents and archaeological evidence*, London, 1948.

Ashby, Robert H., *The Guidebook for the Study of Psychical Research*, London, 1972.

Ashe, Geoffrey, *Miracles*, London and Henley, 1978.

Auerbach, Lloyd, *ESP, Hauntings and Poltergeists*, New York, 1986.

Bagnall, O., *The Origin and Properties of the Human Aura*, New York, 1970.

Barrett, W., and T. Besterman, *The Divining Rod*, London, 1926; New York, 1968.

Bascom, William Russell, *Sixteen Cowries: Yoruba divination*, Indiana, 1980.

Berlitz, Charles Frambach, and J. Manson Valentine, *The Bermuda Triangle*, New York, 1974.

Besterman, Theodore, *Crystal-Gazing: a study in the history, distribution, theory and practice of scrying*, New York, 1965.

Blacker, Carmen, *The Catalpa Bow: Shamanistic practises in Japan*, London, 1975.

Bord, Janet and Colin, *The Bigfoot Casebook*, Harrisburg, Pa, 1982

Mysterious Britain, N.Y. and London, 1973

Modern Mysteries of the World, London, 1989.

Brennan, James Herbert, *Reincarnation*, Wellingborough, 1981.

Briazack, Norman J., and Simon Mennick, *The UFO Guidebook*, New Jersey, 1978.

British College of Psychic Science, *Transactions*.

Brougham, Henry, *Autobiography*, London, 1871.

Brown, Rosemary, *Unfinished Symphonies: Voices from the Beyond*, London, 1971.

Browning, Norma Lee, *The Psychic World of Peter Hurkos*, New York, 1970.

Brunton, Paul, *A Search in Secret India*, London, 1935.

Butler, Walter Ernest, *How to Read the Aura*, London, 1971.

Byrne, Peter, *The Search for Bigfoot*, New York, 1976.

Calloway, Hugh G., *Astral Projection: a record of out-of-the-body experiences*, New York, 1962.

Campbell, Stewart, *The Loch Ness Monster: the evidence*, Wellingborough, 1986.

Carrington, Whately, *Telepathy: an outline of its facts, theory and implications*, London, 1945.

Catoe, Lynn E., *UFOs and Related Subjects: an annotated bibliography*, Detroit, 1978.

Cavendish, Richard, (ed.), *The Encyclopaedia of the Unexplained*, New York, 1974.

Christopher, Milbourne, *Houdini: the Untold Story*, London, 1969.

Clark, Adrian V., *Psycho-Kinesis: moving matter with mind*, New York, 1973.

Coates, James, *Photographing the Invisible*, London, 1922.

Condon, U., and Daniel S. Gillmor, [ed.], *Scientific Study of U.F.O.s*, London, 1970.

Costello, Peter, *In Search of Lake Monsters*, London and New York, 1974.

Cott, Jonathan, *Omm Sety*, London, 1987.

Covina, Gina, *The Ouija Book*, New York and London, 1981.

Crookall, Robert, *Case-book of Astral Projection*, New Jersey, 1972

Out-of-the-body Experiences, New Jersey, 1970

The Study and Practice of Astral Projection, New Jersey, 1960.

Daniken, Erich von, *Chariots of the Gods?*, New York, 1970; London, 1971

In Search of Ancient Gods, New York, 1973.

Davis, Winston, *Dojo: magic and exorcism in modern Japan*, California, 1980.

Demaitre, Edmond, *The Yogis of India*, London, 1937.

Dixon, Jeane, *My Life and Prophesies*, New York, 1969.

Downing, Barry H., *The Bible and Flying Saucers*, New York, 1970.

Ernst, Bernard, and Hereward Carrington, *Houdini and Conan Doyle*, London, 1938.

Evans-Pritchard, Edward E., *Witchcraft, Oracles and Magic among the Azande*, Oxford, 1976.

Eysenck, Hans J., and Carl Sargent, *Explaining the Unexplained*, London, 1982.

Finucane, R.C., *Appearances of the Dead*, London, 1983.

de France, Vicomte Henri, *The Modern Dowser*, London, 1930.

Freud, Sigmund, *A note on the Unconscious in Psycho- analysis*, London, 1912.

Fuller, John G., *Origo: surgeon of the rusty knife*, London, 1966.

Gaddis, Vincent H., *Mysterious Fires and Lights*, New York, 1967

Garrett, Eileen, *Adventures in the Supernormal*, New York, 1949.

Gauld, Alan, and A.D. Cornell, *Poltergeists*, London, 1979.

Geley, Gustave, *Clairvoyance and Materialisation: a Record of Experiments*, London, 1927.

Geller, Uri, and Guy Lyon Playfair, *The Geller Effect*, London, 1986.

Green, Andrew, *Ghost Hunting: a practical guide*, St Albans, 1976.

Green, Celia, and Charles McCreery, *Apparitions*, London, 1975.

Ghandi, Mohandas K., *Letters to a Disciple*, New York.

Grumbine, J.C.F., *Telepathy*, London, 1915.

Hansel, C.E.M., *ESP: a Scientific Evaluation*, New York, 1966

ESP and Parapsychology: a critical re-evaluation, New York, 1980.

Head, Joseph, and S.L. Cranston, *Reincarnation in World Thought*, New York, 1967.

Hitching, Francis, *Earth Magic*, New York, 1978

Dowsing: the PSI Connection, New York, 1978.

Hobana, Ian, and Julien Weverbergh, *UFOs from Behind the Iron Curtain*, London, 1974, New York, 1975.

Houdini, Harry, *A Magician among the Spirits*, New York, 1924

"Margery": the medium exposed, New York, 1924.

Hynek, J. Allen, *The UFO Experience*, Chicago, 1971; London, 1974.

Hyslop, James H., *Contact with the Other World*, London, 1919.

Inglis, Brian, *Natural and Supernatural*, London, 1981

Science and Parascience, London, 1984

Trance, London, 1989.

Iverson, Jeffrey, *More Lives than One?*, London, 1977

Jahn, Robert G., and Brenda J. Dunne, *Margins of Reality: the role of consciousness in the physical world*, New York, 1987.

Jeffery, Adi-Kent Thomas, *The Bermuda Triangle*, Pennsylvania, 1973; New York, 1975.

Johnson, Kendall, *The Living Aura: radiation field photography and the Kirlian effect*, New York, 1976.

Jung, Carl, *Modern Man in Search of a Soul*, London, 1934

Memories, Dreams, Reflections, London, 1975.

Keyhoe, Donald Edward, *Flying Saucers from Outer Space*, London, 1973.

Kilner, W.J., *The Human Atmosphere*, London, 1911.

Klass, Philip J., *UFOs Explained*, New York, 1974.

Krippner, Stanley, ed., *Advances in Parapsychological Research*, New York, 1984.

Kubler-Ross, Elisabeth, *On Death and Dying*, New York, 1969

To Live until we say Goodbye, New Jersey, 1978.

Lambert, R.S., *Exploring the Supernatural: the Weird in Canadian Folklore*, London, 1955.

Leeds, Morton, and Murphy Gardner, *The Paranormal and the Normal*, New Jersey and London, 1980.

Leroy, Oliver, *Levitation*, London, 1928.

LeShan, Lawrence L. *The Medium, the Mystic and the Physicist*, London and New York, 1974.

Lethbridge, T.C., *The Power of the Pendulum*, London, 1976.

Levi, Eliphas, *Transcendental Magic, its doctrine and ritual*, London, 1923.

Lodge, Sir Oliver, *Survival of Man*, London, 1909

Raymond, London, 1916

Past Years, London, 1931

My Philosophy, London, 1933.

Maby, J.C., and Franklin, B.T., *The Physics of the Divining Rod*, London, 1939.

MacKenzie, Andrew, *Dracula Country*, London, 1977

Hauntings and Apparitions, London, 1982

Maloney, Clarence, ed., *The Evil Eye*, New York, 1976.

Marwick, Max G., *Sorcery in its Social Setting: a study of the Northern Rhodesia Cewa*, Manchester, 1965.

Melville, John, *Crystal Gazing and Clairvoyance*, New York, 1970.

Middleton, John, and Winter, E.H., *Witchcraft and Sorcery in East Africa*, New York, 1963.

Mitchell, John, *The Story of Astroarchaeology*, Harmondsworth, 1977.

Moberly, C.A.E., and E.F., Jourdain, *An Adventure*, London, 1911 (5th ed., London, 1955)

Monroe, Robert A., *Journeys out of the Body*, New York, 1971.

Moody, Raymond A., *Life after Life*, London, 1975.

Morrison, Tony, *Pathway to the Gods: the mystery of the Andes lines*, New York, 1979.

Muldoon, Sylvan, and Hereward Carrington, *The Phenomena of Astral Projection*, New York, 1981

The Projection of the Astral Body, New York, 1986.

Murphy, Gardner, and Robert Ballou, *William James on Psychical Research*, London, 1961.

National Laboratory of Psychical Research, *Proceedings*.

Nolen, William A., *Healing*, New York, 1974.

Oldfield, Harry, *The Dark Side of the Brain*, London, 1988.

Ostrander, S., and Schroeder, L., *Psychic Discoveries Behind the Iron Curtain*, New Jersey, 1971

Handbook of PSI, New York, 1974.

Owen, A.R.G., *Can we Explain the Poltergeist?*, New York, 1974.

Panati, Charles, ed., *The Geller Papers*, Boston, 1976.

Parker, Derek, and Julia, *The Future Now*, London and New York, 1988.

Parker, Julia, and Derek, *Dreaming*, 1985.

Playfair, Guy Lyon, *The Flying Cow*, London, 1975.

Pleasants, Helene, *Biographical Dictionary of Parapsychology with Directory and Glossary*, New York, 1964.

Plessis, I.D. de, *Poltergeists of the South*, Cape Town, 1966.

Price, Harry, *Fifty Years of Psychical Research*, London, 1939

Most Haunted House in England, London, 1940

The End of Borley Rectory, London, 1946.

Ramakrishna Rao, K., (ed.) *J.B. Rhine: on the Frontiers of Science*, New York, 1982.

Randall, John, *Parapsychology and the Nature of Life*, London, 1975
Psychokinesis, London, 1982.
Randi, James, *Flim-Flam!*, Buffalo, New York, 1982
The Magic of Uri Geller, New York, 1975.
Raudive, Konstantin, *Breakthrough*, New York, 1971.
Regush, Nicholas and June, *The New Consciousness Catalog*, New York, 1979.
Reiche, Maria, *Mystery of the Desert*, Stuttgart, 1976.
Rhine, J.B., *Extra-Sensory Perception*, Boston, 1934
New Frontiers of the Mind, London, 1938.
Ring, Kenneth, *Heading Towards Omega*, New York, 1984
Life at Death: a scientific Investigation of the Near-death Experience, New York, 1980.
Ritchie, George G., and Elizabeth Sherrill, *Return from Tomorrow*, New Jersey, 1978.
Rogo, D. Scott, *Parapsychology: a century of enquiry*, New York, 1975
Miracles, New York, 1982
Mind Beyond the Body: the mystery of ESP projection, Harmondsworth, 1979.
Roll, W.G., *The Poltergeist*, New York, 1972.
Roll, William George, *The Poltergeist*, New Jersey, 1976.
Rose, Louis (ed. Bryan Morgan), *Faith Healing*, London, 1968.
Sargant, William, *The Mind Possessed*, London, 1973.
Schaffranke, Rolf, *Spirit Voices Tape-Recorded*, Illinois, 1970.
Seabrook, W.B., *The Magic Island*, London, 1935.
Searle, Frank: *Nessie: seven years in search of the Monster*, London, 1976.
Sitwell, Sacheverell, *Poltergeists*, London, 1940.
Smythies, J.R. (ed.), *Science and ESP*, London, 1967.
Sprenger, Jacobus, and Heinrich Kramer, *Malleus Maleficarum*, [tr. Montague Summers] London 1968.
Steiger, Brad, *Project Blue Book*, New York, 1976
Gods of Aquarius: UFOs and the transformation of man, New York, 1976, London, 1980.
Sudré, Rene, *Treatise on Parapsychology* [tr. C. E. Green], London, 1960.
Summers, Montague, *The Vampire, his Kith and Kin*, London, 1928; New York, 1960.
Symposium on UFOs: hearings before the Committee on Science and Astronautics, U.S. House of Representatives, Washington. 1968.
Tabori, Paul, *Harry Price*, London, 1950.
Tchernine, Odette, *In Pursuit of the Abominable Snowman*, London, 1971.
Temple, Robert Kyle Grenville, *The Sirius Mystery*, New York, 1975.
Tenhaeff, W.H.C., *Telepathy and Clairvoyance*, Springfield, Ill., 1965.
Thalbourne, Michael A., *A Glossary of Terms used in Parapsychology*, London, 1982.
Tomkins, Peter, *Secrets of the Great Pyramid*, New York, 1971; London, 1973.
Trento, Salvatore Michael, *The Search for Lost America: mysteries of the stone ruins in the United States*, Harmondsworth and New York, 1979.
Umland, Craig and Eric, *Mysteries of the Ancients: early spacemen and the Mayas*, New York, 1954, London, 1975.
Unidentified Flying Objects: hearing by the Committee on Armed Services of the House of Representatives, Washington, 1966.
Valentine, Tom, *Psychic Surgery*, Chicago, 1973.
Van der Post, L., *Jung*, London, 1976.
Vaughan, Alan, *The Edge of Tomorrow*, New York, 1981.
Warcollier, Rene, *Experiments in Telepathy* (ed. Murphy, Gardner), London, 1939.
Watkins, Guy, *The Old Straight Track*, London, 1970.
West, D.J., *Eleven Lourdes Miracles*, London, 1957
Psychical Research Today, London, 1962.
Williams, Harley, *A Doctor Looks at Miracles*, London, 1959.
Wilson, Colin, *The Occult*, London, 1973
Mysteries, London, 1978
The Encyclopaedia of Unsolved Mysteries, London, 1987 (with Damon Wilson)
Wilson, Ian, *Reincarnation?*, London, 1981
Wolman, B.B. (ed.), *Handbook of Parapsychology*, New York, 1977.

JOURNALS

A great number of journals is published, world-wide, on supernatural and paranormal phenomena. Some are highly serious, others more popular. There follows a selective list, together with editorial addresses at the time of publication.

IN THE U.K. –

Anomaly – The Association for the Scientific Study of Anomalous Phenomena, 65, Amersham Road, High Wycombe, Buckinghamshire, HP13 5AA, England.
The British and Irish Skeptic, 71, Bury and Bolton Road, Radcliffe, Manchester M26 0LF, England.
The British Journal of Experimental and Clinical Hypnosis – British Society of Experimental and Clinical Hypnosis, Department of Psychology, Portsmouth Polytechnic, Portsmouth PO1 2ER, England.
The Christian Parapsychologist – Christian Fellowship for Psychical and Spiritual Studies, The Priory, 44 High Street, New Romney, Kent TN28 8BZ, England.
Flying Saucer Review, FSR Publications, PO Box 12, Snodland, Kent ME6 5JZ, England.
The Fortean Times – (The Journal of Strange Phenomena), 96, Mansfield Road, London NW3 2HX, England.
The Journal of the Society for Psychical Research – The Society for Psychical Research, 1, Adam and Eve Mews, London W8 6UG, England.
The Journal of Transient Aerial Phenomena – 8, Jones Drive, Whittlesey, Peterborough, PE7 2HW, England.
Magonia – John Dee Cottage, 5, James Terrace, Mortlake Churchyard, London SW14 8HB, England.
Psychic News, 20, Earlham Street, London WC2H 9LW, England.
Two Worlds – Two Worlds Publishing Co Ltd, 5, Alexandria Road, West Ealing, London W13 0NP, England.
UFO Times – 3, Hove Avenue, London E17 7NG, England.

IN THE U.S.A. –

Artifex, a Journal of Cyberbiology, The Archaeus Project, 2402 University Avenue, St Paul, MN 55114.
The British Journal of Experimental and Clinical Hypnosis – Department of Psychology, University of Connecticut, Box U22, 406, Cross Campus Road, Storrs, Connecticut 06268
Bulletins Boston Society for Psychical Research
Fate, Karaban/Labiner Association Inc, 130 W. 42nd Street, New York, NY 10036.
The Global Link Newsletter, 800 Third Avenue, 31st Floor, New York, NYT 10022.
The Journal of the American Society for Psychical Research – The American Society for Psychical Research, 5 West 73rd Street, New York, NY 10023.
The Journal of Parapsychology – The Parapsychology Press, PO Box 6847, College Station, Durham, NC 27708.
The Journal of Religion and Psychical Research – The Academy of Religion and Psychical Research, PO Box 614, Bloomfield, Connecticut 06002 U.S.A.
The Journal of Scientific Exploration, The Society for Scientific Exploration, Department of Engineering-Economic Systems, Terman Engineering Center, Stanford CA 94305-4025.
Near-Death Studies – International Association for Near-Death Studies, Human Sciences Press Inc, 72 5th Avenue, New York, NY 10011-8004.
Newsletter for the History and Sociology of Marginal Science, 4635-E, Hope Valley Road, Durham, NC27707.
The Skeptical Inquirer, The Committee for the Scientific Investigation of Claims of the Paranormal, 3025, Palo Alto Drive, N.E., Albuquerque, NM 87111.
Theoretical Parapsychology – Gordon & Breach Science Publishers Ltd., PO Box 786, Cooper Station, New York, NY 10276.

ARGENTINA

Cuadernos de Parapsicologia, Instituto de Parapsicologia, Calle Ramon Lista 868, 1706 Domingo F. Sarmiento (Haedo), Prov. Buenos Aires.

AUSTRALIA

A.I.P.R. Bulletin, Australian Institute of Parapsychological Research, P.O. Box 445, Lane Cove, NSW 2066.
The British Journal of Experimental and Clinical Hypnosis – School of Behavioural Sciences, Maquarie University, Sydney, NSW 2109.

CANADA

ASD Newsletter, Association for the Study of Dreams, Hopital du Sacre-Coeur, Centre d' etude du sommeil, 5400 Boulevard Gouin Ouest, Montreal, Quebec.

FRANCE

Révue Francaise de Psychotronique, Organisation pour la Récherche en Psychotronique, Bureau 644, U.E.R. de Mathematiques, Universite Toulouse le Mirail, 31058 Toulouse.
La Revue de Parapsychologie, 8 Rue Octave Dubois, 95150 Taverny.

GERMANY

Grenzgebiete der Wissenschaft, Organ des Instituts fur Grenzegebiete der Wissenschaft und von Imago Mundi, Maximilianstrasse 8, Postfach 8, A-6010 Innsbruck.

ITALY

Il Bollettino del E.S.P., Organo di Informazione del Centro Studi Parapsicologici, Via Valeriana 39, 40134, Bologna.
Luce e ombra, Organo dell'Associazione Archivo di Documentazione Storica della Ricerca Psichica, Biblioteca Bozzano-de Boni, Via Orfeo, 15, 40124 Bologna.
Notiziario A.I.S.M., Associazione Italiana Scientifica di Metapsichica, Via S. Vittore 19, 20123 Milano.
Vita Nuova, Via Venini 67, 20127 Milano.

JAPAN

Journal of the Japanese Psychic Science Association, 12-12, Kamiochiai Shinjuku-ku, Tokyo.

THE NETHERLANDS

The European Journal of Parapsychology – Parapsychology Laboratory, University of Utrecht, Sorbonnelaan 16, 3584, CA Utrecht.
Parapsychologische Nieuwsbrief, Nieuwsbrief van get Parapsychologische Institut, Springweg 5, 3511 CH Utrecht.

SPAIN

PSI-Communicacion, Revista de la Sociedad Española de Parapsicologia, Belen, 15, 1 derescha, Madrid 4.

INDEX

Page numbers in italics refer to captions

PICTURE CREDITS AND ACKNOWLEDGMENTS

KEY
b bottom c centre l left r right t top

CP – Camera Press, London
ET – *E.T. Archive*
Fortean – *Fortean Picture Library*
HL – *The Hutchison Library*
HPC – *Harry Price Collection, University of London*
Hulton – *The Hulton Picture Company*
JB – *John Beckett*
MEPL – *The Mary Evans Picture Library*
SI – *Syndication International*
SPL – *Science Photo Library*
Spooner – *Gamma/Frank Spooner Pictures.*

Cover: Al Francekevich/ZEFA (UK)
1 Stefan Richter/CP; 3 Sybil Sassoon/Robert Harding Library; 5 Hulton; 8-9 Margaret Ponting & Ron Curtis/Janet & Colin Bord; 10 Yoram Lehmann/ Robert Harding Library; 11 Rex Features; 12t/b MEPL; 13 Mansell Collection; 14-15 SI; 16 Pat Hodgson; 17b MEPL; 17t SI; 18 Pat Hodgson; 20t/b Mansell Collection; 21t/b, 22l SI; 22r Psychic News/SI; 23 Michael Charity/CP; 24 Popperfoto; 25 JB; 27 Andrew Rafferty, from *The Stones Remain*, by Andrew Rafferty and Kevin Crossley Holland, published by Rider, London, 1989; 28-29 Fortean; 29 ET; 30 Rex Features; 31b Pat Hodgson; 31t Popperfoto; 32b MEPL; 32c Rex Features; 32t S.Ferry/ Spooner; 33 CP; 34bl MEPL; 35l Jean-Loup Charmet; 34r Werner Forman Archive; 34tl SPL; 35tr/br Aventurier/Spooner; 36 CP; 37 René Grosjean/ Spooner; 38 Bachberle Jens/Spooner; 39t/c/bl JB; 40 MEPL; 41t Paul Broadhurst/Fortean; 44, 45t/b Fortean; 46t/b David Barritt/Spooner; 47t/b Guy Playfair/MEPL; 48b MEPL; 48t HPC/MEPL; 49tl/tr/br/bl Dr. Elmar R.Gruber; 50 Tom Blau/CP; 50-51 Hulton; 51 Popperfoto; 52b JB; 52t Alain Morvan/Spooner; 53b Claire Leimbach; 53t Mansell Collection; 54 MEPL; 55b Werner Forman Archive; 55t Robert Hunt Library; 57l/r Dr. Elmar R. Gruber; 59b ET; 59tl/tr JB; 60 MB/Photo Guglielmo Galvin; 61t/b Hinniger/Abacus Presseteam; 62b ET; 62c MEPL; 62T Jean-Loup Charmet; 63b ET; 63t MEPL; 64b JB; 64t Dr. Elmar R. Gruber; 65b JB; 65t R. Slade/CP; 66b Rex Features; 66cl/cr JB; 66t Bob Gammon/Sunday Correspondent/Katz Pictures; 70 Topham Picture Library; 71b Werner Forman Archive; 71t/c Popperfoto; 72-73 Julian Baum/SPL; 72b/c Fortean; 72t, 73 MEPL; 74-75 Popperfoto; 74b MEPL; 74tl/tr, 79t/b SPL; 78-79 Arecibo Observatory, part of the National Astronomy and Ionosphere Center, operated by Cornell University under contract with the National Science Foundation. 80l Dr. Elmar R. Gruber; 80r Dennis Stacy/Fortean; 81b James Bolen/SI; 81t John L. Hughes/CP; 86 Royal Observatory, Edinburgh; 88-89 ZEFA; 90-91 Hanny El Zeini; 90b The Griffith Institute/Ashmolean Museum, Oxford; 91 Hulton; 92-93 MacQuitty International; 92t/b, 93b Hulton; 93t Topham Picture Library; 94 MEPL; 95, 96t/b The Mansell Collection; 97 Sarah Errington/HL; 98b John Ryle/HL; 99 Hulton; 100-101 Camerapix; 101 Tim Dackus/Robert Harding Library; 102-103 Victor Lamont/HL; 103b Juliet Highet/HL; 103t Hamish M. Brown/Janet & Colin Bord; 104-105T/b Peter Magubane/Spooner; 105 Louise Gubb/JB/Katz Pictures; 107 P. Goycolea/HL; 110-111 HPC/MEPL; 111b MEPL; 111t SI; 112 J.F. Lefèvre/Spooner; 113c Leszek Matela; 113l/r Popperfoto; 114-115 Laberine/Spooner; 116, 116-117 Hans Verkroost; 117 Frank Fischbeck/Stock House; 118t/b Dr. Elmar R. Gruber; 119r/c/l Spencer Museum of Art, University of Kansas, Gift of H. Lee Turner/Photo: Jon Blumb; 120 J.G. Fuller/HL; 121 Curt Gunther/CP; 123 Paul Broadhurst/Janet & Colin Bord; 124, 124-125, 127 Robert Estall; 128 Fay Godwin/Barbara Heller Photo Library; 129r Andrew Thorpe/MB; 129l Ken Hoskin/Kitchenham Limited; 130-131 HPC/MEPL; 130bl Popperfoto; 130tl Fortean; 130tr HPC/MEPL; 132-133 Anthony Shiels/Fortean; 132b Nicholas Witchell/Fortean; 133 Hamish M. Brown/Janet & Colin Bord; 134, 135t/b MEPL; 138t/bl/br Dr. Erlendur Haraldsson; 139 Popperfoto; 140-141, 141b Lars Thomas/Fortean; 140 MEPL; 141t Dr. Elmar R. Gruber; 142t MEPL; 142b Popperfoto; 143t Larry Mangino/CP; 143b Guido Mangold/CP; 144l MEPL; 144r Thomas Photo; 145 Mansell Collection; 146t Topham Picture Library; 147l Dr. Guenter Unbescheid; 147r MEPL; 148 Karsh of Ottawa/CP; 149 Swiss National Tourist Office; 150b HPC/MEPL; 150t Popperfoto; 151 Dr. Elmar Gruber; 152l Fortean; 152r JB; 153 Sipa/Rex Features; 155r, 156 Europa Press Reportajes SA; 157b Fortean; 160-161 Jean-Loup Charmet; 160t MEPL; 161b Henry Gris/CP; 161t V. Jacina/CP; 162b Julian Baum/SPL; 162t G. Hadjo/SPL; 163b MEPL; 163t Leszek Matela; 164 Piquenal/France Soir Spooner; 165b ET; 165t Kobal Collection; 166 ET; 167 Art Zamur/Spooner; 168, 169 SI; 172-173 Topham Picture Library; 173 Steve McCurry/Magnum; 174-175 JB; 174 ET; 176l MEPL; 176r, 177r Hulton; 178b Kaluzny/Spooner; 178t Paul Fusco/Magnum; 179b Reinstein/Spooner; 179t Dr. J.T. Richards/ Fortean; 181 Derek Palmer/SI; 183bl/br/t JB; 184 Vautier-Decool; 185 Jürgen Schadeberg/Rex Features; 186l Maggie Steber/JB Katz Pictures; 186r David Tindall/CP; 188b Tony Morrison/South American Pictures; 189 Claire Leimbach; 192 Axel Poignant Archive; 193 Claire Leimbach; 195 Pat Hodgson; 196b Chin Show Cultural Enterprise; 196t Claire Leimbach; 197 Chin Show Cultural Enterprise; 198-199 Topham Picture Library; 199 Axel Poignant Archive.

The authors and publishers would like to thank the following for their help: Paul Devereaux, and the librarians of the London Society for Psychical Research and the London Library.